The Manuscripts of Early Norman England

(*c.* 1066–1130)

The Manuscripts of Early Norman England

(*c.* 1066–1130)

by

Richard Gameson

A British Academy Postdoctoral Fellowship Monograph

Published for THE BRITISH ACADEMY
by OXFORD UNIVERSITY PRESS

Oxford University Press, Great Clarendon Street, Oxford OX2 6DP

Oxford New York
Athens Auckland Bangkok Bogota Bombay
Buenos Aires Calcutta Cape Town Dar es Salaam
Delhi Florence Hong Kong Istanbul Karachi
Kuala Lumpur Madras Madrid Melbourne
Mexico City Nairobi Paris Singapore
Taipei Tokyo Toronto Warsaw

and associated companies in
Berlin Ibadan

Published in the United States by
Oxford University Press Inc., New York

British Library Cataloguing in Publication Data
Data available

0–19–726190–6

Phototypeset by Intype London Ltd
Printed in Great Britain
on acid-free paper by
Bookcraft (Bath) Ltd
Midsomer Norton, North Somerset

For Fiona

CONTENTS

LIST OF ILLUSTRATIONS

In most cases the photograph was supplied, and permission to reproduce it was kindly granted by the repository in question. Illustrations 13, 16 and 21 were taken by the Courtauld Institute of Art, University of London, by whose permission, along with that of the British Library and Lambeth Palace Library, they are published here.

Following page 190

ABBREVIATIONS AND SIGLA

A	Arabesque initial
Bedae Pseudepigraphia	C. W. Jones, *Bedae Pseudepigraphia: scientific writings falsely attributed to Bede* (Ithaca, 1939)
BHL	*Bibliotheca Hagiographica Latina Antiquae et Mediae Aetatis*, 2 vols. (Brussels, 1898–1911), cited by item number.
Bloomfield	M. Bloomfield, B.-G. Guyot, D. R. Howard and T. B. Kabealo, *Incipits of Latin Works on the Virtues and Vices* (Cambridge, Mass., 1979), cited by item number.
Bursill-Hall	G. L. Bursill-Hall, A *Census of Medieval Latin Grammatical Manuscripts* (Stuttgart, 1981), cited by item number.
CC (CM/SL)	*Corpus Christianorum* (Continuatio Mediaevalis/Series Latina (Turnhout, 1954–), cited by volume.
Councils and Synods	*Councils and Synods with other Documents relating to the English Church*, ed. D. Whitelock, M. Brett, and C. N. L. Brooke, 2 vols. (Oxford, 1981), cited by document number.
CPG	M. Geerard and F. Glorie, *Clavis Patrum Graecorum*, 5 vols. (Turnhout, 1983–7), cited by item number.
CPL	E. Dekker, *Clavis Patrum Latinorum*, 3rd ed. (Turnhout, 1995), cited by item number.
CSEL	*Corpus scriptorum ecclesiasticorum latinorum* (Vienna, 1866–), cited by volume.
CSLMAAG	M.-H. Jullien and F. Perelman, *Clavis Scriptorum Latinorum Medii Aevi, Auctores Galliae 735–987*, 1 vol. to date (Turnhout, 1994–), cited by item code.
D	Drawings, painted miniatures or major diagrams
E	Embellished initial(s).
EBL	*English Benedictine Libraries: The Shorter Catalogues*, ed. R. Sharpe, J. P. Carley, R. M. Thomson, and A. G. Watson (London, 1996).
EEMF	Early English Manuscripts in Facsimile (Copenhagen, 1951–).
I	Decorated initial(s).
I(f)	Decorated initial(s) including human figures.
Jackson and Lapidge	P. Jackson and M. Lapidge, 'The Contents of the Cotton-Corpus

	Legendary' in P. Szarmach (ed.), *Holy Men and Holy Women: Old English Prose Saints' Lives and their Contexts* (Albany, 1996), 131–46.
Lapidge, 'Booklists'	M. Lapidge, 'Surviving Booklists from Anglo-Saxon England' in *Learning and Literature: Studies presented to Peter Clemoes*, ed. M. Lapidge and H. Gneuss (Cambridge, 1985), 33–89.
MGH	*Monumenta Germaniae Historica.*
MLGB	N. R. Ker (ed.), *Medieval Libraries of Great Britain*, 2nd ed. (London, 1964); with *Supplement*, ed. A. Watson (London, 1987).
MMBL	N. R. Ker, *Medieval Manuscripts in British Libraries*, 4 vols (vol. IV ed. A. Piper) (Oxford, 1969–92)
OE	Old English.
P	Decoration planned but not executed.
PL	*Patrologiae Cursus Completus*, ed. J. P. Migne (Paris, 1841–64), cited by volume number.
Richards, *Texts and Traditions*	M. P. Richards, *Texts and Their Traditions in the Medieval Library of Rochester Cathedral Priory* (= *Transactions of the American Philosophical Society* 78/3 (Philadelphia, 1988)).
RS	Rolls Series: *Rerum Britannicorum Medii Aevi Scriptores* (London, 1858–96), cited by volume.
SC	F. Madan, H. H. E. Craster *et al.*, *A Summary Catalogue of Western Manuscripts in the Bodleian Library at Oxford*, 7 vols. (Oxford, 1895–1953).
Stegmüller	F. Stegmüller, *Repertorium Biblicum Medii Aevi*, 11 vols. (Madrid, 1940–80), cited by item number.
Thorndike and Kibre	L. Thorndike and P. Kibre, *A Catalogue of Incipits of Medieval Scientific Writings in Latin*, rev. ed. (London, 1963), cited by column number.
Walther	H. Walther, *Initia Carminum ac Versum Medii Aevi Posterioris Latinorum*, 6 vols. (Gottingen, 1959–69), cited by item number.
Warner and Gilson, *Catalogue*	G. F. Warner and J. P. Gilson, *Catalogue of Western Manuscripts in the Old Royal and King's Collection*, 4 vols. (London, 1921).
Webber, *Scribes and Scholars*	T. Webber, *Scribes and Scholars at Salisbury Cathedral c. 1075-c. 1125* (Oxford, 1992).
U	Undecorated.
X	Decoration excised.
*	Manuscript of Continental origin.
†	Manuscript identifiable with an item on one of the book-lists inventoried here.
§	Illustrated in this volume.

PREFACE

The present volume is a first attempt to compile an inventory of the surviving manuscripts which were written in England, or acquired by English collections, during the sixty years after the Norman Conquest. The function of this preface is to outline the scope of the project and to clarify the nature of the information presented both in the inventory that comprises the main body of the work, and in the various ancillary sections.

The project took shape gradually. Having looked at most of the *saec.* x and xi manuscripts on Helmut Gneuss's pioneering 'A preliminary list of manuscripts written or owned in England up to 1100' (*Anglo-Saxon England* 9 (1981), 1–60) as well as a good number of *saec.* $xii^{1/2}$ English manuscripts in connection with other projects, and having studied all the *saec.* xi and xii manuscripts of Canterbury, Exeter, and Worcester provenance in the course of writing about those scriptoria, why not, I thought, prepare a formal inventory of all the surviving volumes dating from first two or three generations after the Norman Conquest. In fact, the amount of time and effort that has been required to progress from that stage to the inventory presented here has been considerable.

The importance of the material here assembled for the cultural history of early Norman England can hardly be exaggerated; and the value of the exercise—marshalling and describing a mass of dispersed and hitherto not easily accessible manuscript evidence—is clear. The problems that beset it, however, and hence the limitations of the end result, are less immediately obvious. Hence they should be stressed at the outset.

No such inventory could have pretensions to completeness and accuracy unless the compiler had examined not only every manuscript included in it, but also every other volume that might be potentially relevant. This is a Sisyphean task, which I have not fully accomplished. I have examined personally more than four fifths of the manuscripts on the list—which, of course, means that there are more than a hundred of them that I have not seen.

The principal problem that had to be faced was the lack of adequate catalogues for the large collections with potentially numerous relevant manuscripts. The information in M. R. James's catalogues of the Cambridge college collections and in the *Summary Catalogue* of the Bodleian Library was generally adequate to enable me to know whether a given manuscript was potentially relevant, and hence worth inspecting. Catalogues such as that of the Cambridge University Library, by contrast, along with Coxe's catalogue of Oxford College manuscripts, and most of the catalogues of the British Library's vast holdings did not even provide this guidance. On the positive side, while the project was in progress, excellent new catalogues of the manuscripts of Lincoln and Hereford cathedrals (by Rodney Thomson) and a study of the early manuscripts of Salisbury (by Teresa Webber) were published, which greatly eased the task of comprehending those collections.

In the event, after compiling a first list based on the standard published studies and my own notes, my procedure was to scour the existing catalogues of collections that were likely to include early English books, and to draw up vast lists of potentially relevant manuscripts. These I then endeavoured to inspect. In the case of the Cambridge University Library (whose manuscripts are misdated in the catalogue up to four centuries) virtually anything whose text was not composed after 1130 was possibly relevant. During the last five years I have inspected hundreds of manuscripts in search of volumes dating from *c.* 1066–1130. That I persevered in this daunting task was principally due to three factors. First, I had the firm belief that the game was worth the countless candles. Secondly, every manuscript is interesting, and I have profited from every one of the hundreds of 'rejects' I have examined. Thirdly, during the last few years I have received continuous and invaluable help from Michael Gullick, who has generously shared his knowledge of the material, and has saved me countless hours by providing lists of volumes that would be worth inspecting and, no less important, lists of those that could safely be discounted.

I should state quite clearly that this time-consuming process of investigating manuscripts has not been finished. Why, then, publish now? There are two interrelated reasons. First, having started by pursuing those manuscripts and collections which seemed, for one reason or another, to be the most promising, the return for my efforts during the last couple of years has been dwindling steadily. Consequently and secondly, it would seem most sensible to publish what I have accomplished thus far in the hope that others who are working with such material may assist in locating the hopefully fairly small number of books I have missed.

The reader should be aware that the repositories which I know best are those in Cambridge, London, and Oxford, and that I am also reasonably familiar with the collections of Durham, Hereford, Lincoln, Salisbury, and Worcester cathedrals. This is not to say that manuscripts in these places will not have eluded me; rather it is to indicate that relevant volumes elsewhere are more likely to have escaped me. The only continental collections whose holdings I know in any detail are those of the Bibliothèques municipales of Arras, Boulogne, and Rouen.

The inventory of manuscripts itself was in effect 'closed' at the end of 1996 in order to allow work to progress on the indices. Inevitably a few other items subsequently came to light, and these have been included in a short supplement at the end of the inventory. I have inserted a reference in the main body of the inventory at the appropriate point to alert the reader to their presence. The inconvenience of having a few items in a supplement is undoubtedly outweighed by the advantage of greater comprehensiveness.

Given the volume of material involved, the reader must appreciate that I have not been able to check the details of every text in every volume that is included. This is an inventory, not a descriptive catalogue. It was not always possible simply to take the information from printed sources for a fair number of the older catalogues were sadly deficient in this respect too. In the circumstances I generally accepted the identifications provided in the manuscripts themselves (unless I knew them to be wrong) or, where there was none, I undertook swift and rudimentary research. Consequently, I have no doubt that some of the identifications are in need of correction and improvement. There are, it is true, increasing numbers of aids which can facilitate work of this nature: however such tools are only useful if one has access to them. Canterbury libraries are, unfortunately, very poorly equipped in this respect, lacking not only all the modern electronic collections of texts and incipits, but also virtually all of the printed ones that have been produced in the last hundred years—not to mention many of the standard catalogues of manuscripts. Given that I have had to travel to Oxford, Cambridge, or London if I wished to consult any such works, in view of the bulk of material involved, I have had to be highly selective in checking texts. To have pursued individual identifications any further would have, in effect, indefinitely postponed the appearance of the work.

Another taxing problem and one that emerged during the course of the work was that of the dates assigned to manuscripts in modern studies. Increasing numbers of scholars seem to be using manuscript material and ascribing dates to the books as a matter of course. In theory this would seem to offer a welcome source of information. However after inspecting a good number of books which had been ascribed to one particular date-band and which were undoubtedly written in a different one, I have grown deeply suspicious of the ability of many scholars to date books from this period on palaeographical grounds. Indeed, faced with some of the more blatant misdatings in this respect, I was forced to conclude that some, possibly many, contemporary writers simply reiterate or 'paraphrase' dates given in other sources, and do not come to an informed, independent judgement. Now it seems to me that we are in danger of losing our way here in a mass of self-reinforcing erroneous pronouncements; and I would urge those who are merely echoing dates proposed by others to state that this is what they are doing—just as they would (presumably) acknowledge other facts and interpretations they cite. At the very least, future students will then know where they stand.

I have assigned dates to all the manuscripts I have examined personally, and have relied on the expertise of Gullick, Ker, Piper, Thomson and Webber as appropriate for those I have not seen. It should be borne in mind that there is a direct relationship between localising books and dating them: if one knows the origin of a volume and can examine other products of the same centre, then it is easier to estimate its date and that estimate will be better informed. Unlocated manuscripts can only be dated on general palaeographical grounds and in such circumstances the margin of error is obviously greater. Whether or not other scholars will agree with the dates here assigned, this inventory at least offers the advantage of modest consistency. It is the view of one mind and, in so far as is possible given the lengthy period during which it has been compiled, the same features have been assigned the same approximate date. Nevertheless, palaeography is not an exact science and should not be regarded as such.

1130 is, of course, an arbitrary and artificial terminus. In the case of several scriptoria it patently bisects a continuous and productive phase of activity. In order to minimise the violence thus done to the picture of the scriptoria in question, I have treated the boundary flexibly. The designation 'xii^{1}' here indicates a manuscript which one would most naturally assign to the period *c.* 1110–1130; however, I have occasionally included some books of slightly later date if they are patently linked to volumes that fall within the 'official' time band. Such books are clearly distinguished by being ascribed to xii$^{2/4}$. Similarly at the earlier end of the period, I have included the volumes that probably straddle the boundary (those for which this is most likely to be the case are designated $xi^{3/4}$). I have, however, excluded all but one of the books associated with Exeter in the time of Bishop Leofric (d. 1072), although it is probable that some of them date from 1066 or shortly thereafter.

The entry for each manuscript is presented in five columns comprising: item number, shelf-mark, textual content, decoration, date and provenance. Where a column has been left blank, this indicates that at the time of writing I lacked the relevant data. Occasionally I have allowed myself to include extra information (generally presented in smaller type at the bottom of the textual content column), but in the interests of brevity and economy, this has been kept to a minimum. As was said earlier, this is an inventory, not a catalogue. Ultimately the aim of the entries is to let the reader know whether the manuscript in question is one that they should look at themselves, not to save them the obligation of examining it!

A question mark accompanying an item number indicates that there is some uncertainty concerning whether or not the manuscript should be included. These books are generally those I have not seen myself, or alternatively those which could be either English or Continental and lack an early English provenance. An asterisk beside the item number indicates that the volume was probably (in some cases certainly) made outside England but was, or is likely to have been imported at an early date. The reader should be aware, though, that hard proof for the exact date of the arrival of such manuscripts in England is generally lacking. The two other sigla that appear in the first column are: †, which indicates that the manuscript in question is identifiable with an item on one of the early book lists whose information is presented below; and §, which alerts the reader to the fact that a photograph of the manuscript is included in this volume.

I have tried, subject to the limitations outlined above, to provide a fairly full listing of the textual content of each book, reproducing the order in which the texts appear in the volume. The work of a new author always starts on a new line. The main exceptions, when the individual texts have not been detailed, are medical and computistical compilations, and collections of sermons and homilies. In the case of vernacular homiliaries, full information is available in N. R. Ker's *Catalogue of Manuscripts Containing Anglo-Saxon* (Oxford, 1957). Where the contents of other such collections have been described in detail in a convenient publication, I have included this information. Unless otherwise stated, texts are in Latin.

The fourth column provides summary information about the decoration of the manuscripts. The following sigla have been used.

A	arabesque initial(s)
D	drawings, painted miniatures, or major diagrams.
E	embellished initial(s)
I	decorated initial(s)
I(f)	decorated initial(s) including human figure(s)
P	decoration planned but not executed
U	undecorated
X	decoration lost or excised
—	unknown (in the case of fragments)

Generally only one code is given to each volume. Where, as is often the case, a book contains several types of decoration, the designation is based on the most important. Thus a book with drawings, decorated initials, and arabesque initials will be classified as 'D' alone. The exceptions are those manuscripts whose major decoration was planned and not executed, or from which it has been excised (shown by 'P' and 'X' respectively), where a second code is supplied to indicate the nature of the most important extant decoration. A/E implies that the initials are on the borderline between the two classes, and nearer to arabesque than to embellished. Although the system of classification has been consistently applied for those books which I have examined personally, inconsistencies may have crept in where I have had to work from a catalogue description. The reader should also bear in mind that the quality and quantity of a given type of decoration can vary greatly from one book to another. A book designated 'A' may, for instance, have one mediocre arabesque initial, or, like London, British Library, Harley 3680 and Oxford, Bodleian Library, e Mus. 66, it could have a number of particularly fine ones.

The final column records date and provenance. For the most part, as mentioned above, I have assigned the dates myself in accordance with my understanding of the palaeography of the period. Where I am aware of grounds for a more specific date or date-range, I have supplied this in parentheses. In the context of this work, the dating sigla represent intersecting periods of approximately twenty years. Thus xi^{2} indicates a manuscript one would most naturally assign to the range *c.* 1070–90; xi^{ex} represents *c.* 1080–1100; xi/xii, 1090–1110; xi^{in}, 1100–1120; and xii^{1}, 1110–1130.

The location given is generally medieval provenance: this, it should be noted, may or may not be identical with place of origin. Indeed in a few cases the earliest or only known provenance is an institution that was not, in fact, founded until after 1130. Moreover, in many cases, the reader should remember, the certain evidence for provenance dates from long after our period.

To facilitate use of the main inventory, I have supplied a detailed index of texts. A headnote explains its conventions and limitations, but the key point is that it is an index to the inventory, and texts are indexed according to the way they are described there. Thus if the contents of a manuscript are itemised in detail, each element will accordingly feature in the index; but if it is simply described as a 'homiliary' or a 'passional', that is all that will appear there. Consequently the index does not provide a comprehensive list of, for instance, saints' lives, homilies and sermons extant in manuscripts dating from this period—however, intelligent use of the index and inventory together, could greatly expedite the compilation of such lists. There are also indices of early textual additions, of provenance, and of date.

To supplement the inventory of extant manuscripts and to provide a more comprehensive picture of contemporary books and book-ownership, I have provided a companion inventory of the texts that are listed on relevant book-lists. Once again, a headnote explains its limitations and conventions.

The general introduction offers a concise overview of the material as a whole, drawn from and providing a context for, the detailed information in the inventory of manuscripts and on the book-lists. The two main themes it explores are the diachronistic development of our corpus of manuscripts, and the types of texts and authors that were collected at different times. Its appendices provide alphabetical lists of the most popular texts, judged by manuscript survival, and a register of the authors represented in the corpus, arranged by century.

The volume is supplied with twenty-four plates. These were chosen to give a representative impression of the books of the period, including a cross-section of dates and provenances. They are, for the most part, arranged in chronological order, with the exception that in a couple of cases volumes with the same provenance though of different date are juxtaposed. Not the least impediment to the study of manuscripts of this period is the relative paucity of published reproductions from them: scholars who are reluctant to illustrate their work properly, and libraries that charge reproduction fees even for academic works conspire to perpetuate the problem. This small contribution towards filling the gap should enable the reader to see the sort of features that lead me to assign a manuscript to a particular date-band, and hence to understand the dating conventions used here. More generally, the plates are a reminder that this is a work about surviving artefacts, and not about abstract data.

Finally, I wish to reiterate that this is a *first* inventory. It has been published as a major step towards ordering and understanding a mass of important but under-studied material. The next stage must be to eradicate the errors, and make good the omissions; and I propose to publish a supplement with addenda and corrigenda in due course. (Subsequently, if energy and, above all, time and resources, permit, it is my intention to extend the inventory to 1175, and perhaps even to 1200 or 1220.) I would, therefore, urge readers to direct themselves in the first place to helping me improve its accuracy. All corrections and suggestions will be gratefully received (and, of course, acknowledged). Please address them to me at: The School of History, Rutherford College, University of Kent, Canterbury CT2 7NX.

O lector beneuole ora pro scriptore
Qui diu diligenterque laborabat
Noli eum reprehendere
Scripsit quam optime potuit
Tu tantum laborem non temptauisti.

ACKNOWLEDGEMENTS

It is a pleasure to acknowledge my debt of gratitude to those who have helped in the realisation of the project as it now stands. Alan Coates, Christopher de Hamel, David Ganz, Helmut Gneuss, David Howlett, Martin Kauffmann, Michael Lapidge, David Luscombe, Henry Mayr-Harting, Alan Piper, and Teresa Webber have all kindly shared their time and knowledge in various ways. Deserving of particular thanks are: Michael Gullick, who has provided invaluable help and support at every stage of the work; Fiona Gameson, who read through a draft of the entire catalogue and index for discrepancies and inconsistencies (a formidable task by any standards, this was an act of heroism for someone who cannot see); and Christine Gameson, who painstakingly compared the catalogue with the indices for omissions and inconsistencies. I am sincerely grateful to the many librarians who have readily granted me the access to vast numbers of manuscripts without which this work could not even have been contemplated; and I tender further thanks to those who kindly granted permission to publish photographs of volumes in their care (the institutions in question are acknowledged individually in the List of Illustrations). In addition, it is pleasant to be able to offer thanks to Martin Kauffmann (again), Simon and Ruth Loseby, and Claire and Ian Nabney, whose unfailing and unstinting hospitality gave me bases from which to work in Cambridge and, more recently, in Oxford. Finally, I wish to record my gratitude to the British Academy for the award of a Postdoctoral Fellowship, during the tenure of which much of the groundwork was accomplished.

Feast of St Martin, 1997

INTRODUCTION

Current research, as embodied in the inventory that follows, places the number of surviving manuscripts that were written in England or acquired by English collections between *c.* 1066 and *c.* 1130 at well over 900.[1] Although certainly only a fraction of the original number, this is still an enormous body of books; and when one considers the vicissitudes that have depleted the corpus (not to mention disguising parts of it) during the past nine centuries, the total seems additionally impressive. Given that the nearer in time to the present day a book was produced, the greater its chances of survival will have been, it would be a mistake to place too much weight on numerical comparisons with pre-Conquest material, some of which had the additional 'disadvantage' of being written in Old English. Nevertheless, it is undeniably striking that considerably more volumes are extant from the sixty years after the Norman Conquest than from the four and a half centuries before it.

Our period stretches from the arrival of William of Normandy to the later years of Henry I's reign; it begins with the political chaos of the Norman invasion and ends with England a well-organised part of a transmarine empire. Developments in ecclesiastical history were hardly less momentous. Scarcely had the re-ordering of traditional English monasticism, undertaken in the wake of the Conquest, been accomplished, when the ecclesiastical profile changed again with the rise of Cluniac and Augustinian foundations; and our period ends shortly after the establishment of the first Cistercian house in England. At the same time, the geography of active regular life altered: almost exclusively a southern phenomenon in late Anglo-Saxon times, the northern monastic revival of the late eleventh century and the energetic founding of priories in the north, fostered by Archbishop Thurstan of York (1114–40) among others, went some way towards redressing the balance. Indeed, one of the most impressive groups of books on our inventory is that associated with Durham Cathedral Priory, (re)founded in 1083. If the events to which we have just alluded are the general historical setting for the growth of libraries and book collections documented in the inventory, its broader context embraces the changes in regular life, theology, church-state relations and intellectual outlook that spread across Europe as a whole in the eleventh and early twelfth century. Our manuscripts are themselves a valuable source for assessing the speed and degree

[1] I ventured a provisional assessment of this material, based on the state of the inventory in October 1995, in 'English Book Collections in the late Eleventh and early Twelfth Centuries: Durham and its Context' in *Symeon of Durham and his World*, ed. D. Rollason (Stamford, 1998), 230–53. The figures given there differ from those in the present essay not only because additional manuscripts have since come to my attention, but also because the 'cut-off' date was then slightly earlier.

of England's interaction with these developments. Correspondingly, an awareness of the significance of the broader European trends for the growth of English libraries—as opposed to the local political and ecclesiastical changes which can easily monopolise attention—is of fundamental importance for the interpretation of these book collections. This is an issue to which we shall return at various points. Yet whatever the answer, it is clear that older houses had new library needs in our period, while new ones, needless to say, simply needed libraries. To take one example of the latter, the community of regular canons at St Osyth's, Essex, founded by Bishop Maurice of London (1086–1107) could hardly have achieved the reputation for learning it enjoyed by the end of our period[2] without a reasonable number of books. The fact that there is only one potential, identifiable survivor from this library in our corpus[3] is a sobering reminder of the great losses of books, not to mention the problems of localising those that remain, that bedevil attempts to order and evaluate this material.

This essay provides a succinct overview of the surviving books of early Norman England, complementing, and offering an interpretative framework for the raw material assembled in the inventory.[4] There are, as we have just remarked, considerable problems attendant upon such an exercise, and it is important to state them at the outset.[5] Not only has an unknown amount of material been lost, but the losses have been uneven, afflicting some areas more severely than others. The surviving sample is seriously imbalanced—the general dearth of south-western books is an obvious example: the houses at Winchester, for instance, which were undoubtedly important, wealthy, and well-connected are very poorly represented.[6] This was in large measure the result of local circumstances in the sixteenth century, namely the lack of energetic book collectors in the area in the wake of the dissolution of the Monasteries. But other major collections were drastically affected at other times: one thinks, for instance, of Norwich whose early manuscripts were incinerated in the fire of 1272; and of St Paul's, London, a good proportion of whose medieval books survived until the seventeenth century, only to perish in the Great Fire of London in 1666.[7] Then, there can be no doubt that some of the manuscripts which have survived will have eluded me; and there is imbalance here too, for this is more likely to have happened in the case of volumes of unknown origin and provenance than for those which have a known medieval home and which have consequently

[2] William of Malmesbury, *Gesta pontificum*, ed. N. E. S. A. Hamilton, RS 52 (London, 1870), p. 146: '*Erant ibi et sunt clerici litteratura insignes, eorumque exemplo talis habitus hominum laeta, ut ita dicam, totam patriam uestiuit seges*' ('There were and are there clerics who are outstanding for their learning, and by the example of the quality of these men, a bountiful cornfield, so as to speak, clothed the whole country').

[3] No. 620.

[4] For earlier surveys from different points of view see N. R. Ker, *English Manuscripts in the Century after the Norman Conquest* (Oxford, 1960); and R. M. Thomson, 'The Norman Conquest and English Libraries' in *The Role of the Book in Medieval Culture*, ed. P. Ganz, 2 vols., *Bibliologia* 3–4 (Turnhout, 1986), II, 27–40.

[5] Cf. Birger Munk Olsen's comments on a similar exercise: 'The Production of the Classics in the Eleventh and Twelfth Centuries' in *Medieval Manuscripts of the Latin Classics: Production and Use*, ed. C. A. Chavannes-Mazal and M. M. Smith (Los Altos, 1996), 1–17, at 2.

[6] It is sobering to compare the five manuscripts of Winchester, Old Minster provenance with the numbers for Christ Church, Canterbury (89), Durham (111), Rochester (67) and Worcester (49).

[7] The surviving volumes are discussed by N. R. Ker, 'Books at St Paul's Cathedral before 1313' in *Studies in London History presented to Philip Edmund Jones*, ed. A. Hollaender and W. Kellaway (London, 1969), 41–72; and 'Medieval Manuscripts from Norwich Cathedral Priory', *Transactions of the Cambridge Bibliographical Society* 1 (1949–53), 1–28; reprinted in his *Books, Collectors and Libraries: Studies in the Medieval Heritage*, ed. A. Watson (London, *c.* 1984), at 209–42 and 243–72 respectively.

been listed in *Medieval Libraries of Great Britain*.[8] Equally it is possible that some of the manuscripts will have been misdated by a greater or lesser amount. Suffice it to say here that unprovenanced manuscripts are also at a disadvantage in this respect. Palaeographical dating is at its best when a book can be assessed in relation to the known development of the scriptorium responsible—something which is by definition impossible for unprovenanced volumes.

Nevertheless, the parameters of the corpus of manuscripts as mapped out in the inventory, are likely to be broadly correct; and so long as we do not try to place too much weight on points of detail or on individual statistics, we are unlikely to be greatly misled. Much of what follows is couched in fairly general terms, precisely in order to avoid these pitfalls. The key point is that while the numbers themselves have no independent authority, the relationships between them are potentially revealing. The circumstance that there is a total of 126 surviving books from the end of the eleventh century, for instance, does not tell us very much; however, the fact that this is more than twice as many as from the previous time band is significant.

Ideally, in order to gain as three-dimensional a picture as possible one would want to compare the total English figures with those for other countries during the same period, and to view the English count for a particular text in relation to the number of broadly coeval surviving manuscripts as a whole. Unfortunately, the absence of up-to-date inventories compiled along similar lines for other countries, and the lack of exhaustive lists of carefully dated manuscripts for many patristic and other texts renders this difficult at present.[9] The circumstance that in the listings of many editions and handlists, manuscripts are simply assigned to a century whereas our period straddles the late eleventh century and the early twelfth, makes the problem of deploying their information here additionally delicate. Comparisons based on inadequate or inaccurate information would be specious and misleading.

There are two further, more specific caveats to bear in mind. First, as I will often be focusing on diachronistic changes in the corpus of surviving manuscripts, it is important to remember that collections are cumulative things. The acquisitions made in one period were, in many cases, being added to pre-existing book collections. The point is underlined by the account of Ely's books embodied in the inventory of that house's possessions that was probably made for Ranulf Flambard *c.* 1093.[10] At this time Ely had 287 books, including nineteen missals, eight lectionaries, two benedictionals, twenty-two psalters, seven breviaries, nine antiphonals, and twelve graduals: clearly, an uncertain but undoubtedly high percentage of these volumes must have been written before the Conquest. Similarly, it is probable that most if not all of the twelve Malmesbury gospel books which, William of Malmesbury tells us, were stripped of their precious bindings in William Rufus's reign dated from before the

[8] N. R. Ker, *Medieval Libraries of Great Britain*, 2nd ed. (London, 1964) with *Supplement*, ed. A. G. Watson (London, 1987).

[9] This is not to denigrate the immense value of the introductions to various recent editions and studies, many of which are deployed below, not to mention of seminal works such as A. Wilmart, 'La tradition des grands ouvrages de Saint Augustin', *Miscellanea Agostina* II (1931), 257–315; L. Verheijen, 'Contribution à une édition critique améliorée des *Confessions* de Saint Augustine: nouveaux manuscrits, compléments viennois à la "liste Wilmart"', *Augustiniana* 29 (1979), 87–96; M. Oberleitner *et al.*, *Die handschriftliche Überlieferung der Werke des Heiligen Augustinus*, 12 vols. to date (Vienna, 1969–); B. Lambert, *Biblioteca Hieronymiana Manuscripta: la tradition manuscrite des oeuvres de Saint Jérôme*, 4 vols. (Steenbruge, 1969–72); and B. Munk Olsen, *L'étude des auteurs classiques latins aux XIe et XIIe siècles*, 3 vols. (Paris, 1987–9). However, the dates given in such studies are often too broad to permit detailed comparison with the English manuscripts which are here more closely dated.

[10] *Liber Eliensis*, II, 139, ed. E. O. Blake, Camden Soc. 3rd ser. 92 (London, 1962), pp. 223–4, at 224.

Conquest.[11] The texts that were acquired most energetically at a given period could reflect what was then perceived to be most valuable and desirable; but at the same time the selection was obviously also related to the nature of the collection up to that point. One desires and tends to try to acquire what one lacks, and not what one already has. The evidence suggests that most late Anglo-Saxon book collections worthy of the name were well endowed with liturgical and para-liturgical books as well as homiliaries (often in the vernacular), that they had a reasonable amount of Latin Christian poetry, and a fair quantity of Carolingian writings, but that conversely they possessed very little patristics.[12] The fact that, broadly speaking, much the reverse is true of the volumes written during our period may imply a change in attitudes, but cannot in itself be regarded as evidence for a complete *volte face* when the natural wish to complement rather than duplicate existing resources undoubtedly also affected the selection. Far from rejecting the contents of Anglo-Saxon libraries, there is plentiful evidence in the form of additions and corrections that the volumes already in the collections were revised and used. The text of the early eleventh-century psalter, London, British Library, Arundel 155, for instance, was painstakingly corrected *in rasura* after the Conquest from the Romanum to the Gallicanum;[13] while the Old English Parker Chronicle manuscript, begun in the early tenth century at the latest, received a series of additions from the late eleventh century onwards, including the unique text of the *Acta Lanfranci*.[14]

Secondly, it is virtually impossible to take account of the movement of older books during this period. Various ninth-, tenth-, and earlier eleventh-century books may well have entered a particular English collection for the first time between *c.* 1066 and *c.* 1130, and they are likely to have been an important source of exemplars. A well known example is Hereford Cathedral Library, O. iii. 2, a continental manuscript dating from the second half of the ninth century which seems to have been the ultimate source of all the extant English copies of Cassiodorus's *Institutiones* (Book I), the earliest of which date from the end of the eleventh century.[15] Another of the rare identifiable examples is Oxford, Bodleian Library, Bodley 229,[16] a mid-eleventh-century copy of Augustine's sermons probably from northern

[11] *Gesta Pontificum*, ed. Hamilton, p. 432.

[12] The relevant material is listed in H. Gneuss, 'A Preliminary List of Manuscripts Written or Owned in England up to AD 1100', *Anglo-Saxon England* 9 (1981), 1–60. I am very grateful to Professor Gneuss for kindly supplying me, first with an annotated copy of his work, and subsequently with the draft of a fully revised version in advance of publication.

[13] No. 358: N. R. Ker, *Catalogue of Manuscripts containing Anglo-Saxon* (Oxford, 1957), no. 135; E. Temple, *Anglo-Saxon Manuscripts 900–1066* (London, 1976), cat. 66.

[14] No. 62: Ker, *Catalogue*, no. 39; facsimile: *The Parker Chronicle and Laws*, ed. R. Flower and H. Smith, EETS 208 (London, 1973). The *Acta Lanfranci* is published in *Two Saxon Chronicles Parallel*, ed. J. Earle and C. Plummer, 2 vols (Oxford, 1892), I, pp. 287–92. Other relevant items included on the inventory are nos. 303, 377, and 875. From the numerous other Anglo-Saxon books with post-Conquest additions and corrections, it will suffice here to mention: Cambridge University Library, Gg. 3. 28; Cambridge, Sidney Sussex College, 100; Cambridge, Trinity College, O. 4. 10; Canterbury Cathedral, 127/12; Durham Cathedral Library, B. iv. 9; Exeter Cathedral Library, 3507; Lincoln Cathedral Library, 182; London, British Library, Cott. Faust. A. x; Vesp. D x (part i); Vesp. D. xii; Vit. E. xviii; Oxford, Corpus Christi College, 197; and Winchester Cathedral Library, 1.

[15] See *Cassiodori senatoris institutiones*, ed. R. A. B. Mynors (Oxford, 1937), pp. xv–xvi, and xxxix–xlix; and R. A. B. Mynors and R. M. Thomson, *Catalogue of the Manuscripts of Hereford Cathedral Library* (Woodbridge, 1993), pp. 17–18. It contains: Jerome, *De uiris illustribus*; Pseudo-Gelasius, *Decretum de recipiendis et non recipiendis libris*; Gennadius, *De uiris illustribus*; Augustine, *Retractationes*; Cassiodorus, *Institutiones*; Isidore, *In libros Veteris ac Novi Testamenti prooemia, De ecclesiasticis officiis* (excerpts), *De ortu et obitu patrum*, and *Allegoriae*. The earliest English copy of such a bibliographical handbook is Salisbury Cathedral Library, 88 (our no. 846); followed by Oxford, Bodleian Library, Bodley 391 (our no. 668). See also nos. 584 and 810.

[16] SC 2120.

France, but of medieval Exeter provenance. The fact that it does not appear on the inventory of books, lands, and possessions given to the house by Bishop Leofric (d. 1072),[17] but has a couple of annotations by a known Exeter scribe active in the second half of the century and, moreover, bears a (mistaken) title in the same early twelfth-century hand that labelled other acquisitions of the early Norman period, strongly suggests that it was acquired by Exeter between *c.* 1066 and *c.* 1100. In the absence of documentary evidence, however, the role played by such volumes in our period is largely lost to us, even when the books themselves are still extant.

Bearing these caveats in minds, let us now turn to the first main theme we shall consider, namely the general nature of library growth in England during the period *c.* 1066–1130. The potentially important contribution made by the acquisition of older books is irrecoverable, as we have just noted. Conversely, it is possible that some of the continental manuscripts that do date from our period and have an English medieval provenance did not in fact enter the collection in question until after *c.* 1130.[18] However, a fair quantity of them, such as the volumes that came to Durham and Exerter,[19] demonstrably did, and the number of uncertain cases is sufficiently small that it will not seriously distort our findings. We have little alternative but to proceed on the assumption that the approximate date of writing was also by and large the date of acquisition.

The figures are as follows.

The later eleventh century (*s.* xi^{2}, representing items which would most naturally be assigned to the date-band *c.* 1066–90): 60 surviving manuscripts, of which 8 are continental. If we add the volumes of *s.* xi$^{3/4}$ which are included on the inventory, the total rises to 74.

The end of the eleventh century (*s.* xi^{ex}, *c.* 1080–1100): 124 surviving manuscripts, of which 20 are continental.

The turn of the century (*s.* xi/xii, *c.* 1090–1110): 145 surviving manuscripts, of which 30 are continental.

The beginning of the twelfth century (*s.* xii^{in}, *c.* 1100–20): 209 surviving manuscripts, of which 29 are continental.

The early twelfth century (*s.* xii^{1}, *c.* 1110–30): 349 surviving manuscripts, of which 21 are continental. If we add the volumes of *s.* xii$^{2/4}$ that are included on the inventory, the total becomes 387.

Even making allowance for a margin of error, several important points are immediately obvious—and incontrovertible. In the first place, the scale of book production and acquisition in the immediate aftermath of the Conquest would seem to have been fairly limited; indeed

[17] Lapidge, 'Booklists', no. X.

[18] A possible example is Cambridge, Corpus Christi College, 361 (not included in our inventory), a continental copy of Gregory's *Regula pastoralis* which was probably written around the beginning of our period and was still on the continent *c.* 1100, but may conceivably have come to England towards or shortly after the end of our period. See further R. M. Thomson, *William of Malmesbury* (Woodbridge, 1987), p. 79.

[19] For the Norman books that William of St Calais gave to Durham see M. Gullick, 'The Scribe of the Carilef Bible: A New Look at Some Late Eleventh-Century Durham Cathedral Manuscripts' in *Medieval Book Production: Assessing the Evidence*, ed. L. L. Brownrigg (Los Altos, 1990), 61–83. For Exeter see R. G. Gameson, 'Manuscrits normands à Exeter aux xie et xiie siècles', in *Manuscrits et enluminures dans le monde normand XIe–XVe siècles*, ed. P. Bouet and M. Dosdat (Caen, forthcoming). The general question is considered further by M. Gullick, 'Circulation des copistes et des manuscrits vers l'Angleterre aux xie et xiie siècles' in *Manuscrits et enluminures dans le monde normand*, ed. Bouet and Dosdat.

even the number of 'imports' dating from this period is modest. At the end of the eleventh century, however, and around the turn of the century, there was a substantial increase in the rate at which libraries were growing. The growth rate climbed further at the beginning of the twelfth century; and then rose even more dramatically in the early twelfth century.

The hiatus immediately after the Conquest no doubt reflected the disruptions resulting from the process of invasion and settlement itself, not to mention the despoliation of English houses in favour of Norman ones that had supported the Conqueror.[20] Indeed for a brief spell, manuscripts—above all deluxe ones—may have been leaving England faster than they were being imported.[21] Yet church reform was necessarily high on William's agenda; and the speed with which the remodelling of the church began is symbolised by the launch of a series of great rebuilding programmes from 1070 onwards.[22] Just as the new generation of leading ecclesiastics wished to reconstruct the external fabric of their great churches in accordance with the tastes of the time, so correspondingly they wanted to rebuild its internal fibre—of which books were a crucial part—along 'modern' lines. Anglo-Saxon libraries seemed out-of-date: William of Malmesbury, for instance, reports that Godfrey of Jumièges, the first Norman abbot of Malmesbury Abbey (1087×91–1106) found the Anglo-Saxon library he inherited unsatisfactory, and so set about supplementing it.[23] However, as Godfrey's case highlights, Anglo-Saxon abbots and priors were only gradually replaced by Norman ones,[24] staggering the impetus for change. Moreover, the organisation of programmes of copying new texts on an increased scale was a demanding task, which presupposed not only finance and a sufficiency of competent scribes, but also access to relevant exemplars. Arranging this undoubtedly took time, and there can be little doubt that the problem of exemplars was particularly acute in the earlier years of our period. As with the adoption of Romanesque architectural styles, it is debatable to what extent the changes that started to overtake English book collections from the 1070s represented 'normanisation' as opposed to simply moving with the times. And when approaching this question, we should be wary of accepting too readily the Norman view of the Anglo-Saxon church. If the erudite Archbishop Lanfranc characterised St Wulfstan of Worcester, the last Anglo-Saxon bishop (d. 1095), as illiterate (which he clearly was not),[25] the Flemish Goscelin of St Bertin, a long-time 'resident alien' in England, viewed the Normans as ignorant upstarts who despised learning, forbad scholarship and regarded illiteracy as an emblem either of secular wisdom or of holiness.[26] In point of fact, the expansion of book collections in England seems to have been contemporary with, rather than subsequent to comparable developments in Normandy.

Later chronicle sources are in broad agreement with the manuscript evidence to the

[20] See C. R. Dodwell, *Anglo-Saxon Art: a new perspective* (Manchester, 1982), pp. 216–22.

[21] The evidence is reviewed by D. N. Dumville, 'Anglo-Saxon Books: treasure in Norman hands', *Anglo-Norman Studies* 16 (1994), 83–99.

[22] E.g. at Christ Church, Canterbury, 1070×1; Saint Augustine's, Canterbury, 1070×3; Lincoln, 1072×3; Old Sarum, 1075×8; Saint Albans, 1077×88; Rochester, shortly after 1077; Winchester, 1079; Ely, 1081×93; Worcester, 1084; Gloucester, 1089; Durham, 1093; and Norwich, 1096.

[23] William of Malmesbury, *Gesta Pontificum*, ed. Hamilton, pp. 431–2.

[24] See further D. Knowles, *The Monastic Order in England*, 2nd ed. (Cambridge, 1963), pp. 111–24.

[25] William of Malmesbury, *Gesta Pontificum*, ed. Hamilton, p. 284: '*Sub seniore Willelmo inclamatum est in eum a Lanfranco de letterarum inscientia*'.

[26] 'The *Liber Confortatorius* of Goscelin of Saint Bertin', ed. C. H. Talbot, *Studia Anselmiana* 37, Analecta Monastica 3rd ser. (Rome, 1955), pp. 29 and 82.

extent that they portray some of the early Norman abbots as energetic library builders, and tend to place the 'centre of gravity' of the activity in question at the end of the eleventh century or even later. Paul of Caen, abbot of St Albans (1077–93), for instance, is recorded to have given twenty-eight 'notable' books plus eight psalters, a collectar, an epistolar, a book containing the gospel pericopes for the year, two gospel books ornamented with gold, silver and gems, not to mention ordinals, customaries, missals, tropers, collectors and 'other books which can be found in the little cupboards'.[27] His lead was followed by his successor, Abbot Richard (1097–1119), who gave many precious volumes including a great gospel book and a missal which incorporated an image of the abbot himself before Christ in majesty.[28] Similarly, the early-thirteenth-century chronicle of Evesham stated that Abbot Walther (1077×8–1104), 'had many books made';[29] the thirteenth-century chronicler Bartholomew Cotton reported that Herbert Losinga (1090×1–1119) endowed his new see of Norwich with books and other diverse gifts;[30] while the late medieval history of Gloucester related that Abbot Peter (1104–1113), 'enriched the cloister with a plenitude of books'.[31] Yet while the general expansion in the numbers of extant manuscripts from *s.* xi^{ex} onwards encourages us to give credence to such references, it is a striking fact that relevant localisable manuscripts are lacking in every one of these cases. With regard to Norwich, where we have firm contemporary evidence for Herbert Losinga's collecting of manuscripts (in the form of his own correspondence), there is every reason to believe that the relevant books perished in the fire of 1272. As to Evesham and Gloucester, by contrast, where the main expansion of the libraries seems to have been more a twelfth-century phenomenon, one suspects that the number of books added in the late eleventh century was quite small and that the later chroniclers presented this with formulaic hyperbole.

Less problematic are the cases of Durham and Salisbury where documentary references and extant localisable manuscripts are in accord. The scale of William of St Carilef's enrichment of Durham's library is known from the contemporary record of his gift, which itemises forty-nine books;[32] while the number, not to mention the appearance, of surviving late eleventh-century Salisbury books suggests that the canons were indeed led by a bishop (Osmund, 1078–99) who, in William of Malmesbury's words, wrote and bound books himself.[33]

Although a percentage of the volumes that made up this general expansion in reading matter were imported—a group of William of St Carilef's books being a well-documented example—the great majority were written in England. Sometimes they were written in

[27] Matthew Paris, *Gesta Abbatum Monasterii Sancti Albani* in Thomas Walsingham, *Gesta Abbatum Sancti Albani*, ed. H. T. Riley, 3 vols. RS 28/4a (London, 1867–9), I, pp. 57–8.

[28] *Ibid.*, p. 69.

[29] *Chronicon abbatiae de Evesham*, ed. W. D. Macray, RS 29 (London, 1858), p. 97: '*Libros multos fecit*'.

[30] Bartholomaei de Cotton, *Liber de archiepiscopis et episcopis Angliae*, ed. H. R. Luard, RS 16 (London, 1859), p. 391: '. . . *in quam [ecclesiam] ipse stabilierat, possessionibus, libris et diuersi generis ornamentis ditauerat*'.

[31] *Historia et Cartularium Monasterii S. Petri Gloucestriae*, ed. W. H. Hart, 3 vols., RS 33a–c (London, 1863–7), I, p. 13: '*et claustrum copia librorum ditauit*'.

[32] Durham Cathedral Library, A. II. 4, flyleaf (fol. 1r): see A. C. Browne, 'Bishop William of St Carilef's Book Donations to Durham Cathedral Priory', *Scriptorium* 42 (1988), 140–55.

[33] William of Malmesbury, *Gesta Pontificum*, ed. Hamilton, p. 184: '*cum episcopus ipse nec scribere nec scriptos ligare fastidiret*'. When repeated by Ralph Higden (*Polychronicon*, 9 vols., RS 41a–i (London, 1865–86), VII, p. 294), this had been expanded to include illuminating them: '. . . *ipsemet episcopus libros scribere ligare et illuminare non fastidiret*'. Cf. also *Statuta consuetudinis ecclesiae cathedralis B. Marie Virginis Sarisberiensis*, ed. C. Wordsworth and D. Macleane (London, 1915), p. 26.

England by Normans. Various manuscripts produced between *c.* 1066–1100 show the co-operation of Norman (or French) and Anglo-Saxon hands: British Library, Arundel 235 is a case in point (see pls. 6–7), as are several volumes from Canterbury, and one from Exeter.[34] In such instances it is the coexistence of English and Norman participants, along with an English medieval provenance, that enables the production of the book to be assigned to England. The gospel book, Rouen, Bibliothèque municipale, A. 21, by contrast, is entirely Norman in script and decoration, and its medieval provenance was Jumièges; however in this case an original dedication inscription reveals that it was written at Abingdon during the time of Abbot Reginald (1084–97) and then sent to Jumièges where he had formerly been a monk.[35] It is rare, unfortunately, that the matter is so clear-cut, and localising certain Norman-looking books from this period can be a difficult task. Some of the earliest Rochester manuscripts provide more typical examples: here it is the documented early Rochester provenance (pre *c.* 1125), the reappearance of hands in more than one manuscript, plus the occasional, minor Kentish feature that enables work which is almost entirely Norman or French to be assigned to England. The principal scribe of London, British Library, Royal 2 C. iii, for example, has a characterful, distinctly Norman hand,[36] while two of his collaborators have Norman or Northern French ones;[37] however the volume also includes a very brief stint in the prickly script associated with Kent (above all Christ Church, Canterbury).[38] Furthermore, the second Norman collaborator (who has a rather poor hand) reappears in at least two other books, Royal 5 D. i and Royal 6 C. x, both of early Rochester provenance and which also share an artist,[39] and the display script on fol. 1r of the former echoes the style that was then favoured at Christ Church, Canterbury. Such interconnections, along with the early Rochester provenance of all the volumes in question enable us to conclude that these Norman scribes and artists were almost certainly working at Rochester.

The practical implications of an expansion in manuscript production on this scale from the end of the eleventh century should not be underestimated. In the first place, considerably more 'man hours' must have been devoted to writing books. For ecclesiastics this was in itself a devotional activity,[40] but it is no surprise to find that the services of paid, 'professional' scribes were also welcomed. We know that Paul of Caen, abbot of St Albans, benefitted from lay sponsorship (provided by a literate knight) to employ professional scribes at that house in

[34] E.g. from Saint Augustine's: Cambridge, Corpus Christi College, 276 and 291; Canterbury Cathedral, Add. 172; and Rouen, Bibliothèque municipale, A. 44; from Exeter: Oxford, Bodleian Library, Bodley 314 (cf. Ker, *English Manuscripts*, pls. 2–3).

[35] F. Avril, *Manuscrits normands xi–xii*[e] *siècles* (Rouen, 1975), no. 31; *Trésors des Abbayes Normands* (Rouen-Caen, 1979), no. 137; Ch. Samaran and R. Marichal (gen. eds.), *Manuscrits datés*, 7 vols. to date (Paris, 1959–), VII, pt i, p. 263, pt. ii, pl. xxix; M. Dosdat, *Le Livre saint en Normandie* (Avranches, 1995), no. 5. The volume was entirely written by a single scribe, with the exception of the donation inscription which was the work of a different, though contemporary hand.

[36] Fols. 5r–44va/8; 45ra/12–98ra/2; and 98rb/7–105v.

[37] The first wrote: fols. 98ra/3–98rb/6; 106r–123r; and 127ra/11–170r. The second wrote: 123v–127ra/10.

[38] Fols. 44va/9–45ra/11.

[39] See C. M. Kauffmann, *Romanesque Manuscripts 1066–1190* (London, 1975), cat. 16, with ill. 38.

[40] The point is underlined by the start of Herbert Losinga's remarkable letter to Felix (*Epistolae Herberti Losinga, Osberti de Clara et Elmeri*, ed. R. Anstruther (Brussels-London, 1846), ep. 5): 'You were accustomed to write out Augustine to sustain yourself with the bread of so great a doctor, and to gladden your heart with the wine of the divine scriptures'. Metaphors of food had long been applied to spiritual reading (e.g. Jerome, ep. 125: *Sancti Eusebii Hieronymi Epistulae*, ed. I. Hilberg, 3 vols., CSEL 54–6 (Vienna-Leipzig, 1910–18), III, p. 131), and by extension to the business of copying such texts (e.g. Alcuin, 'On Scribes': *Poetry of the Carolingian Renaissance*, ed. and trans. P. Godman (London, 1985), p. 138).

the late eleventh century;[41] Abbot Fabricius of Abingdon (1100–17) hired six professionals to write texts for his foundation in the early twelfth century;[42] while Herbert Losinga alluded to the fact that a certain Alexander who was about to enter the community had hitherto made a living as a scribe.[43] By the end of our period it is sometimes possible to identify the activities of probable itinerant artists and scribes from the books themselves;[44] however the documented case of a monk from Great Malvern who had gone to Worcester to work on a missal and then moved on, apparently without permission, to Westminster, should give one pause:[45] monks, too, could travel. Moreover, as another of Herbert Losinga's letters reminds us, monks also wrote 'professionally';[46] and it will be noted that the inscription in the famous decretal manuscript that Lanfranc gave to Christ Church declares that he *bought* it from the monastery of Bec.[47]

In addition, the expansion in book production meant that the pelts of ever increasing numbers of animals, not to mention other raw material, had to be acquired—an issue about which the available sources are virtually silent[48]—and that literally hundreds of exemplars had to be located and borrowed.[49] We can be quite confident that books were circulating in England during the late eleventh and early twelfth century in much greater numbers, and on a more regular basis than ever before. Herbert Losinga, for instance, asked an Abbot Richard

[41] *Gesta Abbatum Sancti Albani*, ed. Riley, pp. 57–8.

[42] *Chronicon Monasterii de Abingdon*, ed. J. Stevenson, 2 vols., RS 2a–b (London, 1858), II, p. 289; also EBL, B2 (pp. 5–7), whose reading is followed here: '*Abbas Faricius instituit VI scriptores praeter claustres qui missalia, gradualia, antiphonaria, troparia, lectionaria et caeteros libros eccles[iastic]os scribebant. Scriptores uero hos libros scribebant: Austinum de Ciuitate Dei; Homelias Sancti Austini super Johannem, et multa alia uolumina ipsius doctoris; Homelias sancti Gregorii; Homelias super Ezechielem; Expositiones super Psalterium, et multa alia uolumina ipsius doctoris; Hieronymum super Vetus Testamentum; Hegesippum, et multa alia uolumina ipsius doctoris; Ambrosium de Officiis et multa alia uolumina ipsius doctoris; Johannem Chrysostomum super Epistolas Pauli, de Reparatione Lapsi, et alia plurima uolumina eiusdem doctoris; Homelias Bedae, epistolas Cypriani, Cassianum super Psalterium; multos libros de physica. Prouidit et sacristae, cellarario, lignario, et caeteris obedientiariis omnia necessaria*'.

[43] Herbert Losinga, ep. 51, ed. Anstruther: '*Arguebar solidos quos pro suarum scriptuarum laboribus expostulauerat; at idem hoc abnegans, in nostro uictituum claustro, solo cibo et uestitura se contentum fore confirmauit*'. The issue of professional scribes in Romanesque England is studied by M. Gullick, 'Professional Scribes in Eleventh- and Twelfth-century England', *English Manuscript Studies* 7 (1998), 7–24.

[44] The most famous being the 'Alexis Master', for a convient summary of whose known activities see R. M. Thomson, *Manuscripts of Saint Albans Abbey*, 2 vols. (Woodbridge, 1982), I, pp. 24–7. For another case see Kauffmann, *Romanesque Manuscripts*, cats. 48–51; with Mynors and Thomson, *Manuscripts of Hereford Cathedral Library*, p. 36; and R. M. Thomson, 'Books and Learning at Gloucester Abbey in the Twelfth and Thirteenth Centuries' in *Books and Collectors 1200–1700: Essays presented to Andrew Watson*, ed. J. P. Carley and C. G. C. Tite (London, 1997), 3–26, at p. 7.

[45] *Westminster Abbey Charters 1066–c. 1214*, ed. E. Mason, London Record Society 25 (London, 1988), no. 248A. The event is datable to 1124×34.

[46] Herbert Losinga, ep. 46, ed. Anstruther.

[47] '*Hunc librum dato precio emptum ego Lanfranc archiepiscopus de beccensi cenobio in anglicam terram deferri feci et ecclesiae Christi dedi . . .*': Cambridge, Trinity College, B. 16. 44, p. 405: Ker, *English Manuscripts*, pl. 5.

[48] Herbert Losinga (ep. 4, ed. Anstruther) begged Prior Hugh (?of Thetford) for ink and parchment. The *Chronicon Monasterii de Abingdon*, ed. Stevenson, II, p. 153, refers to the allocation of tithes '*ad parcamenum emendum pro librorum ecclesie renouatione*'.

[49] Important headway has been made in the study of the circulation of texts in England during this period by M. P. Richards, *Texts and their Traditions in the Medieval Library of Rochester Cathedral Priory*, Transactions of the American Philosophical Society 78/3 (Philadelphia, 1988), *passim*; T. Webber, *Scribes and Scholars at Salisbury Cathedral c. 1075–c. 1125* (Oxford, 1992), pp. 44–81; also *eadem*, 'The Diffusion of Augustine's *Confessions* in England during the Eleventh and Twelfth Centuries' in *The Cloister and the World: Essays in Medieval History in honour of Barabara Harvey*, ed. J. Blair and B. Golding (Oxford, 1996), 29–45; and 'The Patristic Content of English Book Collections in the Eleventh Century: towards a continental perspective' in *Of the Making of Books, Medieval Manuscripts: their Scribes and Readers; Essays presented to M. B. Parkes*, ed. P. Robinson and R. Zim (Aldershot, 1997), 191–205.

(probably the abbot of Saint Albans of that name) for a Josephus, the Epistles of Augustine, the Epistles of Jerome and the lectionaries that Richard had himself compiled—all in one letter.[50] The 'chains' of volumes which contain identical or closely similar collections of texts shed further light on this process. A closely related collection of Jerome letters and tractates, for example, appears in four manuscripts of our period, which are associated with Bath, Durham, Rochester and Worcester. The fact that the earliest copy was actually written at Christ Church, Canterbury, but had reached Durham before 1096 further underlines the relevance of the example.[51] Even more striking is the recurrence of a sprawling compendium of commentaries and pseudo-scientific texts in three manuscripts, from Christ Church, Canterbury, Durham, and Rochester; and in this case the earliest copy (again the Durham one) had been written in Normandy.[52]

As this last example suggests, a fairly high percentage of the exemplars were presumably acquired from the continent, particularly in the earlier years of our period. The correspondence of Lanfranc, Anselm, and Herbert Losinga gives some insight into this procedure. Herbert, for instance, looked to Fécamp (where he had been first a monk and then prior, and whose customary he attempted to imitate at Norwich) for a copy of Suetonius, specifying that it was impossible to locate the text in England.[53] (The evidence of the surviving manuscripts and book-lists suggests that this was probably true.[54]) Lanfranc had asked Anselm, then abbot of Bec (where, of course, Lanfranc himself had resided for over twenty years (1042–63)) to procure copies of Gregory's *Moralia* and of unspecified works by Ambrose and Jerome—a task which, in the event, proved problematic.[55] Anselm also sent Lanfranc an early copy of his *Monologion*, and given that Anselm was the contemporary author whose works enjoyed the best circulation in England during our period, it is worth noting that one of them had certainly reached England as early as 1076.[56] An undoubted survivor of Lanfranc's activities in this respect is the aforementioned decretal manuscript which bears a contemporary inscription stating that the archbishop bought it from Bec and gave it to Christ Church, Canterbury.[57] Furthermore, some of the texts that Lanfranc acquired rapidly circulated beyond Canterbury: the Durham Jerome mentioned above is probably a case in point;[58] the various

[50] Herbert Losinga, ep. 10, ed. Anstruther.

[51] Nos. 221, 528, 529, and 530. Further on the Durham manuscript (B. II. 10) see R. A. B. Mynors, *Durham Cathedral Manuscripts to the End of the Twelfth Century* (Oxford, 1939), no. 38, with pl. 26, where other copies of the same collection are noted.

[52] Nos. 136, 167, and 222. Further on the Durham manuscript (B. II. 11) see Mynors, *Durham Cathedral Manuscripts*, no. 39, with pl. 27, where, once again, other copies of the collection are noted. Other 'sets' of books with similar collections of texts include the following: a) 24, 475, and 842; b) 70, 185, 251, 504, 692, 694, 808, and 809; c) 147, 313, 473, 667, and 862; d) 164 and 500; e) 523, 524, 686, 687, 704, and 873; f) 584, 668, 809, and 846; and also perhaps: g) 184, 263, 309, 329, 407, and 754. Some of these groups have been commented on by Webber, *Scribes and Scholars*, pp. 50–8.

[53] Herbert Losinga, ep. 5, ed. Anstruther: '*Suetonium quem in Anglia inuenire non possum, facite transcribi, et transcriptum mittite mihi per Dancardum presbyterum, uel per alium quem uolueritis seruientem*.' For his comments on the customary see ep. 34.

[54] There are three copies on the inventory; however it is uncertain when two of them (nos. 271 and 348) reached England, and in any case the latter only contains extracts; while the third copy (no. 563) was not written until around the time Herbert was making his request. No copies are mentioned on the extant book-lists.

[55] *S. Anselmi Cantuariensis Archiepiscopi Opera Omnia*, ed. F. S. Schmitt, 5 vols. (Edinburgh, 1946–61), III, epp. 23, 25, and 26. The traffic also went the other way: epp. 42–3.

[56] *Ibid.*, ep. 72.

[57] See n. 47 above.

[58] See n. 51 above.

copies of Lanfranc's Decretal Collection certainly are;[59] as also, seemingly, are most of the manuscripts which contain both Augustine's *De nuptiis et concupiscentia* and his *Contra Iulianum*.[60] In addition, although the relevant manuscripts do not appear to survive, the *Gesta Abbatum S. Albani* records that the books written at Saint Albans in the time of Abbot Paul were copied from exemplars that had been supplied by Lanfranc.[61]

Some of the imported books were destined to remain in English collections; however the circumstance that the number of such volumes that can still be identified is comparatively small would seem to imply that most were returned after copying. As far as we can tell, only Durham and, above all, Exeter stocked their collections by actually acquiring substantial numbers of manuscripts from the Continent.[62] In both cases, Normandy was the principal (though not the only) source of supply. The Durham acquisitions are firmly associated with Bishop William of St Carilef: the house chronicler Symeon of Durham, writing less than twenty years after the events in question, recorded that William sent books to Durham from Normandy before his return from exile in November 1091.[63] The relevant Exeter volumes (which are not similarly documented and are, it must be admitted, more difficult to isolate) date from the episcopacies of Osbern FitzOsbern (1072–1103) and William Warelwast (1107–37), the first 'Norman' bishops of the see.[64] Moreover, amongst a group of texts listed as 'the books of Bishop William' on the 1327 Exeter inventory are at least two which, although they no longer survive, were almost certainly imported from Normandy, namely, '*Communis liber sanctorum de usu rotomagensi* (i.e. Rouen)' and '*Unus liber sanctorum de eodem usu in duobus uoluminibus*'.[65]

If the numbers of identifiable continental manuscripts written in our period which have an English medieval provenance are a reasonable guide, they suggest that the practice of importing books rose sharply towards the end of the eleventh century and peaked around the turn of the century.[66] Although the quantity involved remained stable in the early twelfth

[59] Z. N. Brooke, *The English Church and the Papacy from the Conquest to the Reign of John* (Cambridge, 1931), pp. 57–83, and 231–5; Gullick, 'Scribe of the Carilef Bible', pp. 81–2 (nn. 57–8); M. Brett, 'The *Collectio Lanfranci* and its Competitors' in *Intellectual Life in the Middle Ages: Essays Presented to Margaret Gibson*, ed. L. Smith and B. Ward (London, 1992), 157–74; and M. Gullick, 'The English-owned Manuscripts of the *Collectio Lanfranci*' in *The Legacy of M. R. James*, ed. L. Dennison (forthcoming).

[60] See Ker, *English Manuscripts*, pp. 12–13, with Webber, *Scribes and Scholars*, pp. 46–7. The relevant manuscripts are nos. 637, 640, 843, and 871.

[61] *Gesta Abbati Sancti Albani*, ed. Riley, I, pp. 57–8.

[62] See Gullick, 'Scribe of the Carilef Bible', and Gameson, 'Manuscrits normands à Exeter'. The two Mont-Saint-Michel manuscripts of Saint Augustine's provenance (nos. 549–50) most probably arrived there in the time of Scotland, the first Norman abbot of the house, who had formerly been a monk (and scribe) at the Mount. Further on these books see J. J. G. Alexander, *Norman Illumination at Mont-Saint-Michel 966–1100* (Oxford, 1970); and *Trésors des Abbayes Normands*, no. 118.

[63] Durham University Library, Cosin V. ii. 6, fol. 84r (Symeon of Durham, *Historia ecclesiae dunelmensis*, ed. T. Arnold, 2 vols., RS 75a–b (London, 1882–5), I, p. 128): '*At ille nequaquam uacuus rediit, sed non pauca ex auro et argento sacra altaris uasa et diuersa ornamenta, sed et libros plurimos ad ecclesiam praemittere curauit*'.

[64] On the latter, with comments on the former, see D. W. Blake, 'Bishop William Warelwast', *Transactions of the Devonshire Association* 104 (1972), 15–33.

[65] Exeter Cathedral Library, 3671, printed in G. Oliver, *Lives of the Bishops of Exeter* (Exeter, 1861), pp. 301–10 at 304–5. All the titles are included in my inventory of texts in book-lists as 'E'. They are all liturgical or para-liturgical books. The titles of the others provide no comparable clues as to their country of origin.

[66] *Saec.* xi^{2}: 8. xi^{ex}: 20. xi/xii: 29. xii^{in}: 30. xii^{1}: 21. xii$^{2/4}$: 2. As noted above, older continental volumes were undoubtedly also imported at this time, but the relevant manuscripts, if they survive, are naturally much more difficult to identify. Probable examples include: Cambridge, Pembroke College, 81, 83, and 91; Hereford Cathedral, O. III. 2; London, British Library, Add. 23944A; and Add. 40165A; and Oxford, Bodleian Library, Bodley 229.

century, the percentage of the total output that such volumes represent declines very sharply: but then by this time, of course, the numbers of available English manuscripts, and hence exemplars, had increased enormously.

The principal source of supply, as evidenced by the extant manuscripts was, unsurprisingly, Normandy, which accounts for some seventy, or just under 3/5 of the volumes in question. It is equally clear, however, that the Duchy was by no means the only source, for a further fifty-one books (or just over 2/5 of the total) came from elsewhere on the Continent, mainly from France or the Low Countries.[67] In fact, given that some of the wholly Norman books may actually have been written in England, while non-Norman continental books are less likely to be identified as possible early imports, the ratio between these two groups (Norman, non-Norman) was probably closer to fifty-fifty. The English church had enjoyed close contacts with Northern France and Flanders since the tenth century, which were strengthened by the Lotharingian appointments of Edward the Confessor's reign, and can be seen to continue during our period, not least in the person of Goscelin of Saint Bertin.[68] On historical as well as geographical grounds, therefore, libraries in these conveniently accessible areas are likely to have been important sources of books and exemplars after 1066,[69] and, significantly, we know of several relevant houses, such as Saint Vaast, Arras, Gembloux, Lobbes and Saint Bertin, which had built up impressive book collections at an earlier date in the eleventh century.[70]

Furthermore, even in the immediate aftermath of the Conquest, Normandy was by no means the only recruiting ground for the English church: the Conqueror's foundation of Battle Abbey, to mention a well-known example, was initially staffed from Marmoutier, Tours;[71] Lewis (1077) and Castle Acre (1089) priories were established by monks from Cluny;[72] Much Wenlock (1080×1), Bermondsey (1089), Pontefract (1090) and Northampton

[67] Normandy: nos. 6, 80, 87, 93, 124, 143, 149, 162, 198, 210, 222, 224, 225, 227, 233, 236, 237, 245, 293, 297, 306, 348, 389, 391, 416, 427, 495, ?499, 549, 550, 561, 576, 582, 630, 631, 638, 639, 641, 642, 648, 652, 654, 656, 657, 658, 660, 674, 678, 681, 683, 684, 686, 693, 694, 697, 698, 699, 701, 706, 734, 744, 756, 771, 847, 877, 878, 901, 904, and 925.

France: nos. 48, 101, 105, 107, 110, 111, 121, 126, 127, 191, 296, 418, 432, 450, 498, 548, 574, 591, 635, 680, 712, 736, 738, 739, 743, 802, 881, and 909.

Continental (unspecific): nos. 25, 89, 214, 239, 240, 242, 243, 244, 271, 276, 296, 373, 394, 512, 578, 600, 602, 615, 619, 731, 786, 787, 789, and 804.

France or Normandy: 497.

[68] See in general P. Grierson, 'Relations between England and Flanders before the Norman Conquest', *Transactions of the Royal Historical Society* 4th ser. 23 (1941), 71–112, repr. in *Essays in Medieval History*, ed. R. W. Southern (London, 1968), 61–92; and V. Ortenberg, *The English Church and the Continent in the Tenth and Eleventh Centuries* (Oxford, 1992), pp. 21–40.

[69] One Salisbury scribe of the first generation also worked in the Low Countries, contributing to Utrecht, Universiteitsbibliotheek, 86: Webber, *Scribes and Scholars*, p. 14, and 'Patristic Content of English Book Collections', pp. 201–3; with K. van der Horst, *Illuminated and Decorated Medieval Manuscripts in the University Library Utrecht: an illustrated catalogue* (Cambridge, 1989), no. 1.

[70] See respectively: S. Schulten, 'Die Buchmalerei des 11. Jahrhunderts im Kloster St Vaast in Arras', *Münchner Jahrbuch der bildenden Kunst* 7 (1956), 49–90; A. Boutemy, 'Un grand abbé du xie siècle: Olbert de Gembloux', *Annales de la Société archéologique de Namur* 41 (1934), 43–85; F. Dolbeau, 'Un nouveau catalogue des manuscrits de Lobbes aux xie et xiie siècles', *Recherches augustiniennes* 13 (1978), 3–36 and 14 (1979), 191–248; and A. Wilmart, 'Les livres de l'abbé Odbert', *Bulletin historique de la Société des Antiquaires de la Morine* 14 (1929), 169–88.

[71] *The Chronicle of Battle Abbey*, ed. E. Searle (Oxford, 1980), pp. 36–8 and 42; also E. M. Hallam, 'Monasteries as "war memorials": Battle Abbey and La Victoire', *Studies in Church History* 20 (1983), 47–57.

[72] Cf. Knowles, *Monastic Order*, pp. 151–8; and B. Golding, 'The Coming of the Cluniacs', *Anglo-Norman Studies* 3 (1980), 65–77 and 208–12.

(1093×1100) were founded from La Charité-sur-Loire (Cluniac); while Bardney Abbey was refounded (*c.* 1087) by monks from Charroux in Poitou.[73] Correspondingly, some of the high-ranking clergy had a French background: one thinks, for instance, of Ernulf, successively prior of Christ Church (1096–1107), abbot of Peterborough (1107–14) and bishop of Rochester (1115–24), who had been a monk of Beauvais. Furthermore, such monastic connections were complemented by contacts with cathedral schools in northern France. Archbishop Thomas of York (1070–1100) and Bishop Samson of Worcester (1096–1112), for example, had both been to the schools at Liège; while other English and Norman clerics attended those in northern France, notably Laon, Paris and Reims.[74]

But were more people reading larger numbers of texts than previously? This is a very difficult question to answer. Close examination of the fairly small number of new works that were composed in England during this period can at best demonstrate that a few key figures had read a particular selection of texts,[75] which is not especially helpful for the issue at hand. William of Malmesbury (*c.* 1095–1143), precentor and librarian of that house, to take a celebrated example, had first-hand knowledge of an enormous range of works;[76] however, not only was he outstanding among contemporary ecclesiastics in this respect, but furthermore, his reading cannot even be regarded as evidence for the nature of the library at Malmesbury, given that he is known to have travelled widely and to have read extensively in other centres. The value of the evidence provided by the writings of individuals like Lanfranc and Anselm, whose education and intellectual development were accomplished, and much of whose adult life was spent abroad, is even more circumscribed.

The average monk or canon living in the early twelfth century almost certainly had a greater choice of literature available to him than his mid-eleventh-century predecessors; but whether he actually read more than they is a different matter altogether. There was no doctrinal reason why he should have done so; nor did he have any more time to devote to reading than his forebears. Like the *Regula S. Benedicti* before it, Lanfranc's *Constitutiones* only assumed that a monk would read one book a year, and it acknowledged that not all would manage to accomplish that.[77] Correspondingly, Herbert Losinga knew people who, in his opinion, read in a very superficial way and were content, he maintained, simply to know the name of the book they 'read' and how many pages they had 'got through'.[78] This philistine attitude is seemingly reflected in the Ely inventory of 1143 which after a lengthy and admiring description of the many treasures of the church, concluded bluntly: 'These and many other things Bishop Nigel found in the church as well as a large number of books in a chest which,

[73] G. Beech, 'Aquitainians and Flemings in the Refoundation of Bardney Abbey (Lincolnshire) in the Later Eleventh Century', *The Haskings Society Journal* 1 (1989), 73–90.

[74] F. Barlow, *The English Church 1066–1154* (London, 1979), pp. 248–51; P. Demouy, 'Des Anglais à Reims au xiie siècle', *La Champagne, terre d'accueil*, Transactions Universitaires de Nancy (Nancy, 1995), 175–87, esp. 176–8.

[75] See, for example, R. W. Southern, *St Anselm and his Biographer* (Cambridge, 1963), pp. 274–333, esp. 320–8; *The Life of Gundulf, Bishop of Rochester*, ed. R. M. Thomson (Toronto, 1977), esp. pp. 13–16; and R. W. Hunt, '*Liber Florum*: A Twelfth-Century Theological Florilegium', in *Sapientiae Doctrina: Mélanges offerts à Dom. Hildebrand Bascour: Recherche de théologie ancienne et médiévale, numéro special 1* (Louvain, 1980), 137–47.

[76] R. M. Thomson, *William of Malmesbury* (Woodbridge, 1987), esp. pp. 39–75, 139–73, and 197–207.

[77] *The Monastic Constitutions of Lanfranc*, ed. D. Knowles (London, 1951), 19.

[78] Herbert Losinga, ep. 49, ed. Anstruther.

if we paused to list them, would weary the reader'.[79] On the other hand, certain individuals and communities had scholarly reputations. William of Malmesbury's favourable view of the canons of St Osyth's, for example, was mentioned earlier;[80] he similarly lauded the learning of the Salisbury canons, and in this case where we have the independent evidence of a reasonable number of their manuscripts, it corroborates his view.[81] The reality of the situation no doubt varied from place to place, from person to person, and sometimes from one generation to the next. The key point was that, irrespective of whether they were used very much, the best houses were now fortified with weighty collections of reading books which were perceived to be supremely authoritative, with fashionable new libraries as well as with Romanesque architecture.[82]

Although it is, inevitably, institutional ownership that can best be documented, not all the books of our period belonged initially to institutions. Secular clerics and learned individuals such as Gilbert the Universal (bishop of London 1128–34) doubtless possessed books during their lifetimes, even if these can no longer be identified. Probably the most famous extant manuscript that can be associated with an individual is the lavishly decorated St Albans Psalter, which was probably owned by Christina of Markyate;[83] and occasional documentary references allude to other books in 'private hands'. The literate Norman knight who had underwritten the employment of professional scribes at Saint Albans in the late eleventh century, himself received the first batch of books copied as a result of his sponsorship, and Abbot Paul had also given him 'other books for his court chapel at Hatfield'.[84] Geoffrey Gorron, who subsequently became abbot of St Albans (1119–46), was formerly a schoolmaster in Dunstable, entering the house to make reparation for the fact that some of its vestments which he had borrowed for a play were accidentally incinerated, and the same fire, we are told, burned books that were then in his possession.[85] It is equally a reasonable assumption that there were a fair number of volumes in royal hands: Matilda, Henry I's queen, for instance, doubtless possessed some, including presumably copies of the Vita of her mother, Queen Margaret of Scotland, which was written at her request,[86] and of the *Nauigatio S. Brendani* that was translated into French at her command.[87]

Within the overall schema of growth outlined earlier, the individual houses about which more is known can be seen to have had their own patterns of library development, as one would expect. The book collection of Saint Augustine's Abbey, Canterbury, for example, is

[79] *Liber Eliensis*, III, 50, ed. Blake, p. 294: '*Hec et alia multa inuenit episcopus Nigellus in ecclesia, sed et in armario numerum librorum ualde, qui lectorem fastidiret si narrando suspenderetur*'. In fact, the documentation of Ely's medieval library as a whole is extremely poor: see EBL, pp. 127–31.

[80] See n. 2 above.

[81] *Gesta Pontificum*, ed. Hamilton, p. 184.

[82] Cf. R. G. Gameson, 'Alfred the Great and the Destruction and Production of Christian Books', *Scriptorium* 49 (1995), 180–210, esp. 208–10.

[83] Hildesheim, St Godehard's Church, 1, plus Cologne, Schnütgen Museum, 5 (our no. 325). See O. Pächt, C. R. Dodwell, and F. Wormald, *The St Albans Psalter* (London, 1960), esp. pp. 27–30 and 276–80; cf. also Kauffmann, *Romanesque Manuscripts*, cat. 29; Thomson, *St Albans*, I, p. 25; and K. E. Haney, 'The St Albans Psalter: a reconsideration', *Journal of the Warburg and Courtauld Institutes* 58 (1995), 1–28.

[84] *Gesta Abbatum S. Albani*, ed. Riley, I, pp. 57–8.

[85] *Ibid.*, I, p. 73. Further on his activities as abbot see Thomson, *St Albans* I, pp. 20–7.

[86] See L. L. Honeycutt, 'The Ideal of the Perfect Princess: the Life of St Margaret in the Reign of Matilda II', *Anglo-Norman Studies* 12 (1990), 81–97.

[87] M. D. Legge, *Anglo-Norman Literature and its Background* (Oxford, 1963), pp. 8–18.

characterised by continuous but fairly leisurely growth throughout the period, after, seemingly, a fairly barren stretch in the couple of generations before the Conquest (a representative early twelfth-century volume is reproduced as pl. 19).[88] Local resources were swelled by at least a few imports from Mont-Saint-Michel, presumably under Abbot Scotland (1070–87) who had come from that house; while a few passages of script and decoration in locally produced volumes imply that some Norman scribes and artists worked at Saint Augustine's in the late eleventh century.[89]

At Worcester, book production had been fairly piecemeal for much of the late Anglo-Saxon period, and the scriptorium seems only to have achieved maturity towards the middle of the eleventh century. However, the impetus it acquired, and the 'house style' it developed on the eve of the Conquest were then sustained into the late eleventh century, apparently little disturbed by the events of 1066 (pls. 2 and 3 show relevant late eleventh-century volumes).[90] There seems to have been an appreciable slackening in local production around the turn of the century (following the death of St Wulfstan), with a revival in the early twelfth century (see pl. 23).[91] One of the interesting aspects of Worcester's situation is that the foundation can boast some of the earliest post-Conquest copies of patristic writings (such as the manuscript of John Cassian's *Collationes* illustrated in pl. 3), yet it was undoubtedly one of the most conservative, Anglo-Saxon centres throughout the late eleventh century.[92] This underlines the point made earlier, that the desire for such texts was part of a universal trend and was not simply the result of the Norman incursion.

In contrast to Saint Augustine's Abbey, Canterbury, to Worcester, and to other houses which had an appreciable heritage of Anglo-Saxon books in 1066, Salisbury (Old Sarum) was only founded in 1075 when Bishop Herman moved his see thither from Sherborne, and it began our period with next to nothing. This situation goes some way towards explaining the speed and energy with which the canons began to copy their own manuscripts (though the rather different reaction of the canons of Lincoln in a similar circumstance implies that other factors, such as personal taste, the scholarly leanings of the leadership and the literary connections of the community, also came into play). Salisbury's book collection thus grew very rapidly and, in some ways, exotically at the end of the eleventh century, almost exclusively it would seem as a result of local production (pl. 10 reproduces a volume of this phase). Following, apparently, a hiatus at the beginning of the twelfth century, book production then resumed with vigour, again the work of the canons themselves.[93]

That the transfer of a see and the associated foundation of a community of canons did not necessarily have this result is demonstrated by the case of Lincoln, to which Bishop Remigius moved his see from Dorchester in 1072. The handful of surviving manuscripts (the

[88] R. G. Gameson, 'English Manuscript Art in the late Eleventh Century: Canterbury and its Context', in *Canterbury and the Norman Conquest*, ed. R. Eales and R. Sharpe (London, 1995), 95–144, esp. 122–9.

[89] See n. 34 above.

[90] R. G. Gameson, 'Book Production and Decoration at Worcester in the Tenth and Eleventh Centuries' in *St Oswald of Worcester: Life and Influence*, ed. N. Brooks and C. Cubitt (Leicester, 1996), 194–243.

[91] R. G. Gameson, 'St Wulfstan, the Library of Worcester, and the Spirituality of the Medieval Book', in *St Wulfstan of Worcester*, ed. N. Brooks and J. Barrow (London, forthcoming).

[92] See further E. Mason, Change and Continuity in Eleventh-Century Mercia: the experience of St Wulfstan of Worcester', *Anglo-Norman Studies* 8 (1986), 154–76; and *eadem*, *St Wulfstan of Worcester c. 1108–1095* (Oxford, 1990), pp. 108–232.

[93] Webber, *Scribes and Scholars, passim.*

finest and most ambitious of which is illustrated on pl. 12), suggest that the collection grew slowly, remained small and that its content was very conservative; and this impression is reinforced by the section of the twelfth-century booklist which enumerates the volumes that were present by 1148—a modest total of forty-four.[94]

At Christ Church, Canterbury, whose library in 1066 had a long history behind it, we see a generation of frantic but piecemeal writing and collecting in the late eleventh century, probably fostered by the arrival of Lanfranc and further encouraged by losses sustained in the fire of 1067 (which, according to Eadmer, destroyed almost all the foundation's valuable books 'sacred and secular alike').[95] This was superseded from *c.* 1100 by more orderly and less hasty work (see pl. 14),[96] and there followed a steady stream of volumes in a distinctive house style. Such books continued to be produced to the end of our period, by which time the main phase of 'in-house' copying had passed.

At Bury St Edmunds, where Anglo-Saxon traditions of script remained strong, there seems to have been a modest growth in the late eleventh century, with some continental acquisitions augmenting local production; however, the types of text acquired during this phase (largely homiliaries and liturgica) were characteristic more of the pre-Conquest than the post-Conquest era. This impression of conservatism is reinforced by the content, not to mention language (Old English), of a late eleventh-century book-list—if its association with Bury be correct.[97] Such activity dwindled around the turn of the century, only to pick up noticeably in the early twelfth century, when the texts being collected, patristics and Boethius, were more 'fashionable'. The concerted impetus for library growth, however, seems to have come even later, in the second quarter of the twelfth century, and hence largely outside our period.[98]

Despite its antiquity, Rochester does not appear to have had a very extensive Anglo-Saxon literary heritage in 1066. Book production seems to have begun in Gundulf's episcopacy (1077–1108),[99] the first phase (of which the so-called 'Gundulf Bible' is the *magnum opus*[100]) being characterised by the strong presence of Norman or northern French hands. The process of acquiring and copying texts would seem to have accelerated in the early twelfth century,[101]

[94] Printed in *Giraldi Cambrensis Opera*, ed. J. F. Dimock, VII (London, 1877), pp. 165–71; cf. R. M. Thomson, *Catalogue of the Manuscripts of Lincoln Cathedral Chapter Library* (Cambridge, 1989), pp. xii–xv.

[95] Eadmer, *Vita S. Bregwini* in *Anglia Sacra*, ed. H. Wharton, 2 vols. (London, 1691), II, p. 188. See also *The Letters of Lanfranc Archbishop of Canterbury*, ed. H. Clover and M. Gibson (Oxford, 1978), ep. 4 (p. 52).

[96] Gameson, 'English Manuscript Art in the late Eleventh Century', esp. pp. 110–21; T. Webber, 'Script and Manuscript Production at Christ Church, Canterbury, after the Norman Conquest', in *Canterbury and the Norman Conquest*, ed. Eales and Sharpe, 145–58. See also, more generally, C. R. Dodwell, *The Canterbury School of Illumination* (Cambridge, 1954).

[97] Lapidge, 'Booklists', no. XII; cf. Ker, *Catalogue*, no. 290.

[98] *Saec.* xi^{2}: nos. 53, 110, 111, 112, 115, and 199. *S.* xi^{ex}: nos. 21, 119, and 636. *S.* xi/xii: nos. 120, and 720. *S.* xii^{in}: nos. 52, 113, 403, 522, 531, 532, 717, 718, 719, and 916. *S.* xii^{1}: nos. 114, 122, 177, 179, 606, 722, and 928. See further R. M. Thomson, 'The Library of Bury St Edmunds Abbey in the Eleventh and Twelfth Centuries', *Speculum* 47 (1972), 617–45, esp. 617–27; and E. P. McLachlan, *The Scriptorium of Bury St Edmunds in the Twelfth Century* (New York, 1986).

[99] Nos. 899–900: cf. C. W. Dutschke, *Guide to the Medieval and Renaissance Manuscripts in the Huntington Library*, 2 vols. (San Marino, 1989), I, pp. 124–30, with II, pls. 40–1; also Richards, *Texts and their Traditions*, pp. 62–77.

[100] On whom see R. A. L. Smith, 'The Place of Gundulf in the Anglo-Norman Church' in his *Collected Papers* (London, 1947), 83–102.

[101] Richards, *Texts and their Traditions*, pp. 1–11; K. Waller, 'Rochester Cathedral Library: an English Book Collection on Norman Models' in *Les Mutations socio-culturelles au tournant des xie–xiie siècles*, ed. R. Foreville, Études Anselmiennes ive session (Paris, 1974), 237–50.

this main impetus being accompanied by the adoption of the prickly style of script associated with Christ Church, Canterbury, a centre which was also an important source of supply of exemplars.[102] A high percentage of the volumes in question survive, and they include some handsome work (see pls. 17 and 18). The masterpiece from the end of our period was a second bible.[103]

Saint Albans is another ancient foundation whose pre-Conquest books, now extremely elusive, may not have been very numerous; and here the problem of interpretation continues after the Conquest. We have exceptionally clear documentary evidence that a significant body of books was produced at Saint Albans in the late eleventh century, the work in question being accomplished by professional scribes, and underpinned by access to the textual resources of Christ Church, Canterbury. Yet the surviving attributable manuscripts from the period are an impoverished group; while the evidence of the extant books implies that, as at Rochester, the main period of expansion was the early twelfth century.[104] One possible though purely hypothetical explanation for the apparent discrepancy is that the volumes produced during the first generation of the Norman régime were subsequently replaced with better copies, and were passed on to dependent cells.

The book collection at Exeter (which had been non-existent when the foundation was elevated to a see in the 1050s[105]) mushroomed at the end of the eleventh century and around the turn of the century, thanks largely, it would seem, to imported Norman books (pl. 5 shows one of the small number of volumes which were probably written at Exeter itself in the late eleventh).[106] It continued to grow in the twelfth century with local production becoming increasingly important. This was a more conservative library than that built up at Salisbury in the same period, suggesting once again that it was the character of the Salisbury community itself rather than the fact that they were secular canons that lay behind the scope of their collection.

Durham's library grew substantially in the late eleventh century through a combination of local production on the one hand, and acquisition from Normandy on the other, sponsored by the energetic Bishop William of St Carilef.[107] A significant percentage of the volumes in question are visually impressive, above all the great bible in which the details of Carilef's bequest were recorded.[108] This phase of rapid expansion was followed around the turn of the

[102] Richards, *Texts and their Traditions*, esp. pp. 5–6 and 61–84. The point is underlined by volumes such as Cambridge, Trinity College, B. 2. 34 and O. 4. 7 (our nos. 136 and 167), the former from Christ Church, the latter from Rochester (both *s.* xii^{1}), which preserve a virtually identical collection of texts by Jerome. Another related pair (where the principal author is John Chrisostom) is Cambridge, Trinity College, B. 2. 36, and London, British Library, Royal 6 A. xii (our nos. 137 and 511). See also nos. 63 and 929.

[103] Nos. 7 and 459: Kauffmann, *Romanesque Manuscripts*, cat. 45, with ills. 123–6; Richards, *Texts and their Tradtions*, pp. 77–84; *eadem*, 'A Decorated Vulgate Set from Twelfth-Century Rochester', *Journal of the Walters Art Gallery* 39 (1981), 59–67.

[104] Thomson, *Manuscripts from St Albans Abbey*, esp. I, pp. 11–27.

[105] This view, challenged by P. Conner, *Anglo-Saxon Exeter: A Tenth-Century Cultural History* (Woodbridge, 1993), *passim*, is upheld by R. G. Gameson, 'The Origin of the Exeter Book of Old English Poetry', *Anglo-Saxon England* 25 (1996), 135–85.

[106] See further Gameson, 'Manuscrits normands à Exeter'.

[107] The fundamental study remains Mynors, *Durham Cathedral Manuscripts*. New precision has been brought to the material by Gullick, 'Scribe of the Carilef Bible', and 'Scribes of the Durham Cantor's Book and the Durham Martyrology Scribe' in *Anglo-Norman Durham*, ed. D. Rollason, M. Harvey and M. Prestwich (Woodbridge, 1994), 93–109; and by various of the contributions to *Symeon of Durham and his World*, ed. Rollason.

[108] Mynors, *Durham Cathedral Manuscripts*, no. 40, with pls. 16–18.

century with a slack period, after which acquisition and production revived (pls. 8 and 9 show local products of the late eleventh and the beginning of the twelfth century respectively). It seems likely that Norman scribes actually worked at both Durham and Exeter in the late eleventh century, as was also the case at Abingdon, Saint Augustine's, Canterbury, and Rochester.[109]

The surviving manuscripts suggest that, notwithstanding some previous activity, several western houses, such as Gloucester, Evesham, Lanthony, Pershore and Winchcombe, only began to expand their libraries in earnest towards the end of our period (two Lanthony books are reproduced as pls. 20 and 21).[110] Whatever the reality of these cases, it is certainly true of Reading, which was only founded in 1121.[111] This house is here represented by a single liturgical fragment which, if the attribution be correct, is almost certainly one of its very earliest books.[112]

A comparative dearth of extant manuscripts renders it impossible to offer similar sketches for other major centres such as Abingdon (see pl. 16),[113] Battle (see pl. 4),[114] Chichester (see pl. 15),[115] Ely,[116] Glastonbury,[117] Hereford,[118] Norwich (see pl. 11),[119] Peterborough,[120] Saint

[109] See nos. 232, 641, 686, 694, and 699.

[110] On Gloucester see further Thomson, 'Books and Learning at Gloucester Abbey'.

[111] On the foundation of Reading: William of Malmesbury, *Gesta Pontificum*, ed. Hamilton, p. 193.

[112] The library of Reading is studied in a forthcoming monograph by Alan Coates. Another early manuscript, datable just after our period (*c.* 1132) is Cambridge, St John's College, A. 22 (James, 22): see S. Harrison Thomson, *Latin Bookhands of the Later Middle Ages, 1100–1500* (Cambridge, 1969), no. 84; and P. R. Robinson, *Catalogue of Dated and Datable Manuscripts c. 737–1600 in Cambridge Libraries*, 2 vols. (Woodbridge, 1988), I, no. 293; II. pl. 58.

[113] The relevant manuscripts are nos. 410, 445, 708, 709, 710, 711, and 818. Documentary sources attest to the rapid growth of the collection under Abbot Fabricius (1100–17): see n. 42 above.

[114] Nos. 319, 320, 349, 470, and 803. The early community also had a copy of Jerome's *Epistolae* which they presented to Chichester in the time of Bishop Ralph (1091–1123): *Chronicle of Battle Abbey*, ed. Searle, p. 126. Despite the post-Conquest foundation of the house and its initial association with Marmoutier, Tours, one of the two earliest manuscripts of Battle provenance (Oxford, University College, 104 (our no. 803)) is quintessentially English in appearance (see pl. 4). Still in a medieval binding, it is ruled in hard-point and written by a single scribe in a neat late English Caroline minuscule comparable to that of coeval hands from Saint Augustine's Abbey, Canterbury; it is decorated with an arabesque initial on fol. 2r.

[115] Nos. 93, 94, 166, 661, and 795. Cambridge, Emmanuel College, 25 (see pl. 15) is written by a single scribe with a characterful, spiky Norman-type hand, and is decorated with large, embellished initials in red and green at the major textual divisions.

[116] Nos. 88, 367, 368, 369, 679, 689, 906, 907, and 930. For the large book collection at the end of the eleventh century, presumably of pre-Conquest date for the most part, see *Liber Eliensis*, II, 139, ed. Blake, pp. 223–4. For a further allusion to the books, dating from 1143 see *ibid.*, p. 294.

[117] Nos. 441, 442, 627, and 713. The devastation of the collection by fire in 1184 and egregious losses in the sixteenth century are, no doubt, important factors in this very poor showing. However, Glastonbury may not have enlarged its library overmuch during our period: the unhappy circumstances of the house immediately after the Conquest under Thurstan (William of Malmesbury, *Gesta Pontificum*, ed. Hamilton, pp. 196–7) are unlikely to have been conducive to literary activites; Henry of Blois was deeply unimpressed by the literary resources of the house he inherited in 1126. His own energetic enrichment of the library (as attested by EBL, B37) falls outside our period.

[118] Nos. 304, 305, 306, 308, 310, 317, 318, 323, and 394. See further Mynors and Thomson, *Manuscripts of Hereford Cathedral Library*, pp. xvii–xix. Cf. William of Malmesbury, *Gesta Pontificum*, ed. Hamilton, pp. 300–1.

[119] Nos. 31, 35, 42, 345, and 346. The artist who drew the one decorated initial in the volume illustrated as pl. 11 (Cambridge University Library, Ii. 2. 19) was also responsible for the decorated initial on fol. 1r of the second part, Cambridge University Library, Kk. 4. 13. The best evidence for early literary activity at Norwich is the correspondence of Herbert Losinga.

[120] Nos. 404, 448, 646, and 757. The dearth of early books doubtless reflects the fact that the foundation was decimated by fire in 1116. If the attribution be correct, the best evidence for the nature of its library in *s.* xii^{in} is the booklist on fol. 251r of Oxford, Bodleian Library, Bodley 163 (Lapidge, 'Booklists', no. XIII). Comprising sixty-five items, it has a strong showing of patristics, above all Augustine and Jerome.

Paul's,[121] and Winchester.[122] Bath may be taken to typify the problems one encounters in such circumstances. Written evidence hints that the house may have lost a few of its Anglo-Saxon books to the Abbey of Saint Vaast at Arras immediately after the Conquest,[123] and unambiguously credits Bishop John (1088–1122) and his successor Geoffrey (1123–35) with building up a library at Bath, whither the former had moved his see.[124] However, the small cluster of extant, attributable manuscripts are inadequate to develop, modify, or even to substantiate this picture.[125]

The fact that expanded collections required a degree of ordering and organisation not hitherto so necessary would seem to be reflected in the fact that the first surviving English library catalogues worthy of that title (as opposed to 'book-list') date from the end of our period. The shorter and simpler of the two, associated with Peterborough, is written continuously on a single page and dates from the early twelfth century.[126] The document lists sixty-five titles, of which nearly half are works by the Fathers: indeed it begins with a run of texts by Augustine, followed shortly afterwards by a run of Jerome. There is a sprinkling of Carolingian writing (Amalarius, Haimo of Auxerre, Hrabanus Maurus, and Smaragdus), a smattering of history (Bede, Cassiodorus, and Eusebius), and a strong presence of hagiography. The Rochester catalogue included in the *Textus Roffensis* is altogether more sophisticated and spacious: it occupies thirteen pages as it survives, and lists ninety-nine items (twelve of them being early additions), providing a clear insight into the nature of one English benedictine library *c.* 1125.[127] Probably now lacking the initial section on biblical books, it lists works by author (based on the first text in the volume), beginning with Augustine, followed by Jerome, then Ambrose and Gregory. These sections, along with that devoted to Bede's work, are

[121] Nos. 1, 2, 3, 85, 561, and 562.

[122] Old Minster: 78, 406, 675, 676, and 677. New Minster (Hyde Abbey): 326, 356. Nunnaminster: 672. Unspecific: 62, 79, 368, 369, 407, 546, 634, 713, 799, 913, and 914. The Winchester houses suffer also from a lack of medieval library catalogues and book-lists. The fact that the prior of Old Minster from *c.* 1082 was Godfrey of Cambrai, '*qui religione et litteratura insignis fuit*' (William of Malmesbury, *Gesta Pontificum*, ed. Hamilton, p. 172) makes one optimistic about the early post-Conquest development of its library.

[123] Through the donation of Abbot Sæwold (see Lapidge, 'Booklists', no. VIII, pp. 58–62); however all but two of the possibly relevant manuscripts now at Arras, Médiathèque that I have seen are of continental origin and show no sign of ever having been in England. The English volumes are Médiathèque 867 (346) and 1029 (812). The continental ones are Médiathèque 435 (326), 644 (572), 732 (684), 899 (590), 1068 (276), and 1079 (235); and, in fact, it is doubtful whether at least one of these (732 (684)) could have been part of Sæwold's donation, given that it was produced at Saint Vaast itself in the second quarter of the eleventh century: Schulten, 'Die Buchmalerei des 11. Jahrhunderts im Kloster St Vaast in Arras', p. 81.

[124] Bishop John of Bath (1088–1122) reputedly gave the monastery '*maximam partem bibliothecae*' (*Two chartularies of the Priory of St Peter at Bath*, p. 153; *Lateinische Schriftquellen zur Kunst in England, Wales und Schottland vom Jahre 901 bis zum Jahre 1307*, ed. O. Lehmann-Brockhaus, 5 vols. (Munich, 1955–60), I, no. 215), and although this may possibly refer to a bible rather than a library, William of Malmesbury (*Gesta pontificum*, ed. Hamilton, p. 195) independently recorded that he collected books for the abbey: '*Multa ibi nobiliter per eum incepta et consummata in ornamentis et libris . . .*'. His successor, Geoffrey (1123–35), is also recorded to have given 'many books' to the house (*Two chartularies*, p. 154; *Lateinische Schriftquellen*, ed. Lehmann-Brockhaus, I, no. 219). Further on Bishop John see R. A. L. Smith, 'John of Tours, Bishop of Bath, 1088–1122' in his *Collected Papers*, 74–82.

[125] Nos. ?372, 462, 475, 483, 492, 493, ?495, 514, and 528. For relevant reproductions see Warner and Gilson, *Catalogue*, IV, pls. 40a and 41d. Nevertheless, these would repay examination as a group.

[126] Lapidge, 'Booklists', no. XIII.

[127] Rochester Cathedral Library, A. 3. 5 (part ii), fols. 224r–30r. Facsimile: *Textus Roffensis*, ed. P. Sawyer, 2 vols., EEMF 7 and 11 (Copenhagen, 1957–62), II; printed and discussed: *EBL*, pp. 469–92. See also Richards, *Texts and Their Traditions*, pp. 7–42; and Waller, 'Rochester Cathedral Library'.

headed by a descriptive rubric ('*Libri beati ambrosii sunt isti*' and so on) which greatly facilitates reference. Thereafter come historical works, the writings of Bede and John Cassian, and a range of other texts including *Vitae sanctorum*, homiliaries, and a smattering of Carolingian writing—Smaragdus's *Diadema monachorum*, Amalarius's *Liber officialis* and, probably, a collection of commentaries by Haimo of Auxerre (a similar selection to that on the Peterborough list). The Rochester catalogue is virtually devoid of the Latin Classics;[128] the Peterborough list entirely so. In both cases, but especially Rochester, not only the titles themselves, but also the arrangement of the material underlines the priority of the Fathers in the collection.

This leads us to the second main theme we shall consider, namely the nature of the texts that were acquired and copied between *c.* 1066–1130. As is well known, the principal concern of English houses during this period seems to have been to obtain the works of the Fathers, a preoccupation which they shared with their immediate continental neighbours. This is clearly reflected in the grand total of 376 surviving volumes (that is, well over a third of the extant books) which comprise or include patristic writings (relevant manuscripts are illustrated in pls. 3, 4, 10, 14, 15, 18–20 and 22). If one were also to count homiliaries and decretal manuscripts which incorporate selections from the Fathers (an example of the former is illustrated as pl. 11) the figure would rise even higher, to over 400. The picture is confirmed by the book-lists: although there is inevitably some doubt concerning how many texts are covered by certain entries and not every title can be identified with confidence, nevertheless some 117 out of approximately 326 identifiable items are patristics—again well over a third of the sample. There are, it should be noted, hardly any patristic manuscripts dating from the later eleventh century. It is at the end of the eleventh century that the number mushrooms, continuing to climb thereafter.[129]

The fact that the overall total is so very high reflects two complementary circumstances. There was, on the one hand, a solid core of texts which were regarded as the *sine qua non* of any respectable ecclesiastical book collection, which every house will have amassed, and which still survive in considerable numbers;[130] but on the other, there was also a plethora of other patristic writings which the larger and more energetic centres could attempt to acquire in addition. This was very much the nature of the book collections of our period, as we shall see.

The class of texts that was second in importance as reflected in the surviving manuscripts is post-patristic theology, that is spiritual writings ranging in date from the seventh century to the early twelfth (pls. 6–8, 16–17 and 23 illustrate some relevant manuscripts).[131] It should be stressed that the presence of such works is appreciably less in numerical terms than that of the Fathers, but then the number of available works was smaller, and very few of them seem to have achieved the same core-text status.[132] Post-patristic theology appears in 157

[128] The only relevant items are 73 and 91, which include respectively: the *Gesta Alexandri* and *Epistola Alexandri*; and Solinus's *De mirabilibus mundi*, along with Dares's *De excidio Troiae historia*.

[129] *Saec.* xi^{2}: 9. xi^{ex}: 67. xi/xii: 55. xii^{in}. 88. xii^{1}: 157.

[130] See further below, with Appendices 1 and 2; also Ker, *English Manuscripts*, pp. 4–5.

[131] That contemporaries did not make a rigid distinction between patristic and post-patristic theology in shown by those volumes (e.g. nos. 471, 474, 725, 749, 770, and 790) which include both.

[132] Those that came closest to this in our period were the writings by Bede that are listed in Appendix 1, Smaragdus's *Diadema monachorum*, and Paschasius's *De corpore et sanguine Domini*, the relevance of the last of which was, doubtless, underlined by the eucharistic controversy of the mid-eleventh century.

books (or almost exactly a sixth of the corpus). Once again the evidence of the book-lists suggests this is a true reflection of reality, for sixty-one out of the 326 items (about a fifth of the corpus) fall into this class. Here the manuscript evidence implies that interest developed, or exemplars become available, a little later than was the case with the Fathers. There is only a trickle of such texts among the surviving books up to the turn of the eleventh century, and the dramatic expansion happens at the beginning of the twelfth century, being sustained thereafter. The fact that new texts of this class were continuously being composed, not least by Anselm (whose work appears in some thirty-six manuscripts[133]), undoubtedly contributed to this particular pattern of growth.

Third in numerical importance as a class are biblical, liturgical and para-liturgical books—that is bibles (or part-bibles), gospel books, psalters, and other service books.[134] One hundred and five such volumes survive, which represents a ninth of the total corpus of surviving manuscripts as a whole (a couple of examples are reproduced in pls. 2 and 12). One should bear in mind that the range of texts here is very considerably smaller than that for either patristics or post-patristic theology, and this necessarily depresses the total. Nevertheless, one might have expected more of such books which must have been widespread, frequently in multiple copies. The evidence of the book-lists, from which fifty-three out of 326 items fall into this class, amounting to a sixth of the total, points in this direction: however, given that such volumes were often stored separately from the main collections and that the Rochester catalogue probably lacks the relevant page, this is undoubtedly still a low statistic. The point is underlined by the Ely record of *c.* 1093: of the 287 volumes alluded to, seventy-nine—that is more than a quarter of the collection—belonged to this class.[135] Yet whatever the overall quantity, there can be little doubt that the relative numerical importance of liturgical books will have declined as our period advanced. Because of the expansion of the other classes of material mentioned above, the amount of time devoted to copying liturgical books in 1130 will almost certainly have been proportionately less than it had been a generation earlier. We will return to this point below.

In the case of sacramentaries, missals and other service books, the comparatively modest numbers undoubtedly reflect the fact that many have been lost through hard use and deliberate destruction: it is no coincidence that a good proportion of the extant specimens survive merely as fragments. The various cuttings from antiphoners, a missal and a breviary in Oslo, and the two leaves in Durham Cathedral Library, B.III. 10 that are all that survive from an early twelfth-century breviary are cases in point; as is the greviously mutilated, multi-volume Canterbury passional, the fragments of which are now bound up as Canterbury Cathedral Lit. E. 42.[136] Equally, it is sobering to compare the one surviving pontifical that dates from

[133] Nos. 5, 81, 106, 107, 128, 130, 131, 296, 363, 365, 391, 498, 505, 506, 581, 592, 597, 601, 611, 653, 678, 685, 722, 768, 798, 811, 911, and 934. In addition, the following manuscripts contain one or more letters: 34, 104, 116, 129, 269, 312, 376, 774. The most frequently occurring text is the *Epistolae.* Anselm, *Opera Omnia*, ed. Schmitt, includes the following relevant plates: vol. I (Paris, Bibliothèque nationale, lat. 13413); vol. III (London, British Library, Cott. Nero A. vii); vol. IV (British Library, Royal 5 F. ix); and vol. V (London, Lambeth Palace Library, 59).

[134] This does not include homiliaries.

[135] See n. 10 above. Incidentally, twenty-five out of the fifty-nine books (i.e. *c.* 4/10) that Bishop Leofric acquired for Exeter in the third quarter of the eleventh century were liturgical or para-liturgical (see Lapidge, 'Booklists', no. X).

[136] Nos. 194, 237, and 613–18. For Canterbury Cathedral, Lit. E. 42 see MMBL, II, 289–97; and Gameson 'English Manuscript Art in the Late Eleventh Century', p. 119, with pls. 4a, 5b, and 6a.

our period[137] with Lanfranc's mention of the many pontificals of diverse origins to which he apparently had access at Canterbury alone.[138]

Similar factors may have affected the survival rate of gospel books, psalters, and bibles, although probably to a lesser extent.[139] Here, however, it is possible that the number of copies made was indeed comparatively small, at least during the first generation after the Conquest. Why might this have been the case? It was, it is true, becoming increasingly fashionable in the eleventh century for communities to possess a giant bible,[140] a point reflected in the circumstance that in several English houses, notably Durham, Lincoln and Rochester, it was among the first books acquired under the new régime (one volume of the Lincoln copy is illustrated in pl. 12).[141] Nevertheless, producing a pandect or a multi-volume bible was a major undertaking, the sheer scale of which will necessarily have restricted the number that could have been made,[142] particularly given that it is questionable whether many complete texts were readily available for copying in 1066.[143] Conversely, by 1066 England undoubtedly had plenty of gospel books and psalters, which were still usable. There is evidence that the Normans admired fine Anglo-Saxon liturgical books, acquiring them before as well as after the Conquest if they could; while post-Conquest additions and alterations to Anglo-Saxon volumes like the psalters, London, British Library, Arundel 155[144] and Salisbury Cathedral Library, 150[145] reveal that they were still seeing active service after 1066. More copies will, of course, have been needed as new houses and cells were established; but pre-existing manuscripts may sometimes have been redeployed for such purposes in the first place; and the heyday of expansion came in the twelfth century rather than the eleventh.

Although, as we have seen, it would be unwise to place much faith in the general statistics

[137] Dublin, Trinity College, 98, fols. 1–72 (our no. 200). See further M. L. Colker, *Descriptive Catalogue of the Medieval and Renaissance Latin Manuscripts of Trinity College, Dublin*, 2 vols. (Aldershot, 1991), I, pp. 195–8, with II, pl. X. The handful of other pontificals that appear on the inventory (nos. 45e, 58 (supplement), 61, 66e, ?115, and 423 (addition)) are either fragments or supplements to pre-existing manuscripts.

[138] '*In nostris episcopalis ordinis codicibus, quos ex diuersis regionibus multos habemus*': *The Letters of Lanfranc*, ed. Clover and Gibson, ep. 14 (p. 86).

[139] Psalters: 47, 86, 325, 356, 358 (corrections), 406, 748, 819, ?906, and ?912. Gospel books: 120, 198, 304, 458, 607, 734, 806, 813, 818, and 820. Bibles: 7, 154, 186, 210, 311, 328, 351, 459, 570, 574, 576, 733, 899, and 900.

[140] See in general W. Cahn, *Romanesque Bible Illumination* (Ithaca, 1982), pp. 93–119.

[141] Durham: no. 210; see further Mynors, *Durham Cathedral Manuscripts*, no. 30. Lincoln: nos. 154 + 328; see Kauffmann, *Romanesque Manuscripts*, cat. 13, ills. 30–1; and Thomson, *Manuscripts of Lincoln Cathedral*, pp. 3 and 212, with frontispiece and pls. 37a–b. Rochester: nos. 899–900; see Dutschke, *Medieval and Renaissance Manuscripts*, I, pp. 124–30, with II, ills. 40–1.

[142] On the practicalities of making bibles in the early Middle Ages see R. G. Gameson, 'The Cost of the Codex Amiatinus', *Notes and Queries* 237 (1992), 2–9; and D. Ganz, 'Mass Production of Early Medieval Manuscripts: the Carolingian Bibles from Tours', in *The Early Medieval Bible: Its Production, Decoration and Use*, ed. R. Gameson (Cambridge, 1994), 53–62.

[143] Twelve bibles or part-bibles apparently survive from before 1066. They are conveniently listed by R. Marsden, 'The Old Testament in Late Anglo-Saxon England: Preliminary Observations on the Textual Evidence' in *The Early Medieval Bible*, ed. Gameson, 101–24, at 123.

[144] The volume was originally written between 1012×1023 by Eadwig Basan and comprised calendar, tables, preface, psalms, canticles and prayers. In *s.* xi^{med} a less skilful scribe added further prayers (fols. 191v/9–192v/6). These, along with Eadwig's prayers, received an interlinear Old English gloss *s.* xi^{med}. In *s.* xi^{2} further hymns, creeds and prayers were added (fols. 192v/7–193v). Subsequently (*s.* xi^{ex}) the Psalter text was extensively corrected *in rasura*, further corrections being made in *s.* xii^{med}. An entire additional section, comprising prayers, litany and hymns, was added *s.* xii^{2} (fols. 137r–44v, 147r–170v; plus 136v and the re-written 135r/18–136r). An additional late medieval supplement was subsequently inserted between the prayers and the hymns (fols. 145r–6v).

[145] This Gallican Psalter, written in *s.* x^{2}, received a continuous interlinear Old English gloss in *s.* xi/xii; the litanies were rewritten in *s.* xii. See further Ker, *Catalogue*, no. 379.

for this class of material, the differences between the totals for the individual chronological periods are still informative. The percentage that liturgical and para-liturgical texts represent of the total output for each chronological band declines steadily throughout our period: almost a third of the later eleventh-century corpus, it sinks to about a sixth at the end of the century, an eleventh at the turn of the century and the beginning of the twelfth century, slumping further to a fourteenth of the early twelfth-century material. Such 'demotion' was the inevitable result of the rapid expansion of the other classes of writing we have just discussed, and it helps to bring into focus the changing relative effort devoted to these different types of material.

Close together in fourth and fifth position we find history and hagiography with a total of eighty and seventy-five volumes respectively (see pls. 5, 8, 9 and 21). Needless to say, at their extremities these two categories blend imperceptibly one into the other;[146] nevertheless they are in general sufficiently distinct to justify their being counted separately. The production of hagiographical material remained stable in the later eleventh century, increasingly slightly at the turn of the century, and then a little more dramatically at the beginning of the twelfth century, falling slightly thereafter.[147] One factor that undoubtedly contributed to this pattern was the composition of a whole range of new works in the late eleventh century, principally by Goscelin of Saint Bertin.[148] A handsome, comprehensive collection of his works for Saint Augustine's Abbey, Canterbury, where he was based in his later years, survives as London, British Library, Cotton Vespasian B. xx.[149] More generally it reflects the stimulus provided by the Norman Conquest for individual houses to garner, guard, and promote their local traditions of sanctity.[150] Bury St Edmunds can boast a series of such books which straddles our period. The earliest, Copenhagen, Kongelige Bibliotek, G. K. S. 1588 (4°) is a small, neat copy of Abbo of Fleury's *Vita S. Edmundi*, followed by a neumed office for the saint.[151] The manuscript was written by a single scribe in a well-controlled, conservative, late English Caroline minuscule; and though the volume has no decoration apart from a couple of modest arabesque initials, Edmund's name is presented in Rustic Capitals whenever it appears. The next manuscript, British Library, Cotton Tiberius B. ii, was made a generation later, at the beginning of the twelfth century.[152] In addition to Abbo's *Vita Edmundi*,[153] this collection includes the new *Miracula S. Edmundi* associated with Hermann the Archdeacon, which related the story of the saint, his miracles, and the history of the community up to the present day, and which was designed, *inter alia*, to defend the foundation's independence from the

[146] Cf. e.g. nos.: 173 and 432. In addition, at the other extremity, hagiography blurs into liturgy.

[147] *Saec.* xi^{2}: 8. xi^{ex}: 8. xi/xii: 14. xii^{in}: 24. xii^{1}: 21.

[148] A. Gransden, *Historical Writing in England c. 550 to c. 1307* (London, 1974), pp. 107–111, provides a convenient summary; see also *The Life of King Edward who rests at Westminster*, ed. F. Barlow, 2nd ed. (Oxford, 1992), pp. 133–49. Goscelin's work appears in nos. 197, 203, 204, 367, 414, 438, 452, and 486.

[149] No. 414. For reproductions see Gameson, 'English Manuscript Art in the late Eleventh Century', pl. 11, and R. Gem (ed.), *St Augustine's Abbey, Canterbury* (London, 1997), ill. 9.

[150] For recent discussion see S. J. Ridyard, '*Condigna veneratio*: Post-Conquest Attitudes to the Saints of the Anglo-Saxons', *Anglo-Norman Studies* 9 (1987), 179–206; and D. Rollason, *Saints and Relics in Anglo-Saxon England* (Oxford, 1989), 215–39.

[151] No. 199. For comment on its text and on its textual relationship to British Library, Cott. Tib. B. ii see *Three Lives of English Saints*, ed. M. Winterbottom (Toronto, 1972), pp. 8–9 and 91–2.

[152] No. 403. See A. G. Watson, *Catalogue of Dated and Datable Manuscripts c. 700–1600 in the Department of Manuscripts in the British Library*, 2 vols. (London, 1979), I, no. 553; II, pl. 54.

[153] Printed from this manuscript in *Three Lives of English Saints*, ed. Winterbottom, pp. 67–87.

encroachments of the Bishop of East Anglia.[154] This volume is larger and more ambitiously conceived than its predecessor in Copenhagen, with the main initials and Edmund's name written in gold; however its decoration was never finished.[155] Visually it is overshadowed in its turn by the third volume designed to promulgate the saint, New York, Pierpont Morgan Library, M 736,[156] which was produced at the very end of our period. In addition to Abbo's *Vita* and some lessons and hymns, this elaborately illuminated book contains the text of the *Miracula S. Edmundi* ascribed to Osbert of Clare. The glory of the volume, however, and the first thing which the reader encounters is a spectacular pictorial cycle of thirty-two full-page miniatures, which recounts the saint's story, complementing and glossing the texts that follow. In particular, the images stress the unpleasant consequences of violating the saint's shrine, an emphasis which has reasonably been seen as a response to King Henry I and Bishop Herbert Losinga's financial and jurisdictional encroachments on the abbey.[157] The supreme authority of Bury's patron saint is especially underlined by the final, highly charged miniature of the cycle, which shows the coronation of Edmund, king and martyr, in heaven.[158]

There seems to have been very little copying of historical texts until the turn of the century, and the numbers then rose noticeably in the early twelfth century. The percentage that historical texts represent of the total output for each chronological period also varies considerably—as was almost inevitable given that the numbers are very small—ranging between 1/9 and 1/21, though the general impression is that proportionately more effort was being devoted to such writings as time went on.[159] Nevertheless, history was subsidiary to the main thrust of collecting, and it is not difficult to understand why.[160] The key points are that it had only a marginal place in the contemporary educational curriculum,[161] and that there were very few texts apart from the 'classics' by Josephus (see pl. 21) and Bede (see pl. 8) which were felt to be an essential part of any good book collection. William of Jumièges's *Gesta Normannorum* was, it is true, widely copied at an early date,[162] but in this it was fairly exceptional; moreover it dealt with national not local history. The majority of house chron-

[154] Printed as '*Liber de Miraculis Sancti Edmundi*' in *Memorials of St Edmund's Abbey*, ed. T. Arnold, 3 vols., RS 96a–c (London, 1880), I, pp. 26–92.

[155] Spaces for decoration on fols. 2r and 3v remained unfilled; the gold initials and Edmund's name were only intermittently supplied.

[156] No. 606: Kauffmann, *Romanesque Manuscripts*, cat. 34; all the miniatures are reproduced in McLachlan, *Scriptorium of Bury St Edmunds*, pls. 22–53, with discussion at pp. 74–119.

[157] B. Abou-el-Haj, 'Bury St Edmund's Abbey between 1070 and 1124: a history of property, privilege and monastic art production', *Art History* 6 (1983), 1–29.

[158] For comment see *ibid.*, pp. 14–17. For further possible resonances of the cycle see C. Hahn, '*Peregrinatio et Natio*: the illustrated Life of Edmund King and Martyr', *Gesta* 30 (1991), 119–39.

[159] *Saec. xi*^{2}: 6. xi^{ex}: 6. xi/xii: 13. xii^{in}: 13. xii^{1}: 42. Moreover, as Ker points out ('The Migration of Manuscripts from the English Medieval Libraries' reprinted in his *Books, Collectors and Libraries*, 459–70 at 464), historical writings had a better chance of being preserved in the sixteenth century than various other classes of material.

[160] Even in those continental collections whose holdings of history seem reasonably rich by contemporary standards (such as Saint Bertin) it is but a small percentage of the total (in this case 12 items out of 305 or *c.* 1/25: see G. Becker, *Catalogi Bibliothecarum Antiqui* (Bonn, 1885), no. 77 (pp. 181–4); with E. Lesne, *Les Livres, Scriptoria et Bibliothèques du commencement du viii à la fin du xi siècle, Histoire de la propriété ecclésiastique en France* IV (Lille, 1938), pp. 632–3).

[161] See P. Riché, *Écoles et enseignement dans le Haut Moyen Age* (Paris, 1979), pp. 252–4; and L. Boje Mortensen, 'The Texts and Contexts of Ancient Roman History in Twelfth-Century Western Scholarship' in *The Perception of the Past in Twelfth-Century Europe*, ed. P. Magdalino (London, 1992), 99–116, esp. 101–11.

[162] For a convenient list of the manuscripts see *The Gesta Normannorum Ducum of William of Jumièges, Orderic Vitalis, and Robert of Torigni*, ed. E. M. C. van Houts, 2 vols. (Oxford, 1992–5), I, pp. xcv–cxx.

icles, by contrast, were by nature local in subject-matter and focus, and were consequently of little interest outside the immediate circle of the community that produced them. Symeon of Durham's *Libellus de exordio atque procursu istius hoc est Dunelmensis ecclesie* was just such a text, and the fact that only two copies survive from our period, one certainly, the other probably, of Durham origin, is fairly typical (see pl. 9).[163] Similarly, although Bede was a generally popular author and his *Historia ecclesiastica* was widely transcribed, his 'local' account of the abbots of Wearmouth-Jarrow survives in only one copy from our period and that was made at Durham as one of the early twelfth-century additions to a late eleventh-century manuscript of the *Historia ecclesiastica* (pl. 8 illustrates a page from the earliest part of the book).[164]

When we turn to the two remaining principal classes of texts, the numbers become very much smaller. However suspicious one may be of statistics, there is no doubt that these were minority areas. With a total of thirty-six and twenty-two respectively, we find two very different types of texts: on the one hand, those wholly or substantially in Old English; on the other, the Latin Classics. Old English was at its strongest, unsurprisingly, in the later eleventh century: twenty-four of the volumes in question date from this period, representing about a third of contemporary book production (two examples are reproduced as pls. 1–2). It then dwindles. Interestingly, however, it has a very discreet swansong in the early twelfth century[165] (the period, incidentally, to which the one and only French text in the corpus belongs).[166] There are seven manuscripts containing Old English dating from the early twelfth century: though an interesting group, as 1/77 of the contemporary output, there can be little doubt that they were marginal to the main thrust of scribal activity.

The Latin Classics, by contrast, maintain a very discreet presence up to the turn of the century (being represented by one volume from xi^{2}, and two each from xi^{ex} and xi/xii), growing slightly in popularity at the beginning of the twelfth century. Nevertheless the nine *s.* xii^{in} and the eight *s.* xii^{1} volumes represent an unimpressive 1/24 and 1/48 of the corpus for their respective time-bands. Even allowing for the fact that the survival rate of such texts may have been less favourable than that of theology, such literature was still peripheral to English book collections in *c.* 1130; and with a couple of exceptions England was still fairly peripheral to the transmission of classical literature.[167] Contemporary French benedictine

[163] Durham University Library, Cosin V. ii. 6; and London, British Library, Cotton Faustina A. v, fols. 24–97 (our nos. 283 and 380). See further *Symeon of Durham and his World*, ed. Rollason, *passim*.

[164] Durham Cathedral Library, B. II. 35: Mynors, *Durham Cathedral Manuscripts*, no. 47; D. Rollason (ed.), *Anglo-Norman Durham: a catalogue for an exhibition of manuscripts in the Treasury, Durham Cathedral* (Durham, 1993), no. 6. The *Historia abbatum* was added to fols. 123v–9r. In addition, parts of a couple of the vitae were included in the collection of *vitae sanctorum* in Oxford, Bodleian Library, Digby 112 (our no. 713).

[165] Ker, *Catalogue*, pp. xv–xix, provides a convenient tabulation of the extant Old English manuscripts arranged by date.

[166] Namely the *Chanson* of St Alexis in the St Alban's Psalter (Hildesheim, St Godehard's Church, 1, pp. 57–68). See Pächt *et al.*, *St Albans Psalter*, pp. 126–46. For the text see *La Vie de Saint Alexis*, ed. C. Storey (Paris and Geneva, 1968); for discussion of its rationale in this context see R. Bullington, *The Alexis in the Saint Albans Psalter* (New York, 1991). See further in general, I. Short, 'Patrons and Polyglots: French Literature in Twelfth-Century England', *Anglo-Norman Studies* 14 (1991), 231–49. An Anglo-Norman chronicle was added to the margins of fols. 86v–90v of the Peterborough Chronicle (no. 757), but this was done long after our period (*s.* xiii$^{2/2}$): see the facsimile, *The Peterborough Chronicle*, ed. D. Whitelock, EEMF 4 (Copenhagen, 1954), with comment (by Cecily Clark) at pp. 39–43.

[167] *Texts and Transmissions*, ed. L. D. Reynolds (Oxford, 1983), pp. xiii–xliii provides a survey of broad patterns in the copying of classical texts (see esp. pp. xxxi–xxxviii), which is complemented for our period by B. Munk Olsen, 'La popularité des textes classiques entre le ixe et le xiie siècle', *Revue d'Histoire des Textes* 14–15 (1986), 169–81, reprinted in his *La réception de*

libraries were not greatly dissimilar in this respect, judging by the available book-lists.[168] The authors represented by more than extracts in our corpus are Aesop, Cicero, Dioscorides, Frontinus, Galen, Juvenal, Persius, Plautus, Pliny the Younger, Seneca, Statius, Suetonius, Terence, and Virgil, most of whom are present by courtesy of a single work. This modest total may be set against the fact that extant manuscripts show that the works of some sixty antique and late antique authors were copied in Europe as a whole during the eleventh and twelfth centuries.[169] And even making due allowance for the fact that our inventory stops at an early date in the twelfth century, it remains striking that a number of classical authors who, manuscript evidence suggests, were reasonably popular in Europe in the eleventh to twelfth centuries, namely Horace, Lucan, Sallust, and, more controversially, Ovid[170] are virtually or entirely unrepresented here.[171] Correspondingly, of the commonest late Antique authors, Boethius, Macrobius, Martianus, and Solinus, only the second and the fourth seem to have achieved a respectable circulation in England in our period.[172] With the exception of Solinus (whose *Collectanea rerum memorabilium* had evidently supplanted Pliny the Elder's *Historia naturalis* as a source of information on the natural sciences[173]), those authors who are represented appear by dint of their place in the 'school' curriculum.[174] It is difficult not to conclude that the restricted nature of the list reflects the limitations of the schooling generally available in England in our period. Given this picture, Herbert of Losinga's interest in the Classics, and William of Malmesbury's knowledge of them seem all the more impressive.[175] Interestingly, the one palimpsest amongst our material actually contains Latin Classics (Cicero, Sallust, and Pseudo-Atticus) written over Christian texts (fragments of Augustine, Gregory, a

la littérature classique au moyen âge (Copenhagen, 1995), 21–34 (whence cited here). Several of the most interesting and 'significant' works were associated with Salisbury whose range of texts was exceptional: see Webber, *Scribes and Scholars*, pp. 63–5; also R. M. Thomson, 'British Library Royal 15 C. xi: a Manuscript of Plautus' Plays from Salisbury Cathedral (*c.* 1100)', *Scriptorium* 40 (1986), 82–7.

168 See B. Munk Olsen, 'Les bibliothèques bénédictines et les bibliothèques des cathédrales: les mutations des xie et xiie siècles' in A. Vernet (ed.), *Histoire des bibliothèques françaises* I: *Les bibliothèques médiévales du vi^e siècle à 1530* (Paris, 1989), 30–43. One notable exception was the library of Saint-Èvre-Lès-Toul which had a fairly strong showing of antique and late antique authors in this period: R. Fawtier, 'La Bibliothèque et le trésor de l'abbaye de Saint-Èvre-Lès-Toul à la fin du xie siècle', *Mémoires de la société d'archéologie de Lorraine* 61 (1911), 123–56, esp. 144–6 and 149–52.

169 Munk Olsen, *L'Étude des auteurs classiques latins*, I, p. x.

170 On their general popularity, see Munk Olsen, 'Popularité des textes classiques', esp. pp. 29–34; *idem*, 'Ovide au Moyen Age (du ixe au xiie siècle)', *Le Strade del testo*, ed. G. Cavallo (Bari, 1987), 65–96, reprinted in his *Réception de la Littérature Classique au Moyen Age*, 71–94; and *idem*, 'Production of the Classics in the Eleventh and Twelfth Centuries'.

171 The only one to appear at all is Horace, represented by a single extract from his *Epistolae* which appears in our no. 290. In addition, a 'Lucanus' is documented on one booklist: Lapidge, 'Booklists', no. XI, 13.

172 For the extant manuscripts of Macrobius as a whole see B. Eastwood, 'Manuscripts of Macrobius's *Commentarii in Somnium Scipionis* before 1500', *Manuscripta* 38 (1994), 138–55. The approximate totals for each century up to the twelfth are as follows: *s.* viii: one; *s.* ix: nine; *s.* x: eight; *s.* xi: thirty-three; and *s.* xii: ninety-seven.

173 Pliny is only represented by two extracts (in nos. 404 and 545). There are five Solinus manuscripts, nos. 52, 375, 415, 450, and 560. For a list of Solinus manuscripts in general (assigned to a single century) see M. E. Milham, 'A Handlist of the Manuscripts of C. Julius Solinus', *Scriptorium* 37 (1983), 126–9. Of these, nine are ascribed to *s.* ix, sixteen to *s.* x, nineteen to *s.* xi, and thirty to *s.* xii.

174 For primary descriptions see Richer, *Histoire de France (888–995)*, ed. R. Latouche, 2 vols (Paris, 1937) II, pp. 56–8; and P. Vossen, *Der Libellus scolasticus des Walther von Speyer: Ein Schulbericht aus dem Jahr 984* (Berlin, 1962), p. 39. For further comment, see P. Riché, Écoles et enseignement dans le Haut Moyen Age (Paris, 1979), pp. 246–66; *Gerbert d'Aurillac* (Paris, 1987), pp. 40–53; and 'La Vie scolaire et la pédagogie au Bec au temps de Lanfranc et de Saint Anselme', *Mutations Socio-Culturelles*, ed. Foreville, 213–27; also M. Gibson, *Lanfranc of Bec* (Oxford, 1978), pp. 39–50.

175 Cf. Thomson, *William of Malmesbury*, pp. 47–61, with 197–207.

passion, and a service book).[176] If, however, one were to draw any general conclusion from this, it would have to be that it was only for such peripheral, profane literature that re-used parchment would be countenanced.[177]

What we have considered so far (with the exception of liturgica) have been umbrella groups embracing large numbers of texts. The remaining volumes, on the other hand, belong to groupings which are considerably smaller—namely Latin Christian poetry, grammatical and pedagogical works, medical texts, computistical treatises, decretals, and Rules—whose total numbers are necessarily much lower. Accordingly, it would be meaningless to quantify their place in the corpus as we have done with the large umbrella groups. We can, however, legitimately look for internal trends in each of these classes; and some can, in fact, be perceived. Latin Christian poetry, for instance, (Ambrose, Arator, Juvencus and, above all, Prudentius) is notable as an area whose totals compare unfavourably with pre-Conquest ones. To take one example, there are perhaps as many as ten extant manuscripts of Prudentius's *Psychomachia* which were written or owned in late Anglo-Saxon England;[178] by contrast there are but two from our period,[179] to which only one other, no longer extant, can be added from all the book-lists.[180] If on the one hand this would seem to suggest that interest in the genre had passed its peak, on the other hand the very strength of pre-Conquest holdings may have been a factor that militated against extensive further copying. At the same time, it is interesting to note that Herbert Losinga took a dim view of the young monks, Otto and William, reading Sedulius.[181] The gospel accounts themselves were generally better; but at this stage in their development, he maintained, lighter literature was preferable, and they should turn to 'the flowery meadows' of the classical poets. First of all, however, they should master their Donatus.

There is a very small number of grammatical texts, fairly evenly spread throughout our period as a whole—we have but one copy of Phocas's popular *Ars de nomine et uerbo*, for instance, and even the Grammar by the 'local' author Ælfric is only present in three manuscripts[182]—and the same is true of computistical treatises and medical texts. (Two relevant manuscripts are reproduced as pls. 13 and 24.) With regard to purely pedagogical works, the poor showing could reflect the fact that most of the relevant manuscripts were 'worked to death', though it is also possible that late Anglo-Saxon copies of the standard texts were still being employed. Donatus is arguably a case in point. His *Ars minor* and the more comprehensive *Ars*

[176] No. 291: E. A. Lowe, *Codices Latini Antiquiores*, Supplement (Oxford, 1971), nos. 1689–91; I. Cunningham, 'Latin Classical Manuscripts in the National Library of Scotland', *Scriptorium* 27 (1973), 64–90 at 88–9.

[177] Cf. E. A. Lowe, 'Codices Rescripti', as reprinted in his *Palaeographical Papers*, ed. L. Bieler, 2 vols. (Oxford, 1972), II, 480–519, esp. 483–4.

[178] G. Wieland, 'The Anglo-Saxon Manuscripts of Prudentius's *Psychomachia*', *Anglo-Saxon England 16* (1987), 213–31. See also his entry in *Sources of Anglo-Saxon Literary Culture: a trial version*, ed. F. M. Biggs, T. D. Hill, and P. E. Szarmach (New York, 1990), pp. 150–6.

[179] Nos. 411 and 453. There is also an extract in 222. For the first, which is an illustrated copy, see Kauffmann, *Romanesque Manuscripts*, cat. 30; and Thomson, *St Albans*, I, cat. 19.

[180] Lapidge, 'Booklists', no. XI, 11.

[181] Herbert Losinga, ep. 9, ed. Anstruther. By contrast, the elderly Herbert had himself renounced the poets in order to meditate upon the gospels (ep. 32).

[182] Respectively: no. 623; and nos. 178, 383, and 562. On Phocas's work see C. Jeudy, 'L'*Ars de nomine et verbo* de Phocas: manuscrits et commentaires médiévaux', *Annuaire de l'École pratique des Hautes Études* ive section (1973–4), 849–56; and 'L'*Ars de nomine et verbo* de Phocas', *Viator* 5 (1974), 61–156.

maior remained standard elementary texts (as Herbert Losinga's reference, which we have just noted, attests), but no copies from our period are extant, although Anglo-Saxon ones still survive.[183] At the same time, it must be admitted that Donatus seems to have been superseded by Priscian in Europe as a whole during the eleventh and twelfth centuries (the peak period of the latter's popularity),[184] and the English manuscript evidence is certainly in accord with this: our inventory includes no fewer than nine copies of Priscian's *Institutiones grammaticae* (one is illustrated as pl. 24).[185] We may note in passing that three of the English copies are strikingly handsome manuscripts, decorated far in excess of the needs of 'school' books.[186]

Grammatical primers were only one part of the pedagogical range. Study of the Latin Classics was justified by its key role in forming literary style, and when Herbert Losinga praised their value in this respect[187] he was echoing a universal conviction.[188] More generally, Herbert exhorted his protégés to study the Trivium and the Quadrivium;[189] however the other parts of the curriculum are no more strongly represented among the surviving manuscripts than are Grammar and its classical models. Isidore's *Etymologiae*, the long-established basic compendium for the liberal arts as a whole, survives, it is true, in four copies plus a couple of fragments,[190] but more specialised literature is in much shorter supply. For Rhetoric, two of the key texts that were used to illustrate good Latin practice, Cicero's *De inuentione* and the anonymous *Rhetorica ad Herennium* (which was also attributed to Cicero in the Middle Ages), are present in double copies;[191] however there is no Quintilian, and of the 'primers' we have only Bede's *De schematibus et tropis* (devoted to metre) and Alcuin's *De dialectica*, the first extant in one copy, the second in two.[192] The fundamental texts for Logic are comparably scarce: there are no copies of the Boethian translation of Aristotle's *Categoriae*, although it appears on one book-list, was well-known to Lanfranc and Anselm, and is mentioned by Herbert Losinga.[193] The extant manuscript material suggests that the main sources of knowl-

[183] See also Lapidge, 'Booklists', no. III, 4 and 7. On the manuscript tradition of these works in general see L. Holtz, *Donat et la tradition de l'enseignement grammatical* (Paris, 1981), pp. 445–97.

[184] See in general, R. W. Hunt, 'Studies on Priscian in the Eleventh and Twelfth Centuries', *Medieval and Renaissance Studies* 1, part ii (1943), 194–231. For a convenient conspectus of the manuscripts as a whole see M. T. Gibson, 'Priscian, *Institutiones grammaticae*: a handlist of manuscripts', *Scriptorium* 26 (1972), 105–25. The totals there given are as follows: *s.* viii: 3; *s.* ix–x: 61; *s.* xi–xii: 283; *s.* xiii–xiv: 137; and *s.* xv: 44. For descriptions of the manuscripts see M. Passalacqua, *I Codici di Prisiano*, Sussidi Eruditi 29 (Rome, 1978); and G. Ballaira, *Per Il Catalogo del Codici di Prisciano* (Torino, 1982).

[185] Nos. 30, 35, 109, 165, 327, 771, 791, 804, and 935. Also represented are the OE *Disticha Catonis* (nos. 178 and 759), 'Cato Nouus' (290, 759), and Phocas (623).

[186] Nos. 165, 327, and 934; on which see respectively: Kauffmann, *Romanesque Manuscripts*, cat. 8, ills. 13–16; Thomson, *St Albans*, I, no. 62 with II, pls. 11, 17–25; and M. Dell'Omo (ed.), *Virgilio e il Chiostro: Manoscritti di autori classici e civilta monastica* (Rome, 1996), no. 8.

[187] Herbert Losinga, epp. 9, 30, and 39, ed. Anstruther. On the other hand, when trying to avoid the obligation to write verse himself, he underlined the point that prose was the medium of spiritual writing (ep. 32); while in ep. 23 he articulated the 'traditional' conflict between classical literature and christian values.

[188] Cf. *inter alia*, Anselm, *Opera Omnia*, ed. Schmitt, III, ep. 64. See, more generally, G. Evans, *Old Arts and New Theology* (Oxford, 1980), pp. 57–137.

[189] Herbert Losinga, epp. 49 and 20, ed. Anstruther; also ep. 53.

[190] Nos. 264 (provenance: Durham), 521 (Canterbury, Saint Augustine's), 652 (Normandy, Exeter) and 853 (Salisbury). In addition, the fragments 571 (provenance unknown) and 737 (Canterbury, Christ Church) probably represent originally complete copies. The work was frequently excerpted and numerous short extracts appear in other contexts.

[191] Respectively nos. 443 and 767; 443 and 766.

[192] Respectively nos. 163; 163 and 254.

[193] Lapidge, 'Booklists', no. XI, 47; Lanfranc's knowledge of it is attested by his *De corpore et sanguine Domini*; Anselm's principally by his *De grammatico*.

edge here were the section '*De arte dialectica*' in Isidore's *Etymologiae*, Alcuin's *De dialectica* and *De fide sanctae et indiuiduae Trinitatis* (which, though primarily theological, treats the Categories), and Anselm's *De grammatico* (which the author himself described as an introduction to Logic). The book-lists add a single copy of another work in which logic is treated, namely Hrabanus Maurus's *De clericorum institutione*.[194] Moving on to the Quadrivium, the coverage becomes even thinner. Apart from the brief treatment in Martianus Capella's *De nuptiis Philologiae et Mercurii* (of which but one copy survives, plus one attested on a book-list[195]), Arithmetic only appears in the context of the computus—Hrabanus Maurus's *De computo*, Helperic of Grandval and Herman Contractus's treatises of the same name, and, most popular, Bede's *De temporum ratione* being the main relevant texts.[196] For Astronomy, aside from the sections in Martianus Capella's *De nuptiis*, Isidore's *Etymologiae* and Macrobius's *Interpretatio in somnium Scipionis*, the main sources of knowledge were the computistical works just mentioned; there is only a single copy of the *Aratea*.[197] Apart from the section in Macrobius, Music is represented by two copies of Boethius's *De musica*,[198] an extract from Aurelianus of Réomé's *Musica disciplina*, and excerpts from Remigius of Auxerre's commentary on Martianus Capella and from two works by Guido of Arezzo. Geometry seems to have been effectively neglected.

Even allowing for losses, and granted that there are discrepancies in Europe as a whole between the known or implied importance of 'school' texts and their manuscript surival,[199] this remains an unimpressive haul. The unavoidable but hardly surprising conclusion must be that the liberal arts as such fell largely outside the scope of English ecclesiastical libraries at this stage. Their corresponding absence from the lengthy Peterborough book-list and the comprehensive Rochester library catalogue supports this contention.[200]

Turning to the other 'minority' areas, the quantity of surviving decretal and conciliar manuscripts increases noticeably in the twelfth century, mainly due to the energetic dissemination of Lanfranc's collection.[201] By contrast, there are no complete copies of Burchard of Worm's great *Decreta*,[202] and only a couple of copies each of Ivo of Chartres's *Decretum* and the pithier *Panormia*.[203] The number of Rule manuscripts, that is copies of the *Regula S.*

[194] Lapidge, 'Booklists', no. XIII, 63.

[195] No. 80; there is also an extract in 140; Lapidge, 'Booklists', no. XI, 6. On the manuscript tradition in general see C. Leonardi, 'I codici di Marziano Capella', *Aevum* 33 (1959), 443–89, and 34 (1960), 1–99 and 524.

[196] Nos. 419; 370; 74, 302, 544, 626, and 794. There are only, seemingly, sixteen extant manuscripts of Hrabanus's work: *Rabani Mogontiacensis Episcopi, De computo*, ed. W. M. Stevens, CCCM 44 (Turnhout, 1979), pp. 163–332 at 190–4.

[197] No. 541; there is also an extract in 104.

[198] Nos. 409, 548, 626, and 794. For the extant manuscripts as a whole see C. M. Bower, 'Boethius's *De institutione musica*: a Handlist of Manuscripts', *Scriptorium* 42 (1988), 205–51. Of the 137 principal manuscripts there inventoried, twenty-seven are ascribed to *s.* xi, and forty to *s.* xii. Descriptions of copies in British collections, as indeed of other Boethian works, are conveniently assembled in *Codices Boethiani* I: *Great Britain and the Republic of Ireland*, ed. M. T. Gibson and L. Smith (London, 1995).

[199] Munk Olsen, 'Production of the Classics in the Eleventh and Twelfth Centuries', pp. 3–4.

[200] Compare the case of Moissac which, according to a *s.* xi note in Paris, Bibliothèque nationale, lat. 17002, fol. 221 (cited by Lesne, *Livres et scriptoria*, p. 499) then had in its *armarium* 60 '*libri diuini*' and 11 '*libri de arte*'.

[201] See n. 59 above.

[202] No. 305 contains an extract.

[203] *Decretum*: nos. 55 and 802, with extracts in 102 and 104. *Panormia*: nos. 56 and 773. The extant manuscripts of the *Decreta* as a whole (P. Landau, *Das Decret des Ivo von Chartres*, Zeitschrift der Savigny—Stiftung für Rechtsgeschichte, Kanonistische Abteilung, 70 (1984), pp. 1–44) do not suggest that the work achieved particularly great European popularity.

Benedicti, Chrodegang of Metz's *Regula canonicorum*, and Lanfranc's *Constitutiones*, is tiny: there is a total of ten scattered throughout our sixty or so years (part of a bilingual copy of Chrodegang's text is illustrated as pl. 1).[204] Though in the abstract one might have expected more, here too the apparent under-representation probably reflects losses through hard use on the one hand, and the pre-existing availability of the first two of these works on the other. In 1066 each Anglo-Saxon community will presumably have had at least one copy of its Rule, a manuscript which may well have had a good deal of 'life' still left in it. Indeed at least ten Anglo-Saxon copies of the *Regula S. Benedicti* still survive.[205]

Up to this point we have been examining the material in terms of the classes of texts represented. A useful complementary perspective is provided by considering the works diachronistically, that is according to the dates of the writers that feature in our corpus. Appendix 3 provides a list of the authors in question, arranged by century according to the date of their death. Although simplified and schematic and necessarily omitting anonymous texts, this nevertheless provides a convenient conspectus of the general chronological contours of our field.

It is immediately apparent how few known authors there are from the first three centuries AD (seven, six, and five respectively), as is also the case from the pre-Christian era in general (a cumulative total of ten). By contrast, the 'golden age' of Latin patristic literature, the fourth to sixth centuries, is well populated, being represented by a collective total of sixty-nine writers (twenty from the fourth century, thirty-three from the fifth, and seventeen from the sixth). The succeeding two centuries are a little thinner (a cumulative total of twenty authors, nine from the seventh century, eleven from eighth), with a strong revival in the ninth century (twenty-seven authors—a showing which exceeds all the centuries so far, except the fifth). After a 'relapse' to ten writers in the tenth century, the eleventh and twelfth centuries both have a good showing (with thirty and thirty-two figures respectively). It is particularly noteworthy that the twelfth century, only thirty years of which are embraced in the inventory, has the second largest number of authors, and is only just exceeded by the fifth century.

Thus far, one might argue, the contours of our material simply follow the general flow of Christian literature; and, obviously, those centuries in which more authors were at work necessarily have a better chance of being strongly represented than those in which fewer were active. If, however, one also takes some account of the number of copies that were made of individual works, the picture becomes more revealing. Now, a large number of the texts by many of our authors appear in only one or two copies, as we shall see: their statistical presence is negligible. A convenient way to gauge which chronological periods are most strongly represented, therefore, is to consider the distribution of the more popular texts. These are listed in Appendices 1 and 2. If one plots the works in question by century, the results are as follows. (The first column gives the century; the second shows the number of texts from that century which are represented by six or more copies; while the third column presents the number of texts represented by five or more copies.)

[204] *Regula S. Benedicti*: nos 45, 269, 387, and 932; (Old English) 269, and 384. Chrodegang: nos. 187 and 350. Lanfranc: nos. 268, and 319.

[205] Cambridge, Corpus Christi College, 57, 178, and 368; Cambridge, Trinity College, O. 2. 30; London, British Library, Cotton Tiberius A. iii, Cotton Titus A. iv, and Harley 5431; Oxford, Bodleian Library, Hatton 48; Oxford, Corpus Christi College, 197; and Wells Cathedral, 7.

B.C. (general)	0	0
A.D. I:	0	0
II:	2	2
III:	1	2
IV:	12	14
V:	22	37
VI:	1	1
VII:	10	13
VIII:	8	9
IX:	3	5
X:	0	0
XI:	2	5
XII:	7	8

The result significantly modifies the pattern we have just outlined. The huge predominance of the fourth and, above all, the fifth century is accentuated: between them they have almost as many 'popular' works as do all the other periods put together. They are now followed not by the eleventh and twelfth centuries, but by the seventh and the eighth. And it is worth pointing out that in the case of the seventh century, all but one of the relevant texts date from before 640 (being written either by Gregory the Great or by Isidore); in the case of the eighth, most of them date from before 740 (and were written by Bede). The only other century that produced 'best-sellers' in any quantity was the twelfth.

The two main results of this exercise are firstly to underline how strong was the presence of certain works of the Fathers, and secondly to show how comparatively poorly represented were the writers of the Carolingian Renaissance. The only ninth-century texts to appear with any frequency are Berengaudus Ferrariensis's *In Apocalypsin*, Helperic of Grandval's *De computo*, Paschasius Radbertus's *De corpore et sanguine Domini* (a copy of which is reproduced as pl. 16), and Smaragdus's *Diadema monachorum*. The evidence of the book-lists confirms this picture; and, it may be added, broadly contemporary French monastic and collegiate libraries show similar characteristics.[206] Indeed Carolingian works were not much copied in eleventh- and twelfth-century Europe as a whole. Was this because Carolingian works were better represented in the pre-existing book collections; or because they were perceived to be distinctly inferior to the Fathers? Both factors probably came into play, but there can be little doubt, surely, that the latter was the more important.

Armed with this impressionistic picture of the relative popularity of different classes and periods of writing, let us now look in slightly more detail at the fate of individual authors and of particular texts.

In the league of popularity, judged according to the frequency with which works were copied, Augustine towers head and shoulders above every other author. He is represented in 171 volumes (excluding homiliaries and decretal collections), that is more than 1/5 of the surviving manuscripts from our period; and his writings appear in more than twice as many manuscripts as do those of his nearest 'rival' (pl. 10 shows one copy of his most popular work

[206] Munk Olsen, 'Bibliothèques bénédictines', esp. pp. 36–9.

the *Confessiones*[207]). Moreover, in early medieval eyes, Augustine's total would have been even higher, for these figures do not include pseudonymous tracts that were commonly attributed to him. This overwhelming presence is partly a reflection of Augustine's great stature as a Father and of the authority with which his works were regarded; but equally it is an inevitable side-effect of the fact that he wrote so much. There were, quite simply, far more of his writings to copy. Furthermore, his oeuvre included a large number of shorter texts that enjoyed independent circulation in varying combinations, sometimes travelling alongside the work of other authors.[208]

It is also striking that Augustine was consistently popular throughout our period. Subject to the general 'flow' of manuscript production summarised above, Augustine's work was copied steadily from the later eleventh century to the early twelfth century. Inevitably the details vary slightly from one text to another, but the overall profile remains fairly consistent. Of the ten copies of his *Confessiones*, for instance, three date from xi^{2}–xi^{ex} (see pl. 10), one from xi/xii–xii^{in}, and six from xii^{1}; while the six copies of *De agone christiano* are distributed—one from xi^{2}–xi^{ex}, two from xi/xii–xii^{in}, and three from xii^{1}. Of the six complete copies of *De ciuitate Dei*, one is from xi^{2}–xi^{ex}, three from xi/xii–xii^{in}, and two from xii^{1}; and the distribution of the six complete copies of *De Genesi ad litteram* is exactly the same. The thirteen copies of *In euangelium Iohannis* are divided three from xi^{2}–xi^{ex}, seven from xi/xii–xii^{in}, and three from xii^{1}; while of the twenty-four volumes of *Enarrationes in Psalmos*, four date from xi^{2}–xi^{ex}, nine from xi/xii–xii^{in}, and eleven from xii^{1}.

The next most popular author after Augustine—a long way behind admittedly—is not, as one might perhaps have expected, another of the Fathers, but rather the greatest scholar of Anglo-Saxon England, the Venerable Bede. His work appears in eighty-four manuscripts. Bede's local connections may have helped to enhance his popularity; it is not impossible that more of his writings were lurking at the bottom of Anglo-Saxon book-chests waiting to be copied than the surviving pre-Conquest manuscripts suggest; and his *Historia ecclesiastica* in particular was evidently much in demand (a Durham copy is reproduced as pl. 8). Be all that as it may, ultimately the crucial factor in his strong presence was, as with Augustine, the sheer number of his works. There was a large number of his writings to copy: although the *Historia ecclesiastica* is the best represented, some thirty-two further texts or independent part-works appear in the corpus of surviving manuscripts.[209] Unlike Augustine, who was consistently copied throughout our period, Bede's popularity was, above all, a twelfth-century phenomenon: of the eighty-two manuscripts in question, eight date from *s.* xi^{2} or xi^{ex} (see pl. 8), eleven from xi/xii, seventeen from xii^{in}, and an impressive forty-eight from xii^{1}. Volumes including Bede's writings thus represent 1/25 of late eleventh-century production, 1/12 of that of the turn of the century,

[207] Its English circulation is studied by Webber, 'Diffusion of Augustine's *Confessions*'.

[208] Cf. e.g. nos. 474, 476, 512, 667, 691, 841 and 850.

[209] *Chronica maiora; De arte metrica; De die iudicii; De locis sanctis; De natura rerum; 'De ratione computi'; De schematibus et tropis; De tabernaculo; De templo Salomonis; De temporibus; De temporum ratione; Epistola ad Egbertum; Epistola ad Pleguinam de aetatibus saeculi; Epistola ad Wicthedum de aequinoctio uel de paschae celebratione; Historia abbatum; Homiliae euangelii; In Actus Apostolorum; In Apocalypsin; In Canticum Canticorum allegorica expositio; In Epistolas Catholicas; In Euangelium Lucae expositio; In Euangelium Marci expositio; In Genesim; In Prouerbia Salomonis; In Regum libros xxx quaestiones; In Samuelem propheta allegorica expositio; In Tobiam; Libellus retractationes in Actus Apostolorum; Nomina regionum atque locorum de Actibus Apostolorum; Super Canticum Abacuc allegorica expositio; Vita Cuthberti* (prose and verse). For the general manuscript survival of these texts see M. L. W. Laistner and H. H. King, *A Hand-List of Bede Manuscripts* (Ithaca, 1943).

as also of the start of the twelfth century, and 1/8 of the early twelfth-century output. Here again, developments in England were part of a more general trend, for the twelfth century was the universal peak for the copying of Bede's writings in Europe as a whole.[210]

After Bede, the most frequently occurring authors are (in descending order): Jerome (whose writings appear in sixty-three manuscripts: two examples are reproduced in pls. 15 and 22), Gregory the Great (represented in sixty-one books, of which about a quarter, it should be noted, are single parts of three-volume sets of the *Moralia in Iob*: the manuscripts reproduced as pls. 18 and 20 are cases in point.[211]), Ambrose (fifty-three volumes), and Isidore (forty-eight). Although the total numbers for Gregory are modest in comparison with those for Augustine, and he also lags behind Bede and Jerome, they nevertheless attest to very considerable interest since, unlike those writers (as also Ambrose and Isidore), the great pope did not pen many works. Indeed his total 'canonical' output comprised only six texts: the *Dialogi*, the *Homiliae in Euangelia*, the *Homiliae in Ezechielem, the Moralia in Iob*, the *Registrum epistolarum*, and the *Regula pastoralis*.[212] Moreover, these works did not lend themselves to excerption and subdivision to the extent that some of Augustine's works, for instance, did. Although Gregory's total was boosted by the *excerpta* that travelled as the seventh book of Bede's Commentary on the Song of Songs,[213] and extracts are by no means unknown elsewhere,[214] it was not enhanced by the independent circulation of numerous little tractates. If, incidentally, we based our calculations on the number of surviving pages by the author in question (i.e. taking the length of the works into account), and not on the number of separate codices in which he appears, Gregory would certainly rise into third place above Jerome, and might even rival Bede for second place.

Discounting Paul the Deacon, whose popularity was largely due to the circulation of his homiliary, a para-liturgical book compiled from the works of the Fathers (one volume of the Norwich copy is reproduced as pl. 11),[215] the only other author who achieved anything like

[210] Laistner and King, *Hand-List of Bede Manuscripts*, pp. 4 and 7 compute the chronological distribution of manuscripts of Bede's biblical commentaries and the *Historia ecclesiastica* (in percentage terms) as follows. Commentaries: *s.* viii–ix: 1.5%; *s.* ix: 15%; *s.* x: 7.5%; *s.* xi: 10%; *s.* xii: 38.5%; *s.* xiii: 11%; *s.* xiv: 4%; *s.* xv: 10%; *s.* xvi: 0.5%; and 'doubtful': 2%. *Historia ecclesiastica*: *s.* viii–ix: 3.4%; *s.* ix: 7%; *s.* x: 5%; *s.* xi: 9%; *s.* xii: 31%; *s.* xiii: 10%; *s.* xiv: 17%; *s.* xv: 12%; *s.* xvi: 1.2%; and 'doubtful': 4.4%.

[211] Further on the *Moralia* manuscripts see N. R. Ker, 'The English Manuscripts of the *Moralia* of Gregory the Great', in *Kunsthistorische Forschungen, Otto Pächt zu seinem 70. Geburtstag*, ed. A. Rosenauer and G. Weber (Salzburg, 1972), 77–89, esp. 81–3 on format.

[212] There were, in addition, the *In Canticum Canticorum* (which breaks off after 1, 8) and the *In Librum Primum Regum*, but these were only known in the version transmitted by the monk Claudius of Ravenna; moreover, serious doubts have recently been raised over the authenticity of the attribution of the latter to Gregory. See further *Sancti Gregorii Magni Expositio in Canticum Canticorum*, ed. P. Verbraken, CCSL 144 (Turnhout, 1963); *Grégoire le Grand, Commentaire sur le Cantique des Cantiques*, Sources Chrétiennes 314 (Paris, 1984); with P. Meyvaert, 'The Date of Gregory the Great's Commentaries on the Canticle of Canticles and I Kings', *Sacris Erudiri* 23 (1978–9), 191–216; and A. de Vogüé, 'L'auteur du Commentaire des Rois attribué à Saint Grégoire: un moine de Cava?', *Revue bénédictine* 106 (1996), 319–31. In fact, neither of these works appears in our corpus, although the first, at least, had a reasonably strong manuscript tradition: see Verbraken's edition, plus his 'La tradition manuscrite du Commentaire de saint Grégoire sur le Cantiques des Cantiques', *Revue bénédictine* 73 (1963), 277–88; and 'Un nouveau manuscrit de commentaire de saint Grégoire sur le Cantique des Cantiques', *Revue bénédictine* 75 (1965), 143–5.

[213] See *Bedae Venerabilis in Cantica Canticorum*, ed. D. Hurst, CCSL 119B (Turnhout, 1985).

[214] Discounting unitary homiliaries which included Gregory, the relevant items are nos. 112, 250, 266, 364, 561 and 744.

[215] Nos. 30 + 42. On the collection in general see C. Smetana, 'Paul the Deacon's Patristic Anthology' in *The Old English Homily and its Background*, ed. P. Szarmach and B. Huppé (New York, 1978), 75–97; also Richards, *Texts and their Traditions*, pp. 95–120.

the circulation of Bede, Jerome, Gregory, Ambrose, and Isidore, was St Anselm. He is represented by twenty-eight manuscripts containing substantial works, plus a further eight volumes with a small quantity of his letters.[216] Although this total is much less than that of any of the previous figures, it should be remembered that the works in question were actually written during our period, and thus had a shorter time span in which to be copied than had those of earlier authors. Conversely, however, the years up to *c.* 1130 would seem to be the peak period of interest in Anselm's writings until the fourteenth century, and our 'snap-shot' view therefore gives a rosy impression of his general popularity.[217]

After Anselm, the numbers shrink dramatically: indeed there are only four other writers who are represented in more than ten manuscripts. The figures in question are (in alphabetical order): Ælfric, Alcuin, Ivo of Chartres, and Origen (one of whose works is reproduced as pl. 19). The relevance of each of these writers is sufficiently apparent not to require further comment here; though it is worth noting that their writings embrace different functions and address contrasting audiences—vernacular preaching (Ælfric), teaching (Ælfric again, and Alcuin), theology (Alcuin, Ivo, and Origen), and Canon Law (Ivo). As with Anselm, the rapidity with which the recently composed works of Ivo of Chartres (d. 1116) were put into circulation in England is worthy of note;[218] unsurprisingly, all but three of the manuscripts in question date from the latest of our time-bands. In contrast to this (and also in contrast to Bede incidentally), Ælfric's popularity was much more an eleventh-century than a twelfth-century phenomenon, a circumstance which undoubtedly reflects the fact that he wrote in Old English.[219]

As a point of interest, the writers who fell immediately below the thresh-hold of ten manuscripts were only four in number: Cicero and Fulbert of Chartres, Abbo of Fleury and Macrobius, the first pair with nine volumes to their credit each, the second pair with eight each. Cicero is thus the only one of the Ancients who could in any sense be considered to have achieved a respectable circulation in our period, and this he owed, like the late Antique writer Macrobius, to his role as a 'school' author.[220] If this circumstance helps to explain how William of Malmesbury could have managed to compile an anthology of twenty-two Ciceronian works (plus the pseudonymous *Inuectiua in Sallustinum*),[221] it simultaneously underlines how remarkable was such an achievement.

Which individual texts seem to have been particularly popular? If we arbitrarily set the criterion for popularity as being represented by ten copies or more, we have a list of fourteen works, as follows: Ambrose, *De mysteriis* (ten copies) and *De sacramentis* (ten copies); Augustine,

[216] See n. 56 above.

[217] Cf. R. W. Southern, *St Anselm: a portrait in a landscape* (Cambridge, 1990), pp. 367–71 and 479.

[218] Nos. 55, 56, 101, 102e, 104, 122, 188, 515, 644, 738, 749, 773, 798, 802, and 924. For the manuscripts of Ivo's *Epistolae* in general see J. Leclercq, 'La collection des lettres d'Yves de Chartres', *Revue Bénédictine* 56 (1946), 108–25.

[219] *Saec.* xi^{2}–xi^{ex}: 65, 300, 370, 383, 562, 728, 729, 732, and 755. xi/xii–xii^{in}: 75, and 178. xii^{1}: 76, 382, 384, 730.

[220] Cicero appears in nos. 182, 291, 404e, 443, 541, 564, 625, 760, and 767, two of which (404e and 541) are the *Aratea*. For Macrobius manuscripts in general see Eastwood, 'Manuscripts of Macrobius'.

[221] Known from Cambridge University Library, Dd. 13. 2, a copy made in 1444 for William Gray: see Thomson, *William of Malmesbury*, pp. 50–5. At a slightly later date Wibald of Corvey instigated a comparable collection: Berlin, Staatsbibliothek, Preussischer Kulturbesitz, lat. fol. 252: T. Brandis, *Glanz alter Buchkunst: Mittelalterliche Handschriften der Staatsbibliothek Preussischer Kulturbesitz, Berlin* (Wiesbaden, 1988), no. 30.

Confessiones (ten copies, one of which is reproduced as pl. 10),[222] *De Trinitate* (ten), *In Psalmos* (25), *In Euangelium Iohannis* (thirteen), and *Sermones* (nineteen); Pseudo-Augustine, *Dialogus quaestionum lxv Orosii et Augustini respondentis* (ten); Bede, *De tabernaculo* (ten)[223] and *Historia ecclesiastica* (nine, plus one restoration, plus four excerpts: see pl. 8); Gregory, *In Ezechielem* (thirteen) and *Moralia in Iob* (sixteen: two of which are reproduced as pls. 18 and 20);[224] Jerome, *Epistolae* (ten); and, finally, Paul the Deacon's Homiliary (fifteen: see pl. 11). It will be noted that the great majority of these texts achieved the bare ten required for inclusion. Apart from Paul the Deacon's Homiliary, Augustine's *In Psalmos* and Gregory's *Moralia* (multi-volume works and therefore having an additional advantage) and Augustine's *Sermones* (which travelled in varying combinations), there are only two works which 'score' more than ten, namely Gregory's *In Ezechielem* and Augustine's *In Euangelium Iohannis*. If we take into consideration volumes that are mentioned on the book-lists but which do not seem to have survived, this adds one copy each of Ambrose's *De sacramentis*, Augustine's *Confessiones*, Bede's *De tabernaculo*, and Jerome's *Epistolae*; two copies of Gregory's *In Ezechielem* and *Moralia*, and of Augustine's *In Euangelium Iohannis*; and four of Bede's *Historia ecclesiastica*. The combined evidence of the manuscripts and book-lists thus suggests that Augustine's *In Euangelium Iohannis*, Bede's *Historia ecclesiastica* and Gregory's *In Ezechielem* were the most popular texts of all.[225]

If we reduce the requirement to being represented in more than five copies, then we add a further sixty-one works—of greatly differing length incidentally. These are set out at the end of this Introduction, in Appendix 1. Inevitably this expanded list revolves around the authors whose general high profile has just been remarked: there are four texts by Isidore, five texts by Gregory the Great (who, it will be remembered, only really has six to his credit), six by Anselm, seven by Bede, eleven by Ambrose (some of which, it should be noted, circulated together), and sixteen by Augustine. Augustine is also represented indirectly in the form of his biography by Possidius; while Ambrose reappears via a pseudonymous text that regularly travelled with a group of his own works. The other writers involved are (in alphabetical order): Ælfric, Berengaudus Ferrariensis, Eutropius, Gelasius, Gratianus Augustus, Guitmund of Aversa, Helperic, Ivo of Chartres, Jerome, Josephus, Julian of Toledo, Macrobius, Origen, Priscian, and Sulpicius Severus. It will be noted that most of the works by these other authors only just qualified for inclusion.

If we lower the boundary once again to include those works that survive in a bare five copies, the number of extra texts that is thereby incorporated is fairly modest. This is, in

[222] *Sancti Augustini Confessionum libri XIII*, ed. L. Verheijen, CCSL 27 (Turnhout, 1981), pp. lix–lxv, details the manuscripts up to the eleventh century, the totals being as follows: *s.* vi: 2; *s.* viii: 1; *s.* ix: 13; *s.* x: 7; and *s.* xi: 19. For a conspectus of the manuscripts as a whole see Wilmart, 'Grands ouvrages de Saint Augustin', pp. 259–68 (listing 258 items); with Verheijen, 'Nouveaux manuscrits' (adding a further 75).

[223] For the manuscripts as a whole see Laistner and King, *Hand-list of Bede Manuscripts*, pp. 70–4, where the totals are as follows: *s.* ix: 8; *s.* x: 2; *s.* xi: 9; *s.* xii: 32; *s.* xiii: 10; *s.* xiv: 1; and *s.* xv: 5.

[224] For the manuscripts as a whole see *S. Gregorii Magni, Moralia in Iob*, ed. M. Adriaen, CCSL 143, 3 vols. (Turnhout, 1979–85), I, pp. xiv–xxix. The totals are as follows: *s.* vii: 1; *s.* viii: 29; *s.* ix: 41; *s.* x: 27; *s.* xi: 90; *s.* xii: 173; *s.* xiii: 86; *s.* xiv: 42; *s.* xv: 78; and *s.* xvi: 5.

[225] *Sancti Gregorii Magni, Homiliae in Hiezechihelem Prophetam*, ed. M. Adriaen, CCSL 142 (Turnhout, 1971), pp. xiv–xxi, provides a conspectus of the manuscripts, assigned to a single century. This shows very clearly a great increase in the circulation of the text in the eleventh century, rising to a peak in the twelfth century: *saec.* vii, 5 copies; *saec.* viii, 14; *saec.* ix, 16; *saec.* x, 10; *saec.* xi, 32; *saec.* xii, 79; *saec.* xiii, 31; *saec.* xiv, 31; and *saec.* xv, 36.

fact, symptomatic of the nature of English book collections during our period. The thirty-two works in question are itemised in Appendix 2 below. This list, too, is dominated by Augustine, who is represented by six works (with another pseudonymous one). In fact, one further work appears by virtue of Augustine, namely the *Sermo Arianorum*, since it habitually travelled as an integral part of a collection of his texts.[226] Five other authors who were present on the first list also reappear, namely Ambrose, Anselm, Bede, Isidore, and Jerome. Eleven further writers, Abbo of Fleury, Alcuin, Berengar, Dionysius Exiguus, Eusebius of Caesarea, Pseudo-Hegesippus, 'Nennius', Orosius, Osbern of Canterbury, Smaragdus, and Solinus, appear for the first time, all but one of them represented by a single work.

These, then, were the texts that were most frequently copied and most widely distributed in early Norman England, the texts that most reasonable book collections were likely to have possessed. It is notable that Gregory the Great's revered spiritual classic, the *Regula pastoralis*, is not among them, a phenomenon which is all the more striking given that the work enjoyed a vigorous circulation in Europe as a whole in the twelfth century.[227] A probable explanation is that this was the one patristic text of which England probably had a good number of copies (in Latin and Old English) by 1066.[228]

Only one historical text seems to have been transcribed in great numbers, namely Bede's *Historia ecclesiastica* (pl. 8). It survives in nine complete copies (one being of the Old English translation); in addition there is one earlier manuscript which received substantial additions in our period, plus four other manuscripts with extracts from the work.[229] Seven of the nine complete copies date from the end of our period.[230] The popularity implied by the manuscript evidence fits into a context of continuing relevance and use which is attested by other sources. Bede's work, which was very highly regarded by contemporary historians such as Symeon of Durham and William of Malmesbury,[231] was extremely valuable to older foundations as documentary evidence of their antiquity, not to mention of their past glories. Furthermore, reading the text was apparently a catalyst for the northern monastic revival in

[226] Nos. 147, 313, 473, 667, and 862. Webber, *Scribes and Scholars*, pp. 51–3, describes the English circulation.

[227] See R. W. Clement, 'A handlist of manuscripts containing Gregory's *Regula pastoralis*', *Manuscripta* 28 (1984), 33–44. The approximate totals up to the twelfth century are as follows: *s.* vi: 1; *s.* vii: 1; *s.* viii: 11; *s.* ix: 20; *s.* x: 28; *s.* xi: 27; and *s.* xii: 76.

[228] There are five copies of the *Regula pastoralis* from the period *c.* 1066–1130, namely nos. 36, 303 (supplement), 693, ?877, and 901, of which one is uncertain and another a supplement to a pre-existing copy. It is worth noting that the Durham and Exeter manuscripts were certainly duplicates. Bishop Leofric's acquisitions for Exeter (1069×72) included a copy, which still survives (Oxford, Bodleian Library, Bodley 708); Bishop Carilef's bequest to Durham also included a copy, but this does not appear to survive. The book-lists include two further copies, one of which is probably identical with a surviving manuscript.

The extant pre-Conquest copies (or fragments) are: Cambridge University Library, Ii. 2. 4 (OE); Cambridge, Corpus Christi College, 12 (OE), and 361; Cambridge, Trinity College, R. 5. 22; Glasgow, University Library, Hunterian 431 (V. 5. 1); Kassel, Landesbibliothek, MS Theol. Fol. 32; London, British Library, Cotton Otho B. ii (OE), Cotton Tiberius B. xi (OE); Oxford, Bodleian Library, Bodley 708, and Hatton 20 (OE); Oxford, St John's College, 28; Paris, Bibliothèque nationale, lat. 9561; and Worcester Cathedral Library, Add. MS 3.

[229] Nos. 68, 175, 176 (additions), 232, 320, 353, 449, 589e, 707e, 711e, 716, 723, 751, and 805e.

[230] Nos. 175, 320, 353, 449, 716, 723, and 751.

[231] Symeon, *Historia Ecclesiae Dunhelmensis*, cc. xiv–v (*Symeonis Monachi Opera Omnia*, ed. Arnold, I, pp. 41–4); also the *Epistola ad Hugonem* (esp. *ibid.*, pp. 227–8); William of Malmesbury, *De Gestis Regum Anglorum*, I, cc. 54–62, ed. W. Stubbs, 2 vols., RS 90a–b (London, 1887–9), I, pp. 58–67.

the late eleventh century;[232] and it was also useful for resolving contemporary ecclesiastical disputes.[233]

The only other historical texts that achieved something approaching a respectable circulation were the late antique 'classics': Josephus's *De antiquitate iudaica* (six copies) and *De bello iudaico*[234] (four copies, plus five of Pseudo-Hegesippus's version: see pl. 21),[235] Eusebius's *Historia ecclesiastica* (five copies), and Eutropius's *Breuiarium historiae romanae* (six copies, plus one manuscript with extracts).[236] These were all widely copied in Europe as a whole during this period. The most generally popular 'Roman' history book, incidentally, Orosius's *Historiae aduersus paganos*, of which over a hundred manuscripts survive dating from before *c.* 1200, lags behind slightly in our English corpus, being represented by four copies.[237]

Yet if comparatively few individual historical texts seem to have achieved wide circulation, a modest range of historical writings was nevertheless available in England as a whole. Between them these texts covered a broad chronological and geographical field, ranging from Classical Antiquity (Orosius, Eutropius, Justinus) and Jewish antiquity (Josephus) through the early Christian period (Eusebius) to the 'Barbarian West' (Victor of Vita and Paul the Deacon), Freculphus presenting a mélange of all these; and on through the Carolingian period (Einhard, Ado of Vienne) to the 'present day' (William of Jumièges). There is, unsurprisingly, some weighting towards writings about Britain (Bede, 'Nennius', and the *Anglo-Saxon Chronicle*), but it is not overwhelming. Be that as it may, it is no surprise to find that Norman history is also represented (in the form of Dudo of St Quentin and William of Jumièges); and it is striking that, whilst there is only one manuscript preserving Anglo-Saxon royal genealogies, there are three that contain the genealogy of the Kings of France, and three with that of the Dukes of Normandy.[238]

The spread of historical works can fairly be characterised as broad and thin for the most part, with a deeper 'centre'. That is, the majority of the works are represented by a tiny number of copies, while just a few appear in greater strength. To some extent, as we have seen, this was a result of the nature of the genre; however precisely the same is true of the

[232] *Symeonis Monachi Opera Omnia*, ed. Arnold, I, pp. 106 and 108. See futher Knowles, *Monastic Order*, pp. 165–71; L. Butler, 'The Desert in the North', *Northern History* 5 (1970), 1–11; and A. Dawtry, 'The Benedictine Revival in the North: the last bulwark of Anglo-Saxon monasticism', *Studies in Church History* 18 (1982), 87–98.

[233] E.g. in the Canterbury-York dispute *The Letters of Lanfranc*, ed. Clover and Gibson, ep. 4 (p. 50). See further A. Gransden, 'Bede's Reputation as an Historian in Medieval England', *Journal of Ecclesiastical History* 32 (1981), 397–425; reprinted in her *Legends, Traditions and History in Medieval England* (London, 1992), 1–29, esp. 8–16.

[234] Herbert Losinga (ep. 10, ed. Anstruther) begged Abbot Richard to send him his Josephus, something which he had clearly been avoiding doing for some time on the grounds that its binding was in poor condition.

[235] Cf. A. Bell, 'Josephus and Pseudo-Hegesippus' in *Josephus, Judaism and Christianity*, ed. L. H. Feldman and G. Hata (Detroit, 1987), 349–61.

[236] For the general tradition: *Texts and Traditions*, ed. Reynolds, pp. 159–62.

[237] Nos. 49, 53, 168, and 621; also 348e For the extant manuscripts as a whole see J. M. Bately and D. J. Ross, 'A Checklist of Manuscripts of Orosius's *Historiarum aduersum paganos libri septem*', *Scriptorium* 15 (1961), 319–34; with Mortensen, 'Texts and Contexts of Ancient Roman History', esp. pp. 105–6 and 110.

[238] CCCC, MS 290 (*s.* xii^{1}; St Albans): Dukes of Normandy, Merovingians, Carolingians. Hereford Cathedral Library, MS P. I. 3 (*s.* xii^{in}; Gloucester), Kings of France, Dukes of Normandy. BL, MS Royal 13 A. xxiii (*s.* xi^{2}; Mont Saint-Michel; Canterbury, St Augustine's): Emperors to Constantine V, Dukes of Normandy, Kings of France. BL, MS Royal 15 B. xvi (*s.* xii^{in}; Normandy; London, St Paul's): Emperors. Bodl.L., MS Bodley 163 (*s.* xii^{1}; Peterborough): Counts of Flanders, Kings of France. Oxford, Lincoln College, MS lat. 100 (*s.* xii^{1}; Malmesbury): Emperors in East and West. Rochester Cathedral Library, MS A. 3. 5 (*s.* xii^{1}; Rochester): West Saxons, Anglo-Saxon kings, Popes, Emperors, Patriarchs, English archbishops and bishops.

Latin classical texts. More than twenty different authors appear in the corpus of surviving manuscripts, but their individual works are for the most part found in one or occasionally two copies. It is noteworthy, incidentally, that those classical authors who are known to have been copied in late Anglo-Saxon times, such as Persius, Statius and, probably, Vitruvius, are no more strongly represented in the sixty years after the Conquest than are the apparent 'newcomers' such as Lucan, Plautus, and Terence[239] (though it must be said that, judged by the extant manuscripts as a whole, the general circulation of Persius and Statius was hardly impressive at this time).[240] Correspondingly, of the two particularly eminent authors, Ovid and Virgil, who were certainly available in late Anglo-Saxon England,[241] the first does not reappear at all in the extant manuscripts of our period, while the second is represented by a single fragment.[242]

Now, the pattern that is sketched out in these 'minority' areas is in fact a microcosm of what we see in the fields of patristics and post-patristic theology, where the numbers of surviving manuscripts are very much greater. Here, of course, the range of writings is considerably wider; nevertheless, highly significantly the vast majority of the works are still represented by one or two copies. In fact, perhaps the most interesting single point to emerge from the exercise of surveying the texts in all these books is this pattern, namely the breadth of the material, but the shallowness of the presence of most of it. Substantial numbers of different texts seem to have been acquired and copied between 1066 and 1130, but, even making allowance for great losses, very few of them appear to have been produced in more

[239] Persius's *Saturae* appear in nos. 290 and 623: for a description of the former see Cunningham, 'Latin classical manuscripts in the National Library of Scotland', pp. 84–5; for the latter see Ker, *Catalogue*, no. 295, and R. W. Hunt *et al.*, *The Survival of Ancient Literature* (Oxford, 1975), no. 120. Statius's *Achilleid* appears in no. 623, his *Thebaid* in no. 121; Vitruvius's *De architectura* in no. 450.

A pre-Conquest copy of Persius's *Saturae* survives as Oxford, Bodleian Library, Auct. F. 1. 15 (part. ii); while the *Thebaid* survives in Worcester Cathedral Library, Q. 8 etc. (for which see T. A. M. Bishop, *English Caroline Minuscule* (Oxford, 1971), no. 20). The Vitruvius appears in London, British Library, Cotton Cleopatra D. i, fols. 2–82*, the first part of a composite volume, of which this and the following part are of Saint Augustine's Abbey medieval provenance. These pages were written in *s.* x^{in-1} by an English and a continental scribe working in intimate collaboration. Whether the volume was produced in England or on the continent is therefore uncertain. The work of the English scribe is reproduced in Gem (ed.), *St Augustine's Abbey*, ill. 24.

Lucan's *Pharsalia* is no. 174; Plautus's *Comoediae* no. 565, and Terence no. 559.

[240] For Statius manuscripts in general see P. M. Clogan, 'A preliminary list of the manuscripts of Statius's *Achilleid*', *Manuscripta* 8 (1964), 175–8; and 'Medieval glossed manuscripts of the *Thebaid*', *Manuscripta* 11 (1967), 102–12. On Persius manuscripts see P. S. Piacentini, *Saggio di un censimento dei manoscritti contenenti il testo di Persio e gli scoli e i commenti al testo*, Studi su Persio e la scoliastica Persiana 3/1 (Rome, 1973). For Vitruvius see C. H. Krinsky, 'Seventy-eight Vitruvius manuscripts', *Journal of the Warburg and Courtauld Institutes* 30 (1967), 36–70; with Reynolds (ed.), *Texts and Transmission*, pp. 440–4.

[241] A Welsh copy of Ovid's *Ars amatoria* (Bk I) occupied fols. 37r–47r of St Dunstan's 'Classbook' (Oxford, Bodleian Library, Auct. F. 4. 32); see W. M. Lindsay, *Early Welsh Script* (Oxford, 1912), pp. 8–10; and the facsimile, *Saint Dunstan's Classbook from Glastonbury*, ed. R. W. Hunt (Amsterdam, 1961). A copy of Virgil's works was produced at Worcester *s.* x/xi (Vatican City, Biblioteca Apostolica Vaticana, Reg. lat. 1671); see Bishop, *English Caroline Minuscule*, no. 19; and Gameson, 'Book Production and Decoration at Worcester', esp. pp. 205–10, where the fragmentary copy Oxford, Bodleian Library, Lat. class. c. 2, fol. 18 (+ *membra disiecta*) is also discussed. I have not seen London, College of Arms, Arundel 30.

[242] No. 762. B. Munk Olsen, 'Ovide au moyen âge', highlights the discrepancy between the literary evidence for Ovid's increasing influence in Europe as a whole in the late eleventh and twelfth centuries, and the comparatively modest quantity of extant manuscripts from that period. Nevertheless, the numbers of copies of the *Metamorphoses* at least are not negligable (eleven from *s.* xi, and thirty-four from *s.* xii) and the dearth of copies of any of his works in our corpus remains remarkable. Ovid was evidently known to Herbert Losinga, who particularly recommended him to Willelm and Otto as a stylistic model (ep. 39); and who quoted from the *Tristia* in his ep. 10. For an introduction to Virgil manuscripts see G. C. Alessio, 'Medioevo: Tradizione manuscritta', *Enciclopedia Virgiliana*, III (Rome, 1987), 432–43.

than tiny quantities. As we have seen, most of the authors who dominated the corpus in numerical terms did so as much because of the bulk of their writings as owing to the frequency with which particular works were copied. Ten of the nineteen works by Isidore, for example, exist merely in single or double copies; and the same is true of ten of the twenty-five or so works by Jerome. Thirty-two of Augustine's works (not including individual sermons) are only extant in single or double copies, as are twenty of the works of Pseudo-Augustine, seventeen of Bede, and thirteen by Ambrose. Equally symptomatic of this pattern are the cases of Cicero, who features in seven manuscripts by courtesy of seven different works; and Alcuin, who is represented in thirteen books via ten works. In point of fact, a staggering 569 different texts are represented by one copy only.

Bearing this in mind, the special status of those works that do survive in five or more copies is all the more apparent. And to revert to a point made earlier, the fact that three of Gregory the Great's works (that is, half of his oeuvre) exist in more than five copies is a striking testimony to an outstanding popularity (cf. pls. 18 and 20).[243]

The characterisation of the period *c.* 1066 to *c.* 1130 in the history of English libraries as one when religious houses tried to build up collections of patristics is certainly valid, but equally certainly it is oversimplistic. Patristics were undoubtedly copied in great numbers (alongside other texts, as we have seen), but the surviving volumes do not, with a restricted number of exceptions, seem to imply comprehensive and systematic acquisition. As we have noted, apart from the restricted number of core texts listed in Appendix 1, and, to a lesser extent, those in Appendix 2, the great majority of such works are represented by a couple of copies at most. The evidence of the book-lists confirms this 'two tier' system—a small number of widely copied works surrounded by a vast penumbra of other, much rarer texts. Of course, many volumes have been lost, but even if we still possessed the libraries of such centres as Norwich, St Paul's, and Winchester, it seems unlikely that they would alter the basic picture. Some single copies would, of course, now become multiple ones; but further otherwise unattested texts would probably be added, and the number of copies of the 'core' texts would doubtless further increase. One can reasonable speculate that the original situation was a more populous and varied version of what the surviving evidence shows us, with an even more marked contrast between the 'core' texts on the one hand, represented in yet larger numbers, and on the other hand, a greater range of very much rarer, peripheral ones.

The overall impression one gets, therefore, is of communities collecting fairly enthusiastically, trying to acquire works by the Fathers along with those of Bede and certain more recent theological writers, but doing so semi-independently and without much order. Against the suggestion that this is merely an accident of survival, one can point to the prevalence of the pattern. It is common to every author 'great' and 'small' alike, and applies to every class of text except liturgica. The period *c.* 1066 to *c.* 1130 is characterised by the simultaneous acquisition of a small number of texts in large quantites and a large number of other texts in very small quantities. Looking backwards from the middle of the twelfth century, we see a good number of fairly coherent libraries. This should not, however, lead us to assume that they were accumulated easily or in an orderly way. Looking forward from 1066, quite the

[243] In addition, the *Excerpta in Cantica Canticorum* which travelled as part of Bede's Commentary on the Song of Songs is extant in seven copies.

reverse would appear to have been the case. The nature of the collections individual centres could create in the late eleventh and early twelfth century was the product of the exemplars they could lay their hands on. The available selection could vary considerably from place to place and from year to year, and it was undoubtedly very much less in 1066 than it was in 1130.[244]

What, surely, we are seeing here is a situation where the base of available material was too small, the means of replication too slow, and the methods of locating and circulating texts too unreliable to support more efficient, orderly growth. English book collections were undoubtedly increasing in size, in some cases rapidly; but apart from in the best connected and most energetic houses, they were doing so on a fairly *ad hoc* basis. In reality, of course, this is precisely what we should expect. The libraries of the continental region with which England had strongest political ties, namely Normandy,[245] will hardly have been able to support anything else: with the exception of Mont-Saint-Michel and Fécamp,[246] they were hardly over-endowed with resources themselves.[247] In such circumstances, the energy of a religious community and its leaders, its geographical location, and the extent of its intercourse with the rest of the continent, above all, perhaps northern France and Flanders,[248] could make a decisive difference to the size and nature of the book collection it could amass, and the speed at which it could do so. These were pioneering generations.

Assuming this is indeed a fair sketch of the situation, it has very important implications. Beyond the comparatively small selection of readily accessible works mentioned earlier, the contents of one collection could differ appreciably from that of another. In the case of patristics, one could expect the same authors, but often different works. In other areas, one

[244] Cf. Thomson, 'Norman Conquest and English Libraries', pp. 37–40 (though the manuscript evidence does not support his postulated hiatus between *c.* 1100 and *c.* 1120).

[245] The fundamental account of Norman libraries is G. Nortier, *Les bibliothèques médiévales des abbayes bénédictines de Normandie*, 2nd ed. (Paris, 1971). The *s.* xi inventory of Fécamp's books list eighty-seven items: *Catalogue général des manuscrits des bibliothèques publiques de France, Departements I: Rouen*, ed. H. Omont (Paris, 1886), pp. xxiv–v; with B. Branch, 'Inventories of the Library of Fécamp from the Eleventh and Twelfth centuries', *Manuscripta* 23 (1979), 159–72. The list from Rouen Cathedral dating from the time of Archbishop Geoffrey (1111–28) (Rouen, Bibliothèque municipale, Y. 27, p. 128; printed: *Catalogue général, Rouen*, ed. Omont, pp. x–xi) comprises fifty-eight items. On the other hand, the emphasis in the latter is in strong contrast to that of contemporary English libraries: here patristics are very thinly represented while works relating to the Trivium and Quadrivium are a strong presence, with the Latin Classics present in some force.

[246] See J. J. G. Alexander, *Norman Illumination at Mont Saint Michel 966–1100* (Oxford, 1970); and Branch, 'Inventories of the Library of Fécamp'.

[247] As the letters of Anselm (*Opera Omnia*, ed. Schmitt, III, epp. 23, 25, 66, and 74) attest.

[248] The Cambrai inventory, dating from the second half of the tenth century, lists sixty-six items with a good collection of patristics, plus Martial, Ovid (two volumes), Pliny, and Valerius Maximus (Cambrai, Bibliothèque municipale, 685, fol. 1r: ed. A. Molinier in *Catalogue des manuscrits des bibliothèques publiques de France, Départements 17* (Paris, 1891), pp. vii–viii; see also the discussion of D. Nebbiai-Dalla Guarda in *Le Christianisme en occident du début du vii*e *siècle au milieu du xi*e *siècle*, ed. F. Bougard (Paris, 1997), pp. 119–27, with a facsimile of the relevant folio at p. 121). The 1105 Stavelot catalogue (*Corpus Catalogorum Belgii II*, ed. A. Derolez and B. Victor (Brussels, 1994), no. 68) records a collection of 152 items with an extensive and orderly selection of patristics (items 13–37, 45–7 and 49), certain Carolingian commentaries, some other theology, and an extensive range of hagiography (items 58–74). The catalogue of Saint Vaast, Arras, as written by the first hand (which the editor dates to *c.* 1120–30), numbers 210 items (this does not include biblical and liturgical books). It begins with an impressive collection of works on the liberal arts (nos. 1–47), followed by a solid block of core patristics (nos. 48–110), with thereafter good runs of other fathers along with early medieval and Carolingian works (111–210). On the other hand, 'modern' authors are limited to Anselm. See P. Grierson, 'La bibliothèque de St-Vaast d'Arras au xiie siècle', *Revue bénédictine* 52 (1940), 117–40. Surviving identifiable local products show that there was a reasonable collection of patristics by *c.* 1066: see Schulten, 'Buchmalerei des 11. Jahrhunderts im Kloster St Vaast in Arras'. See also n. 70 above.

was as likely to find different authors. The modern scholar must thus be extremely wary of deducing from the presence of a particular text in the corpus of survivors that it was *generally* available in early Norman England. Quite the reverse was probably true. The point is underlined by the fact that at the beginning of the twelfth century Herbert Losinga had to work hard to acquire some of the texts he sought, including even Josephus; while at a slightly later date William of Malmesbury was forced to travel extensively to find a good deal of his reading matter.[249]

By the 1120s, on the other hand, the situation was arguably rather different. A large number of texts were now available somewhere in the country, and several distinguished centres had, by the standards of the day, fairly comprehensive libraries. Consequently, other communities with sufficient determination and good connections could build up an orderly collection, targeting gaps in their holdings, in a way that had hitherto been impossible, or at least extremely difficult. Rochester, whose library grew rapidly and fairly systematically during the later years of our period, benefitting from proximity to Canterbury, provides an early example of the phenomenon.

One may reasonably wonder whether this was, in essence, what happened on a larger scale in the second quarter and middle of the twelfth century. Did the well-established Benedictine houses systematically fill the gaps in their holdings? At the same time, however, one must ask how rapidly they were replaced as the central foyers of book acquisition by newer foundations, notably Augustinian and Cistercian ones. And turning to the contents of the libraries, it would be interesting to know at what point the Fathers were toppled from their pinnacle as the focus of scribal effort, with the increasing availability of new theological works, not to mention glossed books of the Bible. There can be little doubt that the picture becomes more complicated and diffuse as the centres of production and acquisition increase, and the numbers of texts proliferate. It would, however, be premature to approach these and related questions until the present inventory has been extended to embrace subsequent periods.

[249] Cf. Thomson, *William of Malmesbury*, pp. 72–5.

APPENDIX 1
Texts Represented by Six or More Extant Copies

The counting is on the basis of the number of complete copies of the text in question, and the exact figure is given in brackets at the end of each entry. If, however, a text qualified for inclusion on these grounds, the number of additional manuscripts containing extracts from the work is noted, where applicable, in a separate formula. Texts represented by ten copies or more are distinguished by an asterisk. For multi-volume works such as Gregory the Great's *Moralia*, the figure given is the number of extant volumes, not the number of complete copies. Biblical and liturgical books, and decretal/legal collections have not been included.

Ælfric, *Homiliae* (9 + 1e)
Ambrose, *De fide* (7)
  De incarnationis dominicae sacramento (6)
  * *De mysteriis* (10)
  De officiis ministrorum (6)
  * *De sacramentis* (10)
  De Spiritu Sancto (8)
  De uiduis (8)
  De uirginibus (6)
  De uirginitate (9)
  Epistolae (7)
  Exhortatio ad uirgines (6)
Pseudo-Ambrose, *Consolatio ad uirginem lapsam* (6)
  De lapsu uirginis consecretae (9)
Anselm, *Cur Deus homo* (6)
  De conceptu uirginali et originali peccato (7)
  De incarnatione uerbi (7)
  De libertate arbitrii (6)
  Epistolae (6 + 9e)
  Monologion (6)
Augustine, * *Confessiones* (10)
  Contra mendacium (6)
  De agone christiano (6)
  De ciuitate Dei (8)
  De cura pro mortuis gerenda (6)
  De Genesi ad litteram (8)
  De natura et origine animae (6)
  De octo Dulcitii quaestionibus (6)
  * *De Trinitate* (10)
  De uera religione (6)
  * *Enarrationes in Psalmos* (25)
  Enchiridion (7)
  Epistolae (9 + 12e)
  In epistolam Iohannis (8 + 2e)
  * *In euangelium Iohannis* (13 + 2e)
  * *Sermones* [varying combinations] (19 + 7e)
Pseudo-Augustine, *Contra Felicianum Arianum* (6)
  * *Dialogus quaestionum lxv Orosii percontantis et Augustini respondentis* (10)
  Hypomnesticon (7)
Bede, * *De tabernaculo* (10)
  De temporibus (6)
  De temporum ratione (7)
  Historia ecclesiastica (9 + 5e)
  In Cantica Canticorum (7)
  In Epistolas Catholicas (8)
  Vita S. Cuthberti (8)
Berengaudus Ferrariensis, *In Apocalypsin* (6)
Eutropius, *Breuiarium historiae romanae ab urbe condita* (6)
Gelasius (attrib.), *Decretum de recipiendis et non recipiendis libris* (6)
Gratianus Augustus, *Epistola ad Ambrosium* (6)
Gregory, *Excerpta in Cantica Canticorum* (7)
  Homiliae xl in Euangelia (6)
  * *In Ezechielem* (13)
  * *Moralia in Iob* (16)
  Registrum epistolarum (9)
Guitmund of Aversa, *De corpore et sanguine Domini contra Berengarium* (6)
Helperic of Grandval, *De computo* (7)
Isidore, *De natura rerum* (6)
  De nominibus legis et euangelii (6)
  De ortu et obitu patrum (6)
  Etymologiae (6 + 15e)
Ivo of Chartres, *Sermones* (7)
Jerome, * *Epistolae* (10 + 4e)
  In Prophetas minores (7)
Josephus, *De antiquitate iudaica* (6 + 5 of Pseudo-Hegesippus's recension)
Julian of Toledo, *Prognosticon futuri saeculi* (7)
Macrobius, *Interpretatio in somnium Scipionis* (7)
Origen, In *Cantica Canticorum* (8)
Paul the Deacon, * *Homiliarium* (15)
Possidius, *Vita Augustini* (9)
Priscian, *Institutiones grammaticae* (9)
Sulpicius Severus, *Dialogi* (6)
  Epistolae (6)
  Vita S. Martini (6)

APPENDIX 2
Texts Represented by Five Copies

In a few cases, only four of the manuscripts contain the complete work, the fifth volume having merely an extract from it. The texts to which this applies are distinguished by being presented within brackets.

Abbo of Fleury, *Vita S. Edmundi*
[Alcuin, *De fide sanctae et indiuiduae Trinitatis* (4 + 1e)]
[Ambrose, *Hexaemeron* (4 + 1e)]
Anselm, *De casu Diaboli*
Proslogion
Augustine, *Contra aduersarium legis et prophetarum*
Contra Iulianum
De diuersis haeresibus
De doctrina christiana
Retractationes (5 + 27e)
Sermones de uerbis domini et apostoli
Pseudo-Augustine, *Contra sermonem Arianorum*
Bede, *In Tobiam*
Berengar of Tours, *Recantation*
Dionysius Exiguus, *Epistolae duae de ratione festi paschae*
Eusebius of Caesarea, *Historia ecclesiastica*
[Fulbert of Chartres, *Epistolae* (4 + 1e)]
Pseudo-Hegesippus, *Historia libri V de bello iudaico*
Isidore, *De libris Noui Testamenti et Veteri prooemia*
De uiris illustribus
Jerome, *Aduersus Heluidium de Mariae perpetua uirginitate*
Contra Iouinianum
Contra Vigiliantium
De diuersis generibus musicorum
De interpretatione Hebraicorum nominum
De uiris illustribus
In Ieremiam
Quaestiones hebraicae in Genesim
'Nennius', *Historia Brittonum*
Orosius, *Historiae aduersus paganos*
Osbern of Canterbury, *Epistola de uita S. Dunstani*
Vita S. Dunstani
Sermo Arianorum
Smaragdus, *Diadema monachorum*
Solinus, *Collectanea*

APPENDIX 3
Authors Represented, Arranged by Century

In this highly simplified presentation, each author is listed under a single century according to his date of death. Thus Gregory the Great, who died in 604, appears under *s.* vii. The exceptions are those authors who died in the centuries before Christ, all of whom appear in a union 'B.C.' entry.

B.C. (general)

Aesop, Cicero, Dioscorides, Horace, Plato, Plautus, Sallust, Terence, Virgil, Vitruvius

A.D. I

Lucan, Persius, Pliny the Elder, Pliny the Younger, Seneca, Statius, Valerius Maximus

II

Aulus Gellius, Frontinus, Galen, Josephus, Juvenal, Suetonius

III

Cyprian, Justinus, Origen, Solinus, Tertullian

IV

Ambrose, Ambrosiaster, Athanasius, Ausonius, Avianus, Basil the Great, Chalcidius, Didymus of Alexandria, Ephraim the Syrian, Eusebius of Caesarea, Eusebius of Vercelli, Eutropius, Gregory Nazianzenus, Pseudo-Hegesippus, Hilary of Poitiers, Lactantius, Martin of Tours, Phocas Grammaticus, Potamius of Lisbon, Victorinus of Petovium

V

Arnobius, Augustine of Hippo, Dares the Phrygian, Eucherius of Lyon, Faustus of Reiez, Gaudentius of Brescia, Gelasius, Gennadius of Marseilles, Hilarius, Jerome, John Cassian, John Chrysostom, Leo the Great, Macrobius, Martianus Capella, Maximus of Turin, Nicetas of Remesiana, Orosius, Palladius Helenopolitanus, Paulinus of Milan, Pelagius, Possidius, Prosper of Aquitaine, Prudentius, Rufinus of Aquileia, 'Sextus Placitus Papyriensis', Sidonius Apollinaris, Sulpicius Severus, Symphosius, Theodore of Mopsuestia, Vegetius, Victor of Vita, Vigilius of Thapsus

VI

Agnellus of Ravenna, Alexander Trallianus, Arator, Benedict of Nursia, Boethius, Caesarius of Arles, Cassiodorus, Ps.-Dionysius Areopagita, Eutropius Episcopus Valentinensis, Fulgentius of Ruspe, Gregory of Tours, Jordanes, Julianus Pomerius, Martin of Braga, Priscian, Sedulius

VII

Cummian, ?Dionysius Exiguus, Eugenius II of Toledo, Gregory the Great, Isidore of Seville, Julian of Toledo, Leontius of Naples, Mansuetus, Venantius Fortunatus

VIII

Aethicus Ister (Virgil of Salzburg), Aldhelm, Ambrosius Autpertus, Bede, Boniface, Chrodegang of Metz, Cuthbert of Wearmouth-Jarrow, Defensor, 'Eddius', Felix of Crowland, Paul the Deacon

IX

Ado of Vienne, Alcuin, Amalarius of Metz, Anso of Lobbes, Aurelianus of Réomé, Berengaudus Ferrariensis, Dungalus, Einhard, Florus of Lyon, Freculphus of Lisieux, 'Gariopontus of Salerno', Haimo of Auxerre, Heiric of Auxerre, Helperic of Grandval, Hilduin, Hrabanus Maurus, John the Deacon, John Scotus Erigena, Mico of Saint Riquier, 'Nennius', Paschasius Radbertus, Paulinus of Aquileia, Ratramnus of Corbie, Smaragdus of Saint-Mihiel, Theodulf of Orléans, ?Theodulus, Usuardus

X

Abbo of Saint-Germain, Adalbert of Metz, Adso of Montier-en-Der, Æthelwold of Winchester, John of Salerno, ?Lantfred of Winchester, Letald of Micy, Odo of Cluny, Regino of Prüm, Remigius of Auxerre

XI

Abbo of Fleury, Adelard of Ghent, Ælfric of Eynsham, Berengar of Tours, Burchard of Worms, Byrhtferth of Ramsey, Constantinus Africanus, Dudo of Saint Quentin, Folcard of Saint Bertin, Fulbert of Chartres, Gaunilo, Gauzlin of Fleury, Guido of Arezzo, Guitmund of Aversa, Heriger of Lobbes, 'Hermann the Archdeacon', Hermannus Contractus, Hugh of Langres, Hugh of Tours, Lanfranc, Marianus Scotus, Odilo of Cluny, Osbern of Canterbury, Otloh of Saint Emmeram, Patrick of Dublin, Peter Damian, Robert Losinga, Robert de Tumbalena, William of Jumièges, Wulfstan of Winchester, Wulfstan of Worcester and York

XII

Ælmer of Canterbury, Alexander of Canterbury, Anselm of Canterbury, Anselm of Laon, Baudri of Bourgueil, Bernard of Clairvaux, Bruno of Asti, Eadmer of Canterbury, Ernulf of Canterbury, Franco of Afflighem, Fulgentius of Afflighem, Gilbert Crispin, Goscelin of Canterbury, Gregory of Ely, Herbert Losinga, Honorius Augustodunensis, Hugh of Fleury, Hugh of Saint Victor, Ivo of Chartres, John of Bari, Marbod of Rennes, Odo of Asti, Osbert of Clare, Peter Pictor, Ralph of Battle, Ralph d'Escures, Richard of Préaux, Serlo of Bayeux, Symeon of Durham, Walcher of Great Malvern, William of Malmesbury, ?William of Saint Hilary

INVENTORY OF TEXTS INCLUDED IN BOOK-LISTS

Documentary sources describing books that were in circulation during our period are not plentiful, and the majority are limited to passing references to individual manuscripts. Nevertheless, there are a handful of relevant book-lists which usefully supplement the evidence of the extant manuscripts. Their information must, however, be used with caution. The identity of individual texts, for instance, is not always certain. Moreover, unless the manuscript in question has survived and is identifiable, or the text in question was composed after 1066, there is always the possibiltiy that the entry refers to a book that predated our period. Although the great majority of the items on the Rochester library catalogue (R), for example, were undoubtedly produced during our period, at least one of them, which survives as Oxford, Bodleian Library, Bodley 340 + 342, dates from the early eleventh century. The unspecified Old English translation of L13 is another possible case in point. Yet despite such reservations, it is undoubtedly worth presenting a list of the relevant texts, in so far as they can be identified, in this context.

The book-lists in question and the sigla used here to identify them are as follows.

A — The books acquired for Abingdon by Abbot Fabricius (1100–17). These are included in the brief history of the abbots of Abingdon, seemingly composed in the time of Abbot Hugh (*c.* 1190–1220) and surviving as London, British Library, Cott. Vit. A. xiii, fols. 83r–87r. The list is printed with commentary in EBL as no. B2.

D — The items listed on the front flyleaf (fol. 1) of Durham Cathedral Library, A. II. 4, as donated to the Cathedral Priory by Bishop William of St Carilef (d. 1096). The most recent publication and discussion of the list is A. C. Browne, 'Bishop William of St Carilef's Book Donations to Durham Cathedral Priory', *Scriptorium* 42 (1988), 140–55.

E — The books listed as '*libri Wilhelmi episcopi*' in the 1327 inventory of Exeter Cathdral and which are probably to be associated with William Warelwast, Exeter's second 'Norman' bishop (1107–37). The inventory is published in G. Oliver, *Lives of the Bishops of Exeter* (Exeter, 1861), pp. 301–10, the relevant section appearing at pp. 304–5.

L11 — A *s.* xi/xii or xii^{in} book-list added to fol. 198v of Oxford, Bodleian Library, Tanner 3, a *s.* xi^{in} copy of Gregory's *Dialogi*. The medieval provenance of the volume was Worcester. The text is printed and discussed in Lapidge, 'Booklists' as no. XI (pp. 69–73); and in EBL as B115.

L12 — A *s.* xi^{ex} booklist which was added to the *s.* vii Italian gospel book, Oxford, Bodleian Library, Auct. D. 2. 14, fol. 173r, probably at Bury St Edmunds. It is printed and discussed in Lapidge, 'Booklists' as no. XII (pp. 74–6); and in EBL as B12 (pp. 49–50).

L13 — A *s.* xii^{in} booklist written on fol. 251r of Oxford, Bodleian Library, Bodley 163, probably from Peterborough. It is printed and discussed in Lapidge, 'Booklists' as no. XIII (pp. 76–82).

R — The early twelfth-century Rochester library catalogue which occupies fols. 224r–30r of Rochester Cathedral Library, A. 3. 5, part ii (the '*Textus Roffensis*'). Although conventionally dated to 1123, doubts have recently been cast on this (P. Wormald, '*Laga Eadwardi*: The *Textus Roffensis* and its Context', *Anglo-Norman Studies* 17 (1995), 243–66 at 260), and a slightly looser dating to 1123 × *c.* 1130 is perhaps more prudent. The manuscript has been reproduced in facsimile: *Textus Roffensis*, ed. P. Sawyer, 2 vols., EEMF 7 and 11 (Copenhagen, 1957–62); the list is printed and discussed in EBL as B77 (pp. 469–92). 'Ra' is here used to distinguish the early additions (principally on fol. 230r) from the original strata.

The inventory that follows provides a union list of authors and texts, drawing on the identifications proposed in the editions cited above, the source of each entry being identified by the appropriate siglum. Where the manuscript in question is known to survive, its shelfmark is supplied (in the inventory of manuscripts, such volumes are signalled by the presence of '†' in the first column). A small number of works are not represented in any extant manuscript of the period, and these are flagged with an asterisk. They are also supplied with a reference to a secondary source. A query indicates that the text in question is probably rather than certainly the one to which the relevant entry refers. The items listed here are not included in the main index of texts.

Three lists that have deliberately been excluded are those of Sæwold of Bath (Lapidge, 'Booklists', no. VIII), Leofric of Exeter (*Ibid.*, no. X), and Henry of Blois for Glastonbury (EBL, B37). Although listed at the very beginning of our period, it is clear that most of the books that Leofric gave to Exeter were written before 1066; conversely, the majority of the items on Henry's list must have been donated after 1130. Sæwold's inventory lists books he left to the Abbey of Saint-Vaast, Arras. Not only are these therefore by definition books that were not in England during our period, it is also open to doubt whether many of them were ever in England. Several of the items have been identified with extant manuscripts. Only two of the volumes in question which I have seen (Arras, Médiathèque, 867 (Cat. gén. 346) and 1029 (812)) were written in England; the others, by contrast (Arras, Médiathèque, 435 (326), 644 (572), 732 (684), 899 (590), 1068 (276), and 1079 (235) are continental manuscripts which show no sign of having had a sojourn in England. If these are indeed the Sæwold books, which is by no means certain (particularly in the case of 732 (684) which was made at Saint Vaast itself in the second quarter of the eleventh century), it is more likely that he acquired them on the Continent.

ADALBERT OF METZ,
 Speculum Gregorii R
ALCUIN
 De dialectica R (Cambridge, Trinity College, O. 2. 24)
 De fide sanctae et indiuiduae Trinitatis R (London, British Library, Royal 6 A. xii)
 Unspecified text L11
ALFRED THE GREAT,
 Unspecified Old English translation L13
AMALARIUS OF METZ,
 **Aliis pluribus minutis opusculis* R
 De ecclesiasticis officiis/Liber officialis L13; R
AMBROSE,
 De bono mortis R (London, British Library, Royal 5 A. xv)
 De fide R (London, British Library, Royal 6 C. iv)
 De Ioseph patriarcha D (Durham Cathedral Library, B. II. 6)
 'De morte fratris' = De excessu fratris Satyri D (Durham Cathedral Library, B. II. 6)
 De mysteriis R (London, British Library, Royal 6 B. vi)
 De officiis ministrorum A; R (London, British Library, Royal 6 A. iv)
 De paenitentia D (Durham Cathedral Library, B. II. 6); R
 De sacramentis L13; R (London, British Library, Royal 6 B. vi)
 De uiduis R
 De uirginitate L13
 Epistolae R
 Expositio euangelii secundum Lucam R
 Hexaemeron L13; R (London, British Library, Royal 6. A i + 7 A. xi)
Pseudo-AMBROSE,
 (Pseudo-Ildefonsus), *De assumptione BVM* R (Cambridge, Corpus Christi College, 332)
 (?Nicetas of Remesiana) *De lapsu uirginis consecratae* R
AMBROSIUS AUTPERTUS,
 De conflictu uitiorum atque uirtutum R (London, British Library, Royal 5 A. vii)
ANSELM,
 Cur Deus homo R
Antiphoner D [two copies]; L11
Apollonius of Tyre (*Historia Apolloni regis Tyri*) L11
ARATOR,
 Historia apostolica (*De actibus apostolorum*) L11

ARISTOTLE,
*(trans. Boethius), *Categoriae* L11
ATHANASIUS OF ALEXANDRIA,
(trans. Evagrius), *Vita S. Antonii* R
AUGUSTINE,
Confessiones D; R (London, British Library, Royal 5 B. xvi)
Contra aduersarium legis et prophetarum R (Oxford, Bodleian Library, Bodley 387)
Contra Faustum Manichaeum R (London, British Library, Royal 5 B. x)
Contra Iulianum R (Oxford, Bodleian Library, Bodley 134)
De adulterinis coniugiis R (Oxford, Bodleian Library, Bodley 387)
De agone christiano R [2 copies] (Cambridge, Trinity College, O. 2. 24)
De baptismo contra Donatistas R (Cambridge University Library, Ff. 4. 32)
De blasphemia in Spiritum Sanctum (Sermo 71) R (Rochester Cathedral Library, A. 3. 16)
De bono coniugali L13
De ciuitate Dei A; D (Durham Cathedral Library, B. II. 22); L13; R (London, British Library, Royal 5 D. ix)
De consensu euangelistarum R (Rochester Cathedral, A. 3. 16)
De cura pro mortuis gerenda R
De diuersis haeresibus R (London, British Library, Royal 5 B. xvi)
De diuersis quaestionibus lxxxiii L13
De doctrina christiana R (London, British Library, Royal 5 B. xii)
De fide et symbolo R
De mendacio R (Oxford, Bodleian, Library, Bodley 387)
De natura boni R
De natura et origine animae R (Oxford, Bodleian Library, Bodley 387)
De nuptiis et concupiscentia R (Oxford, Bodleian Library, Bodley 134)
De oratione dominica (Sermo 56) R (London, British Library, Royal 6 A. xii)
De ouibus R (Cambridge University Library, Ff. 4. 32)
De pastoribus R (Cambridge University Library, Ff. 4. 32)
De peccatorum meritis et de remissione et de baptismo paruulorum R (Cambridge University Library, Ff. 4. 32)
De periurio (Sermo 180) R
De paenitentia R (London, British Library, Royal 5. B. xii)
De praesentia Dei R (Cambridge, Corpus Christi College, 332)
De sancta uirginitate L13
De sermone Domini in monte L13; R (Rochester Cathedral, A. 3. 16)
De spiritu et littera R (Cambridge University Library, Ff. 4. 32)
De symbolo (Sermo 215) R (London, British Library, Royal 6 A. xii)
De Trinitate R (London, British Library, Royal 5 B. iv)
De uera religione L13; R (London, British Library, Royal 5 B. xii)
De uidendo Deo (Epistola 47) L13
De unico baptismo R (Cambridge University Library, Ff. 4. 32)
De urbis excidio R
De utilitate agendae paenitentiae L13
De utilitate credendi R
Enarrationes in Psalmos D [in 3 vols.] (Durham Cathedral Library, B. II. 13; B. II. 14); R [in 3 vols.] (London, British Library, Royal 5 D. i–iii)
Enchiridion D; R (London, British Library, Royal 5 A. xv)
Epistola ad Armentarium de uoto reddendo (ep. 127) R
Epistolae D (Durham Cathedral Library, B. II. 21)
Excerpta R (London, British Library, Royal 5 B. xiii)
In epistolam Iohannis ad Parthos tractatus X R [2 copies] (London, British Library, Royal 5. B. vi and 5 B. xiii)
In Euangelium Iohannis A; D (Durham Cathedral Library, B. II. 17); L13
Retractationes L13; R (London, Lambeth Palace, 76)
Sermones R (London, British Library, Royal 5 A. vii)
Sermones de caritate (nos 349–50) R
Sermones de timore Dei (nos 347–8) R
Soliloquia L11
Unspecified works ('*multa alia uolumina ipsius doctoris*') A
Pseudo-AUGUSTINE,
Ad inquisitiones Ianuarii R
(Quoduultdeus) *Contra quinque haereses* (sermo 10) R (London, British Library, Royal 5 B. vii)
(Syagrius) *Contra sermonem Arianorum* R (Oxford, Bodleian Library, Bodley 387)
De fide ad Petrum → Fulgentius of Ruspe

De generalitate elemosinarum (CPL, 376) R
De paenitentibus R
Dialogus quaestionum lxv Orosii percontantis et Augustini respondentis R (Cambridge, Trinity College, O. 2. 24)
Hypomnesticon contra Pelagianos et Caelestianos R
(Quoduultdeus) *Sermo contra Iudaeos, paganos et Arianos* (sermo 4) R (London, British Library, Royal 5 B. vi)
(Caesarius of Arles) *Sermo de decem praeceptis legis et de decem plagis Aegyptii* (Pseudo-Augustine sermo App. 21) R (Rochester Cathedral, A. 3. 16)
Sermo de muliere forti (Sermo 37) R (London, British Library, Royal 5 B. vii)

BEDE,
De arte metrice R (Cambridge, Trinity College, O. 2. 24)
De schematibus et tropis R (Cambridge, Trinity College, O. 2. 24)
De tabernaculo R
De templo Salomonis R (London, British Library, Royal 5 B. vii)
De temporibus L11; R
Epistola ad Wicthedum de aequinoctio uel de paschae celebratione R
Historia ecclesiastica D (Durham Cathedral Library, B. II. 35); L11 [2 copies]; L13; R
Homiliae euangelii A
In Actus Apostolorum R
In Apocalypsin R
In Cantica Canticorum allegorica expositio D
In Euangelium Lucae expositio D
In Euangelium Marci expositio D; R
**In Ezram et Nehemiam prophetas allegorica expositio* (CPL, 1349) R
In Regum libros XXX quaestiones R (London, British Library, Royal 5 B. vii)
In Tobiam R
(attrib.) Martyrology → ?Usuardus
Super Canticum Abacuc allegorica expositio R (London, British Library, Royal 5 B. vii)
Vita S. Cuthberti R (Cambridge, Trinity College, O. 2. 24)
Benedictional R

BERENGAUDUS,
Expositio super septem uisiones libri Apocalypsis R (Berlin, Staatsbibliothek, theol. lat. fol. 224)

BERNARDUS MONACHUS (*s.* ix),
**Itinerarium* (PL, 121) R

Bible D [2 vols] (Durham Cathedral Library, A. II. 4); E [two in 2 vols, one in 1 vol.]; R [2 vols] (San Marino, Huntington Library, HM 62)

**Blake had boc* L12

BOETHIUS,
*Commentary on Aristotle's *Categoriae* (PL, 64) L11
*Commentary on Aristotle's *Peri Hermeneias* (*De interpretatione*) (ed. C. Meiser (Leipzig, 1877)) L11
De consolatione philosophiae L11
See also Aristotle

Breviary D [2 copies]

Pseudo-CALLISTHENES (trans. Julius Valerius),
Gesta Alexandri R (London, British Library, Royal 12 C. iv)

Canons L13; R

CASSIODORUS SENATOR,
?*Expositio psalmorum* A; L11
Institutiones (Book I) R (London, Lambeth Palace, 76)
**Tripartita historia ecclesiastica* (PL, 69) L13

Chronicon (unspecified) L12

Pseudo-CLEMENT,
(trans. Rufinus of Aquileia) *Recognitiones* L13; R

Collationes diuersorum auctorum Ra

Collectar L12

Commentary on Juvenal (?by Remigius of Auxerre) L11

Commentary on the Psalter L13

Commentary on the Psalter (50 psalms) L13

CYPRIAN OF CARTHAGE,
Epistolae A; L13

Pseudo-CYPRIAN,
**De singularitate clericorum* (CPL, 62) L13

Daniel (biblical book) L11

DARES THE PHRYGIAN (trans. assoc. with Cornelius Nepos),
De excidio Troiae historia Ra (London, British Library, Royal 15 A. xxii etc.)
Decreta pontificum (Lanfranc's collection) D; R

DEFENSOR OF LIGUGE,
Liber scintillarum R

Dialogus (?Colloquy or ?Gregory, *Dialogi*) L11

DIONYSIUS PERIEGETES → Priscian

DIDYMUS OF ALEXANDRIA,
(trans. Jerome) *De Spiritu Sancto* R (London, British Library Royal 5 B. vii)

DONATUS
*unspecified L12

EADMER OF CANTERBURY,
De beatitudine coelestis patriae R (Cambridge, Corpus Christi College, 332)

EDDIUS (?Stephen of Ripon),
Vita S. Wilfridi L11; L13
EPHRAIM THE SYRIAN,
De compunctione cordis R (London, British Library, Royal 5 A. vii)
**Vitae Egyptiorum monachorum* D
Unspecified R
Epistolae Pauli L13; R [2 copies] (Manchester, John Rylands University Library, lat. 109)
*Epistolary L11; L12
EUSEBIUS OF CAESAREA,
(trans. Jerome) *De situ et nominibus locorum hebraicorum* R (Cambridge, Trinity College, O. 4. 7)
(trans. Rufinus) *Historia ecclesiastica* L11; L13; R (Cambridge, Corpus Christi College, 184)
EUSEBIUS GALLICANUS,
Homiliae xii de pascha (Sermones 12–23) R (Cambridge, Trinity College, O. 2. 24)
Expositio super psalterium (mistakenly attributed to Gregory) A
FELIX OF CROWLAND,
Vita S. Guthlaci L13 (London, British Library, Harley 3097)
FOLCARD OF ST BERTIN,
Vita S. Botulfi L13 (London, British Library, Harley 3097)
FRECULPHUS OF LISIEUX,
Chronicon L13
FULBERT OF CHARTRES,
De eo quod tria sunt necessaria ad perfectionem christianae religionis R (London, British Library, Royal 6 A. xii)
Epistola R (London, British Library, Royal 6 A. xii)
(Pseudo-Ambrose) *Sermo de natiuitate BVM* R (Cambridge, Corpus Christi College, 332)
FULCHER OF CHARTRES (Fulcherius Carnotensis) (d. 1127),
**Historia Hierosolimitana* (ed. H. Hagenmeyer (Heidelberg, 1913)) R
FULGENTIUS OF RUSPE,
De fide Trinitatis ad Petrum R
GELASIUS I,
(attrib.) *Decretum de recipiendis et non recipiendis libris* R (London, Lambeth Palace, 76)
GENNADIUS OF MARSEILLES,
De uiris illustribus R (London, Lambeth Palace, 76)
Liber siue diffinitio ecclesiasticorum dogmatum L13
Gloss on Genesis L13
Glossary L11 [3 copies]
Gradual D (?Durham University Library, Cosin V. v. 6); L11; L12
Grammatical texts L11 [2 copies]
Gospel Book L11
GREGORY THE GREAT,
Dialogi D; L11
Homiliae xl in Euangelia A; D (Durham Cathedral Library B. III. 11); L11
In Ezechielem A; D (Durham Cathedral Library, B. IV. 13); R [2 copies, one in two vols] (London, British Library, Royal 4 B. i)
Moralia in Iob D [in 2 vols] (Durham Cathedral Library, B. III. 10); L13; R [in 2 vols] (London, British Library, Royal 3 C. iv and 6 C. vi)
Registrum epistolarum D (Durham Cathedral Library, B. III. 9); R (London, British Library, Royal 6 C. x)
Regula pastoralis D; L13; R (?London, British Library, Royal 5 E. ii)
Regula pastoralis (King Alfred's Old English translation) R
Unspecified ('*multa alia uolumina ipsius doctoris*') A
GREGORY NAZIANZENUS,
(trans. Rufinus) *Oratio* II L13
HAIMO OF AUXERRE,
Commentarii (unspecified) R
**Commentarii in epistolas Paulinas* (PL, 117) L13
(attrib.) '*In euangeliis*' L13 [NB: Haimo is not known to have written a gospel commentary]
Unspecific L11
Pseudo-HEGESIPPUS,
Historiae libri V de bello Iudaico A; R (Edinburgh, National Library of Scotland, Adv. 18. 3. 9)
HELPERIC OF GRANDVAL/ST GALLEN,
De computo R
Heptateuch Ra
Homiliary D [2 vols] (Durham Cathedral Library, ?A. III. 29; B. II. 2); E [3 vols]; L11; L12 [2 vols]; R [2 vols] (Edinburgh, National Library of Scotland, Adv. 2.4; London, British Library, Royal 2 C. iii)
HRABANUS MAURUS,
De clericorum institutione ad Heistulphum archiepiscopum L13
In Mattheum D (Durham Cathedral Library, B. III. 16)
HUGH OF TOURS,
De quodam miraculo beati Martini quod contigit in festo translationis eius R (London, British Library, Royal 6 A. xii)

HYGINUS,
De sphaera mundi R (London, British Library, Royal 12 C. iv)
Hymnal L11; L12
*Ioseph et Aseneth (ed. M. R. James in *Studia Patristica* 2 (1890)) R
ISIDORE OF SEVILLE,
Allegoriae sanctae scripturae → *De nominibus legis et euangelii*
**De differentiis uerborum* (CPL, 1187) L13
De libris Noui Testamenti et Veteri prooemia L11; R (London, Lambeth Palace, 76)
De natura rerum L11; L13
De nominibus legis et euangelii R (London, Lambeth Palace, 76)
De ortu et obitu patrum R (London, Lambeth Palace Library, 76)
De uiris illustribus R (London, Lambeth Palace, 76)
*?*Historia Gothorum* (CPL, 1204) R
Liber sententiarum L13
Quaestiones in Vetus Testamentum L13 [?two copies]; R (London, British Library, Royal 3 B. i)
Pseudo-ISIDORE,
**De ordine creaturarum* (CPL, 1189) Ra
*?*Liber de numeris* (work of *s.* viii; PL, 83) L13
Institutiones regum anglorum R (?Rochester Cathedral. A. 3. 5, fols 58–87)
IVO OF CHARTRES,
Decretum Ra
Epistolae R
JEROME,
Commentarii in quattuor epistolas Paulinas R (London, British Library, Royal 3 B. i — Tit. and Phil. only)
Contra Iouinianum L13; R (Eton College, 80)
De interpretatione Hebraicorum nominum D (Durham Cathedral Library, B. II. 11); R (Cambridge, Trinity College, O. 4. 7)
De xlii mansionibus filiorum Israhel in deserto (ep. 78) R (Cambridge, Trinity College, O. 4. 7)
De uiris illustribus R (London, Lambeth Palace, 76)
Epistolae D (Durham Cathedral Library, B. II. 10); L13; R (London, British Library, Royal 6 D. ii)
In Danielem L13; R
In Ecclesiasten Salomonis R
In Ezechielem L13; R
In Ieremiam R
In Isaiam L13; R
In Mattheum R
In Prophetas minores D (Durham Cathedral Library, B. II. 9); L13; R
?*In Psalmos* R
Quaestiones hebraicae in Genesim R (Cambridge, Trinity College, O. 4. 7)
Vita S. Hilarionis R
**Vita Malchi* (CPL, 619) R
Vita S. Pauli R
Unspecified works ('*multa alia uolumina ipsius doctoris*') A
Pseudo-JEROME
Commentarium in Canticum Deborae R (Cambridge, Trinity College, O. 4. 7)
Commentarium in Lamentationes Jeremie R (Cambridge, Trinity College, O. 4. 7)
De decem temptationibus populi Israeli in deserto R (Cambridge, Trinity Colllege, O. 4. 7)
De essentia diuinitatis (Ep. supp. 14) R
**Dialogus de origine animae* (Ep. supp. 37) R
Quaestiones hebraicae in libros Regum et Paralipomenon R (Cambridge, Trinity College, O. 4. 7)
JOHN CASSIAN,
Collationes L13 (extracts); R [2 copies]
De coenobium institutis R (London, British Library, Royal 8 D. xvi)
JOHN CHRYSOSTOM,
Cum de expulsione eius ageretur R (London, British Library, Royal 6 A. xii)
De compunctione cordis R (London, British Library, Royal 6 A. xii)
De eo quod nemo laeditur nisi a semet ipso R (London, British Library, Royal 6 A. xii)
(attrib.) *De psalmo quinquagesimo* R (London, British Library, Royal 6 A. xii)
De reparatione lapsi A; R (London, British Library, Royal 6 A. xii)
**De sacerdotis* L13
**In epistolam ad Hebraeos* (CPG, 4440) A
Unspecified works ('*multa alia uolumina ipsius doctoris*') A
JOHN THE DEACON,
Vita S. Gregorii L13
JOSEPHUS,
De antiquitate judaica L13; R
De bello judaico R
See also Pseudo-Hegesippus
Joshua, Judges and Ruth (biblical books) R
JULIANUS POMERIUS
(Pseudo-Prosper of Aquitaine) *De uita contemplatiua et actiua* D; R (London, British Library, Royal 5 E. x)

JULIAN OF TOLEDO,
Prognosticon futuri saeculi D; L11; L13; R [2 copies] (London, British Library, Royal 5 A. vii)
JULIUS VALERIUS → Pseudo-Callisthenes
JUSTINUS, MARCUS IUNIANUS,
Epitome historiarum (of Pompeius Trogus) R
See also Pompeius Trogus
LANFRANC OF BEC / CANTERBURY,
Constitutiones R
Epistolae R (?London, British Library, Cott. Nero A. vii)
Laws → *Institutiones regum anglorum*
Lectionary L13; R [2 vols]; Ra [3 vols]
Legendary E
**Liber miraculorum* L13
LUCAN,
Pharsalia L11
LUCIFER OF CAGLIARI (fl. *c.* 356–60)
*unspecified L11
MANSUETUS,
Epistola ad Constantinum R (London, British Library, Royal 5 B. vii)
MARTIANUS CAPELLA,
De nuptiis Philologiae et Mercurii L11
Martyrology D (Durham Cathedral Library, B. IV. 24); L12 See also Usuardus
*Matitudinal D [2 copies]
Medical books ('*multos libros de physica*') A
Medical collection L12
Missal D [3 copies]; L11
NENNIUS (attrib.),
Historia Brittonum Ra (London, British Library, Royal 15 A. xxii)
New Testament Ra (?Baltimore, Walters Art Gallery, 18)
Ordines Romani L11
ORIGEN,
(attrib.) *De singularitate clericorum* → Pseudo-Cyprian
Homiliae in Iosue L13; R (Oxford, Bodleian Library, Bodley 387)
Super Vetus Testamentum D (Durham Cathedral Library, B. III. 1)
OROSIUS,
Historiae aduersum paganos L11; R
OSBERN OF CANTERBURY,
Vita S. Dunstani R (Vatican City, Biblioteca Apostolica Vaticana, Reg. lat. 458 + 646 etc.)
Vita S. Ælphegi R (Vatican City, Biblioteca Apostolica Vaticana, Reg. lat 458 + 646 etc.)
OTLOH OF ST EMMERAM,
Vita S. Nicholai L13 (London, British Library, Harley 3097)
PALLADIUS,
Historia Lausiaca (Heraclides, *Paradisus* recension) R
PASCHASIUS RADBERTUS,
De corpore et sanguine domini R (London, British Library, Royal 5 A. vii)
In Mattheum R (Cambridge, Corpus Christi College, 332)
Passional E [3 vols]; R [4 vols] (?Oxford, Worcester College, 273)
PAUL THE DEACON,
Historia Langobardorum R (London, British Library, Royal 12 C. iv)
Paul, St, Epistles of → *Epistolae Pauli*
See also Seneca
PAULINUS OF NOLA,
**Vita S. Felicis* (ex *Carmina*) (CPL, 203) L13
Pentateuch R
PERSIUS,
Saturae L11 [2 copies]
POMPEIUS TROGUS,
Historiae (presumably Justinus's epitome) D
PRISCIAN,
Institutiones grammaticae L11
Periegesis (Latin version of Dionysius Periegesis, *Periegesis*) Ra (London, British Library, Royal 15 A. xxii)
PROSPER OF AQUITAINE,
De uita contemplatiua et actiua → Julianus Pomerius
**Epigrammata* (CPL, 518) L11 [three copies]
**Epitoma chronicorum* (CPL, 2257) L13
PRUDENTIUS,
Psychomachia L11
Psalter L11; L12 [2 copies, one glossed in Old English]; L13; R ['tripartite']
RALPH OF BATTLE,
De peccatore qui desperat R (London, British Library, Royal 12 C. i)
'Pluribus opusculis' R (London, British Library, Royal 12 C. i)
RATRAMNUS OF CORBIE,
De anima R (Cambridge, Corpus Christi College, 332)
De natiuitate Christi R (Cambridge, Corpus Christi College, 332)
Regula S. Benedicti D (Durham Cathedral Library, B. IV. 24); R
REMIGIUS OF AUXERRE,
**Commentarium* on Sedulius's *Carmen paschale* L11

Sedulius,
Carmen paschale L11 [2 copies]
Sedulius Scotus (*fl. s.* xi^{med}),
*Grammatical commentary (unspecified) L11
Pseudo-Seneca,
fictitious correspondence between Seneca and St Paul R (Cambridge, Corpus Christi College, 332)
Sergius,
*?*De littera* L11
Sermo Arianorum R (Oxford, Bodleian Library, Bodley 387)
Sermones R (?Vatican City, Biblioteca Apostolica Vaticana, lat. 4951)
Sermons (Old English) R (Oxford, Bodleian Library, Bodley 340, 342 [of *s.* xi^{in}])
Sibylla Tiburtina Ra (London, British Library, Royal 15 A. xxii)
Sidonius Apollinaris,
Panigericus (ex *carmina*) D
Smaragdus of Saint-Mihiel,
Diadema monachorum D; L13; R
Solinus,
Collectanea rerum memorabilium R
Sulpicius Severus,
Vita S. Martini L13
Super Vetus Testamentum (mistakenly attributed to Jerome) A
Terence,
Comoediae L11
Tertullian,
Apologeticum D
Theobald of Estampes (Stampensis) (d. *c.* 1129),
**Improperium ciuisdam ad monachos* (ed. R. Foreville and J. Leclercq in *Studia Anselmiana* 41 (1957)) R
(anon) *Responsio cuiusdam pro monachos* (ed. *ibid*) R
Troper L12 [two copies]
Pseudo-Turpinus (*s.* xii),
**Historia Caroli Magni* (ed. C. Meredith Jones (Paris, 1936), and H. M. Smyser (Cambridge, Mass., 1937)) R
?Usuardus,
Martyrology R (attributed to Bede)
Victor of Vita,
Historia persecutionis Africanae prouinciae L13
Virgil,
**Eclogues, Georgics* L11
Vigilius of Thapsus,
(attrib.) *Contra Felicianum Arianum de unitate Trinitatis* R
Visio Baronti L13
Vita S. Æthelwoldi L13
**Vita S. Ciarani* (BHL 46564–5, or 4657–8) L11
**Vita S. Eustachii* (verse) L13
Vita S. Fursei L13
**Vita S. Gisleni* (BHL, 3552–61) L13
Vitae sanctorum E [two copies, one of one volume, the other of two]
Vitae sanctorum anglice (?Ælfric) L13
Vitas patrum D; L13
William of Jumièges,
Gesta Normannorum ducum R

INVENTORY OF MANUSCRIPTS

1	Aberdeen University Library, 4	Augustine, *Enarrationes in Psalmos* (I–L). ?Companion to Aberdeen University Library, 5 (no. 2 below).	P; A	xii$^{1-2/4}$ London, St Paul's
2	Aberdeen University Library, 5	Augustine, *Enarrationes in Psalmos* (CI–CL). ?Companion to Aberdeen University Library, 4 (no. 1 above).	I(f)	xii$^{1-2/4}$ London, St Paul's
3	Aberdeen University Library, 9	Excerpts on the salvation of Solomon (by Augustine, Jerome, Ambrose). Augustine, *Sermones de uerbis Domini et apostoli.*	E	xii^{in} London, St Paul's
4	Aberdeen University Library, 216	Bede, *In Apocalypsin.* Victorinus of Petovium, *In Apocalypsin* (Jerome's recension).	U	xi^{ex} Salisbury
5	Arras, Médiathèque, 484 (Cat. gén. 805)	Anselm, *De processione Spiritus Sancti.*	U/E	xii^{in} Kent; Arras
6 ?	Avranches, Bibliothèque Municipale, 81	Augustine, *In Epistolam Iohannis (De caritate).* Pseudo-Faustus, *Sermo.* Pseudo-Augustine, *Sermones* (85, 74, 79). Alcuin, *De uirtutibus et uitiis ad Widonem comitem.*		xi^{2} Mont Saint Michel
7 †	Baltimore, Walters Art Gallery, 18	New Testament. Companion to London, British Library, Royal 1 C. vii (no. 459 below).	I	xii^{1} Rochester
8	Bergen, Universitets-bibliothek, 1549.5	Missal (frag.).	–	xi/xii
9	Berlin, Staatsbibliothek Preussischer Kulturbesitz, theol. lat. fol. 224 (Rose no. 350)	Berengaudus, *In Apocalypsin.*	I(f)	xii^{1} (?pre 1124) Rochester
10 ?	Bloomington, University of Indiana, Lily Library, Poole 43	Anso of Lobbes, *Vita S. Ermini* (frag.).	–	xi/xii
11	Brussels, Bibliothèque Royale inv. no. 444–52 (cat. no. 1103)	Augustine, *De perfectione iustitiae hominis; De natura et gratia; De gratia et libero arbitrio; De correptione et gratia.* Prosper of Aquitaine, *Pro Augustino responsiones ad capitula obiectionum Gallorum calumniantium.* Hilarius, *Epistola ad Augustinum de querela Gallorum.* Augustine, *De praedestinatione sanctorum; De dono perseuerantiae.* Pseudo-Augustine, *Hypomnesticon contra Pelagianos et Caelestinos.* Jerome, *Contra Iouinianum.*	A	xi/xii Canterbury, St Augustine's
12	Brussels, Bibliothèque Royale inv. no. 8794–99 (cat. no. 1403), fols 1–17	Ernulfus of Canterbury/Rochester (Thomellus), *De incestis coniugibus.* Decretum, 'Si monasterium sancti Theodori fines de quibus causatio mota est'. Addition *s.* xii/xiii (post 1191): fol. 1r: epistola ('Gaufridus eboracensis episcopus ad Gilebertum Roffensem episcopum').	E	xi/xii Rochester

13 §	Brussels, Bibliothèque Royale inv. no. 8794–99 (cat. no. 1403), fols 18–71	Augustine, *De Trinitate* (excerpts); *In euangelium Iohannis* (excerpts); *Enarrationes in Psalmos* (excerpts). Gilbert Crispin, *De monachatu.* Gregory, *Moralia in Iob* (very short extract). Gilbert Crispin, *Probatio de illa peccatrice que unxit pedes Domini; Disputatio Iudei cum Christiano.* Medical tract: '*A leguminibus praeter lenticulum cum cedro aut coriandro decoctam omnino abstineatis*'. See PLATE 17.	A	xii^{in} Rochester (possibly item 93 in ?1123/4 catalogue: *Collationes diuersorum auctorum in uno uolumine*)
14	Cambridge University Library, Add. 3206	Wulfstan's Canons of Edgar OE (frag.).	–	xi^{2}
15 ?	Cambridge University Library, Add. 4406, part ?1 + Columbia, Missouri, University of Missouri Library, Rare – L/PA/ 3381.A1/F 7	Cassiodorus, *Expositio psalmorum.*	–	xii^{in}
16	Cambridge University Library, Add. 4406 (63)	? *Vitae sanctorum.* Ten binding strips of varying sizes.	–	xii^{in}
17	Cambridge University Library, Dd. 1. 4	Josephus, *De antiquitate iudaica* (I–XIV). Companion to Cambridge, St John's College, A. 8 (no. 118)	X I(f)	xii^{1} Canterbury, Christ Church
18	Cambridge University Library, Dd. 2. 7	Jerome, *Epistolae* (122) including *Aduersus Heluidium de Mariae perpetua uirginitate; Contra Vigilantium.* Origen (trans. Jerome), *In Cantica Canticorum.* Pelagius, *Epistola ad Demetriadem* (Pseudo-Jerome ep. 1). Pseudo-Jerome, *De tribus uirtutibus* (= Origen (trans. Jerome), *Homiliae 5 in Hieremiam*). '*Symboli explanatio ad Dardanum.*' Pseudo-Jerome, *Ad Oceanum de uita clericorum* (ep. 42).	E	xii^{in} Canterbury, Christ Church
19	Cambridge University Library, Dd. 8. 15	Haimo of Auxerre, *Expositio in Isaiam.* Augustine, *De sancta uirginitate.*	I	xii^{in} Canterbury, Christ Church

20	Cambridge University Library, Ee. 1.23	Jerome, *Epistola ad Paulam et Eustochium*. Ephraim the Syrian, *Sermones: De compunctione cordis; De die iudicii et de resurrectione et de regno caelorum; De beatitudine animae; De paenitentia; De luctaminibus; De die iudicii; 'Beatus uir qui Deum in toto corde dilexerit'; 'Beatus homo qui inuenerit fratris uitam in illa hora'; 'Beatus homo qui habet compunctionem'*. Possidius, *Vita S. Augustini* (fol. 71 ff.). Addition, *s.* xii^{1}, fols 69r–70r: *Translatio S. Augustini* (inc.: '*Beatus Augustinus dum Ypponensi sepultus esset regione*').	I	xi/xii
21	Cambridge University Library, Ff. 2. 33, fols i, ii, vi, vii	*Concilium africanum* (frag. = two bifolia used as endleaves).	–	xi^{ex} ?Bury St Edmunds
22	Cambridge University Library, Ff. 3. 9	Ezechiel (extract). Gregory, *In Ezechielem*.	I	xi^{ex} Canterbury, Christ Church
23	Cambridge University Library, Ff. 3. 29, fols 13–162	Isidore, *Quaestiones in Vetus Testamentum (Genesis, Exodus, Leuiticus, Numeri, Deuteronomium, Jesu Naue, Judices, Ruth)*. Bede, *In Regum libros XXX quaestiones; De templo Salomonis; Super Canticum Abacuc allegorica expositio* (incomplete).	I(f)	xii^{in} Canterbury, Christ Church
24 †	Cambridge University Library, Ff. 4. 32	Augustine, *De ouibus* (imperfect: the end only); *De baptismo contra Donatistas; De peccatorum meritis et remissione et de baptismo paruulorum; De unico baptismo* (imperfect: the beginning only). The volume wants leaves at the beginning and end. It originally also contained: Augustine, *De pastoribus; De ouibus* (the remainder); *De spiritu et littera — teste* contents list on fol. 1v; and cf. Rochester library catalogue (EBL, 77), no. 14.	A	xii^{1} (? pre 1124) Rochester
25 ?*	Cambridge University Library Ff. 5. 27, fols ii, 1–54	**A)** Palladius, *Historia Lausiaca* (Heraclides, *Paradisus* recension). Addition, *s.* xii^{med}, fol. 54r: '*Primus itaque gradus humilitatis est: quemque cognoscere contemtibilem se esse*'. Addition, *s.* xii$^{2/4-med}$, fol. 54v: litanic verses: '*Supplicatio utilis in memoria trinitas et unitas*'. **B)** Fol. ii (flyleaf) gloss on Psalms (frag.) (?Origen), written *s.* xii^{1}.	E	**A** xi/xii **B** xii^{1} ?Continent; England (by xii^{1})
26	Cambridge University Library, Gg. 4. 2	Jerome, *Epistolae* (127). Pseudo-Jerome, *Explanatio fidei ad Cyrillum* (= Pseudo-Jerome ep. 17) (incomplete).	E	xii^{1}
27	Cambridge University Library, Gg. 4. 15, fols 1–108	Bede, *In Epistolas Catholicas*. Addition, *s.* xii, fols 108r–111r: Methodius (attrib.), *De principio saeculi et de regnis gentium et fine saeculorum*.	U	xii^{in} Eynsham
28	Cambridge University Library, Gg. 4. 28	Jerome, *In Prophetas minores* (*Osee, Amos, Ion., Abd., Mich., Nah.*) (?Part one of a two-volume set). Account of a *libellus* of Athanasius, read by Peter, bishop of Nicomedia at the Council of Cappadocia.	E	xi/xii

29	Cambridge University Library, Gg. 4. 33, fols 49–92	*Florilegium* excerpting or reporting, *inter alios*, Ambrose, Aristotle, Augustine, Bede, Councils, Cyprian, Isidore, Jerome, Paul, Plato; with the fictitious letters of Pseudo-Seneca and St Paul. Inc.: '*Hominem deum dici multis testimoniis approbatur ut duorum hominum testimonium uerum est . . .*'. Fol. 87r, lower margin: the remnants of a crude but contemporary ink drawing of a creature, mainly cut away by the binder's knife.	U; D	xii^{1} Durham
30	Cambridge University Library, Ii. 2. 1	Priscian, *Institutiones grammaticae* (1–18) plus gloss (imperfect: text lost at the end — lacks fols 167–8 and breaks off at 174, the final leaf). Gloss begins with '*liberalibus artibus arguitur a iunioribus*'.	A	xii^{in} Canterbury, St Augustine's
31 §	Cambridge University Library, Ii. 2. 19, fols 1–216	Paul the Deacon, *Homiliarium* (contents inventoried in Richards, *Texts and Traditions*, pp. 104–8). Addition, *s.* xii^{in}, fols 217–40: Herbert Losinga, *Sermones*. Companion to Cambridge University Library, Kk. 4. 13 (no. 42). See PLATE 11.	I	xi/xii Norwich
32	Cambridge University Library, Ii. 3. 12, fols 62–133	Boethius, *De musica*. Fols 135–7: *s.* xii^{2}, library catalogue (fragment).	D	xii^{1} Canterbury, Christ Church
33	Cambridge University Library, Ii. 3. 28	Augustine, *In Euangelium Iohannis*.	U/E	xii^{1}
34	Cambridge University Library, Ii. 3. 33	Gregory, *Symbolum fidei; Registrum epistolarum* (14 books, not 13 as stated in the CUL catalogue). Berengar of Tours, Recantation at Council of Rome (1079). Additions: *s.* xii^{in}, fols 1–3r: *De natiuitate Sanctae Mariae* (Inc. 'Petis a me petitiunculam opere quidem leuem'). (Fol. 4: blank.) Fols 194–5, *s.* xii^{in}: Paschal II to Henry I of England, '*Contra inuestituras ecclesiasticas*'; Paschal to Anselm, '*Excommunicatos esse inuestiturarum in Anglia fautores*'; Anselm to Ernulf of Canterbury; Paschal to Henry V of Germany '*De inuestituris*' (imperfect).	I(f)	xi/xii (1079–1101) Canterbury, Christ Church
35 §	Cambridge University Library, Ii. 4. 34	Priscian, *Institutiones grammaticae* plus gloss. Most of the glossing is contemporary with the text, but fol. 1r is a notable exception. See PLATE 24.	I(f)	xii^{1} Norwich
36	Cambridge University Library, Ii. 4. 36, fols 1–65	Gregory, *Regula pastoralis. Decretum*. Versus: '*Eripe, caute piis monitis precibusque sacratis*'.	E/A	xii^{in}
37	Cambridge University library, Ii. 4. 36, fols 66–142	Palladius, *Historia Lausiaca* (Heraclides, *Paradisus* recension).	A	xii^{1}
—	Cambridge University Library, Ii. 6. 5, fols 112–27	See Supplement		

38 §	Cambridge University Library, Kk. 1. 17	Origen (trans. Rufinus), *Expositio libri Iesu Naue.* Jerome, *Commentarii in quattuor epistolas Paulinas* (sections *ad Titum* and *ad Philemon* only). This volume seems never to have had any more of the Jerome: the text stops half-way down 140r, and 140v was originally blank; while the late medieval contents list on 1v only includes the three texts that are actually in the book. See PLATE 19.	A	xii^{in-1} Canterbury, St Augustine's
39	Cambridge University Library Kk. 1. 23, fols 1–66	Ambrose, *Hexaemeron.* Fols 1–66 and 67–135, were clearly written separately, but were evidently together by *s.* xii (*teste* contents list on fol. 2v).	I(f)	xi/xii Canterbury, Christ Church
40	Cambridge University Library, Kk. 1. 23, fols 67–135 (the last leaf is actually numbered '138', '135–7' being cancelled blanks)	Ambrose, *De paenitentia.* Augustine, *De paenitentia; De utilitate credendi; De fide et symbolo; Retractatio.* Pseudo-Augustine, *Ad inquisitiones Ianuarii* (I–II). Augustine, *Epistola ad Armentarium et Paulinam* (ep. 127); *Sermones* (*De periurio* (180); *De urbis excidio; De faciendis elemosynis* (389). Pseudo-Augustine, *De fide.* Augustine, *Sermones* 350, 346, 347, 348, 259 (incl. *De timore Dei; De octauis paschae*). See note on previous item.	U	xi^{ex} Canterbury, Christ Church
41	Cambridge University Library, Kk. 3. 18	OE Bede, *Historia ecclesiastica.*	U	xi^{2} Worcester
42	Cambridge University library Kk. 4. 13	Paul the Deacon, *Homiliarium* (contents inventoried in Richards, *Texts and Traditions*, pp. 98–101). Companion to Cambridge University Library, Ii. 2. 19 (no. 31).	I(f)	xi/xii Norwich
43	Cambridge University Library Kk. 4. 22	Ambrose, *De officiis ministrorum* (ends imperfectly at III, 133).	I	xii^{in} St Albans
44	Cambridge University Library, Kk. 5. 32, fols 61–72, 76	Computistical tables (mutilated), including names of popes, emperors, kings and bishops. The obits include Wulfstan II and William II. Though probably not in the main hand responsible for the tables, they appear to be contemporary with them. A unit comprising two quires, the second mutilated by the excision of three leaves (73–5); the foliation *includes* these lost leaves.	U	xii^{in} (?post 1100) West Country
45	Cambridge University Library, Ll. 1. 14, fols 70–108	*Regula S. Benedicti; Memoriale qualiter; Indicium Regulae; 'Ad clericum faciendum'* (from pontifical service).	U	xi^{ex}
46	Cambridge University Library, Mm. 3. 31	Bede, *In Cantica Canticorum allegorica expositio*, ?including Gregory, *Excerpta in Cantica Canticorum* (ends imperfectly).	I(f)	xii^{1} Winchcombe
47	Cambridge University Library, Mm. 4. 25 + *membrum disjectum*	Psalter with gloss (extensively mutilated). A fragment of the same manuscript was no. 46 in an album of script specimens in the Phillipps library, subsequently passing to Sydney Cockerell.	X; E	xii^{1}

48 ?	Cambridge, Clare College, James's Catalogue no. 17 (Shelfmark: N′2.2)	Smaragdus of Saint-Mihiel, *Diadema monachorum.* Corrections in a xii$^{2/4}$ English hand.	I(f)	xii^{in} England or France; England
49 ?*	Cambridge, Clare College, 18 (N′1.9)	Orosius, *Historiae aduersus paganos.* Justinus, *Epitome Historiarum Philippicarum* (of Pompeius Trogus's lost *Historiae Philippicae*) beginning in Book XVIII. Addition, fol. 62: Hrabanus Maurus, Dedication to Lothar for Vegetius's *Epitome rei militaris*. Vegetius, *Epitome rei militaris*, prologue and first five capitula of Book I only. Norman type script; St Albans style artwork.	I	xii^{in} ?Exeter
50	Cambridge, Clare College, 30 (N′1.8), part I Quires 1–13	Gregory, *Dialogi.* NB: this volume is unfoliated.	I	xi^{2+} Worcester
51	Cambridge, Clare College, 30 (N′1.8), part II Quires 14–21	Defensor of Ligugé, *Liber scintillarum.* Julian of Toledo, *Prognosticon futuri saeculi.* Alcuin, *De fide sanctae et indiuiduae Trinitatis* (frag.). See note on previous item.	U	xi^{2+} Worcester
52	Cambridge Clare College, s.n. (pastedown)	Solinus, *Collectanea rerum memorabilium* (frag.)	–	xii^{in} Bury St Edmunds
53 ?	Cambridge, Clare College, s.n.	Orosius, *Historiae aduersus paganos* (frag.)	–	xi^{2} Bury St Edmunds
54	Cambridge. Corpus Christi College, 9	Additions to an *s.* xi^{med} legendary (original contents inventoried by Lapidge and Jackson, 'Contents of the Cotton-Corpus Legendary'): fols. 9r–23v, *Vita S. Saluii, s.* xi^{2}; fols. 27r–30v, *Vita Rumwoldi; Passio SS. Quiriaci et Iulittae, s.* xi^{2}; fols. 23v–6v (pp. 46–52), *Vita et miracula S. Nicholai, s.* xii^{1}. Fol. i = incomplete leaf from *s.* xii$^{2/4\text{-}med}$ passional. Endleaf 'ii' (p. 459) = part of a *Vita S. Oswaldi* (imperfect); *In translatione S. Oswaldi*, both *s.* xii$^{2/4}$. Original volume includes a tiny sketch of Hysimbardus and Wyngardus on 13r. Companion to London, British Library, Cott. Nero E. i (no. 397 below), which also received major additions post 1066.	D	xi^{2} and xii^{1} additions to xi^{med} volume Worcester
55	Cambridge, Corpus Christi College, 19, fols 1–333	Ivo of Chartres, *Decretum.* Papal letter. Near-contemporary additions, fols 333v–4: Extracts from papal councils; Council of Westminster (1127); Henry I's confirmation of Council of Westminster; List of Popes to Honorius II (1124–30).	I	xii^{1} (before *c.* 1127) Canterbury, Christ Church
56	Cambridge, Corpus Christi College, 94	Ivo of Chartres, *Panormia* (revised version).	X; A	xii^{1} Canterbury, St Augustine's

57	Cambridge, Corpus Christi College, 130	*Decreta pontificum et concilia* (Lanfranc's collection). Lanfranc, *Epistola ad episcopum Hiberniae* (Domnall Ua h-Enna). The first initial, which was presumably decorated, has been excised. Early additions, fols 219–23: List of Popes to Calixtus II (1118–24) with short biographies of Paschal II, Gelasius II and Calixtus II; Papal document of 1143.	X; I	xii^{in} Canterbury
58	Cambridge, Corpus Christi College, 146, pp. 1–60, 319–30	*Supplementa* to a pontifical of *s.* xi^{in} (the 'Samson Pontifical'). The main additional work is xi^{ex}, with additions continuing to xii^{1} and beyond. NB: *pace* Robinson, *Dated and Datable MSS in Cambridge Libraries*, this is *not* datable to 1096 × 1112.	E	xi^{ex+} Worcester
59	Cambridge, Corpus Christi College, 149	Pseudo-Hegesippus, *Historiae libri V de bello iudaico*.	I	xii^{1} ?Hexham
60	Cambridge, Corpus Christi College, 160	Bede, *In Epistolas Catholicas*. NB: *pace* James, *Catalogue* and Ker, *MLGB*, there is seemingly no evidence of provenance. The *ex libris* inscription reported by James (p. 358: 'At top of f. 1 erased and revived, "— liber Refectorij burg"') is not visible, even under u.v. As the binding is *s.* xviii, it cannot have been trimmed away subsequent to his examination of the MS. The other inscriptions he records are, however, visible.	A	xii^{in}
61	Cambridge, Corpus Christi College, 163	Pontifical; Blessings; Benediction; Versus: '*Gloria uictori sit Christo laude perenni*'; Sermo for Office for the dead; Office for the dead.	E	xi^{2} Worcester
62	Cambridge, Corpus Christi College, 173, additions	Additions to, and revisions of, a copy of the *Anglo-Saxon Chronicle* and *Laws* (the 'Parker Chronicle', MS 'A') started *s.* ix/x or x^{in}, including: OE entry for 1070 devoted to Lanfranc. *Acta Lanfranci* (Latin) (fol. 32r–v). List of Popes to Marinus (53r). (Fols 53v–4r: blank). List of Archbishops of Canterbury to Anselm (1093–1109), with Ralph d'Escures (1114+) added subsequently (54v). Additions to episcopal lists: Bishops of Lindisfarne/Durham to Ranulf Flambard (1099–1128); Bishops of York to Thomas II (1109–14) (55v).	U	Additions: xi^{2+}–xii^{in} *s.* x provenance and possible origin: ?Winchester. Subsequent provenance: Canterbury, Christ Church (by *c.* 1070)
—	Cambridge, Corpus Christi College, 184	See Supplement		
63	Cambridge, Corpus Christi College, 187	Eusebius of Caesarea (trans. Rufinus), *Historia ecclesiastica*. Addition, *s.* xii, fols 131v–3r: previously omitted portions of Book XI (= cc. xxiii–xxix).	A	xi/xii Canterbury, Christ Church
—	Cambridge, Corpus Christi College, 206, fol. 1	Addition to *s.* x^{2} copy of Martianus Capella, *De nuptiis Philologiae et Mercurii*, iv.	I	Addition: xii^{1}

64	Cambridge, Corpus Christi College, 253, fols 1–132	Augustine, *Retractatio; Confessiones.* Fols 131–2: blank. Fols. 133r–40r, Ferrandus of Carthage, *De bono duce*, is a discrete unit produced to a different format, *s.* xii$^{2/4}$, with U/E. Addition, *s.* xii$^{med-3/4}$, fols 140v–1r, Hymn for St Augustine, '*Interni festi gaudia nostra sonet armonia*'.	I(f) U/E	xii^{1}
65 §	Cambridge, Corpus Christi College, 265, pp. 209–268	Map (partially executed). Excommunication Laws: IV Edgar (Latin and OE). *Liturgica.* Ælfric, Letter to monks of Eynsham (*Excerpta ex institutionibus monasticis*). This is a matching supplement to pp. 1–208 (a collection of penitentials and canons of *s.* xi^{med+}). Direct additions to this original section include: a) (p. 1) a formula for the profession of a monk dating from the time of St Wulfstan (1062–95); and b) (p. 197) a little sketch of a head (*s.* xi^{2-ex}). See PLATE 2.	D; E D	xi^{2} Worcester
66	Cambridge, Corpus Christi College, 265, pp. 269–329	Amalarius, *De ecclesiasticis officiis* (extracts). *Ordo Romanus* (pp. 298–326) taken from Romano-Germanic pontifical). *Liturgica.* Includes marginal drawing of a man's head on p. 325. Addition *s.* xii$^{1-2/4}$, pp. 329–442: Amalarius, *Eclogae; Micrologus.*	D; I	xi^{2+} Worcester
67	Cambridge, Corpus Christi College, 267, fols 4–120	Freculphus of Lisieux, *Chronicon.* Near-contemporary addition, fols 119v–120r: Peter Damian (Pseudo-Jerome, Pseudo-Bede), *De quindecim signis.* Near-contemporary but separate: fols i, 1–3 with Hymn to St Mellitus.	I	xi/xii Canterbury St Augustine's
68	Cambridge, Corpus Christi College, 270, fols 1, 199	Bede, *Historia ecclesiastica* (frag.). Formerly pastedowns: the surfaces of 1v and 199v are rubbed and damaged.	–	xi^{ex}
69	Cambridge, Corpus Christi College, 270, fols 2–173	Sacramentary ('The Missal of Saint Augustine's Abbey'). Additions: further *liturgica*, *s.* xii^{1}, fols 174r–82r; *s.* xii^{med}, fols 182v–96r; *s.* xii^{ex}, fol. 196v. The original text and the first two supplements were corrected throughout *s.* xiii, many passages being re-written *in rasura.*	A	xi^{ex}–xi/xii (after 1091; ?before 1100) Canterbury, St Augustine's
70	Cambridge, Corpus Christi College, 274	Ambrose, *De uirginitate; De uiduis.* Pseudo-Ambrose, *De lapsu uirginis consecratae; Ad corruptorem uirginis; Consolatio ad uirginem lapsam.* Anon., *De uitiis et uirtutibus* (Inc.: '*Radix cuncti mali superbia est . . . Quia per superbiam cecidimus . . .*' = Bloomfield 5095).	I(f)	xii^{in} Canterbury, St Augustine's
71	Cambridge, Corpus Christi College, 276, fols 1–54	Eutropius, *Breuiarium historiae romanae ab urbe condita.* Paul the Deacon's continuation of Eutropius. Spurious charter of Leo VII.	U/E	xi^{ex} Canterbury, St Augustine's

72	Cambridge, Corpus Christi College, 276, fols 55–134	Dudo of St Quentin, *Historia Normannorum*.	A	xii^{in} Canterbury, St Augustine's
73	Cambridge, Corpus Christi College, 290	Ado of Vienne, *Chronicon* (*De sex aetatibus mundi*). Annals (inc.: 'Ab orbe condito usque ad urbem conditam anni quattuor milia CCCC octaginta quatuor . . .'). Genealogy of the Dukes of Normandy from Rollo to William I. Genealogies of Merovingians and Carolingians. Vision of Eucherius of Lyons on the punishment of Charles Martel.	I	xii^{1} St Albans
74	Cambridge, Corpus Christi College, 291	Bede, *De temporum ratione*. Pseudo-Bede, '*De ratione anni*' (Computus). Isidore, '*De positione septem stellarum errantium*' (= *De natura rerum*, 23). Bede, *Epistola ad Wicthedum de aequinoctio uel de paschae celebratione*. Tables.	I	xi/xii Canterbury, St Augustine's
75	Cambridge, Corpus Christi College, 302	Ælfric, *Hexameron*. OE Homilies (mainly by Ælfric).	E	xi/xii
76	Cambridge, Corpus Christi College, 303	OE Homilies (including 42 from Ælfric's *Sermones catholici*). Incomplete: lacks 44 leaves at the beginning.	U	xii$^{2/4}$ Rochester
77	Cambridge, Corpus Christi College, 322	Gregory (trans. Wærferth), OE *Dialogi*	E	xi^{2} Worcester
78	Cambridge, Corpus Christi College, 328, pp. 1–80	Osbern, *Epistola de uita S. Dunstani; Vita S. Dunstani*. *Missa de S. Dunstano; Prosa de Sancto Dunstano*. Addition ?*s*. xii^{1}: miracles from Eadmer, *Vita S. Dunstani*. NB: Although Christ Church *provenance* is rejected in Ker, *MLGB*, external features support a Christ Church *origin*. It was at Winchester by *s*. xiii.	I	xi/xii ?Canterbury, Christ Church; Winchester, Old Minster
79	Cambridge, Corpus Christi College, 328, pp. 81–230	John of Salerno, *Vita S. Odonis Cluniacensis*. Odilo of Cluny, *Vita S. Maioli Cluniacensis*. Peter Damian, *Vita S. Odilonis*.	E	xii$^{1-2/4}$ Winchester
80 ?*	Cambridge, Corpus Christi College, 330, part I	Martianus Capella, *De nuptiis Philologiae et Mercurii*. Addition at Malmesbury *s*. xii^{1} by William of Malmesbury: Interlinear and marginal gloss, extracted from that of Remigius of Auxerre.	D	xi/xii ?Normandy; Malmesbury

81 †	Cambridge, Corpus Christi College, 332	*Theologica miscellanea:* Augustine, *De praesentia Dei* (ep. 187). Fictitious correspondence between Seneca and St Paul. Ratramnus of Corbie, *De natiuitate Christi*; *De anima.* Ambrosius Autpertus (Pseudo-Augustine), *Sermo* 28. Pseudo-Augustine (?Fulbert of Chartres), *De assumptione BVM.* Paschasius Radbertus, *De assumptione BVM* (Sermones 2–3). Pseudo-Ildefonsus, *De assumptione BVM.* Pseudo-Paschasius, *De partu uirginis.* Paschasius Radbertus, *In Mattheum* (Preface and Bk I). Fulbert of Chartres (Pseudo-Ambrose), *Sermo de natiuitate BVM* (Sermo 4). Pseudo-Ildefonsus (Pseudo-Ambrose), *De assumptione BVM* (extract). Eadmer, *De beatitudine coelestis patriae.* Anselm, *De conuersatione monachorum.*	E/A	xii^{1} (? pre 1124) Rochester
82	Cambridge, Corpus Christi College, 341, fragments a and b	**A)** Eadmer, *Historia nouorum* (frag. = one leaf). **B)** Eadmer, *Vita S. Anselmi*, capitula (frag. = one leaf).	–	xii^{1} Canterbury, Christ Church
83	Cambridge, Corpus Christi College, 367, part II, fols 45–54, addition	*Visio Leofrici* (OE) (fols 48v–50v) added to the end of a now fragmentary *Vita S. Kenelmi* of *s.* xi^{med}, following a *s.* xi^{med} booklist. Further additions: *s.* xi/xii, Sequence for Epiphany; *s.* xii$^{2/4}$, letter about recusant monk.	–	xi^{2} Worcester
84	Cambridge, Corpus Christi College, 371	Eadmer, [*Versus de S. Dunstano; Ymnus de S. Edwardo rege; Epistolae* — early additions]; *Vita S. Wilfridi; Breuiloquium uitae eiusdem patris; Vita S. Odonis; Vita S. Dunstani; Quaedam de miraculis Dunstani; Ascriptum de ordinatione beati Gregorii; Consideratio de excellentia gloriosissimae uirginis matris Dei; Vita S. Oswaldi; Quaedam de miraculis Oswaldi; Scriptum quoddam de beatitudine perennis uitae;* [*Historia nouorum* (removed by Eadmer at an early stage: see Cambridge, Corpus Christi College, 452 (no. 90 below))]; *Vita S. Bregowini; Vita et conuersatio Anselmi; Miracula Anselmi.* Second strata of additions: *De conceptione S. Mariae; Vita beati Petri primi abbatis; De memoria sanctorum quos ueneraris; Scriptum Eadmeri peccatoris ad commouendum super se misericordiam beati Petri; De reliquiis sancti Audoenii* (i.e. Ouen) *et quorundam aliorum sanctorum; Insipida quaedam diuinae dispensationis consideratio.*	E/A	xii^{1} (?1113×30) Original strata: ?pre 1116. Additions 1121–30. Canterbury, Christ Church (Eadmer's personal manuscript)
85	Cambridge, Corpus Christi College, 383	OE Laws.	U	xi/xii London, St Paul's
86	Cambridge, Corpus Christi College, 391	Calendar; Psalter; Hymnal; Litany; Collectar (the 'Portiforium of St Wulfstan'). Additions and corrections, *s.* xi^{2+}, including: extensive correction of the Psalter text, *s.* xi^{ex}; additions to hymnal, *s.* xii^{in} (p. 252), and xii$^{2/4}$ (pp. 264–5); additions to Common of Saints, *s.* xii^{1}.	D	xi$^{3/4}$ (partly datable *c.* 1065) Worcester

—	Cambridge, Corpus Christi College, 393	See Supplement		
87 ?*	Cambridge, Corpus Christi College, 415	The 'Norman anonymous'. Ecclesiastical tracts.	U	xii^{in} (after 1095) Normandy or England
88	Cambridge, Corpus Christi College, 416	Amalarius, *De ecclesiasticis officiis.*	E	xii^{1} Ely
89 ?*	Cambridge, Corpus Christi College, 442	*Excerpta theologica* including: Alcuin, *De fide sanctae et indiuiduae Trinitatis* (excerpts). Excerpts from Julian of Toledo, John Chrysostom, Augustine, Jerome, Gregory, Isidore, Bede, Hrabanus Maurus. Excerpts from *Concilia et decreta* (Pseudo-Isidorean collection).	U	xii^{in} ?Continent
90	Cambridge, Corpus Christi College, 452	Eadmer, *Historia nouorum in Anglia.* ?Originally part of Cambridge, Corpus Christi College, 371 (no. 84 above), removed by Eadmer.	E/A	xii^{1} (*c.* 1122–30) Canterbury, Christ Church
91	Cambridge, Corpus Christi College, 457	Alexander of Canterbury, *Liber ex dictis beati Anselmi.*		xii^{1} ?Canterbury, Christ Church
92 ?	Cambridge, Corpus Christi College, 496, rear pastedown	Service book (frag.) with lesson for St Godwaldus.	–	xii$^{2/4}$?Worcester
93 ?* §	Cambridge, Emmanuel College, Cat. no. 25 (Shelf-mark I. 2.4)	Jerome, *Epistolae* (nos. 83, 84, 81 and 80); *Contra Rufinum.* Rufinus, *Apologia ad Anastasium; Apologia contra Hieronymum.* Jerome, *Epistola ad Nepotianum de uita clericorum* (no. 52). See PLATE 15.	E	xii^{in} ?Normandy; Chichester
94 §	Cambridge, Emmanuel College, 26 (I. 2. 5)	Jerome, *Contra Iouinianum.* Augustine, *De bono coniugali; De sancta uirginitate; Retractatio in libro de doctrina christiana; Retractatio in libro de sancta uirginitate.* See PLATE 22.	I	xii^{1} Chichester
95	Cambridge, Emmanuel College, 143 (II. 2. 18)	Gregory, *In Ezechielem.* Versus: 'Tu miserere mei pater inclite sancte sacerdos'. Addition, *s.* xii^{1}: *De situ Ierusalem*, inc.: 'Ab occidente est introitus Iherusalem per portam David . . .'.	I	xii^{in}
96	Cambridge, Fitzwilliam Museum, 88–1972, fols 2–43	Mass lectionary (incomplete): temporale, sanctorale, common of saints.	E	xii^{in} ?Shrewsbury
97	Cambridge, Fitzwilliam Museum, 88–1972, part ii	Mass lectionary (incomplete): sanctorale, temporale.	E/A	xii^{1} ?Shrewsbury

98	Cambridge, Jesus College, Shelfmark Q. A. 14 (Cat. no. 14), fols 1–120	Bede, *In Genesim* (with rejected leaves of the same text as flyleaves). NB: Although bound together at an early date (the present binding probably dates from *s.* xii) and produced to a matching format, both parts of Q. A. 14 have their own quire signatures (and they were written by different scribes), showing that they were originally separate.	I	xii$^{1-2/4}$ Durham
99	Cambridge, Jesus College, Q. A. 14 (14), fols 121–54	Bede, *De tabernaculo* (incomplete). See note on previous item.	A	xii^{1} Durham
100	Cambridge, Jesus College, Q. B. 8 (25), fols 1–18	Anon., '*Egyptii autem ex initio noctis sequentis diei originem tradunt . . .*' (Thorndike and Kibre, 484).	P	xii^{1} Durham
101 ?*	Cambridge, Jesus College, Q. G. 4 (52), fols 1–29*	Ivo of Chartres, *Sermones* (6–20)= *Corruptum peccatis; De aduentu Domini; De natiuitate Domini; De circumcisione Domini; De epiphania Domini; De purificatione BVM; De septuagesima; De capite ieiunii; De quadragesima; De annunciatione BVM; In ramis palmarum; In cena Domini; De pascha; De ascensione Domini; De pentecosten.* Pseudo-Augustine (Pelagius), *De uita christiana ad sororem suam uiduam.* Companion to Cambridge, Jesus College, Q. G. 5 (53), and Oxford, Bodleian Library, Laud. Misc. 52 (nos. 104 and 749).	U/E	xii^{in} England or France; Durham
102	Cambridge, Jesus College, Q. G. 4 (52), fols 31–7	Excerptiones ecclesiasticarum regularum = Ivo of Chartres, *Prologus in Decretum.*	U	xii^{1} Durham
103	Cambridge, Jesus College, G. 4 (52), fols 39–44	Pseudo-Augustine (Caesarius of Arles), *Sermo de decem praeceptis legis et de decem plagis Aegyptii.* Martin of Braga, *Formula honestae uitae* (*prologus*).	U	xii^{1} Durham
104	Cambridge, Jesus College, Q. 5 (53)	Ivo of Chartres, *Epistolae.* Paschal II, *Epistolae.* Anselm, *Epistola.* Ivo of Chartres, *Decretum* xvii, 1; *Epistolae.* Companion to Cambridge, Jesus College, Q. G. 4, and Oxford, Bodleian Library, Laud. Misc. 52 (nos. 101 and 749).	U	xii^{1} Durham
105 ?*	Cambridge, Jesus College, Q. G. 16 (64), fols 1–15	Boethius, *De Trinitate; Utrum Pater et Filius et Spiritus Sanctus de diuinitate substantialiter praedicentur; Quomodo substantiae in eo, quod sint, bonae sint; De fide catholica; Liber contra Eutychen et Nestorium.*	U	xii^{1} England or France; Durham
106	Cambridge, Jesus College, Q. G. 16 (64), fols 16–85	Anselm, *Monologion; Proslogion.* Gaunilio, *Pro insipiente aduersus Anselmum.* Anselm, *Liber apologeticus contra Gaunilionem; De incarnatione Verbi; De ueritate; De libertate arbitrii; De casu Diaboli.*	U	xii^{1} Durham
107 ?*	Cambridge, Jesus College, Q. G. 16 (64), fols 86–120	Anselm, *Cur Deus homo; De conceptu uirginali et originali peccato.*	U	xii^{1} England or France; Durham

108	Cambridge, King's College, 19	Prologue to Matthew (Stegmüller, 591). Bede, *In Cantica Canticorum allegorica expositio* (including Gregory, *Excerpta in Cantica Canticorum*).	I(f)	xii^{1} St Albans
109 ?	Cambridge, Magdalene College, Pepys 2981(8)	Priscian, *Institutiones grammaticae* (fragment).	–	xi^{2}
110 ★	Cambridge, Pembroke College, 23	Paul the Deacon, *Homiliarium* (*de tempore*; Easter to Advent [contents itemised by James, *Catalogue*, pp. 20–2]). Companion to Cambridge, Pembroke College, 24 (no. 111).	I	xi^{2} France; Bury St Edmunds (in England by xi/xii)
111 ★	Cambridge, Pembroke College, 24	Paul the Deacon, *Homiliarium* (*de sanctis*; Sanctorale; Commune sanctorum [contents itemised by James, *Catalogue*, pp. 22–5]). Companion to Cambridge, Pembroke College, 23 (no. 110).	I	xi^{2} France; Bury St Edmunds (in England by xi/xii)
112	Cambridge, Pembroke College, 25	Homiliary of Saint-Père de Chartres, drawing on, *inter alia*: Caesarius of Arles and Pseudo-Caesarius, *Sermones*. Gregory, *Homiliae xl in Euangelia*. Amalarius, *De ecclesiasticis officiis*. Alcuin, *De uirtutibus et uitiis ad Widonem comitem; De uita S. Martini Turonensis*. Theodulf of Orléans, *Capitula ad presbyteros parochiae suae*. Hrabanus Maurus, *De clericorum institutione ad Heistulphum archiepiscopum*.	U	xi^{2} Bury St Edmunds
113	Cambridge, Pembroke College, 84, fols 1–31	Boethius, *De Trinitate; Utrum Pater et Filius et Spiritus Sanctus de diuinitate substantialiter praedicentur; Quomodo substantiae in eo, quod sint, bonae sint; De fide catholica; Liber contra Eutychen et Nestorium*. The text was planned for all-round glossing; the first page alone received a near-contemporary gloss.	U	xii^{in} Bury St Edmunds
114	Cambridge, Pembroke College, 84, fols 32–9	Scholia on Boethius's *De consolatione Philosophiae* III, metrum 9, inc.: '*O admirantis est non uocantis*'. Contemporary addition, fol. 39v: Definitions: '*Quot sunt species qualitatis iiii . . . Scientiae species sunt hae . . .*'.	U	xii^{1} Bury St Edmunds
115	Cambridge, Pembroke College, 313 (20)	Service book: ?Pontifical (frag.). Bifolium from the binding of Pembroke College, 20.	–	xi^{2} Bury St Edmunds
116	Cambridge, Peterhouse, 74	*Decreta pontificum et concilia* (Lanfranc's collection). Additions, *s.* xii^{in-1}: Eadmer, *Historia nouorum in Anglia* (extracts). Anselm, *Epistola ad Henricum regem Anglorum*. *Concilium lateranense* (1123). Thurstan of York, *Notificatio de consecratione episcopi S. Andree*. Lanfranc, *Epistola ad episcopum Hiberniae* (Domnall Ua h-Enna). Paschal II, *Epistolae* (2). *Canones de penitentibus de secunda uxore*. NB: further additions were made *s.* xii^{med}; these are not itemised here.	X; A	xi^{ex} (pre 1096; ?1080×88) Durham

117	Cambridge, Peterhouse, 251, fols 106–91	Galen, *Ad Glauconem de medendi methodo; Liber tertius.* '*Aurelius de acutis passionibus.*' '*Esculapius de chronicis passionibus.*' Galen (attrib.), *De podagra.*	X	xi/xii Canterbury, St Augustine's
118	Cambridge, St John's College, Shelfmark: A. 8 (James, *Catalogue* no. 8), vol. I	Josephus, *De antiquitate iudaica* (XV–XX); *De bello iudaico.* Colophon-portrait of Samuel. Companion to Cambridge University Library, Dd. 1. 4 (no. 17).	I(f)	xii^1 Canterbury, Christ Church
119	Cambridge, St John's College, B. 13 (35)	Gregory, *In Ezechielem.*	E/A	xi^{ex} Bury St Edmunds
120	Cambridge, St John's College, C. 23 (73)	Gospels.	P	xi/xii Bury St Edmunds
121 *	Cambridge, St John's College, D. 12 (87), part i	Statius, *Thebaid.* *Glossae super Priscianum*, inc.: '*Circa hanc artem primo considerandum est*'.	P; I	xi^2 France; Dover
122	Cambridge, St John's College, D. 19 (94)	Ivo of Chartres, *Sermones* (8): *De sacramentis neophytorum; De excellentia sacrorum ordinum et uita ordinandorum; De significationibus indumentorum sacerdotalium; De sacramentis dedicationis; De conuenientia noui ac ueteris sacerdotii; De cruce Domini quare Deus natus et passus sit; De aduentu Domini; De natiuitate Domini.*	I(f)	xii^1 (1112×26) Bury St Edmunds
123	Cambridge, St John's College, E. 4 (107), fols 181–96	Plato (trans. Chalcidius), *Timaeus.* Addition, *s.* xii^1, fols 192v–6: Notes on rhetoric and theology, including Sibylline extract, '*In illo tempore surget princeps iniquitatis*' . . .	U	xii^{in}
124 * ??	Cambridge, Trinity College, Shelfmark: B. 1. 16 (James, *Catalogue* no. 15)	Berengaudus, *In Apocalypsin.* Haimo of Auxerre, *Commentarium in Cantica Canticorum* (imperfect). Early additions (*s.* xi/xii), fols 1v–2v, include: Hymn 'Salue uirgo Dei mater'. NB: There is no internal evidence for an early English provenance; however, the fact that it was given to Trinity by John Whitgift, suggests it might have come from Canterbury, Christ Church.	I(f)	xi/xii Normandy; ?England
125	Cambridge, Trinity College, B. 1. 17 (16)	Jerome, *In Mattheum.* Physiologus (extract: on the hyena)	A/E	xii^1 Canterbury, Christ Church
126 ?* ?	Cambridge, Trinity College, B. 1. 29 (27), fols 3–47	Anon., *Notae super Cantica Canticorum* (here attrib. to Jerome, but cf. Durham Cathedral Library. A. IV. 34): inc.: '*Intentio Salomonis est in hoc libro persuadere . . .*'. Probably not written in England. The earliest evidence of English provenance is the *s.* xii/xiii *ex libris* on fol. 2v, written by a known Buildwas hand.	U	xi/xii^+ France or England; Buildwas
127 ?* ?	Cambridge, Trinity College, B. 1. 29 (27), fols 48–103	*Epistolae Pauli*, glossed (gloss derived from School of Laon). See note on previous item. The Buildwas note includes this part of the book, as well as two further originally discrete sections which are too late in date to be included in this inventory.		$xii^{2/4}$ France or England; Buildwas

128	Cambridge, Trinity College, B. 1. 37 (35), fols 1–37, plus 98–105	Anselm, *Cur Deus homo.* The original order of the leaves was 1–27, 98–105, 28–37.	U	xii^{in}
129	Cambridge, Trinity College, B. 1. 37 (35), fols 38–45	Anselm, *Epistolae* (2: to Pope Urban and Abbot William, the second ending imperfectly). One quire.	U	xii^{1}
130	Cambridge, Trinity College, B. 1. 37 (35), fols 46–73	Anselm, *Proslogion; Epistolae* (17). Tracts: '*Quidam christiane ac paterne caritatis obliti intentum*'; '*Quod dominus noster Iesus Christus non pro omnium hominum salute et redemptione sit passus*'. The last four letter and the tracts, fols 67r–73r, were added by several scribes.	U	xii^{in}
131	Cambridge, Trinity College, B. 1. 37 (35), fols 74–97	Anselm, *Monologion* (imperfect).	U	xii^{1}
132	Cambridge, Trinity College, B. 1. 40 (38)	Augustine, *De diuersis quaestionibus lxxxiii.*	I(f)	xi^{ex} Canterbury, St Augustine's
133	Cambridge, Trinity College, B. 2. 3. (46)	Bede, *In Euangelium Lucae expositio.*	I(f)	xii$^{1-2/4}$ Canterbury, Christ Church
134	Cambridge, Trinity College, B. 2. 22 (65)	Gregory, *In Ezechielem* (ending with homily X).		xii^{1} Leicester
135	Cambridge, Trinity College, B. 2. 32 (75)	Bede, *In Epistolas Catholicas.*	U	xii$^{1-2/4}$ Gloucester
136	Cambridge, Trinity College, B. 2. 34 (77)	Jerome, *Quaestiones hebraicae in Genesim; De xlii mansionibus filiorum Israhel in deserto*; Eusebius of Caesarea (trans. Jerome), *De situ et nominibus locorum hebraicorum.* Jerome, *De interpretatione Hebraicorum nominum.* ?Pseudo-Jerome, *Interpretatio alphabeti Hebraeorum.* Anon., *Interpretatio alphabeti Graecorum.* *'Notae diuinae legi necessarie cum suis exemplis.'* Pseudo-Jerome, *Quaestiones hebraicae in libros Regum et Paralipomenon; De decem temptationibus populi Israeli in deserto; Commentarium in Canticum Debborae; Commentarium in Lamentationes Ieremiae prophetae; Ad Dardanum de musicis instrumentis (De diuersis generibus musicorum).* Anon., *'De partibus minus notis Veteris Testamenti.'* *Notulae duodecim signorum secundum chaldeos.* *Multae sententiae expositae utiliter de Nouo et Veteri Testamento.* *'De sphera caeli.'* *'De lapidibus.'* *'De mensuris.'*	I(f)	xii^{1} Canterbury, Christ Church

137	Cambridge, Trinity College, B. 2. 36 (79), fols 1–121	John Chrysostom, *De reparatione lapsi; De compunctione cordis; De Psalmo quinquagesimo; De eo qui nemo laeditur nisi a semet ipso; Cum de expulsione eius ageretur; Post reditum a priore exsilio; Quando de Asia regressus est Constantinopolim ipse Iohannes; De proditione Iudae; De cruce et latrone*; (attrib.), *De cruce; De ascensione Domini.*	I	xii[1] Canterbury, Christ Church
138	Cambridge, Trinity College, B. 2. 36 (79), fols 122–245	Isidore, *De uiris illustribus* (extract on Gregory). Gregory, *Dialogi.*	I	xii[1] Canterbury, Christ Church
139	Cambridge, Trinity College, B. 3. 4 (83)	Jerome, *In Psalmos.*	I(f)	xii^{in} Canterbury, Christ Church
140	Cambridge, Trinity College, B. 3. 5 (84)	Jerome, *In Prophetas minores* (Nah., Hab., Soph., Agg., Zach., Mal.); *In Danielem.* Part two of a two-volume set; the first volume is not known to survive. ?Addition, fols 144r–v: Bede, *De temporibus* (extract).	I	xi^{ex} Canterbury, Christ Church
141	Cambridge, Trinity College, B. 3. 9 (88)	Ambrose, *Expositio Euangelii secundum Lucam.*	I(f)	xi/xii Canterbury, Christ Church
142	Cambridge, Trinity College, B. 3. 10 (89)	Ambrose, *Epistolae; Contra Auxentium de basilicis tradendis; De traditione basilicae; De obitu Theodosii imperatoris.* Pseudo-Ambrose, *De SS. Geruasio et Protasio* (epistola 2). Ambrose, *De Nabutha Israelita.*	I	xi/xii Canterbury, Christ Church
143 ⋆	Cambridge, Trinity College, B. 3. 14 (93)	Richard of Préaux, *In Genesim* (Part II). Companion to London, Lambeth Palace, 62 (no. 582).	I	xi/xii (post 1093) Normandy (Préaux?); Canterbury, Christ Church
144	Cambridge, Trinity College, B. 3. 25 (104)	Augustine, *Retractatio; Confessiones; De diuersis haeresibus* (without prologue).	E	xi/xii Canterbury, Christ Church
145	Cambridge, Trinity College, B. 3. 31 (110)	Augustine, *Retractatio; Epistola ad Aurelium* (ep. 174); *De Trinitate.*	U/E	xii^{in} Canterbury, Christ Church

146	Cambridge, Trinity College, B. 3. 32 (111)	Colophon for 'Thiodricus'. **A)** (fols 1–41) Augustine, *Sermo de aduentu Domini* [= a contemporary addition on endleaves]; *De agone christiano* [original first item]. Pseudo-Augustine, *Dialogus quaestionum lxv Orosii percontantis et Augustini respondentis*. **B)** (fols 42–117) *Sermones* including works by Augustine (*Sermones* App. 117, App. 119, App. 215, App. 317, App. 210, App. 319, App. 154, 303, App. 207, 356 [= *De uita et moribus clericorum suorum*]), Maximus episcopus, Petrus episcopus, Eusebius Gallicanus, Isidore, Leo, and Jerome.	I(f) U	xii^{in} Canterbury, Christ Church
147	Cambridge, Trinity College, B. 3. 33 (112)	Augustine, *De adulterinis coniugiis; De mendacio; Contra mendacium; De cura pro mortuis gerenda; De uera religione; De natura et origine animae. Sermo Arianorum.* Pseudo-Augustine (Syagrius), *Contra sermonem Arianorum.* Augustine, *Contra aduersarium legis et prophetarum.*	I	xi^{ex} Canterbury, Christ Church
148	Cambridge, Trinity College, B. 4. 2 (116)	Gospel of St John ('*iuxta eam translationem quam beatus Augustinus exponit*'). Augustine, *In euangelium Iohannis.*	I	xi^{ex} Canterbury, Christ Church
149 ?*	Cambridge, Trinity College, B. 4. 5 (119)	Florus Lugdunensis (*ex* Augustine), *Expositio in epistolas beati Pauli ex operibus S. Augustini collecta* (Part i: Rom. and 1 Cor.). Companion to Oxford, Bodleian Library, Bodley 317 (no. 660).	I	xi/xii ?Normandy; Canterbury, Christ Church
150	Cambridge, Trinity College, B. 4. 9 (123)	Gregory, *Moralia in Iob* (Books 17–35: i.e. part II of a two volume set). Part I is not known to survive.	I	xi/xii Canterbury, Christ Church
151	Cambridge, Trinity College, B. 4. 25 (139)	Augustine, *De Genesi ad litteram.*	I(f)	xii^{1} Canterbury, Christ Church
152	Cambridge, Trinity College, B. 4. 26 (140)	Augustine, *Epistolae* (incomplete): nos. 132, 135, 137, 136, 138, 92, 143, 81–2, 41, 233–5, 98, 25, 27, 30–1, 24, 32, 109, 243, 26, 16–17, 127, 214, 93, 102, 185, 154–5, 152–3, 117–18, 187, 121, 149, 90–1, 23, 173, 164, 130, 147, 111, 257, 96, 259, 100, 97, 265, 144, 101, 165, 199, 266, 99, 58, 110, 77–8, 122, 245, 260–1, 264, 188, 145, 248, 205, 33, 21, 38, 112, 232, 242, 3, 18, 20, 19, 15, 5–7, 9, 10, 4, 141, 46–7, 258, 131, 190, 43, 105, App. 1–7, App. 11–15, 34–5, 52, 76, 88, 51, 66, 238–40.	I	xi/xii Canterbury, Christ Church
153	Cambridge, Trinity College, B. 4. 28 (142), fols 3–215	Jerome, *In Ezechielem.*	I	xii^{1} Canterbury, Christ Church

154 §	Cambridge, Trinity College, B. 5. 2 (148)	Bible (part II: Proverbs – Paul, *Epistola ad Hebreos*). Companion to Lincoln Cathedral, 1 (no. 328). See PLATE 12.	I(f)	xi/xii–xii^{in} (pre 1110) Lincoln
155	Cambridge, Trinity College, B. 5. 22 (168)	Jerome, *In Ieremiam*.	I(f)	xii^{1} Canterbury, Christ Church
156	Cambridge, Trinity College, B. 5. 23 (169)	Jerome, *In Isaiam* (I–X). Companion to Cambridge, Trinity College, B. 5. 24 (no. 157).	I	xii^{1} Canterbury, Christ Church
157	Cambridge, Trinity College, B. 5. 24 (170)	Jerome, *In Isaiam* (XI–XVIII). Companion to Cambridge, Trinity College, B. 5. 23 (no. 156).		xii^{1} Canterbury, Christ Church
158	Cambridge, Trinity College, B. 5. 24 (172)	Augustine, *Enarrationes in Psalmos* (I–L). Companion to Cambridge, Trinity College, B. 5. 28, and Tokyo, Takamiya Collection, 55 (nos. 159 and 905).	I	xi^{ex} Canterbury, Christ Church
159	Cambridge, Trinity College, B. 5. 28 (174)	Augustine, *Enarrationes in Psalmos* (CI–CL) Companion to Cambridge, Trinity College, B. 5. 26, and Tokyo, Takamiya Collection, 55 (nos. 158 and 905).	X; I	xi^{ex} Canterbury, Christ Church
160	Cambridge, Trinity College, B. 14. 30 (315), fols 1–57 Probably written in three parts, as indicated.	**A)** (fols 1–32) Pseudo-Augustine, *Sermo de purificatione BVM* (= Fulgentius, *Sermo* 2); *Sermo de presentatione Christi*. Anon., *Sermo de natiuitate Domini ('Karissimi fratres qui in eternum est'). 'Ecce homo erat in Hierusalem'*. Pseudo-Augustine, *Sermo de natiuitate BVM* (= Fulbert of Chartres, *Sermo* 6). '*Gloriosam sollemnitatem BVM*'. '*Natiuitatis gloriose genetricis*'. '*Narrat siquidem historia quia die tertio*'. Augustine, *De annunciatione BVM* (= *sermo* App. 194). **B)** (fols 33–47) Odilo of Cluny, *Sermo* xiv (*De uita BVM*). Paschasius Radbertus, *De assumptione BVM* (= Pseudo-Jerome, *Epistola de assumptione BVM*). **C)** (fols 48–57) Lection on the life BVM (including Fulbert of Chartres, *Sermo de natiuitate BVM* (*sermo* 4); with added scribal prayer.	U	xi^{ex} Exeter; Leicester
161	Cambridge, Trinity College, B. 14. 30 (315), fols 58–129	Ambrose, *De uirginitate; Exhortatio ad uirgines*. Pseudo-Ambrose, *De lapsu uirginis consecratae; Ad corruptorem uirginis; Consolatio ad uirginem lapsam*. NB: Although originally separate, fols 1–57 and 58–129 appear as one item (no. 150) in the *s.* xv/xvi Leicester Abbey library catalogue.	U	xi^{ex} Exeter; Leicester

162 *	Cambridge, Trinity College, B. 16. 44 (405)	*Decreta pontificum et concilia* (Lanfranc's collection). Includes (p. 404) a contemporary donation / anathema note, recording Lanfranc's purchase of the book and subsequent gift of it to Christ Church. Additions, *s.* xi^{ex}, pp. 405–7: Letters to Lanfranc; extracts from councils.	E	xi^{2} (written post *c.* 1060; brought to England 1070×89) Normandy (?Bec); Canterbury, Christ Church
163 †	Cambridge, Trinity College, O. 2. 24 (1128)	Alcuin, *De dialectica.* Bede, *De arte metrica; De schematibus et tropis; Vita S. Cuthberti* (verse). Metrical Calendar from York. Diagrams with short verses including Bede, *De die iudicii* (extract). Peter Damian, *Dominus uobiscum.* Marbod of Rennes, *Passio S. Mauricii et sociorum eius.* Pseudo-Augustine, *Dialogus quaestionum lxv Orosii percontantis et Augustini respondentis.* Eusebius Gallicanus, *Homiliae xii de pascha* (Sermones 12–23). Pseudo-Ildefonsus, *De natiuitate Dei genetricis semperque uirginis Mariae* (*Sermo* 7). Augustine, *De agone christiano.*	D; A	xii^{1} (pre ?1124) Rochester
164	Cambridge, Trinity College, O. 2. 30 (1134), fols 1–70	Pseudo-Augustine, *De unitate sanctae Trinitatis.* Extracts in dialogue form from Isidore, *De differentiis rerum* and *Etymologiae* ('*De diuersitate aquarum*'). Isidore, *De fide catholica contra Iudaeos.*		xii^{in} Southwark
165	Cambridge, Trinity College, O. 2. 51 (1155), part ii	Priscian, *Institutiones grammaticae* (i–xviii). (Pseudo-)Priscian, *De accentibus* (incomplete).	I(f)	xi^{ex} Canterbury, St Augustine's
166	Cambridge, Trinity College, O. 3. 35 (1207)	Ambrose, *Hexaemeron.*	A	xi/xii Chichester

167 †	Cambridge, Trinity College, O. 4. 7 (1238)	Jerome, *Quaestiones hebraicae in Genesim; De xlii mansionibus filiorum Israhel in deserto.* Eusebius of Caesarea (trans. Jerome), *De situ et nominibus locorum hebraicorum.* Jerome, *De interpretatione Hebraicorum nominum.* Pseudo-Jerome, *Interpretatio alphabeti Hebraeorum.* Anon., *Interpretatio alphabeti Graecorum.* Pseudo-Jerome, *Quaestiones hebraicae in libros Regum et Paralipomenon; De decem temptationibus populi Israeli in deserto; Commentarium in Canticum Debborae; Commentarium in Lamentationes Ieremiae prophetae; Ad Dardanum de musicis instrumentis* (*De diuersis generibus musicorum*). Anon., *De partibus minus notis Veteris Testimenti.* *Notulae duodecim signorum secundum chaldeos.* *Multae sententiae expositae utiliter de Nouo et Veteri Testimento.* *'De sphera caeli.'* *'De lapidibus.'* *'De mensuris.'* *'Ad estimandum cuiusque rei altitudinem sole lucente.'*	I(f)	xii[1] (?pre 1124) Rochester
168	Cambridge, Trinity College, O. 4. 34 (1264)	Orosius, *Historiae aduersus paganos.* Pseudo-Aethicus Ister (Julius Honorius), *Cosmographia* (frag.). The original volume continued as follows: *Cosmographia* (continued). Jordanes, *De origine actibusque Getarum.* *Itinerarium prouinciarum Antonii Augusti.* These items were in O. 4. 36, now destroyed.	I	xi/xii Canterbury, Christ Church
—	Cambridge, Trinity College, O. 4. 36	*See* Cambridge, Trinity College, O. 4. 34.		
169	Cambridge Trinity College, O. 5. 20 (1301), pp. 1–265a + London, British Library, Royal App. 85, fols 25–6	John Scotus Erigena, *Periphyseon.*	U	xii[1–2/4] (post 1125) Malmesbury
170	Cambridge, Trinity College, O. 7. 41 (1369)	*Sphera Pythagorae* inc.: '*Ratio sphere Pytagorice quam Apuleius descripsit*' Calendar; Tables. Robert Losinga of Hereford's edition of Marianus Scotus's *Chronicon* (*Excerptio Rodberti Herefordensis episcopi de Chronica Mariani*). Walcher of Great Malvern, *De lunationibus.* Tract on arithmetic. Additions *s.* xii, fols 58v–9: Orders of the Church; Hebrew alphabet with numerical equivalents.	U	xii[1] (after 1112) Colchester
171 §	Cambridge Trinity College, O. 10. 23 (1475)	Gregory of Tours, *Liber miraculorum in gloriam sanctorum.* See PLATE 5.	U	xi[ex] Exeter

172	Cambridge, Trinity College, O. 10. 28 (1480)	Eutropius, *Breuiarium historiae romanae ab urbe condita.* Paul the Deacon's continuation of Eutropius.	I(f)	xi/xii Canterbury, Christ Church
173	Cambridge, Trinity College, O. 10. 31 (1483)	*Passio S. Quiriaci.* *Inuentio Sanctae Crucis*, inc.: '*Anno ducentisimo tricesimo post passionem*'. Victor of Vita, *Historia persecutionis Africanae prouinciae.*	A	xi/xii Canterbury, Christ Church
174	Cambridge, Trinity College, R. 3. 30 (610)	Lucan, *Pharsalia.*	I(f)	xii^1 Rochester
175	Cambridge, Trinity College, R. 5. 27 (722)	Bede, *Historia ecclesiastica.* Cuthbert, *Epistola de obitu uenerabilis Bedae.*	X; A	xii^1
176	Cambridge, Trinity College, R. 7. 5 (743), supply leaves: fols ii–iii, 4–5, 46–7, 81v–2v, 151–53/14, 235–7, 246–51	Capitula added, and extensive corrections made, to a copy of Bede, *Historia ecclesiastica* which was started *s.* xi^{1-med}, possibly in two campaigns. Addenda to the text including: Description of the wanderings of the Community of St Cuthbert, inc.: 'Lindisfarne dicitur insula . . .'. Fol. 82v includes an arabesque initial (for the re-written start of Book III). Additions, *s.* $xii^{1-2/4}$ (?1123×28), fols. 250v–51r: *Prognostica archiepiscoporum et episcoporum angliae.* Further additions, *s.* xvi.	– A	xii^1 ?Northern England
177	Cambridge, Trinity College, R. 7. 28 (770), pp. 1–74	Annals of St Neots.	U	$xii^{2/4}$ Bury St Edmunds
178	Cambridge, Trinity College, R. 9. 17 (819), fols 1–48	Ælfric, *Grammar* (abbreviated). OE *Disticha Catonis.* Apothegms (OE).	U	xi/xii
179	Cambridge, Trinity College, R. 14. 34 (906)	Constantine Africanus, *Liber Pantegni.*		$xii^{1-2/4}$ Bury St Edmunds
180	Cambridge, Trinity College, R. 14. 49 (919), front flyleaf	Service book (frag. = one leaf, cropped). Provenance of 'host book' is Bury St Edmunds, Franciscan convent.	–	$xii^{1-2/4}$
181	Cambridge, Trinity College, R. 14. 50 (920)	Medical texts attributed to Galen: 'Gariopontus of Salerno', *Passionarius Galeni* (extensively mutiliated). Additions *s.* $xii^{2/4}$: extensive annotation of margins; addition of '*Ratio uentorum*' on fols 112r–v. Self-contained addition, *s.* $xii^{2/4}$, fols 121–32: tract, *De urinis* (incomplete). NB: the current foliation *includes* the many missing leaves.	X E/U	$xi^{3/4}$

182	Cambridge, Trinity College, R. 16. 34 (982)	Florilegium of extracts from Aulus Gellius, *Noctes Atticae* and Valerius Maximus, *Factorum et dictorum memorabilium libri* (= '*Anthologia Valerio-Gelliana*') [mutilated at the start]. Anon. verses, *De uino et Venere* inc.: '*Nec Veneris nec tu uini tenearis amore*' (Walther, 38622c). Extracts from Seneca, *De beneficiis*. Provisions of Council of Lisieux (1064). Cicero, *De officiis*, i, ii, iii, ix.		xii^{1} Salisbury
183	Cambridge, Trinity Hall, 4	Josephus, *De antiquitate iudaica*.	I(f)	xii$^{2/4}$ Monkland Priory (Herefords.)
184	Cambridge, Trinity Hall, 21	Sulpicius Severus, *Vita S. Martini; Epistolae; Dialogi.* Gregory of Tours, *Epistola de transitu S. Martini.* *Item de transitu Martini.* Ambrose, *Sermo de transitu Martini.* *Quando corpus Martini translatum est.* *Confessio S. Martini de Trinitate.* *Versus in foribus primi celle S. Martini.* *Vita S. Britii.* John the Deacon, *Vita S. Nicholai* (incomplete).	I(f)	xii^{in}
185	Cambridge, Trinity Hall, 26	Ambrose, *De uirginitate; De uiduis; De SS. Vitale et Agricola.* Pseudo-Ambrose, *De lapsu uirginis consecratae; Ad corruptorem uirginis; Consolatio ad uirginem lapsum.* Isidore (attrib.), *Sermo de corpore et sanguine Domini in pascha* (= Eusebius Gallicanus, *Sermo* 16).	E/A	xii^{in}
186 ?	Cambridge (Mass.), Harvard University, Houghton Library, pfMS Typ 704, no. 3	Bible (frag.: one leaf)	–	xii^{1}
187 §	Canterbury Cathedral, Add. 20	Chrodegang of Metz, *Regula canonicorum*, Latin and OE (frag.: part of one bifolium). See PLATE 1.	–	xi$^{3/4}$ Canterbury, Christ Church
188	Canterbury Cathedral, Add. 127/15	Ivo of Chartres, *Epistolae* (frag.: three folios).	– E	xii^{1} (post 1100) ?Canterbury, Christ Church
189	Canterbury Cathedral, Add. 172	*Cantica Canticorum.* *Epistolae Pauli* with Lanfranc's gloss. *Apocalypsis Iohannis* (ruled for a gloss, but none supplied). NB: the binding is contemporary with the text; the rear pastedown is from a *s.* xi^{med} service book.	P; E	xi^{ex} Canterbury, St Augustine's
190	Canterbury Cathedral, Lit. A. 8	Augustine, *Sermones de uerbis Domini et apostoli; Sermones* (151–2).	I(f)	xi/xii Canterbury, St Augustine's

191 * ??	Canterbury Cathedral, Lit. B. 7	Sententiae de primatu Romanae ecclesiae. *Possibly* in England by xii[in]: Ker, *MMBL* II, characterised the early additions as English; this seems open to doubt.	I	xi[ex] France; ?Canterbury, Christ Church
192	Canterbury Cathedral, Lit. D. 4, fols 25–32	Domesday Book: extract for Canterbury, Kent (incomplete). A single quire fragment.	U	xii[1]
193	Canterbury Cathedral, Lit. E. 28, fols 1–7	*Domesday monachorum.*	U	xi/xii Canterbury, Christ Church
194	Canterbury Cathedral, Lit. E. 42, with Maidstone, Kent County Archives, S/Rm Fae. 2	Passional (frags.: parts of four separate volumes from a seven volume set; contents inventoried in *MMBL*, II, pp. 289–96). Companions to London, British Library, Harley 624 + 315 + Cott. Nero C. vii (no. 433).	I(f)	xii[in–1] (?before 1128) Canterbury, Christ Church
195	Canterbury Cathedral, U3/ 162/ 28/ 1	Augustine, *Enarrationes in psalmos* (frag.: one damaged bifolium. The 'Elmstone bifolium').	–	xi/xii Canterbury, St Augustine's
196	Canterbury Cathedral, X. 1. 11 (flyleaves)	Jerome, *In Prophetas minores* (frag.: 2 leaves, with part of *In Habbakuk*).	–	xii[in] Canterbury, St Augustine's
197	Cardiff Public Library, I. 381, fols 81–120	Vitae sanctorum: Goscelin, *Vita Æthelburgae.* Lections for St Hildelitha. *Passio et miracula Eadwardi.* Goscelin, *Vita Edithae.* Addition, *s.* xii[med], fols 121–46: Rhigyfarch/Ricemarch, *Vita S. Davidis.* Hildebert, Metrical life of Mary of Egypt. *Vita Ebrulfi.*	U	xii[in] Barking
198 ?	Colchester and Essex Museum, Colchester Castle Society, s. n.	Gospels. The first scribe and the hand responsible for the initials is English; the other scribes and the artist of the Canon Tables look Norman. Additions to preliminary leaves (fols 1–2v), *s.* xii[2]: Verses, '*surgit defunctus iuuenis quem suscitat unctus* (acephalus); '*Tu Petre me sequere, sis pastor ouesque tuere*'.	D	xii[1] England or Normandy
—	Cologne, Schnütgen Museum, 5	*See* Hildesheim, St Godehard's Church, 1.		
—	Columbia, Missouri, University of Missouri Library, Rare — L/PA/ 3381. A1/F7	*See* Cambridge University Library, Add. 4406.		

199	Copenhagen, Kongelige Bibliotek, G.K.S 1588 (4°)	Abbo of Fleury, *Vita S. Edmundi.* Officium sancti Edmundi (incomplete). Addition s. xii² (fol. 1ʳ), *Sequentiae in honorem S. Nicolai.*	E/A	xi² Bury St Edmunds; Saint-Denis (s. xiii)
—	Copenhagen, Kongelige Bibliotek, N.K.S 1854 (2°)	See Supplement		
200	Dublin, Trinity College, 98 (B. 3. 6), fols 1–72	Pontifical.	U	xiiⁱⁿ Canterbury, Christ Church
201	Dublin, Trinity College, 98 (B. 3. 6), fols 73–155	Benedictional.	U	xiiⁱⁿ Canterbury, Christ Church
202	Dublin, Trinity College, 174 (B. 3.4)	*Vitae sanctorum*; Homilies for Saints' days (including Augustine, *Sermones* 276, 316, 382, App. 217; and Caesarius, *Sermo* 220). Double mass in honour of martyrs (?Achatus and his 10,000 companions). Text about the Apostles' Creed. Litanies; Prayer. ?Companion to Salisbury Cathedral, 223 (no. 898).	U/E	xi/xii–xiiⁱⁿ Salisbury
203	Dublin, Trinity College, 176 (E. 5. 28), fols 1–26	Goscelin, *Vita S. Æthelburgae; Vita S. Wulfhildae.*	U	xi/xii ?Barking
204	Dublin, Trinity College, 176 (E. 5. 28), fols 27–41	?Goscelin, *Textus translationis SS. Æthelburgae, Hildelithae, Wulfhildae.* ?Goscelin, Vision associated with the same; *De translatione S. Æthelburgae, Hildelithae.*	U	xii¹ ?Kent
205	Dublin, Trinity College, 370a, fols 1–6	Antiphoner (frag.) including office of St Guthlac.	–	xiiⁱⁿ ?Croyland
206	Dublin, Trinity College, 371, pp. 1–74	Pseudo-Aethicus Ister (Julius Honorius), *Cosmographia.*	E/A	xii¹
207	Dublin, Trinity College, 371, pp. 149–50	Gradual (frag.).	–	xi² ?Canterbury
208	Durham Cathedral, A. I. 10, fols 1–169	Anselm of Laon, *In Mattheum.*	I(f)	xii¹ Durham
209	Durham Cathedral, A. I. 10, fols 170–242	Berengaudus, *In Apocalypsin.* Cassiodorus, *De anima* (imperfect).	I(f)	xii¹ Durham

210 ★ †	Durham Cathedral, A. II. 4	Bible (Prophets — Apocalypse) (The 'Carilef Bible'). Haimo of Auxerre, *Commentarium in Apocalypsin* (incomplete). The second volume of a two volume set; volume one is not known to survive. Near-contemporary addition to flyleaf (fol. 1r): List of books given to Durham by William Carilef.	I(f)	xi^{ex} (pre 1096) Normandy; Durham
211 †	Durham Cathedral, A. III. 29	Paul the Deacon, *Homiliarium* (Easter to 25th Sunday after Whitsun; Saints' days from 1 May to December). Companion to Durham Cathedral, B. II. 2, and C. IV. 12, frags (nos. 216 and 275).	U	xi^{ex} (pre 1096) Durham
212	Durham Cathedral, A. IV. 15, fols 17–56	Anon., *Commentarium in Iohannem*, inc.: '*In principio erat Verbum — Verbum substantiale intelligitur quod in ipso homine manet intus . . .*'.	U	xii^{1} Durham
213	Durham Cathedral, A. IV. 16, fols 66–109	Augustine, *De Genesi ad litteram* (I–VI) (incomplete).		xii^{in} Durham
214 ?★	Durham Cathedral, A. IV. 34	Anon., *Notae super Cantica Canticorum*, inc.: '*Intentio Salomonis est in hoc libro persuadere*'. NB: the manuscript is unsewn.	U	xii^{1} Continent (Low Countries) or England; Durham
215	Durham Cathedral, B. II. 1	Josephus, *De antiquitate iudaica; De bello iudaico.*	I(f)	xii^{1} Durham
216 †	Durham Cathedral, B. II. 2	Paul the Deacon, *Homiliarium* (Advent to Easter) (incomplete). Companion to Durham Cathedral, A. III. 29, and C. IV. 12, frags (nos. 211 and 275).	X; U	xi^{ex} (pre 1096) Durham
217 †	Durham Cathedral, B. II. 6	Ambrose, *De Ioseph patriarcha; De duodecim patriarchis; De paenitentia; 'De morte fratris'* (= *De excessu fratris Satyri*)*; De bono mortis; De obitu Valentiniani; De paradiso* (unfinished); *De Abraham patriarcha; De Nabutha Israelita.* Addition of *s.* xi/xii: Augustine, *De decem chordis* (*sermo 9*).	A	xi^{ex} (pre 1096) Durham
218	Durham Cathedral, B. II. 7	Prefatory texts to the Psalms including extracts from Augustine, Pseudo-Jerome, Isidore, Gregory of Tours and Cassiodorus. Jerome, *In Psalmos*.	I	xii$^{2/4}$ Durham
219	Durham Cathedral, B. II. 8	Jerome, *In Isaiam*.	I(f)	xii^{1} Durham
220 ★ †	Durham Cathedral, B. II. 9	Jerome, *In Prophetas minores* (Osee, Ioel, Amos, Abd., Ion., Mich., Nah., Hab., Soph., Agg., Zach., Mal.).	I	xi^{ex} (pre 1096) Normandy; Durham
221 †	Durham Cathedral, B. II. 10	Jerome, *Epistolae* (123, including pseudonymous letters and letters to Jerome). Origen (trans. Jerome), *In Cantica Canticorum*. Jerome, *Aduersus Heluidium de Mariae perpetua uirginitate; Contra Vigilantium.* Addition, *s.* xii^{in} fols 183v–6v: ?Pseudo-Sebastianus Casinensis, *Vita S. Hieronymi.*	I/A	xi^{ex} (pre 1096) Canterbury, Christ Church; Durham

222 † ★	Durham Cathedral, B. II. 11, fols 1–108	Jerome, *Quaestiones hebraicae in Genesim.* Eusebius of Caesarea (trans. Jerome), *De situ et nominibus locorum hebraicorum.* Jerome, *De interpretatione Hebraicorum nominum.* Pseudo-Jerome, *Interpretatio alphabeti Hebraeorum.* Anon., *Interpretatio alphabeti Graecorum.* Pseudo-Jerome, *Quaestiones hebraicae in libros Regum et Paralipomenon; De decem temptationibus populi Israeli in deserto. De sex ciuitatibus ad quas homicida fugit.* Pseudo-Jerome, *Commentarium in Canticum Debborae; Commentarium in Lamentationes Ieremiae prophetae.* Prudentius, *Psychomachia* (extract). Pseudo-Jerome, *Ad Dardanum de musicis instrumentis* (*De diuersis generibus musicorum*). Jerome and Pseudo-Jerome, *Epistolae.* '*De sphera caeli.*' '*De mensuris.*' '*Ad estimandum cuiusque rei altitudinem sole lucente.*' '*De lapidibus.*' Short texts on science, music and liturgy. List of Popes (*ex: Liber pontificalis*). See note on next item.	I	xi^{ex} (pre 1096) Normandy; Durham
223	Durham Cathedral, B. II. 11, fols 109–37	Fulbert of Chartres, *Epistolae; Sermones; Versus.* Robert II of France, *Epistola ad Gauzlinum abbatem.* Gauzlin of Fleury, *Rescriptum ad regem Rotbertum.* Fulbert of Chartres, *Hymni; Versus.* Both parts (nos. 222 and 223) were prepared to the same format, and were probably bound together soon after writing.		xi^{ex} Durham
224 ★ †	Durham Cathedral, B. II. 13, fols 7–226	Augustine, *Enarrationes in Psalmos* (LI–C). Companion to Durham Cathedral, B. II. 14 (no. 225). Volume I is not known to survive. NB: Fols 1–6 = index added *s.* xv.	I(f)	xi^{ex} (pre 1096) Normandy; Durham
225 ★ †	Durham Cathedral, B. II. 14, fols 7–200	Augustine, *Enarrationes in Psalmos* (CI–CL). Companion to Durham Cathedral, B. II. 13 (no. 224). Volume I is not known to survive. NB: Fols 1–6 = index added *s.* xv.	I	xi^{ex} (1088×93) Normandy; Durham
226	Durham Cathedral, B. II. 16	Augustine, *In Euangelium Iohannis.* Although Durham Cathedral Library, B. II. 17 (no. 227) is probably the copy of Augustine, *In Euangelium Iohannis* that William Carilef gave to Durham, it is not impossible that it was the present manuscript, for which a date of xi^{ex} would then be necessary.	I(f)	xi/xii (??pre 1096) Canterbury, St Augustine's; Durham
227 ★ †	Durham Cathedral, B. II. 17	Augustine, *In Euangelium Iohannis.* See note on previous item.	E	xi^{ex} (?pre 1096) Normandy; Durham
228	Durham Cathedral, B. II. 18	Augustine, *Sermones de uerbis Domini et apostoli* (*Sermones de uerbis Domini* 1–64; *Sermones de uerbis apostoli* 1, 2, 34, 3–24).	I	xii^{in} Durham

229 †	Durham Cathedral, B. II. 21, fols 10–158	Augustine, *Epistolae* (142): nos. 132, 135, 137, 136, 138, 92, 143, 81–2, 41, 233–5, 98, 25, 27, 30–1, 24, 32, 109, 243, 26, 16, 17, 127, 214–15, 93, 102, 185, 154–5, 152–3, 117–18, 187, 121, 149, 90–1, 23, 173, 164, 130, 147, 111, 257, 96, 259, 100, 97, 265, 144, 101, 199, 266, 99, 58, 110, 77–8, 122, 245, 260–1, 264, 188, 145, 248, 205, 33, 21, 38, 112, 232, 242, 3, 141, 46–7, 258, 131, 190, 139, 134, 133, 176, 49, 43, 87, 44, 53, 105, 89, 34–5, 52, 76, 88, 51, 66, 238–41, 150, 228, 147, Pseudo-Augustine, *Sermo ad Italicum*, App. 1–15, 148, 262, 196, 80, 189, 18, 20, 19, 15, 5–7, 9, 10, 4. Addition, *s.* xi/xii, fol. 9: Augustine, *Epistolae* 60, 48 (excerpts), etc. Fols. 1–8 = index added *s.* xv.	I	xi^{ex} (pre 1096) Durham
230 †	Durham Cathedral, B. II. 22, fols 27–231	Augustine, *Retractatio; De ciuitate Dei.* Lanfranc's *Notae* on *De ciuitate Dei.* Addition *s.* xi/xii, fol. 231v: '*Sententia quam Augustinus de Tymeo Platonis sumit et in xiii*^{o} huius operis libro ponit'. Fols 4–26: *s.* xiii–xv, Capitula and Indices.	I(f)	xi^{ex} (pre 1096) Durham
231	Durham Cathedral, B. II. 26, fols 5–137	Augustine, *Retractatio; Epistola 174; De Trinitate.*	I	xii^{1} Durham
232 † §	Durham Cathedral, B. II. 35, fols 38–118	Bede, *Historia ecclesiastica.* Work of a Norman scribe at Durham? Additions, *s.* xii^{1}: fols 119–23, *Vita Bedae*; fol. 123v, Sergius Papa, *Epistola ad Ceolfridum*; fols 123v–9, Bede, *Historia abbatum.* Further additions. *Saec.* xii$^{2/4\text{–med}}$, fols 129v–36: Nennius, *Historia Brittonum. Saec.* xii^{2}: fols 136–8, Gilbert of Limerick, *De hierarchia ecclesiae*; fols 136v–7, *Nomina regum Britanniae*; fols 137v–8v, Caradoc of Llancarran, *Vita Gildae*; fols 138v–9v, *Regna Israel, Judae, Assyriorum, Persarum et Medorum, Chaldeorum*; fol. 140r, Genealogy Adam-Woden; fols 140r–3v, *De regibus regnorum Anglorum* (to Henry II); fols 144r–7r, *De episcopis prouinciae Cantuariensis*; fols 147–9v *De episcopis prouinciae Eboracensis.* See PLATE 8.	I	xi^{ex} (pre 1096; ?1091×96) Durham
233 ⋆ †	Durham Cathedral, B. III. 1	Origen (trans. Rufinus), *Homiliae in Genesim.* Pseudo-Origen (trans. Rufinus), *De benedictionibus patriarcharum* (extract). Origen (trans. Rufinus), *Homiliae in Exodum; Homiliae in Leuiticum; Homiliae in Iosue; Homiliae in Iudices; Homiliae in Regum libros (I).* Origen (trans. Jerome), *Homiliae in Cantica Canticorum; In Isaiam; In Hieremiam; In Ezechielem.*	I	xi^{ex} (pre 1096) Normandy; Durham
234	Durham Cathedral, B. III. 3, fols 1–56	Augustine, *Retractatio*; *De diuersis quaestionibus lxxxiii.*	E	xii^{1} Durham
235 †	Durham Cathedral, B. III. 9	Gregory, *Symbolum fidei*; *Registrum epistolarum* (14 books plus supplement, books 2 and 3 being joined together).	I	xi^{ex} (pre 1096) Durham
236 † ⋆	Durham Cathedral, B. III. 10 fols 1–236	Gregory, *Moralia in Iob* (I–XVI). Fols 237–8 = rejected version of fols 233–4.	I(f)	xi^{ex} (pre 1096) Normandy; Durham

237 *	Durham Cathedral, B. III. 10, fols i bis, and 243	Breviary (frag.).	–	xii^{in} France; Durham
—	Durham Cathedral, B. III. 10, fols 239 and 242	*See* Durham Cathedral, B. III. 16, fols 159–60.		
238	Durham Cathedral, B. III. 10, fol. ii	Sermones (frag.).	–	xii^{in}
239 †	Durham Cathedral, B. III. 11, fols 1–135	Gregory, *Homiliae xl in Euangelia.* Haimo of Auxerre (Pseudo-Haimo of Halberstadt), Homiliary (*De tempore*).	E	xi^{ex} (pre 1096) Continent; Durham
240 *	Durham Cathedral, B. III. 11, fols 136–59	Antiphoner.		xi^{ex} Continent (?Liège); Durham
241	Durham Cathedral, B. III. 14, fols 1–58	Isidore, *De summo bono.*	A	xii^{1} Durham
242 ?*	Durham Cathedral, B. III. 14, fols 59–64	Peter Damian, *Dominus uobiscum.*		xii^{1} ?Continent; Durham
243 ?*	Durham Cathedral, B. III. 14, fols 65–123	?Anselm of Laon, *In Apocalypsin*, inc.: '*Beatus Johannes apostolus a Domiciano seuerissimo imperatore apud Pathmos insulam*'.		xii^{1} ?Continent; Durham
244 ?*	Durham Cathedral, B. III. 14, fols 124–63	John Chrysostom, *De Psalmo quinquagesimo; De muliere Cananaea. De reparatione lapsi.* Pseudo-Augustine, *Sermo de muliere forti* (sermo 37).		xii^{1} ?Continent; Durham
245 * †	Durham Cathedral, B. III. 16, fols 2–158	Hrabanus Maurus, *Epistola dedicatoria.* *Versus de euangelistis: 'Mattheus leni comitem'* (Walther, 10788). Hrabanus Maurus, *In Mattheum.*	I	xi^{ex} (pre 1096) Normandy; Durham
246	Durham Cathedral, B. III. 16, fols 159–60 + B. III. 10, fols 239 and 242	Augustine, *Sermones* 55, 61, 62, 70 (frag.).	–	xii^{in} Durham
247	Durham Cathedral, B. IV. 1	Gregory Nazianzenus (trans. Rufinus), Orationes (8).	A	xii^{1} Durham
248	Durham Cathedral, B. IV. 4, fol. 1	Tract on sin (frag.).	–	xii^{1} Durham
249	Durham Cathedral, B. IV. 4, fols 2–79	Ambrose, *Hexaemeron* (plus ii *Excerpta*).	I	xii^{in} Durham
250	Durham Cathedral, B. IV. 4, fols 80–90	*Excerpta* (including: Gregory, *Moralia in Iob*, i, 1–3; and Isidore, *Etymologiae* ix, v–vi. 22; and ix, vi. 28–9).	U	xii^{in} Durham

251	Durham Cathedral, B. IV. 5	Ambrose, *De officiis ministrorum; De uirginibus; De uiduis; De uirginitate; Exhortatio ad uirgines.* Pseudo-Ambrose, *De lapsu uirginis consecratae; Ad corruptorem uirginis; Consolatio ad uirginem lapsam.* Ambrose, *De sacramentis.* Eusebius Gallicanus, *Sermo* 17 (olim 16). Additions, *s.* xii^{1}, fols 102v–22v: Ambrose, *De Helia et ieiunia.* Pseudo-Ambrose, *Libellus de dignitate sacerdotali; Sermo* 35 (*De mysterio paschae*).	I(f)	xii^{in} Durham
252	Durham Cathedral, B. IV. 6, fols 1–94	Augustine, *Retractatio; Confessiones; De diuersis haeresibus.*	A	xii^{1} Durham
253	Durham Cathedral, B. IV. 6, fols 99–138	Augustine, *Retractationes.*		xii^{1} Durham
254	Durham Cathedral, B. IV. 6, fols 142–69	'*Augustinus sciebat omnes artes praeter unum*' (short excerpta from Augustine, etc.). Alcuin, *Epistola dedicatoria metrica in De dialectica sua.* Pseudo-Augustine, *Dialectica* (*Categoriae decem*). Alcuin, *De dialectica.* Versus, '*Qui rogo ciuiles cupiat cognoscere*' (Walther, 15640).		xii^{1} Durham
255	Durham Cathedral, B. IV. 7	Augustine, *In epistolam Iohannis ad Parthos tractatus x (De caritate).* Pseudo-Augustine (Pseudo-Cyprian), *De duodecim abusiuis saeculi.*	I	xii^{in} Durham
256	Durham Cathedral, B. IV. 8, fols 2–79	Augustine, *In epistolam Iohannis ad Parthos tractatus x (De caritate).*	P	xii^{1} Durham
257	Durham Cathedral, B. IV. 8, fols 81–98	Josephus, *De bello iudaico* (epitome).		xii^{in} Durham
258	Durham Cathedral, B. IV. 12, fols 1–38	Fulgentius of Ruspe, *Epistola ad Donatum*; (Pseudo-Augustine), *De fide S. Trinitatis ad Petrum.* Gennadius, *Liber siue diffinitio ecclesiasticorum dogmatum.* Augustine, *Sententia de penitentia* (*Sermo* 351); *Sermo* 393. Additions, ?*s.* xii^{med}, fols 36v–9r: four anonymous sermons. Bound with the following items at an early date.	I	xii^{in} Durham

259	Durham Cathedral, B. IV. 12, fols 39–120	Prosper of Aquitaine, *De gratia Dei et libero arbitrio contra Collatorem; Pro Augustino responsiones ad capitula obiectionum Gallorum calumniantium; Pro Augustino responsiones ad excerpta Genuensium*. Augustine, *De octo Dulcitii quaestionibus*. Pseudo-Augustine, *Hypomnesticon contra Pelagianos et Caelestinos; Homeliae*. Augustine, *Sermones* (including *De natiuitate Iesu Christi*). Origen (trans. Jerome), *In Lucam*, 14 (*De circumcisione Domini*). Ambrose, *Expositio Euangelii secundum Lucam*, ii, 55–7. Pseudo-Augustine, *Sermo in natali Domini*. Augustine, *Sermones*. Pseudo-Ambrose, *De tribus difficilimis Salomonis liber*, inc.: '*Mirum satis est, dilectissimi fratres*'. Ambrose, *De mysteriis; De Spiritu Sancto* (prologue); *De apologia prophetae David*. Near-contemporary addition, fols 118v–20v: Pseudo-Augustine, *De essentia diuinitatis*. See note on previous item.	I	xii^in^ Durham
260	Durham Cathedral, B. IV. 12, fols 121–72	Augustine, *De quantitate animae; De praesentia Dei; De paradiso* (= *De Genesi ad litteram*, xii). See note on no. 258.	E	xii¹ Durham
261	Durham Cathedral, B. IV. 12, fols 173–87	Pseudo-Augustine, *Dialogus quaestionum lxv Orosii percontantis et Augustini respondentis*. See note on no. 258.	E	xii¹ Durham
262 †	Durham Cathedral, B. IV. 13	Gregory, *In Ezechielem*.	I	xi^ex^ (pre 1096) Durham
263	Durham Cathedral, B. IV. 14	John the Deacon, *Vita S. Gregorii*. Sulpicius Severus, *Vita S. Martini; Epistolae* (3); *Dialogi*. Gregory of Tours, *Miracula S. Martini*. John the Deacon, *Vita S. Nicholai*. John the Archdeacon of Bari, *Translatio S. Nicholai Barium* (account of the translation of Nicholas to Bari, 1087). Osbern, *Epistola de uita S. Dunstani; Vita S. Dunstani* (incomplete: ends at same point as London, British Library, Harley 56). Possidius, *Vita S. Augustini*. Near-contemporary additions: *Translatio S. Augustini Hipponensis* (inc.: '*Beatus Augustinus dum ypponensi sepultus esset regione*'); Pseudo-Leo, *Translatio S. Iacobi*. Too late in date to be identified with the '*Vitas patrum*' on William Carilef's book-list.	I(f)	xii^in^ (post 1087) Durham
264	Durham Cathedral, B. IV. 15	Isidore and Braulio bishop of Saragossa, *Epistolae*. Isidore, *Etymologiae*.	U	xii¹ Durham
265	Durham Cathedral, B. IV. 16, fols 1–44	Bede, *In Apocalypsin*.	A	xii¹ Durham

266	Durham Cathedral, B. IV. 18	*Decreta* (abridgement of Lanfranc's collection). Gregory, *Registrum epistolarum* (excerpts). Henry V, *Decretum*. Calixtus II, *Decretum de electionibus in Teutonico regno* (1122) Cyprian Gallus, *Cena* (incomplete). *Priuilegia papalia de statu ecclesiae Cantuariensis.* *Concilium Lateranensis* (1123). Additions, *s.* xii^{med}, fols 99–102: *Concilium Remensis* (1148). *Saec.* xii^{2}, fols 77–9: Hugh of St Victor, *De modo orandi*. *Saec.* xii^{ex}: papal bulls.		xii^{1} Canterbury, Christ Church; Durham
267	Durham Cathedral, B. IV. 22, fols 3–5	Annals.		xii^{1} (*c.* 1125) Durham
268 †	Durham Cathedral, B. IV. 24, fols 12–73	Usuardus, *Martyrologium* (obits added in the margins, *s.* xi^{ex}–xii^{in}). Lectionary of gospels for Chapter. Lanfranc, *Constitutiones*. William Carilef, *Epistola ad monachos Dunelmenses*. Additions: *s.* xi/xii, fols 6–11: Calendar without saints. *Saec.* xii^{1}, fol. 72r: liturgical ordinance.	U	xi^{ex} (pre 1096) Canterbury, Christ Church; Durham
269 †	Durham Cathedral, B. IV. 24, fols 74–127 (comprising two coeval sections as indicated)	**A)** (fols 74v–95r) *Regula S. Benedicti*. Additions: 74r, *s.* xi/xii, omitted portion of Prologue to *Regula*; William Carilef, *Epistola*; fol. 95v, *s.* xi/xii, *Regula* c. 62 previously omitted; fols 95v–6r, *s.* xii^{in}, Anselm, *Epistolae* (2); fol. 96r, *s.* xii^{1}, On types of monks; fol. 96r, *s.* xii^{med}, Bernard of Clairvaux, *Epistolae*; fol. 96v, *s.* xii^{med} (1154×59), Maundy ordinance. **B)** (fols 98v–123v) OE *Regula S. Benedicti*. Additions: fol. 124r, *s.* xii^{med}, Peter the Venerable, *Epistola*; fol. 124r–v, *s.* xii^{med}, Liturgica; fols. 126r–v, *s.* xi/xii, Liturgica; fol. 127r, *s.* xi/xii, Miscellaneous. NB: the two main items were clearly written separately, but probably as a pair.	U	xi^{2} (pre 1096) Durham
270	Durham Cathedral, B. IV. 37	*Excerpta* from patristic writers. *Excerpta* from Hrabanus Maurus and Amalarius of Metz. *Excerpta* from patristics and canon law.	U	xii^{1} Durham
271 ?	Durham Cathedral, C. III. 18	Suetonius, *De uita caesarum*. Ausonius, *Versus de duodecim imperatoribus Romanorum*. Date of arrival in England uncertain.	U	xi/xii ?Continent; Durham (late medieval provenance)
272	Durham Cathedral, C. IV. 7, fols 2–49	*Glossae super De inuentione rhetorica Ciceronis*, inc.: '*In primis materia et intentio huius Rethoris*'. *Glossae super De ratione dicendi ad Herennium pseudo-Ciceronis* ('*Etsi in familiaribus*'). Plato (trans. Chalcidius), *Timaeus*, with gloss. This and the following item are coeval but separable. They were clearly bound together by *s.* xii/xiii, *teste* the list of contents on fol. 1 (this also includes a now-lost '*Tractatus super Macrobium*' which preceded the Plato).		xii^{in} Durham
273	Durham Cathedral, C. IV. 7, fols 50–69	*Glossae in Arithmetica Boethii*. Diagrams with verses ('*Ignea uis terrae*'). See note on previous item.	D	xii^{in} Durham

274	Durham Cathedral, C. IV. 10	*Expositiones uerborum in historia Romanorum.* Marbod of Rennes, *De gemmis.* *Dialogus super symbolum Athanasii.* *Explanatio super Psychomachia Prudentii* (inc.: '*Prudentius tria habuisse nomina dicitur*'). *Expositio super uersus Sibyllae de aduentu Domini.* *Expositio super poemata Sedulii* (inc.: '*Sedulius primo laicus fuit*'). *Commentarium in De consolatione Philosophiae Boethii* (inc.: '*Alii auctores solebant prologos in libris suis prescribere*').		xii[1] Durham
275 †	Durham Cathedral, C. IV. 12, binding slips	*Homiliae* (frag.) Companion to Durham A. III. 29 and ? B. II. 2 (nos. 211 and 216).		xi[ex] (pre 1096) Durham
276 ?*	Durham Cathedral, C. IV. 15	*Annales Mettenses priores.* Regino of Prüm, *Libellus de temporibus dominicae incarnationis.*	U	xii[1] ?Continent; Durham
277	Durham Cathedral, Hunter 57	Augustine, *Sermo 350; In epistolam Iohannis ad Parthos tractatus x (De caritate).* Pseudo-Augustine (Quoduultdeus), *Contra quinque haereses* (= *sermo* 10).		xii[1] Hexham
278	Durham Cathedral, Hunter 100, fols 1–42	Isidore, *De natura rerum* (extract). Eugenius II of Toledo, *Versus de septem diebus.* Petrus Pictor (Pseudo-Hildebert), *Versus de decem plagis.* Tables. Calendar. Abbo of Fleury, *Computus.* ?Robert of Losinga, *Expositio de computo.* Tables; Schema. '*De die resurrectionis Christi*'. Dionysius Exiguus, *Epistolae duae de ratione festi paschae.* *Cyclus xxviii annorum* (with annals in margins). Guido of Arezzo, *Micrologus* (extracts). This and the following three items are coeval but separable sections.	D	xii[in] (1100–28) Durham
279	Durham Cathedral, Hunter 100, fols 43–84	Helperic, *De computo.* Bede, *De temporibus* (extract). '*De uertice mundi*'. Pseudo-Bede, *De signis caeli* (extract). *De planetis.* Abbo of Fleury, *De differentia circuli et spherae; 'De duplici ortu signorum dubitantes'; 'Explanatio tabulae'.* Isidore, *Etymologiae* (extract). *De qualitate et quantitate ponderum.* *Ratio ponderum medicinalium.* *De mensuris liquidis et pensis.* *De ponderibus.* Latin-Old English *Glossarium nominum planetarum.* See note on previous item.	D	xii[in] Durham

280	Durham Cathedral, Hunter 100, fols 85–101	*De quattuor humoribus corporis.* Isidore, *Etymologiae* (extract). Ambrose, *Hexaemeron* (extract). See note on no. 278. NB: at one stage this was the start of the compilation.		xii^{in} Durham
281	Durham Cathedral, Hunter 100, fols 102–20	*Remedia.* *De herbis medicinalibus.* *De quattuor humoribus.* *Medicina.* See note on no. 278.	D	xii^{in} Durham
282	Durham University Library, Cosin V. ii. 2, fols 148–74	Augustine, *Contra Iulianum* (IV–VI).	U	xii^{in}
283 §	Durham University Library, Cosin V. ii. 6	Symeon of Durham, *Prefatio.* List of Bishops of Durham to Ranulph Flambard (with subsequent additions). List of Monks of Durham (with subsequent additions). Symeon of Durham, *Libellus de exordio atque procursu istius, hoc est ecclesiae Dunelmensis.* Additions: *s.* xii^{in}: Continuation of Symeon to 1114; *s.* xii^{med}, continuation to Bishop William of St Barbe (1143–52). See PLATE 9.	I(f)	xii^{in} (?1104–09) Durham
284 ?†	Durham University Library, Cosin V. v. 6	Gradual (Prosae de sanctis; Kyriale; Laudes regiae; Graduale; Kyriale; Tonale; Antiphoner; Prosae) [mutilated]. Additions, *s.* xi/xii, fols 2r–8v, Proses; *s.* xii^{in+}, fols. 123v–8, Antiphons and proses.	XI	xi^{ex} (?1079×96) Canterbury, Christ Church; Durham
285 †	Edinburgh, National Library of Scotland, Adv. 18. 2. 4	Paul the Deacon, *Homiliarium* (Homilies from Holy Saturday to the Fourth Sunday after Epiphany) (contents inventoried in Richards, *Texts and Traditions*, pp. 104–8).	I(f)	xii^{1} Rochester
286 †	Edinburgh, National Library of Scotland, Adv. 18. 3. 9	Pseudo-Hegesippus, *Historiae libri V de bello iudaico.*	X	xii^{1} Rochester
287	Edinburgh, National Library of Scotland, Adv. 18. 4. 3, fols 1–83	Palladius, *Historia Lausiaca* (Heraclides, *Paradisus* recension). Victor of Vita, *Historia persecutionis Africanae prouinciae.*	X; A	xi^{ex} (pre 1096) Durham
288	Edinburgh, National Library of Scotland, Adv. 18. 4. 3, fols 84–120	Paschasius Radbertus, *De corpore et sanguine Domini* (which embodies Augustine, *Sermo* 52).		xi^{ex} Durham
289	Edinburgh, National Library of Scotland, Adv. 18. 4. 3, fols 123–49	Guitmund of Aversa, *De corpore et sanguine Domini contra Berengarium.* Augustine, *De sacramentis altaris.*		xi^{ex} Durham

290	Edinburgh, National Library of Scotland, Adv. 18. 6. 12	Persius, *Saturae.* Avianus, *Fabulae.* 'Cato nouus' (= *Disticha Catonis* (incomplete)). Unidentified stanza. *Gesta Ludouici imperatoris.* *'Exemplarii uersus'* (from Horace, *Epistolae*). William of St Hilary, *Contra Clementem* (Anti-pope 1080, 1084–1100). *'Versus maligni angeli'.* Marbod of Rennes, *Vas fractum.* 2 *differentiae.* Mock epithet of a cleric; epigram; 3 riddles. Abbo of Saint-Germain, *Bella Parisiacae urbis* (extracts). Symphosius, *Aenigmata* (incomplete).	A	xii^{in} Thorney
291	Edinburgh, National Library of Scotland, Adv. 18. 7. 8	Cicero, *Orationes in Catilinam.* Sallust (attrib.), *Inuectiua in Ciceronem.* Pseudo-Atticus, *Regula formata.* On Greek letters. NB: this is a palimpsest, for which parts of at least five English MSS, ranging in date from *s.* viii–xi, were used.	A	xi^{ex} Thorney
292 †	Eton College, 80	Jerome, *Contra Iouinianum.*	E	xii^{1} (pre ?1124) Rochester
293 ⋆	Eton College, 97	*Decreta pontificum et concilia.*		xii^{in} Normandy; Exeter
—	Eton College, 220, 1	*See* Oxford, All Souls College, SR 80. G.8		
294	Exeter Cathedral, 3500	Exon. Domesday. Includes work by Salisbury scribes.	U	xi^{ex} (*c.* 1086)
295	Exeter Cathedral, 3512	*Decreta pontificum* (Lanfranc's collection). *Capitula Angilramni.* Proceedings of the Council of Rome (1059). Berengar's Recantation at the Council of Rome (1079). Probably made as the companion to Oxford, Bodleian Library, Bodley 810 (no. 698).	U	xii^{in} Exeter
296 ⋆	Exeter Cathedral, 3520, pp. 1–232	Anselm, *De ueritate; De libertate arbitrii; De casu Diaboli; De incarnatione Verbi; Cur Deus homo; Meditatio animae christianae; De conceptu uirginali et originali peccato; Epistola de sacrificio azimi et fermentati; 'Quomodo grammaticus sit substantia et qualitas'* (*De grammatico*); *Orationes.*	U	xii^{in} France; Exeter
297 ?⋆	Exeter Cathedral, 3520, pp. 232–477	Ambrose, *De mysteriis; De sacramentis.* Eusebius Gallicanus, *De Septuagesima* (*Sermo* 16). Lanfranc, *De corpore et sanguine Domini aduersus Berengarium Turonensem* (embodying attributed quotations from Ambrose, Augustine, Cyprian, Gregory, Jerome and Paul). Guitmund of Aversa, *De corpore et sanguine Domini contra Berengarium.*	U	xii^{in} ?Normandy; Exeter

298	Exeter Cathedral, 3525	Pseudo-Augustine, *Tractatus 'Licet multi'; Dialogus quaestionum lxv Orosii percontantis et Augustini respondentis.* Augustine, *De Genesi contra Manichaeos* (Bk II, chs 28–9). *Excerpta* (from Jerome, Sallust, and Jordanes). Prosper of Aquitaine, *Pro Augustino responsiones ad capitula obiectionum Gallorum calumniantium.* *Sermo de ecclesiastico ordine et figura.* *Sermo de dedicatione ecclesiae.* *Sententiae.* Augustine, *De paenitentia* (excerpts). Significations from Genesis-Kings.	U	xii^{in}
299	Florence, Biblioteca Medicea Laurenziana, Plut. xii. 17	Augustine, *Retractatio*; *De ciuitate Dei.* Lanfranc, *Notae* on *De ciuitate Dei.*	I(f)	xii^{in} ?Canterbury, St Augustine's
300	Geneva, Biblioteca Bodmeriana, Bodmer 2	Ælfric, Homily (frag.).	–	xi^{2}
301	Glasgow, University Library, Hunter 85 (T. 4. 2), fols 11–34	*Tabulae paschales* (with marginal addition, *s.* xii^{in}: the *Annales Lindisfarnenses et Dunelmenses*). '*De ratione computi*' = Dialogue version of Bede, *De temporum ratione.*		xii^{in} Durham
302	Glasgow, University Library, Hunter 85 (T. 4. 2), fols 35+	Bede, *De temporum ratione; Epistola ad Wicthedum de uernali equinocto.* Dionysius Exiguus, *Epistolae duae de ratione festi paschae.* Walcher of Great Malvern, *De lunationibus* (1092 +). Abbo of Fleury, *Computus; De differentia circuli et spherae.* *Tabula lunationum lxxvi annorum.* Near contemporary addition: Hyginus, *Poetica astronomica* (incomplete).	I(f)	xii^{1} Durham
303 ?	Glasgow, University Library, Hunter 431 (V. 5. 1), fols 6, 102v–58	Supplement to a defective *s.* xii^{in} copy of Gregory, *Regula pastoralis* (which was also carefully corrected at this time).		xii^{in} Worcester
304	Hereford Cathedral, O. I. 8	Gospels. ?Perhaps made at St Albans.	D	xii^{1} Hereford
305	Hereford Cathedral, O. II. 7	Canon law collection ('Flores canonum Niceni'). *Decreta* (including abridged version of Burchard of Worms, *Decreta*). Additions, *s.* xii^{1}, fols 150v–2: Council of London (1108); Council of Westminster (1125); Council of Westminster (1127).	A	xii^{in} Hereford
306 ?*	Hereford Cathedral, O. II. 9	Gennadius, *Liber siue diffinitio ecclesiasticorum dogmatum.* Tract, 'De Genesi'. Theological notes and excerpts. Haimo of Auxerre (Pseudo-Haimo of Halberstadt), *In Cantica Canticorum.* Jerome, *Epistola* 108; *Vita S. Pauli.* Isidore, *Chronica.* Eutropius, *Breuiarium historiae romanae ab urbe condita.*	I	xii^{in} ?Normandy; Hereford

307	Hereford Cathedral, O. III. 1	Prosper of Aquitaine, *Epistola ad Rufinum de gratia et libero arbitrio.* Augustine, *De octo Dulcitii quaestionibus; De praedestinatione sanctorum; De uera religione; De gratia et libero arbitrio.* Sermones (7 for Nativity, 2 for Circumcision, 3 for Epiphany, including 6 by or attributed to Augustine).	U	xii^{in} Gloucester
308	Hereford Cathedral, O. IV. 5	*Decreta pontificum* (Lanfranc's collection). Companion to Hereford Cathedral, P. II. 8 (no. 317).	A	xii^{1} Hereford
309	Hereford Cathedral, O. VI. 11	Paschasius Radbertus (Pseudo-Jerome), *De assumptione BVM.* Jerome, *Epistolae* (39, 31, 54, 22). Sulpicius Severus, *Prologus; Vita S. Martini; Epistolae* (I, III). Gregory of Tours, extracts relating to Martin (ex *De uirtutibus S. Martini* and *Historia Francorum*); *Vita S. Bricii* (ex *Historia Francorum*, II, 1). Sulpicius Severus, *Dialogi* (II, III, I). Guitmund of Aversa, *Confessio de Sancta Trinitate, Christi humanitate corporisque et sanguinis Domini nostri ueritate.* Pseudo-Faustus (Odo of Glanfeuil), *Vita S. Mauri.*	E/I	xi/xii–xii^{in} Hereford (St Guthlac)
310	Hereford Cathedral, O. VIII. 8	*Decreta pontificum et concilia* (Lanfranc's collection).	U	xi/xii Hereford
311	Hereford Cathedral, O. IX. 2	Bible (I–IV Regum; Isaias-Ierem., Ezech., Dan., Prophetae minores). Presumably part of a multi-volume bible, none of the rest of which is known to survive. Additions, fol. 203^{v}, *s.* xii^{2} three *versus*; *s.* xii/xiii one *versus*.	I(f)	xi/xii
312	Hereford Cathedral, P. I. 3	Augustine, *De agone christiano.* Genealogies of Kings of France and Dukes of Normandy. *Versus* ('*Sentiat orantem*', '*Rolliger expecta*', '*Qui sunt felices*', '*Si uellet generi*'). Augustine, *De uera religione; De gratia et libero arbitrio.* Anselm, *Epistolae* (65, 2, 37).	I(f)	xii^{in} Gloucesrer
313	Hereford Cathedral, P. I. 5	Augustine, *De natura et origine animae.* *Sermo Arianorum.* Pseudo-Augustine (Syagrius), *Contra sermonem Arianorum.* Augustine, *Contra aduersarium legis et prophetarum.*	U/E	xii^{1} Gloucester
314	Hereford Cathedral, P. I. 10	Didymus of Alexandria (trans. Jerome), *De Spiritu Sancto.* Pseudo-Augustine, *Dialogus quaestionum lxv Orosii percontantis et Augustini respondentis*; (Vigilius of Thapsus) *Contra Felicianum.* Augustine, *De orando Deo.* Anon., '*Sunt quidem sanctae Dei ecclesiae inimici*'. Augustine, *Sermo* 37. Anon., '*Ferunt autem physici natum*'. Augustine, *De octo Dulcitii quaestionibus.*	I	xi/xii–xii^{in} ?Durham

315	Hereford Cathedral, P. II. 5, fols 1–145	**A)** (fols 1–95) Palladius, *Historia Lausiaca* (Heraclides, *Paradisus* recension). **B)** (fols 96–145) Leontius Neapolitanus (trans. Anastasius Bibliothecarius), *Vita S. Iohannis Eleemosynarii.* John the Deacon, *Vita S. Nicholai.* Although the same scribe was responsible both for the end of section A and for the start of section B, the presence of an original quire signature 'iii' on fol. 127^{v} (the correct place if 96 was a new start) and the blank leaves at the end of the final quire of A (93^{v}–95^{v}) show that the two parts were written as separate, albeit matching, volumes.	E A	**A** xi^{ex} **B** xi^{ex}
316	Hereford Cathedral, P. II. 5, fols 146–54	*Passio S. Margaritae.* Odo of Cluny, *Vita S. Mariae Magdalenae.*	E/U	xii^{in}
317	Hereford Cathedral, P. II. 8	*Canones* (Lanfranc's collection). Companion to Hereford Cathedral, O. IV. 5 (no. 308).	A/I	xii^{1} Hereford
318	Hereford Cathedral, P. IV. 11	Ambrose, *De officiis ministrorum.*	U	xii^{in} Hereford
319	Hereford Cathedral, P. V. 1, fols 1–28	Lanfranc, *Constitutiones.* Pseudo-Augustine (Vigilius of Thapsus), *Contra Felicianum Arianum.*	E	xi/xii Battle
320	Hereford Cathedral, P. V. 1, fols 29–152 with Oxford, Bodleian Library, e Mus. 93	**A)** (Hereford) Bede, *Historia ecclesiastica.* Cuthbert, *Epistola de obitu Bedae.* Addition, *s.* xii$^{3/4}$, fol. 152v: List of Archbishops of Canterbury to Theobald, with subsequent additions. **B)** (Oxford) '*Breuis relatio de Willelmo nobilissimo comite Normannorum*' (frag.). Originally also contained: '*De constructione ecclesiae Belli*'. 'Nennius' (attrib.), *Historia Brittonum.*	I	xii^{1} Battle
321	Hereford Cathedral, P. VIII. 4	Augustine, *Epistolae* (132, 135, 137, 136, 138, 92, 143, 81–2, 41, 233–5, 98, 25, 27, 30–1, 24, 32, 109, 243, 26, 16–17, 127, 214, 93, 102, 185, 154–5, 152–3, 117–18, 149, 90–1, 23, 173, 164, 130, 147, 101, 165, 199, 266, 99, 58, 110, 77–8, 122, 245, 260–1, 264, 188, 145, 248, 205, 33, 21, 38, 112, 232, 242, 3, 18, 20, 19, 15, 5–7, 9–10, 4, 141, 46–7, 258, 131, 190, 43, 105, App. 1–7, App. 11–16, App. 8–10, 189, 34–5, 52, 76, 88, 51, 66, 238–41, 150, 228, 147, Pseudo-Augustine, *Sermo 'Ad Italicum'*, 139, 134, 133, 176, 49, 87, 44, 53, 89, 148, 262, 196, 80).	I	xii^{1} ?Winchcombe
322	Hereford Cathedral, P. IX. 5	Augustine, *In Euangelium Iohannis.* Possidius, *Vita S. Augustini.*	I	xii^{1} ?Winchcombe
323	Hereford Cathedral, P. IX. 7, fol. i	Antiphoner (frag.).	–	xii^{in} Hereford
324	Hertford, Hertfordshire Record Office, Gorhambury X.D.4.B and X.D.4.C	Homiliary or Lectionary (frag.).	–	xi^{2}

325	Hildesheim, St Godehard's Church, 1, + Cologne, Schütgen Museum, 5 (a single leaf)	**A)** (pp. 2–15) Calendar; Computistical tables. **B)** (pp. 17–56) Pictorial cycle (scenes from Old Testament, Life of Christ, Life of St Martin of Tours). **C)** (pp. 57–72) *Chanson* of St Alexis (in French); Drawing of scenes from Life of St Alexis. Near-contemporary addition: Gregory, '*Ratio picturarum*' (extracted from *epistolae*), followed by French translation of the same. Drawings of Journey to Emmaus, King David as musician. **D)** (pp. 73–414) Psalter (Gallican); Canticles; Creeds; Litany; Prayers. (pp. 416–17) Miniatures of the martyrdom of St Albans, David with musicians. Comprises four separable sections, as indicated.	D D D D	xii^{1} St Albans; ?Christina of Markyate; Markyate
326	Le Havre, Bibliothèque Municipale, 330	Missal (incomplete).	U	xi$^{3/4}$ Winchester, New Minster
327	Leiden, Universiteits-bibliotheek, B.P.L. 114B	Priscian, *Institutiones grammaticae.*	I(f)	xii^{1} St Albans
328	Lincoln Cathedral, 1 (A. 1. 2)	Bible (Genesis-Job). Additions: fol. 207r, *s.* xii$^{2/4}$, List of psalms for daily recitation; fol. 2r, *s.* xii^{2+}, Book-list; fols 204v–6v, *s.* xii^{2}, Calendar; fol. 207, *s.* xii^{ex}, List of canons of Lincoln. Companion to Cambridge, Trinity College, B. 5. 2 (no. 154).	I(f)	xi/xii (pre 1110) Lincoln (the donation of Nicholas, archdeacon of Huntingdon: *teste s.* xii^{med} inscription, fol. 2r)
329	Lincoln Cathedral, 7 (A. 1. 20), fols 1–43	Sulpicius Severus, *Vita S. Martini; Epistolae; Dialogi.* John the Deacon, *Vita S. Nicholai.* *'Miracula S. Nicholai.'*	X; A	xii^{1} Lincoln
330	Lincoln Cathedral, 9 (A. 1. 22)	Augustine, *In euangelium Iohannis.*	I	xii^{in} Lincoln
331	Lincoln Cathedral, 13 (A. 1. 26)	Augustine, *Retractatio; De Genesi ad litteram; De Genesi contra Manicheos.* Pseudo-Augustine, *Dialogus quaestionum lxv Orosii percontantis et Augustini respondentis.*	E	xi/xii Lincoln
332	Lincoln Cathedral, 52 (A. 6. 3), fols 1, 231–2	Collectar (frag.).	A/I	xii^{in}
333	Lincoln Cathedral, 74 (B. 3. 5)	Gregory, *Moralia in Iob* (I–X). Companion to Lincoln Cathedral, 75–6 (nos. 334–5).	I(f)	xii^{1} Lincoln

334	Lincoln Cathedral, 75 (A. 3. 3)	Gregory, *Moralia in Iob* (XI–XXII). Companion to Lincoln Cathedral, 74 and 76 (nos. 333 and 335).	I	xii^1 Lincoln
335	Lincoln Cathedral, 76 (B. 2. 1)	Gregory, *Moralia in Iob* (XXIII–XXXV). Companion to Lincoln Cathedral, 74–5 (nos. 333–4).	I	xii^1 Lincoln
336	Lincoln Cathedral, 89 (A. 3. 16)	Gregory, *In Ezechielem.*	A	xii^1 Lincoln
337	Lincoln Cathedral, 90 (A. 3. 17)	Augustine, *Sermones de uerbis domini et apostoli.*	I(f)	xii^1 Lincoln
338	Lincoln Cathedral, 134 (C. 5. 10), fols 1–30, 85–125	Ambrose, *De mysteriis; De sacramentis.* Eusebius Gallicanus, *Sermo* 16; '*De Septuagesima*'.	E	xii^{in} Lincoln
339	Lincoln Cathedral, 134, fols 31–84	Fulbert of Chartres, *Epistolae; Opuscula.*	U	xii^{in} Lincoln
340 ? *	Lincoln Cathedral, 158 (C. 2. 2)	Paul the Deacon, *Homiliarium* (Lent to Easter vigil, Sanctorale 25 Jan. to 30 Nov., Commune sanctorum) [contents inventoried in Richards, *Texts and Traditions*, pp. 98–101].	U	xi^{ex} Normandy or England; Lincoln
341	Lincoln Cathedral, 161 (B. 2. 3)	*Decreta pontificum et concilia* (Lanfranc's collection).	I(f)	xii^{in} Lincoln
342	Lincoln Cathedral, 196, fols 1–62	Adalbert of Metz, *Speculum Gregorii.*	A/I	xii^{in} Missenden
343	Lincoln Cathedral, 214, fols 1–8	Pseudo-Ambrose, *Libellus de dignitate sacerdotali.*	U	xii^1
344	Lincoln Cathedral, 214, fols 9–160	Augustine, *Confessiones.*	A	xii^1
345	Lincoln Cathedral, 220, fols 1–44	Alexander, Commentary on Hippocrates, *Aphorismi.* '*Si febricitanti tumore*'; '*Quid est incephalus*'.	E	xii^{in} ?Norwich
346	Lincoln Cathedral, 220, fols 45–61	Pliny the Younger, *De diuersis medicinis.* Sermon on St Patrick (frag.).	U	xii^{in} ?Norwich
347	Lincoln Cathedral, 298, B	OE Heptateuch (frag. = one bifolium).	–	xi^2

348 ★ ?	London, British Library, Add. 19835	Heiric of Auxerre's '*Collectanea*' including: Suetonius, *De uita caesarum* (short extracts on Julius Caesar, Antonius, Tiberius, Germanicus, Nero, Vitellius, Vespasian, Titus and Domitian) followed by two short extracts from Orosius, *Historiae aduersus paganos* (on Trajan and Iouinianus). Valerius Maximus, *Factorum et dictorum memorabilium libri* (extracts). *Sententiae philosophorum* (start). *Scolia quaestionum.* Treatise on Greek alphabet. Treatise, *De uirtute.* Fulbert of Chartres, *Epistolae; Sermones* ('*De natiuitate et uita* BVM'; '*De purificatione* BVM'). Liturgical directions. *Dicta super Psalmos* (ex Jerome and Augustine) (incomplete). ?Written by a Norman scribe some of whose other works were demonstrably in England at an early date.	E/A	xi/xii Normandy or England
349	London, British Library, Add. 22719	Constantinus Africanus, *Liber pantegni* (particula i–x) to which was appended (fols 161^{v}–163^{v}) as part of the original copying: Nemesius, *De elementis* (from the Latin version of his *De natura hominus*). Constantinus Africanus, *Liber pantegni* (practical books). Near contemporary additions: a) 163^{v}–164^{r}, Recipes; b) 200^{v} Qusta ibn Luqa, *De physicis ligaturis* (Latin version of Arabic original).	E	xii^{1} Battle; Exeter, St Nicholas
350	London, British Library, Add. 34652, fol. 3	Chrodegang, *Regula canonicorum* in Latin and OE (frag.).	–	xi^{2}
351	London, British Library, Add. 34652, fol. 6	Bible (frag.: Song of Songs; Wisdom capitula).	–	xii^{in}
352	London, British Library, Add. 34652, fol. 13	Augustine, *Enarrationes in Psalmos* (frag.)	–	xii^{1}
353	London, British Library, Add. 38130	*Vita S. Neoti; Translatione S. Neoti*; *Sermones de translatione S. Neoti.* Abbo of Fleury, dedicatory epistle to St Dunstan (from *Vita S. Edmundi*) (incomplete). Bede, *Historia ecclesiastica.*	U	xii^{1}
354	London, British Library, Add. 46204, plus Cott. Nero E. i, vol. II, fols 181–4	Worcester cartulary (frag.: five leaves and two part-leaves).	–	xi^{ex} Worcester
355	London, British Library, Arundel 16, fols 1–37, and 41–5	Osbern, *Epistola de uita S. Dunstani; Vita S. Dunstani.* According to the 1389 Dover catalogue, there then followed: Osbern, *Vita S. Æphegi*; *Translatio Ælphegi*. Eadmer, *Vita S. Odonis.*	I(f)	xi/xii Canterbury, Christ Church; Dover (by *s.* xiv)

356	London, British Library, Arundel 60	Calendar; Computistica; Psalter; Canticles; Litany; Prayers. Continuous interlinear OE gloss to the Psalms and Canticles. Additions: fols 133–42, *s.* xi^{ex}, Collects and Prayers; fol. 149, s. xi^{ex} (*c.* 1099): Six Ages of the World (in Latin and OE); List of Bishops of Winchester.	D	xi^{2} Winchester, New Minster
357	London, British Library, Arundel 91	Passional, 21 September – 9 November (one part of a seven-volume set). Near-contemporary addition, fols 227v–9v: '*Lectiones de Sancto Nicholao*'. List of contents, fol. 1v, added *s.* xii/xii. Companion and predecessor to Oxford, Bodleian Library, Fell 2 (no. 724).	I(f)	xii^{in} Canterbury, St Augustine's
358	London, British Library, Arundel 155, corrections and additions	Extensive corrections and additions to a Psalter with Calendar, Tables, Preface, Canticles and Prayers which was originally written (by Eaduuius Basan) 1012×1023. Original work = fols 2–136r (135v–6r entirely re-written *s.* xii^{2}) and 171–191v/18. Two scribes added: i) 191v/19–192v/6, further prayers, *s.* xi^{med}; ii) 192v/7–193v: hymn for feast days, creeds, prayer, *s.* xi^{med+}. Eaduuius's prayers and those of scribe ii above (= 171r/21–192v/6) received an interlinear OE gloss *s.* xi^{med+}. Eaduuius's psalter text was extensively corrected *in rasura* (from Romanum to Gallicanum) *s.* xi^{2+}. Further corrections to the psalter text *s.* xii^{med+}. Additional section of prayers, litany, hymns added *s.* xii^{2} (= fols 137r–44v, 147r–70v, plus 136v and the rewritten 135r/18–136r). Late medieval supplement: 145v–6v.	–	xi^{2+} Canterbury Christ Church
359	London, British Library, Arundel 180	Guitmund of Aversa, *De corpore et sanguine Domini contra Berengarium.* Augustine, *De sacramentis altaris* (*Sermo* 52).	E	xii^{1}
360	London, British Library, Arundel 181 (bound with Arundel 180)	Paschasius Radbertus, '*De sacramento eucharistiae*' (= *De corpore et sanguine Domini*). Pseudo-Basil, *Monita ad monachos (Admonitio ad filium spiritualem).*	E	xii^{1}
361 §	London, British Library, Arundel 235	Hugh of Langres, *Commentarium in Psalmos*, inc.: '*Iste liber apud Hebreos intitulatur liber hymnorum, apud latinos psalterium. Est aut(em) ymn(us) laus d(e)i metrice co(m)posita*'. See PLATES 6–7.	U	xi^{ex}
362	London, British Library, Burney 277, fol. 42	Laws of Alfred and Ine (OE) (frag.: severely damaged bifolium).	–	xi^{2}

363	London, British Library, Burney 357	Mico of St Riquier, *Alphabetum uocabulorum* (incomplete). Peter Damian (Pseudo-Jerome, Pseudo-Bede), *De quindecim signis ante diem iudicii.* Eugenius II of Toledo, *De decem plagis Ægypti monosticha* (extract). Anon., *De iisdem plagis uersus quinque heroici.* *Oratio ad Iesum Christum.* *De partibus hominis.* Anselm, *De conceptu uirginali et originali peccato.* Sygerius Lucanus, *Versus in sanctorum laudem monachorum.* Anon., *De diluuio Noe tractatulus.* *Canticum sacrum* (Canticles). *Officii cuiusdam ordo fortassis in festo S. Juliani.* Hugh of St Victor, *Institutiones in Decalogum legis.* Anon., *Meditationes de amore Iesu Christi* (incomplete).		$xii^{2/4}$ Thame
364	London, British Library, Cott. Appendix 26	Augustine, *Retractatio; De doctrina christiana.* Ambrose, *Preces; De officiis ministrorum.* Gregory, *Moralia in Iob* (short extracts). Augustine, short extracts from: *De perfectione iustitiae hominis; De correptione et gratia; De dono perseuerantiae; De doctrina christiana; Enchiridion; In epistolam Iohannis; De libero arbitrio.*	U	xii^{1}
365	London, British Library, Cott. Appendix 56, fols 1–4 with Cott. Vesp. E. iv, fols 203–10	Augustine, *De doctrina christiana* (frag.). *Epistolae episcoporum* (Lanfranc, Thomas of York, Anselm). Anselm (attrib.), '*De malo et nihilo*'.	–	xii^{1} Worcester
366	London, British Library, Cott. Appendix 56, fols 5–60	Pseudo-Augustine, *Hypomnesticon contra Pelagianos et Celestianos.* Athanasius (attrib.), *De processione Spiritus Sancti.*	U	xii^{in}
367	London, British Library, Cott. Calig. A. viii, fols 59–101	Eadmer, *Vita S. Wilfridi.* Goscelin, *Vita S. Werburgae.*	I	xii^{1} Ely
368	London, British Library, Cott. Calig. A. viii, fols 121–4	*Vita S. Birini* (frag.).	I(f)	xii^{in} ?Winchester; Ely
369	London, British Library, Cott. Calig. A. viii, fols 125–8	Wulfstan of Winchester, *Vita S. Æthelwoldi* (frag.).	–	xii^{in} ?Winchester; Ely

370	London, British Library, Cott. Calig. A. xv, fols 120–53 with Egerton 3314	**A)** [Caligula] *Computistica* (mainly in OE). Annals (in OE and Latin) concerned with Christ Church written in one phase to 1073; subsequent additions. Short notes. Ælfric, *De temporibus anni* (OE) (extracts). **B)** [Egerton] Instructions and verses for locating Easter and moveable feasts. Hermannus Contractus, *De computo*, cc. 1–24. *Ratio Gaii Caesaris de ordine anni.* Astronomical calendar. Easter Tables [with later additions]. *De locis septem embolismorum.* Notes on Computus based on Bede. Notes on Computus and Astronomy from, *inter alios*, Bede, Isidore, and Hrabanus. Egerton additions: Fols 1–8, *s.* xii^{ex}: Salomon of Canterbury, Notes on Computus. Fol. 18r, *s.* xii^{med}: *Histis mortiferam cogniscite uersibus horam.* Fol. 34r, *s.* xi/xii: list of Archbishops of Canterbury to Anselm. Subsequently continued to Richard of Dover (1174). Fols 73–5, *s.* xii/xiii: *Quomodo inueniri possint concurrentes et data cuiuslibet anni per manum.* (Includes diagrams). Further late medieval additions, not itemised here.	D D	xi^2 (*c.* 1073) Canterbury, Christ Church
371	London, British Library, Cott. Claud. A. i, fols 41–157	Paulinus, deacon of Milan, *Vita S. Ambrosii.* *Inuentio SS. Geruasii et Protasii.* *Inuentio corporis S. Nazarii.* Pseudo-Sebastian of Monte Cassino, *Vita S. Hieronymi.* Venantius Fortunatus, *Vita et uirtutes S. Hilarii; Epistola ad Pascentium papam.* Hilary, *Epistola; Sermo in depositione Honorati.* Pseudo-Ildefonsus (Pseudo-Jerome), *De natiuitate Dei genetricis semperque uirginis Mariae.* *Conuersio Mariae Egyptiacae.* *Vita S. Martialis.* Leontius Neapolitanus (trans. Anastasius Bibliothecarius), *Vita S. Iohannis Eleemosynarii.* Bede, *Vita S. Cuthberti* (prose).	A	xii^{in}
372	London, British Library, Cott. Claud. D. ix, fols 7–239	*Decreta pontificum et concilia* (Lanfranc's collection).	A	xii^1 ??Bath

373 ?*	London, British Library, Cott. Claud. E. v	*Decreta pontificum* (Pseudo-Isidore: *not* Lanfranc's abridgement) followed by (231v ff.): [Gregory], *Libellus responsionum; Epistola Mellito* (Bede, *Historia ecclesiastica* I, 27 and I, 30). Privileges for Canterbury. Papal decrees. Berengar's Recantation at the Council of Rome. Papal letters to Lanfranc, Anselm, Henry I, Gerard of York, and Ralph d'Escures concerning the Canterbury-York dispute (*post* 1119×22). Tables of the Kings of Israel and Judah. The script of fols 1–232 (Qq. I–XXIX) looks continental, while fols 233–56 (Qq. XXX–XXXII) are written in a Christ Church hand. However the decorated initials which occur up to fol. 93r are in a Christ Church style, and the text of the *Libellus responsionum* (fols 231v–4v) straddles the 'join'. Seemingly, the volume was either largely the work of a continental scribe at Canterbury, or was a continental import which was decorated and augmented at Christ Church.	I(f)	xii^{1} (fols 233–56 = after 1119×22) ??Continent; Canterbury, Christ Church
374	London, British Library, Cott. Cleop. A. vii, fols 107–47	Helperic, *De computo.* Addition, *s.* xii$^{2/4}$, fols 143v–7v plus the supplementary 148: Tract comparing Roman and Arabic computus, inc., '*In singulis igitur lunationibus* . . .'. This has A/E.	U A/E	xi^{ex}
375	London, British Library, Cott. Cleop. D. i, fols 129–98	Solinus, *Collectanea rerum memorabilium.* Late contents list shows that this was once followed by Aethicus Ister, *Cosmographia.* NB: This is the third part of a composite volume whose other parts — fols 2–82* (*s.* xi^{1}, England or France) and fols 83–128** (*?s.* x, Continent) — are of Canterbury, St Augustine's provenance. The appearance of fols 129–98, especially the initial, suggests that it is of St Augustine's origin.	A	xii^{in} ?Canterbury, St Augustine's
376	London, British Library, Cott. Cleop. E. i, fols 17–38, and 40–57	**A)** (Fols 40–57) Papal letters to English kings and bishops. *Narratio de Thoma Eboracensi.* Council of Winchester (1072). Lanfranc, *Epistola.* Alexander II (Pope), *Epistola.* Council of London (1075). Paschal II (Pope), *Epistolae* (to Anselm and Gerard of York). Anselm, *Epistolae.* Paschal, *Epistolae.* Addition, *s.* xii$^{2/4}$, fols 56–7: Alexander II, *Epistola* (to Baldwin of Bury St Edmunds). **B)** (fols 17–38) *Professiones episcoporum Angliae et Cambriae et abbatiarum Cantiae.* (Hand changes on 32r for Everard of Norwich (1121), also Gregory of Dublin (1121). Additions continuing to xii$^{3/4}$: Walter abbot of Boxley, Kent (1162×4). Later addition: Lawrence of Rochester (1250). Both parts were produced to the same format; their original order was as given above.	I(f)	xii^{1} (1120–1) Canterbury, Christ Church
377	London, British Library, Cott. Dom. vii, additions	Durham *Liber Vitae*: substantial additions to book started *s.* ix$^{2/4}$. Additions continued into the later Middle Ages.	U	xi^{2+} Durham

378	London, British Library, Cott. Dom. viii, fols 30–70	Anglo-Saxon Chronicle 'F', with Latin version of each annal.	U	xi/xii Canterbury, Christ Church
379	London, British Library, Cott. Dom. ix, fol. 9	Anglo-Saxon Chronicle (frag.): annals for 1113 and 1114.	U	xii^{1}
380	London, British Library, Cott. Faust. A. v, fols 24–97	Symeon of Durham, *Libellus de exordio atque procursu istius, hoc est ecclesiae Dunelmensis*	I	xii^{in} ?Durham; Fountains (by *s.* xiii^{in})
381	London British Library, Cott. Faust. A. v, fols 99–102	Peter Damian (Pseudo-Jerome; Pseudo-Bede), *De xv signis praecedentibus diem iudicii.* Pseudo-Augustine, *De antichristo.*	U	xii^{in}
382	London, British Library, Cott. Faust. A. ix	OE Homilies (including twenty-two from Ælfric, *Sermones Catholici*).	E	xii^{1}
383	London, British Library, Cott. Faust. A. x, fols 3–101	Ælfric, *Grammar; Glossary.* Additions *s.* xi^{2}–xii, fols 100v–101v: Proverbs and Maxims (in Latin and OE); Grammatical dialogue, '*Prima declinatio quot litteras terminales habet?*' Extensive annotation of the text in Latin, French and English, *s.* xii^{2}; it seems to have been with the originally separate fols 102–51 (no. 384) by this date.	U	xi$^{3/4}$??Worcester (same scribe as Oxford, Bodleian Library, Hatton 115 (no. 729) which was at Worcester by *s.* xiii)
384	London, British Library, Cott. Faust. A. x, fols 102–51	OE *Regula S. Benedicti*. Æthelwold of Winchester, OE account of the monastic revival (incomplete). (Added in the margins on fols 148–9 are five extracts from Ælfric's homily on Gregory the Great, marked for insertion.) Very extensive additions in the margins, esp. on fols 102–111, 147v, and 149r–51v *s.* xii^{med}, including: ?Roger of Caen, '*Quid deceat monachum . . .*' (34 lines: fol. 105r). Theological notes quoting Augustine and Peter Abelard. Maxims. NB: the earlier, separate, fols 3–101 (no. 383) were also heavily annotated, suggesting that the two items had a common provenance in *s.* xii, which is conceivably Worcester.	E	xii^{1} Though too distant to merit even a tentative ascription here, the volume has a tenuous connection with Worcester via its association with no. 383.
385	London, British Library, Cott. Faust. B. iii, fol. 158	Chronological Table (a list of emperors to Constantine IV (668–85)).	–	xii^{1}

386	London, British Library, Cott. Faust. B. vi, fols 95, 98–100	*Epistolae paparum* (on jurisdictions and privileges of Canterbury and York).	–	xii^in Canterbury, Christ Church
387	London, British Library, Cott. Faust. C. i, fols 94–123	*Regula S. Benedicti.*	A	xii¹
388	London, British Library, Cott. Julius A. ii, fols 2–9	Bede, *Chronica maiora* (frag.).	E	xii¹
389 ?* ?†	London, British Library, Cott. Nero A. vii, fols 1–39	Lanfranc, *Epistolae.* Memorandum on primacy of Canterbury. Council of Winchester (1072). Council of London (1075). Possibly item 79 on the early Rochester library catalogue (EBL, 77).	E	xi/xii or xii^in England or Normandy; ?Rochester
390 ??†	London, British Library, Cott. Nero A. vii, fol. 40	'*De coloribus et mixtionibus*' (frag.: only the lower half of one leaf remains). Near-contemporary ?addition: *Epitaphium Lanfranci.* Possibly the '*aliis minutis opusculis*' of item 79 on the early Rochester library catalogue (EBL, 77). If the identification should be correct, it was already bound with fols 1–39 (no. 389) by xii¹.	–	xi/xii ??Rochester
391 ?*	London, British Library, Cott, Nero A. vii, fols 41–112	Anselm, *Epistolae.*	U/E	xi/xii or xii^in (?1092×1100) England or Normandy; Rochester
392	London, British Library, Cott. Nero A. xi, fols 108–42	Pseudo-Jerome, *De essentia diuinitatis.* Sentences on the church, and church discipline.	E/A	xii
393	London, British Library, Cott. Nero C. iii, fols 241–6	Augustine, *Enarrationes in Psalmos* (frag.). ?Part one of a three-volume set.		xii^in ?Worcester
394 ?*	London, British Library, Cott. Nero C. v, fols 1–161	Consular Tables. List of Popes to John XII (955–64). Nineteen-year Tables. Marianus Scotus, *Chronicon* (to 1087). Annals for 1088–1109 (NB: space was prepared for entries for 1110–22, but nothing was written). Additions, *s.* xii¹⁺, fols 160v–61; Computistical tables.	E	xii^in (after 1086; ? *c.* 1105 and *c.* 1110) ?Continent; ?Hereford
—	London, British Library, Cott. Nero C. vii, fols 29–78	*See* London, British Library, Harley 624.		
—	London, British Library, Cott. Nero C. vii, fols 80–4	*See* Oxford, St John's College, 17		

395	London, British Library, Cott. Nero C. ix, fols 19–21, plus London, Lambeth Palace, 430, flyleaves	Necrology (frag.).	E	xii^{in} (post 1087) Canterbury, Christ Church
396	London, British Library, Cott. Nero D. ii, fols 238–41	*Annales abbatiae de Bello.* NB: In *s.* xvi these were part of the *s.* xi$^{2/4}$ 'Miscellany', British Library, Cott. Tib. B. v, and were probably added to it when they were written.		xii^{1} (*c.* 1118)
397	London, British Library, Cott. Nero E. 1, vol. 1, fols 1–53	Additions to *s.* xi^{med} Legendary (original contents inventoried in Jackson and Lapidge, 'Cotton-Corpus Legendary'): Byrhtferth, *Vita S. Oswaldi; Vita S. Ecgwini.* Lantfred, *Translatio et miracula S. Swithuni.* Hymn to Swithun: '*Aurea lux patriae*' (Walther, 1799). Extensive corrections to original text, *s.* xii^{1}. Further additions, *s.* xii$^{2/4}$: Vol. 1, fols 53v–4v: *Passio S. Andreae* (incomplete). Vol. 2, fols 156–65, 174v–76v, 187–8: *Vita S. Fritheswithae*; Rhigyfarch, *Vita S. Davidis*; Anon., *Vita S. Margaretae Antiochenae; Vita Bedae.* Companion to Cambridge, Corpus Christi College, 9 (no. 54 above).		xi$^{3/4}$ Worcester
—	London, British, Library, Cott. Nero E. i, vol. 2, fols 181–4	*See* British Library, Add. 46204		
398	London, British Library, Cott. Otho A. viii, fols 1–6	Goscelin, *Vita S. Mildrethae.* *Textus translationis . . . S. Mildrethae.* Owing to the very badly damaged state of the manuscript, the script is difficult to date with precision. The script, display script and initial, along with the textual content, suggest a Kentish origin, most probably Canterbury, St Augustine's Abbey.	I	xi/xii or xii^{in} (post 1087×91) Kent (?Canterbury, St Augustine's)
399	London, British Library, Cott. Otho A, xii, fols 8–12, 14–16, 18–19	Osbern, *Vita et translatio S. Ælphegi.*	–	xi^{2}
400 ?	London, British Library, Cott. Otho A. xii, fols 13 and 20–7	Ælmer of Canterbury, *Epistolae*; etc. It is difficult to date in its very badly charred state.	–	?xii$^{2/4}$
401	London, British Library, Cott. Otho D. viii, fols 8–173	Passional (31 Jan. - 20 March): *Passio S. Ignatii; Vita S. Brigidae; Passio S. Blasii; Trifonis, Agathae; Vita et miracula S. Vedasti; Vita Amandi; ?Ausberti, Austrobertae, Euphrasiae; Passio S. Valentini, Iulianae, Ananiae; Acta Theophili; Vita S. Wingualoei; Vita et passio Perpetuae; Passio 40 militum;* John the Deacon, *Vita S. Gregorii; Passio Longini; Vita et miracula Geretrudis; Passio S. Theodori;* Bede, *Vita Cuthberti; Vita S. Wulframni.*	I	xii$^{1-2/4}$ Canterbury, Christ Church

402	London, British Library, Cott. Tiberius A. xiii, fols 119–200	Worcester cartulary ('Heming's Cartulary'). Additions and corrections *s.* xii^{in+}. NB: corrections and additions were also made to the *s.* xi^{in} Worcester cartulary, Cott. Tib. A. xiii, fols 1–118, from *s.* xi^{2+}.	U	xi^{ex} (*c.* 1096) Worcester
403	London, British Library, Cott. Tiberius B. ii, fols 2–85	Abbo of Fleury, *Vita S. Edmundi.* 'Hermann the Archdeacon' (attrib.), *Miracula S. Edmundi* (imperfect).	P	xii^{in} (post 1097/8) Bury St Edmunds
404	London, British Library, Cott. Tiberius C. i, fols 2–42, plus Harley 3667	(Tiberius C. i) *Computistica*; *Astronomica* including: '*Continentia circuit paschalis*', '*De circulo decennouenali*' (= Bede, *De temporibus*, 13). Eugenius II of Toledo, *Heptametron de primordio mundi* (8 verses). '*De octo tramitibus cycli decennouenalis*'. '*De partibus mundi*', '*Lectio de mensibus*', '*De nominibus uentorum*', '*De quinque circulis mundi* (= from Isidore, *De natura rerum*, xi, iv, xxxvii, and x). '*De circulis caeli*' (= Isidore, *Etymologiae*, xiii, 6, 2–5). '*De concordia mensium*', '*De positione septem stellarum errantium* (= Isidore, *De natura rerum*, v and xxiii). '*De nominibus stellarum*'. Cicero, *Aratea* (extracts). Pliny the Elder, *Historia naturalis* (extract). Macrobius, *Interpretatio in somnium Scipionis* (extract) (Harley 3667) Annals of Peterborough Abbey. NB: this represents six quires from a volume which originally had at least twenty-one.	D	xii$^{1-2/4}$ (?between 1122 and 1135) Peterborough
405	London, British Library, Cott. Tiberius C. i, fols 43–203, additions	Additions to a *s.* xi^{med} continental pontifical (on fols 89–151, plus additions to original section, 172–9), including: OE homilies; Latin sermons; prayers; benedictions. Canons of councils including the Council of Winchester (1070). *'Penitentiae institutio secundum decreta Normannorum presulum.'* Litany.	U	xi^{2}; xi/xii (post 1070) Sherborne; Salisbury
406	London, British Library, Cott. Tiberius C. vi	Computistical Tables. Pictorial cycle; Prefatory texts, including *Ordo confessionis* and litany. Psalter (with interlinear OE gloss).	D	xi$^{3/4}$ (after 1063) Winchester, Old Minster
407	London, British Library, Cott. Tiberius D. iv, vol. I, fols 1–115	*Vitae sanctorum*: *Vita Siluestri, Basilii, Remigii, Hilarii, Felicis, Vedasti, Amandi, Albini, Walarici, Ambrosii, Vita et conuersio Mariae Egyptiacae, Germani Parisiacensis episcopi, Medardi, Germani Autissiodorensis episcopi, Augustini* (of Hippo), *Egidii*; Sulpicius Severus, *Vita S. Martini*; *Epistolae*; Gregory of Tours, *Narrationes de miraculis in obitu et de prima translatione S. Martini*; Sulpicius Severus, *Dialogi*; Alcuin, *De uita et uirtutibus S. Martini. Vita Britii, Richarii* (Riquier). Fols 116–51 = *s.* xii^{med} addition beginning with the *Miracula S. Martini* (includes A initials). NB: Vol. II = entirely xii^{med}, except fols 158–66 which were originally separate, and belong to Winchester Cathedral, 1 (Bede), *s.* x/xi.	I A	xi/xii ?Winchester

408	London, British Library, Cott. Tiberius E. iv, fols 1–42	Annals; Charters. Text on the winds, '*Ventus est aer commotus*'. Computistical tables; Calendar. One hand or type of hand, wrote the Annals up to 1122 (fol. 22v). A later hand (*s.* xii^{2}) added A.D. 1123–72 (22v–5v). A still later hand (*s.* xii^{ex}) added A.D. 1173–81 (fols 26r–7v). The principal additions (apart from marginal insertions) occupy fols 14v, and 22v–29v, col. a.	D	xii$^{1-2/4}$ (?shortly after 1122) Winchcombe
409	London, British Library, Cott. Tiberius, E. iv, fols 43–181	Bede, *De temporibus; De natura rerum.* Computistical texts including: '*De temporibus horis et momentis.*' Dionysius Exiguus, *Epistolae duae de ratione festi paschae.* Helperic, *De computo.* Addition, *s.* xii^{2}, fols 182–3: Treatise, '*Maiores nostri orbem totius* . . .'.	D I(f)	xii$^{1-2/4}$ Winchcombe
410	London, British Library, Cott. Titus C. xx	Julian of Toledo, *Prognosticon futuri saeculi.* Isidore, *Sententiae.*	E	xi^{in} ?Abingdon
411	London, British Library, Cott. Titus D. xvi, fols 1–36	Prudentius, *Psychomachia* (illustrated). Poem in praise of St Lawrence: '*Reddimus aeternas indulgentissime doctor*'.	D	xii^{1} St Albans
412	London, British Library, Cott. Titus D. xvi, fols 37–69	Gilbert Crispin, *Disputatio Iudei cum Christiano.*	U	xii^{1} St Albans
413	London, British Library, Cott. Titus D. xvi, fols 70–111	*Altercatio Ecclesiae contra Synagogam.*	U	xii^{1} St Albans
414	London, British Library, Cott. Vespasian B. xx, fols 1–284	Privilege for St Augustine's Abbey ('Bulla plumba'). Goscelin, *Historia minor de uita S. Augustini; Historia minor de miraculis S. Augustini; Historia maior de aduentu beatissimi Augustini sociorumque eius in Britannia; Historia maior de miraculis S. Augustini*; (fols 86–93 = xii^{med} insertion — see below); *Historia translationis S. Augustini; Vita S. Mildrethae; Translatio S. Mildrethae; Lectiones de SS. Laurentio, Mellito, Justo, Honorio, Deusdedito, Theodoro, Adriano.* [Gregory], *Libellus responsionum.* Goscelin, *Libellus contra inanes S. uirginis Mildrethae usurpatores.* *Priuilegium Æthelberti* (for St Augustine's). Papal privileges (that on fol. 284v being a *s.* xii$^{2/4}$ addition). Addition, *s.* xii^{med}, fols 86–93: *Sermo in festiuitate S. Augustini* (inserted quire). Fols. 285–6 = late medieval additions.	I(f)	xii^{in} (post 1098×1100) Canterbury, St Augustine's

415	London, British Library, Cott. Vespasian B. xxv	Solinus, *Collectanea rerum memorabilium*. Priscian, Latin verse version of Dionysius, *Periegesis*. Dares the Phrygian (translation ascribed to Cornelius Nepos), *Historia Troianorum*. Verses ascribed to Jerome: '*Nescit mens nostra fixum seruare tenorem*' (= *De mobilitate mentis*: Walther, 11749). *Prophetia Sibyllae* (Prophecy of the Tenth Sibyl/Sibylla Tiburtina). Segardus de Sancto Audomaro (attrib.), *Versus de miseria hominis et poenis inferni* (inc.: '*Debilitas carnis aciem turbat rationis*'). 'Nennius' (attrib.), *Historia Brittonum*. Addition: ?Pseudo-Bede, *De signis uenturis ante finem mundi*.	A	xii[1] Canterbury, Christ Church
416 ?* ??	London, British Library, Cott. Vespasian D. ii	Penitentials. Adso of Moutier-en-Der, *De ortu et tempore Antichristi ad Gerbergam reginam epistola*. Canons; Homilies; *Miracula sanctorum*.	E	xi/xii ?Normandy (no evidence for early English provenance)
417	London, British Library, Cott. Vesp. D. vi, fols 78–125	'Eddius' (?Stephen of Ripon), *Vita S. Wilfridi*.	I	xi[ex]
418 ?	London, British Library, Cott. Vesp. D. xix, fols 71–82	Chronological Tables with Saints, Popes, Emperors, and Kings.	U	xii[1] England or France
—	London, British Library, Cott. Vesp. D. xxi, fols 1–17	*See* London, British Library, Royal 15 A. xxii.		
—	London, British Library, Cott. Vesp. D. xxii, fols 18–40	*See* Oxford, Bodleian Library, Laud. misc. 509.		
—	London, British Library, Cott. Vesp. E. iv, fols 203–10	*See* London, British Library, Cott. Appendix 56, fols 1–4.		
419	London, British Library, Cott. Vitellius A. xii, fols 4–77	*Dialogus Egberti*. Abbo of Fleury, *De differentia circuli et sphaerae*. Hrabanus Maurus, *De computo*. Scientific texts including Greek and Hebrew alphabets with interpretations, 3 runic alphabets. Calendar. Isidore, *De natura rerum*.	I	xi/xii Salisbury
420	London, British Library, Cott. Vitellius A. xii, fols 79–86	Cummian, *Epistola de controuersia paschali*. Bede, *Epistola ad Pleguinam de aetatibus saeculi*.	U	xii[1] Salisbury

421	London, British Library, Cott. Vitellius A. xviii	Calendar; Sacramentary. Corrections and additions, *s.* xi/xii–xii[1] including verses added to each month in the calendar, and a couple of supplementary prayers added in the margins. The hypothetical date range and possible Wells provenance depend on the association of the MS with Bishop Giso of Wells, which is far from certain.	P	xi[2] (??1061×88) ?West Country,?? Wells
422	London, British Library, Cott. Vitellius C. xii, fols 114–57	Usuardus, *Martyrologium.* Additions: obits added at the end of the individual sections, *s.* xii[1+]; sections on fols 115r and 118r rewritten *in rasura.* Fols 154–6 = *s.* xii/xii supplement with additional entries for 24–31 December, and a monastic *conuentio.*	I(f)	xii[in] (or xi[ex]) (*c.* 1100×10; or just conceivably pre 1091) Canterbury, St Augustine's
—	London, British Library, Cott. Vitellius D. xviii, fols 1–3	*See* Oxford, Bodleian Library, Bodley 852		
423	London, British Library, Cott. Vitellius E. xii, fols 153–60	Additions to a Romano-German pontifical (= fols 116–52): Blessings. Poem, '*Gloria uictori sit Christo laude perenni*' (Walther, 7249). Sermon prefacing office for dead. *Laudes regiae.*	–	xi[2] (post 1068) ??York; Exeter
424	London, British Library, Egerton 654	Seneca, *Epistolae.* Fictitious correspondence between Seneca and St Paul.	E	xii[in] St Albans
—	London, British Library, Egerton 3314	*See* London, British Library, Cott. Calig. A. xv, fols 120–53.		
425	London, British Library, Egerton 3721	Calendar. Augustine, *De doctrina christiana* (extracts); *De Trinitate* (extracts). Marbod of Rennes, *De duodecim lapidibus pretiosis.*	A	xii[2/4] (1119×46) St Albans
426	London, British Library, Harley 12, fols 1–140	John the Deacon, *Vita S. Gregorii.* Addition, *s.* xii[in], fol. 140v: '*Versus Gregorii quos fecit sabbato ante Ramis Palmarum*'.	A/E	xi[ex] ?Durham
427 ? *	London, British Library, Harley 12, fols 141–3	*Vita S. Katherinae.*	U	xi/xii England or Normandy
428	London, British Library, Harley 56, fols 2–25	Osbern, *Epistola de uita S. Dunstani*; *Vita S. Dunstani* (incomplete: ends at same place as Durham Cathedral Library, B. IV. 14).	A	xii[1] ?York
429 ?	London, British Library, Harley 271, fols 1, 45	Service book: missal (frag.).	–	?xi[2]
—	London, British Library, Harley 315	*See* London, British Library, Harley 624.		

—	London, British Library, Harley 488	*See* Supplement		
430	London, British Library, Harley 491, fols 3–46, plus two blank unnumbered fols	William of Jumièges, *Gesta Normannorum Ducum.* NB: Front flyleaves (fols 1–2) = *s.* $xi^{2/3}$ text. Endleaves (fols 47–8) = frags. from *s.* $xii^{1/2}$ Mortuary Roll.	U	xii^{in-1} Durham
431	London, British Library, Harley 526, fols 28–37	*Vita Bedae* (Preface, inc.: '*Inter catholicos sacrae scripturae expositores'; Vita* inc.: '*Humanae salutis auctore Christo Iesu in messem crediturae multitudinis mittente operarios*').	E	$xii^{1-2/4}$ Durham
432 ?	London, British Library, Harley 526, fols 38–57	*Vita Edwardi regis* (Edward the Confessor).	U	xii^{in} England or France
433	London, British Library, Harley 624, fols 84–143, with Cott. Nero C. vii, fols 29–78 and Harley 315, fols 1–39	Passional (parts of one volume from a seven-volume set). (Harley 315, fols 16–39, *Vita Anselmi* = datable to after 1123.) Addition, *s.* xii/xiii, Cott. Nero C. vii, fols 78v–79v: *Vita S. Anselmi* (verse). Companion to Canterbury Cathedral, Lit. E. 42, plus Maidstone, Kent County Archives, S/Rm Fae. 2 (no. 194 above).	I(f)	xii^{in-1} (one part datable to after 1123) Canterbury, Christ Church
434	London, British Library, Harley 649, fols 1–104	Bede, *In Cantica Canticorum allegorica expositio* (including Gregory, *Excerpta in Cantica Canticorum*). Homily on Luke 11, 33 written in smaller script, Inc.: *'Sancti euangelii fratris karissimi lectio sollicito et perspicaci consideranda est animo ac bone operationis retinenda studio'.* Addition, *s.* $xii^{2/4}$, fol. 100v: Venantius Fortunatus, *Vita S. Radegundis.* Addition, *s.* xii^{med}, fol. 103v: Homily, inc.: *'Virtutem spiritus signa miraculorum dicit'.* NB: Differences in format, preparation and script, along with independent quire signatures, show that this and the following three items were originally separate.	A	xii^1 Ramsey
435	London, British Library, Harley 649, fols 105–152	Bede, *In Actus Apostolorum.* See note on previous item.	A	xii^1 Ramsey
436	London, British Library, Harley 649, fols 153–222	Bede, *In Epistolas Catholicas.* See note on no. 434.	A	xii^1 Ramsey
437	London, British Library, Harley 649, fols 223–58	Bede, *Homiliae euangelii* (selected); *In Tobiam.* See note on no. 434.	E/A	xii^1 Ramsey
438	London, British Library, Harley 652, fols 1–216	Paul the Deacon, *Homiliarium*, expanded (contents up to fol. 208 are inventoried in Richards, *Texts and Traditions*, pp. 104–8). Goscelin, *Translatio S. Mildrethae uirginis; Lectiones de SS. Laurentio, Iusto, Honorio, Theodoro.*	I(f)	xi/xii Canterbury St Augustine's

439	London, British Library, Harley 865	Ambrose, *De mysteriis; De sacramentis.* Pseudo-Ambrose, *De corpore et sanguine Christi in pascha.* Jerome, *Contra Iouinianum.* Pseudo-Augustine, *Hypomnesticon contra Pelagianos et Caelestianos* (I–IV).	I	xi^{ex} St Albans
440	London, British Library, Harley 988, fols 1–15, 15*–26, plus two original blanks (the first two unfoliated, the third '27*')	*Commentarium in Cantica Canticorum*, inc.: '*Trinomius Salomon fuit editur, id est dilectus ecclesiastes, id est contionator, id est contionum congregator, Salomon id est pacificus, qui secundum hunc numerum tria composuit uolumina singula in se continentia quoque terna uocabula*'.	U	xii^{in}
—	London, British Library, Harley 988, fols 27–71	*See* Supplement.		
441	London, British Library, Harley 1916 with Harley 5958, fol. 87	Augustine, *In Euangelium Iohannis; In Epistolam Iohannis ad Parthos tractatus x.*	X	xii^{1} ?Glastonbury
442	London, British Library, Harley 1918	Paul the Deacon, *Homiliarium*, expanded (Easter to 4th Sunday after Epiphany) [similar but not identical to the version in British Library, Harley 652].	I	xii^{1} Glastonbury
443	London, British Library, Harley 2624	Cicero, *De Inuentione.* Pseudo-Cicero, *Rhetorica and Herennium.*	I	xii^{1} St Albans
444	London, British Library, Harley 2729	Frontinus, *Strategemata* (acephalus). Eutropius, *Breuiarium historiae romanae ab urbe condita.*	U	xi/xii ?Durham
445 §	London, British Library, Harley 3061	Paschasius Radbertus, *De corpore et sanguine Domini* which embodies (fols 28v–35r) Augustine, *Sermo* 52 [NB: the chapter list gives 65 chs., of which 1–57 are Paschasius, and 58–65 Augustine]. Lanfranc, *De corpore et sanguine Domini contra Berengarium Turonensem* embodying attributed quotations from Augustine, Ambrose, Cyprian, Gregory, Jerome and Paul. ?Contemporary addition: Augustine, 'De purgatorio igne' = *Sermo* app. 104). *Saec.* xiv contents list shows that this was once followed by Guitmund of Aversa, *De corpore et sanguine Domini contra Berengarium.* The author portrait on fol. 1v is possibly slightly later than the text: ?added *s.* xii^{1}. See PLATE 16.	I D	xii^{in} ?Abingdon
446	London, British Library, Harley 3066	Augustine, *Enchiridion; In epistolam Iohannis ad Parthos tractatus x.* Although the initial on fol. 47v is flourished, this was done at a much later date: ?*s.* xvi.	U	xii$^{2/4}$ Worcester
447	London, British Library, Harley 3080	Augustine, *Retractatio; Confessiones.*	A	xi^{ex}

448 †	London, British Library, Harley 3097	Jerome, *In Danielem.* Otloh of St Emmeram, *Vita S. Nicholai.* Folcard of St Bertin, *Vita S. Botulfi.* *Vita SS. Tancredi, Torhtredi, Tovae.* Translation of saints who rest in Thorney ('*Translatio sanctorum apud Thorney*'). Felix of Crowland, *Vita S. Guthlaci* (unfinished). Ambrose, *iv sermones.* *Vita et miracula S. Nicholai* (excerpts).	U	xii^{1} Peterborough
—	London, British Library, Harley 3667	*See* London, British Library, Cott. Tib. C. i, fols 2–42.		
449	London, British Library, Harley 3680	Bede, *Historia ecclesiastica.* Cuthbert, *Epistola de obitu uenerabilis Bedae.* Short text on the early Kentish royal family and the monasteries they founded. Latin list of resting places of English saints.	A	xii^{1} Rochester
450	London, British Library, Harley 3659	Vegetius, *Epitome rei militaris.* *Computistica.* Macrobius, *Saturnalia.* Sallust (attrib.), *Inuectiua in Ciceronem.* 'Nennius' (attrib.), *Historia Brittonum.* Augustine, *De diuersis haeresibus* (starts incomplete at c. 51: mutilitated). Solinus, *Collectanea rerum memorabilium.* Aethicus Ister (Virgil of Salzburg), *Cosmographia.* Vitruvius, *De architectura.*	D; E	xii^{in} England or France; subsequently Italy
451	London, British Library, Harley 3864	Bede, *In Epistolas Catholicas.*	A	xii^{in} Durham
452	London, British Library, Harley 3908, fols 1–100	Goscelin, *Vita S. Mildrethae.* Eight lections for the feast of St Mildred. Gospel reading and homily (= Gregory, *Homeliae xl in euangelia* (extract)). *Missa de S. Mildretha.* ?Goscelin, '*Historia de S. Mildretha.*' Goscelin, *Translatio S. Mildrethae.*	E	xii^{1} Canterbury, St Augustine's
453	London, British Library, Harley 4092, fols 1–38 (NB: fols 4–5 = replacement, *s.* xii^{ex})	Prudentius, *Psychomachia* (frag.: begins at 1. 801). Sedulius, *Carmen paschale; Hymni; Versus:* *'Cantemus socii domino cantemus'* (Walther, 2382); *'A solis ortu cardine'* (Walther, 88); '*Hostis Herodes impie*'; *'Sedulius Christi miracula uersibus edens'*. Part of an enlarged volume by *s.* xiv: see next item.	X; A	xii$^{1-2/4}$
454	London, British Library, Harley 4092, fols 87–158	Boethius, *De consolatione philosophiae.* NB: the hand responsible for fols 143–50 looks later (xii$^{2/4-med}$); that responsible for 151–7 is even later. Fol. 158r bears a late medieval contents list for the volume as a whole, i.e. including no. 453.	A	xii^{1+}

455	London, British Library, Harley 4688	Bede, *In Prouerbia Salomonis; Epistola ad Egbertum.*	A	xii[in] Durham
456 ?	London, British Library, Harley 4725, fols 206–13	*Sermones* (frag.) including *'Sermo S. Augustini ad praedicandum cotidianis', inc.: 'O fratres karissimi ut tota mentis intentione inquirere et intelligere studeamus quare christiani sumus et quare signum crucis Christi in fronte portamus'.*	A	xii[1–2/4] Durham
457	London, British Library, Harley 5915, fol.12	Augustine, *Contra mendacium* (frag.: the end); *De cura pro mortuis gerenda* (frag.: the beginning).	X	xi/xii ?Canterbury Christ Church
—	London, British Library, Harley 5958, fol. 87	*See* London, British Library, Harley 1916.		
458	London, British Library Harley 5977, frag. 62	Gospel book or lectionary (frag.: contains Luke 6, 23–8).	–	xii[in]
459	London, British Library, Royal 1 C. vii	Bible (Joshua to Kings). Companion to Baltimore, Walters Art Gallery, 18 (no. 7).	I(f)	xii[1] ?Rochester
460 †	London, British Library, Royal 2 C. iii, fols 5–172	Paul the Deacon, *Homiliarium* (Temporale — Septuagesima to Good Friday; Sanctorale — Stephen to Andrew; Commune sanctorum) (contents inventoried in Richards, *Texts and Traditions*, pp. 98–101). Additions, *s.* xii[in], fols. 170v–71r: *uersus*: a) '*De corpore et sanguine domini: Mysterio magno legali uescimur agno*' (Walther, 11545); b) '*Crimina deploret sua sic peccator et oret*' (Walther, 3451). The work of Norman scribes at Rochester.	I	xi[ex] Rochester
461 †	London, British Library, Royal 3 B. i	Isidore, *Quaestiones in Vetus Testamentum.* Jerome, *Commentarii in quattuor epistolas Paulinas* (only Titus and Philemon here, the latter incomplete). Fol. 124 is a near-contemporary supply leaf (actually a half-leaf), which does not quite bring the last text to completion.	E	xii[in] Rochester
462	London, British Library, Royal 3 B. xvi	Jerome, *In Ieremiam.*	A	xi/xii Bath
463 † §	London, British Library, Royal 3 C. iv	*Liber Iob.* Gregory, *Moralia in Iob* (I–XVI). Companion to London, British Library, Royal 6 C. vi (no. 525). See PLATE 18.	I	xii[in] (pre ?1124) Rochester
464	London, British Library, Royal 3 C. x	John's Gospel. Augustine, *In Euangelium Iohannis.* NB: although not including human figures, both the decorated initials are historiated: that on fol. 3r is surmounted by the eagle of St John holding a codex; that on fol. 14v is surmounted by the Agnus Dei. ?The work of Normans in England.	I	xi/xii Rochester

465 †	London, British Library, Royal 4 B. i	Ezechiel (extract: c. 40). Gregory, *In Ezechielem* (Bk II). The first part is not known to survive.	I	xii^{1} (pre ?1124) Rochester
466	London, British Library, Royal 4 B. iii	Bede, *In epistolas catholicas; In Tobiam.*	I(f)	xii$^{1-2/4}$
467 §	London, British Library, Royal 4 B. iv, fols 1–119	*Epistolae Pauli* with Lanfranc's gloss, preceded by three prologues. *Cantica Canticorum*, glossed, preceded by a prologue [a contemporary addition]. *Apocalypsis Iohannis*, glossed, preceded by a prologue. Pseudo-Atticus of Constantinople, *Regula formata.* See PLATE 23.	A	xii^{1} Worcester
468	London, British Library, Royal 4 B. iv, fols 120–202	Sidonius, *Epistolae.* Ausonius, *Versus de duodecim imperatoribus Romanorum.* *Vita Sidonii.* *Vita Symmachi.* Sidonius, *Carmina.*	E	xii$^{2/4}$ Worcester
469	London, British Library, Royal 4 C. ii	Jerome, *In Prophetas minores* (Nah., Hab., Soph., Agg., Zach., Mal.). Near-contemporary addition: Honorius Augustodunensis, *Sigillum Beatae Mariae*, preface and cc. 1–4. Part two of a two-volume set: the first volume is not known to survive.	A	xii^{1} Worcester
470	London, British Library, Royal 4 C. xi, fols 1–222	Jerome, *In Danielem; In Prophetas minores* (Osee, Ioel, Amos, Abd., Ion., Mich., Nah., Hab., Soph., Agg., Zach., Mal.).	A/E	xii^{in} Battle
471 †	London, British Library, Royal 5 A. vii	Pseudo-Augustine (Ambrosius Autpertus), *De conflictu uitiorum atque uirtutum* (imperfect). Ephraim the Syrian, *De compunctione cordis.* Julian of Toledo, *Prognosticon futuri saeculi.* *Vita S. Fursei* (attrib. to Bede). Augustine, *Sermo.* Caesarius of Arles, *Sermo* 187 (= Pseudo-Augustine, *Sermo* 115). Pseudo-Augustine, *Sermo in natale Domini* (?Sedatus); *Sermo* app. 116. *Sermones* (one on the birth of a bishop and confessor; one on the birth of a virgin). Paschasius Radbertus, *De corpore et sanguine Domini.* Near-contemporary additions, fols 160–61r: *Excerpta* on Solomon (from Augustine, Jerome, Ambrose).	E/A	xii^{in} (pre ?1124) Rochester
472	London, British Library, Royal 5. A. xi, fols 3–46	Augustine, *Enchiridion.*	A	xii^{1} Gloucester

473	London, British Library, Royal 5 A. xiii, fols 1–197	**A)** (fols 1–179) Augustine, *De mendacio; Contra mendacium; De natura et origine animae.* Sermo Arianorum. Pseudo-Augustine (Syagrius), *Contra sermonem Arianorum.* Augustine, *Contra aduersarium legis et prophetarum; De cura pro mortuis gerenda.* Pseudo-Augustine, *De uisitatione infirmorum.* **B)** (fols 180–197) Fulbert of Chartres, *Sermones; Epistolae.* Comprises two sections, as indicated.	E	xii^{1} Worcester $xii^{1-2/4}$
474 †	London, British Library, Royal 5 A. xv	Augustine, *Enchiridion.* Ambrose, *De bono mortis.* Lanfranc, *De corpore et sanguine Domini aduersus Berengarium Turonensem* (embodying attributed quotations from Ambrose, Augustine, Cyprian, Gregory, Jerome and Paul).	X; A	xii^{1} (pre ?1124) Rochester
475	London, British Library, Royal 5. B. ii	Augustine, *De pastoribus; De ouibus; De baptismo contra Donatistas; De peccatorum meritis et remissione et de baptismo paruulorum; De unico baptismo; De spiritu et littera.*	D	xi/xii Bath
476	London, British Library, Royal 5 B. iii	Fulgentius (Pseudo-Augustine), *Epistola ad Donatum; De fide Trinitatis.* Augustine, *De utilitate agendae paenitentiae; De disciplina christiana; De decem chordis.* ?Paulinus of Aquileia, *Liber exhortationis ad comitem quendam.* Gennadius, *Liber siue diffinitio ecclesiasticorum dogmatum.* Additions, *s.* xii, fols 87v–88v: '*Capitula de generalibus conciliis*' = part of the preface to the Isidorean *Collectio canonum.* Paschal II, *Epistolae* (2, of 1102 and 1117) relating to the Canterbury — York dispute.	A	xii^{in} Worcester
477 †	London, British Library, Royal 5 B. iv	Augustine, *De Trinitate.* *Saec.* xiii inscription on fol. 3r attributes the volume to 'Humfridus precentor'; the same hand wrote an *ex libris* and anathema on fol. 2v.	E	xii^{1} (pre ?1124) Rochester
478 †	London, British Library, Royal 5 B. vi	Augustine, *In epistolam Iohannis ad Parthos tractatus x.* Pseudo-Augustine (Quoduultdeus), *Sermo contra Iudaeos, paganos, et Arianos.* *Apocalypsis Iohannis.* *Cantica canticorum.*	A/E	xii^{in} (pre ?1124) Rochester
479 †	London, British Library, Royal 5 B. vii	Pseudo-Augustine (Quoduultdeus), *Contra quinque haereses.* Pseudo-Ambrose, *Libellus de dignitate sacerdotali.* Didymus of Alexandria (trans. Jerome), *De Spiritu Sancto.* Pseudo-Augustine, *Sermo de muliere forti.* Mansuetus (Mediolanensis episcopus), *Epistola ad Constantinum imperatorem.* Bede, *In Regum libros XXX quaestiones; De templo Salomonis; Super Canticum Abacuc allegorica expositio.*	A/I	xii^{1} Rochester

480 †	London, British Library, Royal 5 B. x	Augustine, *Contra Faustum Manichaeum*.	A	xii^{1} (pre ?1124) Rochester
481 †	London, British Library, Royal 5 B. xii, fols 4–165	Schema showing, '*Diuisiones Augustini in libro De doctrina christiana*' (fol. 4r). Augustine, *Retractatio; De doctrina christiana; De uera religione; De paenitentia* (sermo 351 only). Pseudo-Augustine, *De paenitentibus* (Sermo 393). Addition, *s.* xiii^{in} (1202), fols 2–3: Rochester library catalogue. Fol. 1r: Table of contents.	A	xii^{1} (pre ?1124) Rochester
482 †	London, British Library, Royal 5 B. xiii	Augustine, *In epistolam Iohannis* (excerpta in five books). *Excerpta* from Augustine, *De Trinitate; De ciuitate Dei* (in seven books); *De cura pro mortuis gerenda; De natura et origine animae*; and *De uera religione*.	U/E	xi/xii Rochester
483	London, British Library, Royal 5 B. xiv	Augustine, *Retractatio; Confessiones*. NB: fols 1–8 (quire I) = *s.* xii$^{2/4}$ supply leaves containing Book I and part of Book II.	U	xii^{1} Bath (from 1502)
484	London, British Library, Royal 5 B. xv, fols 1–48	Augustine, *Enchiridion*.	I	xii^{1} Canterbury, St Augustine's
485	London, British Library, Royal 5 B. xv, fols 49–56	Pseudo-Augustine (Ambrosius Autpertus [here attributed to Leo]), *De conflictu uitiorum atque uirtutum*. *Excerpta* from Augustine and Ambrose.	U	xii^{1} Canterbury, St Augustine's
486	London, British Library, Royal 5 B. xv, fols 57–64	John Chrysostom, *De muliere Cananaea*. Goscelin, *Miracula S. Lethardi* (= Liudhard).	E	xi^{ex} Canterbury, St Augustine's
487 †	London, British Library, Royal 5 B. xvi	Augustine, *Confessiones; De diuersis haeresibus* (starting imperfectly in c. 1).	A	xii^{1} (pre ?1124) Rochester
488	London, British Library, Royal 5 C. viii	Augustine, *Sermones de uerbis Domini et apostoli* (*De uerbis Domini* 1–64; *De uerbis apostoli*, 1, 2, 34, 3–24).	I	xii$^{2/4}$ Rochester
489 †	London, British Library, Royal 5 D. i	Augustine, *Enarrationes in Psalmos* (LI–C). The work of Normans in England. Companion to London, British Library, Royal 5 D. ii–iii (nos. 490–1).	I(f)	xi/xii (??*c.* 1107×13) Rochester
490 †	London, British Library, Royal 5. D. ii	Augustine, *Enarrationes in Psalmos* (CI–CL). Companion to London, British Library, Royal 5 D. i and iii (nos. 489 and 491).	I(f)	xii^{in} (??1115×24) Rochester
491 †	London, British Library, Royal 5 D. iii	Augustine, *Enarrationes in Psalmos* (I–L). Companion to London, British Library, Royal 5 D. i–ii (nos. 489–90).	I	xii^{1} (pre ?1124) Rochester

492	London, British Library, Royal 5 D. v	Augustine, *Enarrationes in Psalmos* (LI–C). Companion to London, British Library, Royal 5 D. v (no. 493).	A	xii^{in} Bath
493	London, British Library, Royal 5 D. v	Augustine, *Enarrationes in Psalmos* (CI–CL). Companion to London, British Library, Royal 5 D. iv (no. 492).	I	xii^{in} Bath
494	London, British Library, Royal 5 D. vi	Augustine, *Epistolae* (125: itemised in Warner and Gilson, *Catalogue*).	A(f)	xii^{in} Bath
495 ?*	London, British Library, Royal 5 D. vii	Augustine, *Retractatio; De ciuitate Dei* (with marginal summary).	A	xii^{in} ?Normandy ?Bath
496 †	London, British Library, Royal 5 D. ix	Augustine, *Retractatio; De ciuitate Dei.* Lanfranc, *Notae* on *De ciuitate Dei.*	I(f)	xii^{1} (pre ?1124) Rochester
497 ?*	London, British Library, Royal 5 E. iii, fols 3–82	Ephraim the Syrian, *De compunctione cordis; De die iudicii et de resurrectione; De beatitudine animae; De paenitentia; De luctaminibus; De die iudicii.* Versus: '*Hic uitae pastus indeficienter habentur*' (not in Walther). Catena of scriptural and patristic excerpts, quoting 'Albinus', Augustine, Bede, Caesarius, Cassiodorus, Celestinus, Cyprian, Gregory, Hilary, Isidore, Jerome, Laurentius, Maximus, Prosper, Sabinus, Salvius, and Sixtus, inc.: '*Dei omnipotentis filius inter cetera sacra*'.	I	xii^{in} Normandy, Northern France, or England
498 ?*	London, British Library, Royal 5 E. v, fols 50–73	Anselm, *De processione Spiritus Sancti; Epistola de sacrificio azimi et fermentati.*	U	xii^{1} ?France; Worcester
499 † ?*	London, British Library, Royal 5 E. x	Julianus Pomerius (Pseudo-Prosper of Aquitaine), *De uita contemplatiua et actiua.*	I(f)	xi/xii (pre ?1124) Normandy or England; Rochester
500	London, British Library, Royal 5 E. xvi	Pseudo-Augustine, *De unitate sanctae Trinitatis* (acephalus). Extracts in dialogue form from Isidore, *De differentiis rerum* and *Etymologiae* (including '*De diuersitate aquarum*'). Isidore, *De fide catholica contra Iudeos.*	U	xi^{ex} Salisbury
501	London, British Library, Royal 5 E. xix, fols 1–20	Isidore, *Liber synonymorum.* *Homiliae* (two).	U	xi^{ex} Salisbury
502	London, British Library, Royal 5 E. xix, fols 21–36	Twelve homilies from the homiliary of St-Père de Chartres.	U	xi/xii Salisbury
503	London, British Library, Royal 5 E. xix, fols 37–52	Alcuin, *In Cantica Canticorum.* Anon., *Commentarium in Cantica Canticorum* (from Jerome, *In Ecclesiasten Salomonis*) inc.: '*Tribus nominibus uocatus est Salomon*'.	U	xi/xii

504	London, British Library, Royal 5 F. iv	Ambrose, *De uirginitate; De uiduis; De institutione uirginis; Exhortatio uirginitatis.* Pseudo-Ambrose, *De lapsu uirginis consecratae.* Ambrose, *De mysteriis; De sacramentis.*	A	xii¹ Malmesbury
505	London, British Library, Royal 5 F. ix, fols 1–56	Anselm, *De humanis moribus per similitudines.* Versus: '*Vita breuis, casusque leuis*' (Walther, 20660). Anselm (attrib.), *Utrum bono bonum siue malo malum possit esse contrarium; De similitudine temporalis et spiritualis militis; De cellarario domini; Hic ostendit archiepiscopus quid uere appetendum sit uel quid respuendum.*	U/E	xii¹ ?Lanthony or Gloucester
506	London, British Library, Royal 5 F. ix, fols 57–196	Anselm, *De libertate arbitrii; De processione Spiritus Sancti; De incarnatione Verbi; Epistolae* (many of them abbreviated to a greater or lesser extent; NB: fols 177–84 = contemporary addition or insertion.) Addition, s. xii^{med} (post 1135), fol. 196v: Letter from Hugh, bishop of Rouen to Pope Innocent II.	U	xii$^{1-2/4}$?Lanthony or Gloucester
507	London, British Library, Royal 5 F. xiii	Ambrose, *Epistolae; De obitu Theodosii.* Pseudo-Ambrose, *De SS. Geruasio et Protasio.* Ambrose, *De Nabutha Israelita.*	U	xii^{in} Salisbury
508	London, British Library, Royal 5 F. xviii	Tertullian, *Apologeticum* (defective). Pseudo-Methodius, *Reuelationes.*	U	xii^{in} Salisbury
509 †	London, British Library, Royal 6 A. i with 7 A. xi, fols 19–24	(Royal 6 A. i) Ambrose, *Hexaemeron.* *De situ Ierusalem*, inc.: '*Ab oriente est introitus Ierusalem per portam David*'. (Royal 7 A. xi) *Inuentio sanctae crucis* (abbreviated version).	A	xii¹ (pre ?1124) Rochester
510 †	London, British Library, Royal 6 A. iv	Ambrose, *De officiis ministrorum.*	E	xii¹ (pre ?1124) Rochester
511 †	London, British Library, Royal 6 A. xii	John Chrysostom, *De reparatione lapsi; De compunctione cordis; De Psalmo quinquagesimo; De eo qui nemo laeditur nisi a semet ipso; Cum de expulsione eius ageretur; Quando de Asia regressus est Constantinopolim ipse Iohannes; De proditione Iudae; De cruce et latrone;* (attrib.) *De cruce; De ascensione Domini.* Augustine, *De symbolo ad catechumenos* (Sermo 215); *De oratione dominica* (Sermo 56). Hugh, archdeacon of Tours, *De quodam miraculo beati Martini quod contigit in festo translationis eius.* Fulbert of Chartres (attrib.), *De eo quod tria sunt necessaria ad perfectionem christianae religionis; Epistola.* Alcuin, *De fide sanctae et indiuiduae Trinitatis.*	A/E	xii¹ (pre ?1124) Rochester

512 ★	London, British Library, Royal 6 A. xiii	Gregory, *Homiliae xl in Euangelia; Sermo de mortalitate*; Decretal of 595. Augustine, *In euangelium Iohannis* (extract). Sermon on Psalm 84, 11. Alcuin, *Liber generationis Jesu Christi* (imperfect). Homily on the genealogy in Matthew. Bede, homilies for Christmas day (*ex Homiliae euangelii*). Fols 175–81 = *s.* xii^{med}: Bede, *Homiliae euangelii* (extracts). Liturgica for Whitsunday and feast of BVM. Sermon on Psalm 120, 1.	–	xi/xii Continent (Low Countries or Germany). In England by *s.* xii^{1}
513	London, British Library, Royal 6 A. xvi	Ambrose, *Epistolae; De obitu Theodosii imperatoris.* Pseudo-Ambrose, *De SS. Gervasio et Protasio.* Ambrose, *De Nabutha Israelita* (imperfect).	U	xii^{1} Worcester
514	London, British Library, Royal 6 B. i	Gregory, *In Ezechielem.* Isidore, *Quaestiones in Vetus Testamentum* (extract, imperfect).	I	xii^{in} Bath
515 †	London, British Library, Royal 6 B. vi	Ambrose, *De mysteriis; De sacramentis.* Ivo of Chartres, *Sermones* (8, the last incomplete). Bruno of Asti, *De sacramentis ecclesiae.* Ivo of Chartres, *Epistolae* (ninety-two).	I(f)	xii^{1} (?1114 × ?1124) Rochester
516	London, British Library, Royal 6 B. vii	Aldhelm, *De laudibus uirginitatis.* Addition, *s.* xi/xii, fols 54v–55r: Exeter relic list.	I	xi^{ex} Exeter
517	London, British Library, Royal 6 B. viii, fols 39–57	Alcuin, *De fide sanctae et indiuiduae Trinitatis* (conclusion); *De animae ratione liber ad Eulalium.* Supplement to a *s.* xi^{1-med} manuscript of Isidore, *De fide catholica*, bk. 1, and Alcuin, *Epistolae* = fols 1–38. Addition *s.* xii^{med}, fols 57v–73v: Alcuin, *Epistola ad Widonem comitem de utilitate animae; Epistola ad Fredegisum nobilem.*	U	xi^{2}
518	London, British Library, Royal 6 B. xii, fol. 38	Benedictional (frag.: one and one third of a leaf, used as a pastedown).	– E	xi$^{3/4}$
519	London, British Library, Royal 6 B. xiii	Eusebius of Vercelli (Pseudo-Athanasius), *De Trinitate* (I–VIII). '*Libellus fidei Patris et Filii et Spiritus Sancti Athanasii*' (?Pseudo-Gregorius Illiberitanus, *De Fide Nicaena*). Eusebius of Vercelli, *De Trinitate* (XII). Vigilius of Thapsus, *Contra Arianos, Sabellianos, Photinianos dialogus.* Potamius of Lisbon, *Epistola ad Athanasium.* Pseudo-Vigilius of Thapsus, *Solutiones obiectionum Arianorum.* Creed, '*De fide sancti Ieronymi presbyter*'. Creed of Damasus. Pseudo-Augustine, *De duodecim abusiuis saeculi.*	E/A	xii$^{1-2/4}$

520	London, British Library, Royal 6 B. xv	Cyprian, *Ad Donatum; De habitu uirginum; De lapsis; De catholicae ecclesiae unitate; De dominica oratione; De mortalitate; De opere et eleemosynis; Ad Demetrianum; De bono patientiae; De zelo et liuore; Ad Fortunatum; Ad Quirinum; Epistolae; Quod idola dii non sint; Sententiae episcoporum de haereticis baptizandis; Epistolae.* Cyprian (attrib.), *Sermones*: '*De aleatoribus*'; '*De laude martyrii*'. Cyprian, *Epistolae.*	A	xii^{1} Salisbury
521	London, British Library, Royal 6 C. i	Correspondence between Isidore and Braulio, bishop of Saragossa. Isidore, *Etymologiae.*	X; D	xi^{2} Canterbury, St Augustine's
522	London, British Library, Royal 6 C. ii	Gregory, *Symbolum fidei; Registrum epistolarum* (14 books plus supplement). Berengar of Tours, Recantation at Council of Rome (1079). Addition, *s.* xiii^{in}: Account of Papal schism (1159), and Peace of Venice.	E	xii^{in} Bury St Edmunds
523	London, British Library, Royal 6 C. iii	Ambrose, *De fide.* Gratianus Augustus, *Epistola ad Ambrosium.* Ambrose, *De Spiritu Sancto; De incarnationis dominicae sacramento.*	I	xii$^{1-2/4}$
524 †	London, British Library, Royal 6 C. iv	Gratianus Augustus, *Epistola ad Ambrosium.* Ambrose, *De fide; De Spiritu Sancto; De incarnationis dominicae sacramento.*	A	xii^{1} (pre ?1124) Rochester
525 †	London, British Library, Royal 6 C. vi	Gregory, *Moralia in Iob* (XVII–XXXV). Lanfranc, *Notae on the Moralia.* Addition, *s.* xiii, fols 1–5: Extracts from Job. Companion to British Library, Royal 3 C. iv (no. 463).	I	xii^{in} (pre ?1124; ??1108×14) Rochester
526	London, British Library, Royal 6 C. vii	Gregory, *Symbolum fidei; Registrum epistolarum* (14 books plus supplement). Decretum extract on ordination of monks. Additions, *s.* xii^{med}, fols 216v–17v: Papal and episcopal letters to the Bishop of Worcester.	E	xii^{in} Worcester
527 †	London, British Library, Royal 6 C. x	Gregory, *Symbolum fidei; Registrum epistolarum* (14 books plus supplement). ?The work of Normans in England.	I	xi/xii (pre ?1124) Rochester
528	London, British Library, Royal 6 C. xi	Jerome, *Epistolae* (128). Origen (trans. Jerome), *In Cantica Canticorum.* Jerome, *Aduersus Heluidium de Mariae uirginitate perpetua; Contra Vigiliantium.*	E	xii^{in} Bath
529 †	London, British Library, Royal 6 D. ii	Jerome, *Epistolae* (128: same collection as previous item, according to Warner and Gilson, *Catalogue*). Origen (trans. Jerome), *In Cantica Canticorum.* Jerome, *Aduersus Heluidium de Mariae uirginitate perpetua; Contra Vigiliantium.*	A	xii^{in} (pre ?1124) Rochester
530	London, British Library, Royal 6 D. iii	Jerome, *Epistolae* (now imperfect: ? same collection as item 528). Origen (trans. Jerome), *In Cantica Canticorum.* Jerome, *Aduersus Heluidium de Mariae uirginitate perpetua; Contra Vigiliantium.*	E	xii$^{1-2/4}$ Worcester

—	London, British Library, Royal 7 A. xi, fols 19–24	*See* British Library, Royal 6 A. i.		
531	London, British Library, Royal 7 C. ii, fols 166–91	Florus of Lyon, *Opusculum de actione missarum.* *Symbolum apostolorum.* *Expositio symboli apostolorum* (on the Apostles' Creed). *Expositio dominicae orationis.* *Praefatio dominicae orationis.* ?Nicetas of Remesiana, *Expositio symboli apostolorum.*	U	xii^{in} Bury St Edmunds
532	London, British Library, Royal 8 B. iv, fols 102–12, plus two unnumbered blanks	Boethius, *De consolatione philosophiae* (Bks I–II). NB: text on 112v completed *s.* xvi.	P; E	xii^{in} Bury St Edmunds
533	London, British Library, Royal 8 B. xiii, fol. 143	Processional (frag.)	–	xii^1
534	London, British Library, Royal 8 B. xiv, fols 154–6	*Commentarium in Cantica Canticorum* (Frag.).	–	xi/xii Salisbury
535	London, British Library, Royal 8 D. xiii, fols 1, 84	*Actus apostolorum* (frag.).	–	xii^{in} ?Worcester
536	London, British Library, Royal 8 D. xiii, fols 2–83	Smaragdus of Saint-Mihiel, *Diadema monachorum.* Addition, *s.* xii^{med}: A type initial.	U A	xii^{in} Worcester
537 †	London, British Library, Royal 8 D. xvi	John Cassian, *De coenobiorum institutis.*	A/E	xii^1 (pre ?1124) Rochester
538	London, British Library, Royal 9 B. xii, fols 16–273	*Decreta pontificum et concilia* (Lanfranc's collection). Later additions, *s.* xii^2, fols 2–15: Alexander III, Decretal to Theobald of Canterbury (1159). Emperor Frederick I, *Epistola* to Henry II (1159). Encyclical concerning schism of 1159. Creed of Constantinople. Record of First Council of Nicea. Leo, *Epistola ad Flauianum.*	E	xii^{in} Worcester
539	London, British Library, Royal 11 D. viii	*Decreta pontificum et concilia* (Lanfranc's collection). Lateran Council of 1112.	I	xii^1 (post 1112) ?Winchcombe; Gloucester

540 †	London, British Library, Royal 12 C. i	Ralph of Battle, *De peccatore qui desperat; Quod sint octo quae obseruant monachi; Fides exposita de ueritate corporis et sanguinis domini; De perpetua uirginitate BVM; Meditatio cuiusdam christiani de fide* (texts include authorial corrections). Anon., *Fides exposita quomodo creditur unus Deus Trinitas et Trinitas unus Deus.* Guitmund of Aversa, *De corpore et sanguine Domini contra Berengarium.* Publilius Syrus and Pseudo-Seneca, *Prouerbia.* Martianus Capella, '*De litteris*' (= extract from *De nuptiis Philologiae et Mercurii*).	A	xii^{in} (pre ?1124; possibly pre 1107) Rochester
541 †	London, British Library, Royal 12 C. iv, fols 1–43	Hyginus, *Poetica astronomica* (*De sphaera mundi*). Description of constellations (Aratus or Hyginus: Thorndike and Kibre, 473). Macrobius, *Interpretatio in somnium Scipionis* (the abbreviated version). NB: Although listed as one volume in the *c.* 1124 Rochester catalogue (EBL, 77, item 73), the three sets of quire signatures, not to mention the different ruling patterns, show that this and the next two items were initially three separate volumes.	U	xii^1 (pre ?1124) Rochester
542 †	London, British Library, Royal 12 C. iv, fols 44–137a	Paul the Deacon, *Historia Langobardorum.* See note on previous item.	E	xii^1 (pre ?1124) Rochester
543 †	London, British Library, Royal 12 C. iv, fols 138–70	Pseudo-Callisthenes (Julius Valerius), *Historia Alexandri Magni.* Epigrams on Alexander. 'Alexander', *Epistola ad Aristotelem de mirabilibus Indiae.* See note on no. 541.	U	xii^1 (pre ?1124) Rochester
544	London, British Library, Royal 12 D. iv	Calendar; Tables. Helperic, *De computo.* Bede, *De temporum ratione; Epistola ad Wicthedum de aequinoctio uel de paschae celebratione.*	U	xi/xii (not before 1090) Canterbury, Christ Church
545	London, British Library, Royal 12 E. xx	*Commentarium* on Hippocrates, *Aphorisma.* Gariopontus of Salerno, *Passionarius Galeni.* Medical tracts. Pseudo-Oribasius, *Commentarium* on Hippocrates (extracts). Pliny the Elder, extract on medicine from *Historia naturalis.* Latin abridgement of Alexander Trallianus, *Therapeutika.* Isidore, *Etymologiae* (extract).	I(f)	xii^1 ?Rochester
546	London, British Library, Royal 12 F. xiv, fols 1–2, 135 plus Oxford, Bodleian Library, Selden Supra 36*	Antiphoner (frag.: three leaves in London, one leaf (cut down) in Oxford).	–	xi^{ex+} ??Winchester

547	London, British Library, Royal 13. A. i	Pseudo-Callisthenes (Julius Valerius), *Historia Alexandri Magni*. 'Alexander', *Epistola ad Aristotelem de mirabilibus Indiae*. *Epitaphium Alexandri*. *Epistolae Alexandri et Dindymi*. *Parua recapitulatio de Alexandro et de suis*.	D	xi^{ex}
548 §	London, British Library, Royal 13 A. xi	Helperic, *De computo*. *Dies Egyptiaci*. *Ciclus annalis*. Bede, *De natura rerum*. *Ratio de aegris*. Bede, *De temporum ratione*. Aratus (attrib.), *De signis celestibus*. '*De duodecim signis*.' On the measurement of celestial circles. Dungalus, *Epistola ad Carolum Magnum de duplici solis eclipsi anno 810*. '*De eclipsi*' (=Isidore, *Etymologiae* 3, 58–9). Macrobius, *Interpretatio in somnium Scipionis* (extracts on astronomical subjects). Rules for computus. '*Versus Dionisii de annis Iesu Christi*.' '*De notis antiquioribus quae notant numeros*.' *De mensuris et ponderibus*. Diagram and Paschal Tables. Bede, *Epistola ad Wicthedum de aequinoctio uel de paschae celebratione*. Verses on the seven liberal arts. See PLATE 13.	I(f)	xii^{in} England or France
549 ★	London, British Library, Royal 13 A. xxii	Paul the Deacon, *Historia Langobardorum*. Josephus, *Excerpta* (about Moses). Contemporary addition, fol. 71v: Hymn on the preservation of Saint Bertin's Abbey from fire through the intervention of SS. Vincent, Omer and Bertin.	I	xi^2 Mont St-Michel; Canterbury, St Augustine's
550 ★	London, British Library, Royal 13 A. xxiii	Ado of Vienne, *Chronicon* (*De sex aetatibus mundi*). Chronological series of emperors to Constantine V; Dukes of Normandy from Rollo to Robert I; Genealogy of French kings.	I	xi^2 Mont St-Michel; Canterbury, St Augustine's
551	London, British Library, Royal 13 B. iv	Eusebius of Caesarea (trans. Rufinus), *Historia ecclesiastica*.	A	xii^1
552	London, British Library, Royal 13 B. v	Eusebius of Caesarea (trans. Rufinus), *Historia ecclesiastica*.	A	xii^{in} St Albans

553	London, British Library, Royal 13 D. vi	Jerome, *De uiris illustribus* (extract about Josephus). Josephus, *De antiquitate iudaica* (I–XIV). Companion to London, British Library, Royal 13 D. vii (no. 554).	I(f)	xii^{1} St Albans
554	London, British Library, Royal 13 D. vii	Josephus, *De antiquitate iudaica* (XV–XX); *De bello iudaico.* Companion to London, British Library, Royal 13 D. vi (no. 553).	I	xii^{1} St Albans
555	London, British Library, Royal 14 C. viii	Pseudo-Hegesippus, *Historiae libri V de bello iudaico.*	A	xi^{ex}
556	London, British Library, Royal 15 A. v, fols 1–29	*Actus Apostolorum.* NB: fols 1–29 and 30–85 were evidently in the same collection by *s.* xv/xvi: *teste* the note 'telos' (in Greek) added to fols 29v and 85r in the same hand.	U	xii^{in}
557	London, British Library, Royal 15 A. v, fols 30–85	Arator, *Historia apostolica.* Note on the recitation of Arator at Rome in 544. ?Alcuin (Pseudo-Columbanus of Bobbio), '*Monosticha*'. See note on previous item.		xi/xii–xii^{in}
558	London, British Library, Royal 15 A. v, fols 86–147	Commentary on Arator, inc.: '*Arator subdiaconus fuit sanctae romanae ecclesiae tempore Vigilii papae*'.	U	xii^{1}
559	London, British Library, Royal 15 A. xii	Epitaph of Terence. Terence, *Comoediae* (Calliopus's recension).	U	xii^{in} Dover
560 †	London, British Library, Royal 15 A. xxii, plus Cott. Vesp. D. xxi, fols 1–17	Solinus, *Collectanea rerum memorabilium.* Dares the Phrygian (translation ascribed to Cornelius Nepos), *De excidio Troiae historia.* Priscian, Latin verse version of Dionysius, *Periegesis.* *Prophetia Sibyllae* (*Sibylla Tiburtina*). 'Nennius' (attrib.), *Historia Brittonum.* Segardus de Sancto Audomaro (attrib.), *Versus de miseria hominis et poenis inferni.*	A/E	xii^{1} (before ?1124) Rochester
561 ★	London, British Library, Royal 15 B. xvi	Eutropius, *Breuiarium historiae romanae ab urbe condita.* Paul the Deacon's continuation of Eutropius. Table of emperors. Victor of Vita, *Historia persecutionis Africanae prouinciae.* *Passio septem monachorum.* Lections for SS. Benedict and Scholastica (including extracts from Gregory, *Dialogi*).	I	xii^{in} Normandy; London, St Paul's
—	London, British Library, Royal 15 B. xix, fols 200–5	*See* Salisbury Cathedral Library, 115.		
562	London, British Library, Royal 15 B. xxii	Ælfric, *Grammar.*	U/E	xi$^{3/4}$

563	London, British Library, Royal 15 C. iii	Suetonius, *De uita caesarum.*	E	xii^{in} London, St Paul's
564	London, British Library, Royal 15 C. xi, fols 1–58	Cicero, *Disputationes Tusculanae.*	U	xii^{1} Salisbury
565	London, British Library, Royal 15 C. xi, fols 113–94	Plautus, *Comoediae.* Isidore, *Etymologiae* I, 21.	E	xii^{in} Salisbury
—	London, British Library, Royal App. 1	*See* Salisbury Cathedral Library, 197		
566	London, British Library, Sloane 475, fols 1–124	Medical texts (acephalus) including: 'Remius Fauinus', *Carmen de ponderibus et mensuris* (copied as prose). 'Hippocrates', *Epistolae; De cibis (Diaeta).* *Dies Egyptiaci.*	E/U	xii^{in}
567	London, British Library, Sloane 475, fols 125–231	Medical texts (incomplete) including: Isidore, '*De quattuor humoribus*' (= *Etymologiae* IV, 5). Galen, *Epistola de Febribus.* Recipes. *Glossarium medicinale* (Inc.: '*Anesus, id est, herba*'). '*De urinis*' (Inc.: '*Ut per speciem urinarum*'). Gynaecological recipes (Hippocrates, *De mulierum affectibus*). Lunary. *Dies Egyptiaci.* *De significatione somniorum* (Inc.: '*Aues in somnis uidere*'). Recipes (Inc.: '*Antidotum dia pepereos*').	E	xi/xii
568	London, British Library, Sloane 1044, fol. 21	Service book: Missal (frag.: part of one leaf).	–	xi^{ex}
569	London, British Library, Sloane 1044, fol. 28	? (frag.)	–	xii^{1}
570	London, British Library, Sloane 1044, fol. 36	Bible (frag.: part of Maccabees).	–	xii^{in}
571	London, British Library, Sloane 1044, fols 38–9	Isidore, *Etymologiae* (frag.)	E	xii^{1}
572	London, British Library, Sloane 1044, fol. 40	(frag.) unidentified homily drawing on, *inter alia*, Mt. 13, 31 and Lk. 17, 6, and making reference to Plato on the nature of the human soul.	–	xii^{in}
573	London, British Library, Sloane 1086, fol. 42	Jerome, *In Ieremiam* (frag.) Kentish script.	–	xii^{1} ?Kent

574 ?	London, British Library, Sloane 1086, fol. 44	Bible (frag: part of one leaf, Incipit to Daniel).	X; A	xii¹ England or France
575 ?	London, British Library, Sloane 1086, fol. 45	Hrabanus Maurus, *Homiliae* (frag.: part of one leaf).	–	xii^in
576 ?	London, British Library, Sloane 1086, fol. 100	Bible (frag.: Deuteronomy).	X; I	xi/xii Normandy or England
577	London, British Library, Sloane 1086, fol. 108	Service book (frag.)	–	xii¹
578 ?	London, British Library, Sloane 2839	Medical texts: the 'Petrocellus' embodying Hippocrates, *Chirurgia; De cibis* (*Diaeta*). *Dies Egyptiaci.*	D	xii^in England or Continent
579	London, Grays Inn, 3	*Vitae sanctorum* (9 Feb.–29 June) (contents inventoried in *MMBL* I, pp. 52–6.) Volume one of a four-volume set: the other three volumes are not known to survive; however the *s.* xvi^in contents list gives the contents of the lost volumes.	I	xii^in
580	London, Inner Temple, 511.10	Macrobius, *Interpretatio in somnium Scipionis.*	D	xii^in Canterbury, Christ Church
581	London, Lambeth Palace, 59, fols 1–190	Anselm, *Epistolae.* Near-contemporary additions: Anselm, *Epistolae; 'Philosophical fragments'; Epitaphium Hugonis* etc.; *Admonitio moriendi* (× 2); *Versus ad laudem Domini Anselmi archiepiscopi*, inc.: '*Haud habiture parem sumas pater alme salutem*' (Walther, 7673).	I	xii^1–2/4 (post 1122) Canterbury, Christ Church
582 *	London, Lambeth Place, 62	Richard of Préaux, *In Genesim* (part I). Companion to Cambridge, Trinity College, B. 3. 14 (no. 143).	I	xii^in Normandy (?Préaux); Canterbury, Christ Church
583	London, Lambeth Palace, 64	Berengar, Recantation at Council of Rome (1059). Gregory, *Symbolum fidei; Registrum epistolarum* (14 books). Additions, *s.* xii: Papal decretals (extracts).	I(f)	xii¹
584 †	London, Lambeth Palace, 76, fols 1–146	'*Annotatio operum Augustini*'. Augustine, *Retractationes.* Isidore, *De ortu et obitu patrum; De nominibus legis et euangelii.* Jerome, *De uiris illustribus.* Gennadius, *Catalogus uirorum illustrium.* Isidore, *De uiris illustribus.* Gelasius (attrib.), *Decretum de recipiendis et non recipiendis libris.* Cassiodorus, *Institutiones* (Book I). Isidore, *De libris Noui Testamenti et Veteri prooemia.*	A	xii¹ (pre ?1124) Rochester

585	London, Lambeth Palace, 96, fols 1–112	Gregory, *In Ezechielem*. Addition, *s.* xii², fol. 1r: Egidius, bishop of Evreux, *Epistolae*.	E	xi/xii
586	London, Lambeth Palace, 144 (part II = fols 163–314)	Ezechiel (extract). Gregory, *In Ezechielem* (10 homilies). Kentish script. ?Shares artist (initials on fols 164r and 166r) with London, British Library, Cott. Claud. E. v.	I	xii¹⁻²/⁴ ?Canterbury, Christ Church; Lessness (Kent)
587	London, Lambeth Palace, 147 (part I = fols 1–59)	Bede, *In Prouerbia Salomonis*. Kentish script: ?same scribe as no 586.	A/I	xii¹⁻²/⁴ Lessness (Kent)
588 §	London, Lambeth Palace, 173, fols 1–156	Pseudo-Hegesippus, *Historiae libri V de bello iudaico*. See PLATE 21.	X; E	xii^in–1 Lanthony
589	London, Lambeth Palace, 173, fols 157–222	Ephraim the Syrian, *Vita S. Abrahae*. James the Deacon (Eustochius), *Vita S. Pelagiae*. *Vita S. Fursei*. *Visio Baronti*. *Visio Wettini*. *Visio Drihthelmi* (ex Bede, *Historia ecclesiastica*, V, 12). *Visiones* (ex Bede, *Historia ecclesiastica*, V, 13–14). *De Antigono et Eufraxia*.	A	xii¹ Lanthony
590	London, Lambeth Palace, 173, fols 223–32	*Sermo in die omnium sanctorum*.	I	xi/xii ?Lanthony
591 ?*	London, Lambeth Palace, 219	Odo of Asti, *In Psalmos*.	I	xii²/⁴ England or France
592	London, Lambeth Palace, 224	Anselm, *Monologion; Proslogion*. Gaunilo, *Pro insipiente aduersus Anselmum*. Anselm, *Liber apologeticus contra Gaunilonem; De incarnatione Verbi; Cur Deus homo; De conceptu uirginali et de originali peccato; De concordia praescientiae et praedestinationis et gratia Dei cum libero arbitrio; Unde malum; Meditatio de redemptione humana; De grammatico; De ueritate; De libertate arbitrii; De casu Diaboli; Epistolae; De processione Spiritus Sancti* (originally incomplete (completed, and further Anselmiana added *s.* xiv)).	A	xii¹ Malmesbury
593	London, Lambeth Palace, 351, fols 1–131	*Decreta* (abridgement of Lanfranc's collection). Gregory, *Registrum epistolarum* (excerpts). *Decreta: 'Sanctorum patrum uestigiis inherentes'; 'Decime tributa sunt egentium'*. Henry IV (emperor), *Epistola*. Peter Damian, *Epistola*. Additions, *s.* xii²/⁴⁺: Fols 100v–101v: *'Decretum Gregorii Pape ut episcopi nullam molestiam abbatibus uel monasteriis monachorum inferre presumant'; 'Opportet monachum sollicitudinem habere'*. Fols 102r–131r: Further collection of *excerpta* from Canons and the Fathers (including Augustine, Bede, Gregory and Ivo of Chartres).	U	xii¹

594	London, Lambeth Palace, 378 (part II = fols 122–64)	Pseudo-Hegesippus, *Historiae libri V de bello iudaico.*	I(f)	xii$^{1-2/4}$ Lanthony
595	London, Lambeth Palace, 427, fols 210 and 211	OE *Vita S. Mildrethae* (frag.). OE text on Kentish royal saints (frag.) Two originally non-adjacent leaves.	–	xi^{2}
—	London, Lambeth Palace, 430, flyleaves	*See* London, British Library, Cott. Nero C. ix, fols 19–21.		
596	London, Lambeth Palace, 431, fols 146–60	Pseudo-Augustine (Ambrosius Autpertus; here attributed to Leo), *De conflictu uitiorum atque uirtutum.*	U	xi/xii Lanthony
597	London, Private Collection CdH	Anselm, *Meditationes* (frag.: part of one leaf).	–	xii^{1} Canterbury
—	London, Private Collection CdH	*See* Oxford, Bodleian Library, Lat. misc. d. 13.		
598	London, Public Record Office, E 31/1	Little Domesday Book.	U	xi^{ex} (*c.* 1086) Winchester, Exchequor
599	London, Public Record Office, E 31/2	Great Domesday Book.	U	xi^{ex} (*c.* 1086) Winchester, Exchequor
600 ?	London, Public Record Office, E 165/43, fols 296–7	Augustine, *Enarrationes in Psalmos* (frag.).	X; E	xii^{in} England or Continent
601	London, Society of Antiquaries, 7	Anselm and Pseudo-Anselm, *Meditationes; Orationes. Preces.*	A	xii^{1} Durham
602 ?	London, Westminster Abbey, 17	*Tractatus de uirtutibus*, Inc.: '*Philosophia est inquisitio rerum humanarum*'. Arator, *Historia apostolica.*	U	xii^{in} England or Continent; Lincoln (Friars minor)
—	Maidstone, Kent County Archives, S/Rm Fae. 2	*See* Canterbury Cathedral, Lit. E. 42.		
603	Maidstone, Kent County Archives, U 1121 M2B, pp. 103–6	Boethius, *De consolatione philosophiae* (frag.: one bifolium).	I(f)	xii^{in} Rochester

604 †	Manchester, John Rylands University Library, lat. 109	*Epistolae Pauli* with Lanfranc's gloss. Fols i–ii = separable preliminary gathering of two leaves, written *s.* xii¹, containing: Account of the trial on Penenden Heath; Charter of Henry I for Christ Church, Canterbury.	U	xii^{in} (pre ?1124) Rochester
605	New York, Pierpont Morgan Library, G 63	OE version of Exodus (frag.: four leaves).	–	xi^{2}
606	New York, Pierpont Morgan Library, M 736	Pictorial cycle. Osbert of Clare, *Miracula S. Edmundi regis et martyris.* Abbo of Fleury, *Vita S. Edmundi.* Lessons for the Office of St Edmund. Hymns.	D	$xii^{1-2/4}$ Bury St Edmunds
607	New York, Pierpont Morgan Library, M 777	Gospel book ('The Mostyn Gospels').	D	$xii^{1-2/4}$
608 ?*	New York, Pierpont Morgan Library, M 926, fols 1–41	Leontius Neapolitanus (trans. Anastasius Bibliothecarius), *Vita S. Iohannis Eleemosynarii.* NB: This and the following four items were bound together by *s.* xiv.	U	xi/xii ?Continent; St Albans
609	New York, Pierpont Morgan Library, M 926, fols 42–51	Three hymns to St Alban. Office of St Alban. Mass of St Alban. St Albans See note on previous item.	I	xi^{ex}
610	New York, Pierpont Morgan Library, M 926, fols 52–68	Hymn to St Dunstan. Adelard of Ghent, *Vita S. Dunstani.* See note on no. 608.	U	xi^{ex} St Albans
611	New York, Pierpont Morgan Library, M 926, fols 69–73	Anselm's dedicatory *epistola* to Lanfranc (from *Monologion*, incomplete) [?contemporary addition]. *Vita S. Alexii.* See note on no. 608.	U	xii^{in} St Albans
612	New York, Pierpont Morgan Library, M 926, fols 74–8	Versicles, antiphons, responses for feast of St Birinus. Odo of Cluny, *Sermo* for feast of St Benedict. *Sermo* (frag.) (parts of Augustine, *De ordine*). See note on no. 608.	U	xi/xii
613	Oslo, Riksarkivet, Lat. fragm. 145	Calendar (frag.).	–	xii^{1} ?Croyland
614	Oslo, Riksarkivet, Lat. fragm. 223/1 and 2	Antiphoner (frag.).	–	xi^{ex}
615 ?	Oslo, Riksarkivet, Lat. fragm. 225/1 and 2	Antiphoner (frag.).	X; I	xi/xii England or Norway

616	Oslo, Riksarkivet, Lat. fragm. 226/1 and 2	Antiphoner (frag.)	–	xi^{ex}
617	Oslo, Riksarkivet, Lat. fragm. 228/ 1–21	Missal (frag.: twenty-one oblong strips).	–	xi^{2}
618	Oslo, Riksarkivet, Lat. fragm. 1023	Breviary (frag.)	–	xii^{1}
619 ?	Oslo and London, Schøyen collection, 76	Bede, *De tabernaculo* (frag.)	I	xi/xii England or Continent
—	Oslo and London, Schøyen collection, 79	*See* Oxford, Magdalen College, lat. 267, fols 60–1.		
620 ??	Oslo and London, Schøyen collection, 257	*Sermones.*	–	xii^{in} ?St Osyth
621	Oxford, Bodleian Library, Archivum Seldenianum B. 16 (SC 3362)	Dares the Phrygian (translation ascribed to Cornelius Nepos), *Historia Troianorum.* Orosius, *Historiae aduersus paganos.* Conflation of Eutropius, Jordanes and Paul the Deacon. Hugh of Fleury, *Historia ecclesiastica* (*Chronicon*). *Lex Romana Visigothorum* (= '*Breuiarium Alaricum*': Law code of Alaric II).	I	xii^{1} (1129) Malmesbury
622	Oxford, Bodleian Library, Ashmole 1431	Pseudo-Apuleius, *Herbarium.* Dioscorides, *Liber medicinae* (*Herbae foemineae*).	D	xi/xii Canterbury, St Augustine's
—	Oxford, Bodleian Library, Auct. D. infra 2.9, fols 111–142	*See* Supplement.		
623	Oxford, Bodleian Library, Auct. F. 2. 14 (SC 2657)	Wulfstan of Winchester, *Vita S. Swithuni.* Prudentius, *Dittochaeon.* Theodulus, *Ecloga.* Avianus, *Fabulae.* Persius, *Saturae.* Phocas, *Ars de nomine et uerbo.* [Homer] (Italicus), *Ilias Latina.* Pseudo-Ovid, '*Nux elegia*'. Serlo of Bayeux, *Versus contra monachos* (Inc.: '*Que monachi querunt*': Walther, 14995). Verses: Against simony ('*Petre nimis tardas*' (Walther, 14029); On chess ('*Belli cupit instrumentum*': Walther, 2123). Statius, *Achilleid.* Lactantius, *De aue phoenice.* Added to margins, *s.* xii^{in}: alphabetical glossary/vocabulary.	E	xi/xii Sherborne

624	Oxford, Bodleian Library, Auct. F. 2. 20, fols 1–16 (SC 2186)	Isidore, *De natura rerum*. Includes coloured diagrams.	D; U	xi[ex]
625	Oxford, Bodleian Library, Auct. F. 2. 20, fols 17–65 (SC 2186)	Cicero, *Somnium Scipionis*. Macrobius, *Interpretatio in somnium Scipionis*. *De Sibyllis et earum prophetiis* (inc.: '*Sibillae dicuntur generaliter omnes feminae prophetantes*').	A	xi[ex]
626	Oxford, Bodleian Library, Auct. F. 3. 14 (SC 2372) (?Composite)	Isidore, *De natura rerum*. Bede, *De natura rerum; De temporibus; De temporum ratione*. Helperic, *De computo*. Dionysius Exiguus, *Epistolae duae de ratione festi paschae*. Paschal Tables. Robert of Hereford, *Excerpta de Chronicis Mariani Scoti*. Additions, ?*s*. xii/xiii: Hyginus, *De sphaera celesti*. Gerbert of Aurillac (attrib.), *Regulae de astrolabio*. Tracts on the astrolabe.	D	xii[1] (pre 1125) Malmesbury
627	Oxford, Bodleian Library, Auct. F. 4. 32, fols 10–18 (SC 2176)	OE Homily (on the finding of the True Cross). A self-contained quire which was, at some point, added to the composite 'St Dunstan's "Classbook" '.	U	xi[3/4] Glastonbury
628	Oxford, Bodleian Library, Barlow 4, pp. 1–8 (SC 6416)	pp. 1–6: Homily on genealogy of Christ. Addition of *s*. xii[1] to pp. 6–7: Homily (attrib. to Jerome) on the same. This is an extra quire prefixed to a *s*. x copy of Smaragdus, *Expositio libri comitis*.	U	xi[3/4] Worcester
629	Oxford, Bodleian Library, Bodley 63 (SC 2042)	Ephraim the Syrian, *Sermones*: *De compunctione cordis; De die iudicii et de resurrectione et de regno caelorum; De beatitudine animae; De paenitentia; De luctaminibus; De die iudicii; Beatus uir qui Deum in toto corde dilexerit; Beatus homo qui inuenerit fratris uitam in illa hora; Beatus homo qui habet compunctionem*. Addition, fols 69–72: *Excerpta theologica*.	E/A	xii[in]
630 ⋆	Oxford, Bodleian Library, Bodley 92 (SC 1901)	Ambrose, *De officiis ministrorum*.	E/A	xi/xii Normandy; Exeter
631 ⋆	Oxford, Bodleian Library, Bodley 94 (SC 1904)	Ambrose, *De Isaac et anima; De bono mortis; De fuga saeculi; De Iacob et uita beata; De paradiso; De obitu Valentiniani; Epistola ad Vercellensem ecclesiam*. Jerome, *Contra Iouinianum*. Augustine, *Epistolae*.	A/E	xi/xii Normandy; Exeter
632	Oxford, Bodleian Library, Bodley 109, fols 60v–78 (SC 1962)	Substantial addition to an incomplete copy of Bede, *Vitae S. Cuthberti*, started *s*. x/xi.	U	xii[1]
633	Oxford, Bodleian Library, Bodley 120, fols i–iv (SC 27643)	Sacramentary (frag.: four leaves, all badly damaged).	–	xi[ex]

634	Oxford, Bodleian Library, Bodley 126, fols 1–58 (SC 1990)	Julianus Pomerius (Pseudo-Prosper), *De uita contemplatiua et actiua.* ?Written by the scribe of Winchester Cathedral, 2 (no. 913). Fol. 59: *s.* xii^{med} Verses, '*Aduentum Christi patriarchas premonuisse*'. This is structurally separate from the main volume (forming a self-contained bifolium with the endleaf 62) and may not represent an early addition to it. Fol. 58v looks as if it served as the endleaf of the volume, at least during *s.* xii.	A	xi/xii ??Winchester
635	Oxford, Bodleian Library, Bodley 126, flyleaves (fols ii, iii, 60, and 61)	Troper (frag.). Original order of leaves: ii, 60, 61, iii.	–	xii^{in} England or France
636	Oxford, Bodleian Library, Bodley 130 (SC 27609)	Pseudo-Apuleius, *Herbarium.* Dioscorides, *Liber Medicinae* (*Herbae foemineae*). Sextus Placitus, *Medicina de quadrupedibus.*	D	xi^{ex} Bury St Edmunds
637 †	Oxford, Bodleian Library, Bodley 134 (SC 1898)	Augustine, *Epistola* 200; *De nuptiis et concupiscentia; Epistola ad Claudium* (no. 207); *Contra Iulianum.*	A	xii^{1} (pre ?1124) Rochester; Windsor
638 *	Oxford, Bodleian Library, Bodley 135 (SC 1899)	Augustine, *Contra Faustum Manichaeum.*	I	xi/xii Normandy; Exeter
639 *	Oxford, Bodleian Libary, Bodley 137 (SC 1903)	Ambrose, *De apologia prophetae David; De Ioseph patriarcha liber I; De duodecim patriarchis; De paenitentia; De excessu fratris Satyri; Epistolae* (nos. 74, 75, 78, 80).	A	xi^{ex} Normandy; Exeter
640	Oxford, Bodleian, Bodley 145 (SC 1915)	Augustine, *Epistola* 200; *De nuptiis et concupiscentia; Epistola ad Claudium* (no. 207); *Contra Iulianum.*	U	xi^{2}
641 ?*	Oxford, Bodleian Library, Bodley 147 (SC 1918)	Pseudo-Augustine (Vigilius of Thapsus), *Contra Felicianum Arianum de unitate Trinitatis.* Vigilius of Thapsus, *Dialogus contra Arianos, Sabellianos, Photinianos.* Pseudo-Vigilius, *Solutiones obiectionum Arianorum.* Athanasius, *Epistolae.* Jerome, *Credo.* Pseudo-Jerome, *Explanatio fidei ad Cyrillum.* Possibly the work of Normans in England. The first initial (fol. 1r) was never supplied.	P I(f)	xi^{ex} ?Normandy; Exeter
642 *	Oxford, Bodleian Library, Bodley 148 (SC 1920)	Augustine, *Retractatio; De consensu euangelistarum.*	E	xi/xii Normandy; Exeter
643	Oxford, Bodleian Library, Bodley 160, fols 1–52 (SC 2014A)	Bede, *In Actus Apostolorum; Nomina regionum atque locorum de Actibus Apostolorum.*	A	xii^{1} Canterbury, Christ Church

644	Oxford, Bodleian Library, Bodley 160, fols 53–89 (SC 2014A)	Ivo of Chartres, *De modo et origine et ueritate sacramentorum Christi et ecclesiae; Sermones: De ecclesiasticis sacramentis; De clericatu et eius officio; De significationibus sacerdotalium indumentorum; De sacramentis dedicationis; Qualiter uetera sacramenta conueniant nouis; 'Corruptum peccatis'; 'Quoniam presentium'.* *Translatio S. Iacobi*, inc.: '*Nemo putet quod iste sit Iacobus*'.	A	xii^{1} Canterbury, Christ Church
645	Oxford, Bodleian Library, Bodley 161 (SC 2014B)	**A)** (fols 1–110) Bede, *In Cantica Canticorum allegorica expositio* including Gregory, *Excerpta in Cantica Canticorum.* **B)** (fols 112–64) Jerome, *In ecclesiasten Salomonis.*	I U	**A** xii^{in} **B** xii^{in-1} Canterbury, Christ Church
646	Oxford, Bodleian Library, Bodley 163 (SC 2027), fols 228–49	'Nennius' (attrib.), *Historia Brittonum.* Pseudo-Methodius, *Reuelationes.* List of counts of Flanders to Baldwin VII; Kings of France to Louis VI. NB: fols 1–227 = a *s.* xi^{in} copy of Bede, *Historia ecclesiastica*, of which fols 1, 6–7 are *s.* xii^{1} supply leaves, and include a fine arabesque initial. Fols 135v–7v are *s.* xi/xii supply leaves. NB: Fols 250–1, which were originally separate, contain: Glossary, *s.* xi^{med}; Latin homily, *s.* xi^{ex}; Book list, *s.* xii^{in} (= Lapidge, 'Booklists', no. XIII).	U A	xii^{1} (?*c.* 1111–19) Peterborough
647	Oxford, Bodleian Library, Bodley 180 (SC 2079)	OE Boethius, *De consolatione philosophiae.* OE prayer.	E	xii^{1}
648 ★	Oxford, Bodleian Library, Bodley 193 (SC 2100)	Gregory, *Symbolum fidei; Registrum epistolarum* (14 books plus supplement).	I	xi/xii Normandy; Exeter
649	Oxford, Bodleian Library, Bodley 217 (SC 2053)	Bede, *In Euangelium Marci expositio; In Epistolas Catholicas.*	A	xii^{1} Canterbury, Christ Church
650	Oxford, Bodleian Library, Bodley 223 (SC 2106)	Gregory, *In Ezechielem.* Additions, *s.* xii^{med+}: Episcopal letters etc., mainly of Worcester interest.	U	xi^{2} Worcester; Windsor
651	Oxford, Bodleian Library, Bodley 237 (SC 1939)	Florus Lugdunensis (ex Augustine), *Expositio in epistolas beati Pauli ex operibus Augustini collecta* (Rom., I Cor., II Cor., Gal., Eph., Phil., Colos., I. Thess., II Thess., I Tim., II Tim., Tit., Philem., Hebr.).	A	xii^{in} Exeter
652 ★ ?	Oxford, Bodleian Library Bodley 239 (SC 2244)	Isidore and Braulio, bishop of Saragossa, *Epistolae.* Isidore, *Etymologiae.*	E/A	xii^{in} ? Normandy; Exeter
653	Oxford, Bodleian Library, Bodley 271, fols 1–166 (SC 1938)	Anselm, *Monologion; Proslogion; De ueritate; De libertate arbitrii; De casu Diaboli; De incarnatione Verbi; Cur Deus homo; De conceptu uirginali et originali peccato; De processione Spiritus Sancti; Epistola de sacrificio azimi et fermentati; Epistola de sacramentis ecclesiae; Meditatio de redemptione humana; De concordia praescientiae et praedestinationis et gratiae Dei cum libero arbitrio; Orationes siue meditationes; De grammatico; Preces.*	I(f)	xii^{1} Canterbury, Christ Church

654	Oxford, Bodleian Library, Bodley 272 (SC 1941)	Augustine, *Enarrationes in Psalmos* (LI–C). Companion to Oxford, Bodleian Library, Bodley 273 and 289 (nos. 655 and 657).	E	xii[1] England or Normandy; Exeter
655	Oxford, Bodleian Library, Bodley 273 (SC 1941)	Augustine, *Enarrationes in Psalmos* (CI–CL). Companion to Oxford, Bodleian Library, Bodley 272 and 289 (nos. 654 and 657).	U/E	xii[2/4] Exeter
656 ?*	Oxford, Bodleian Library, Bodley 274 (SC 1942)	Augustine, *Epistolae* (132, 135, 137, 136, 138, 92, 143, 81–2, 41, 233–5, 98, 25, 27, 30–1, 24, 32, 109, 243, 26, 16, 17, 127, 214–15, 93, 102, 185, 154–5, 152–3, 117–18, 187, 121, 149, 90–1, 23, 173, 164, 130, 147, 111, 257, 96, 259, 100, 97, 265, 144, 101, 199, 266, 99, 58, 110, 77–8, 122, 245, 260–1, 264, 188, 145, 248, 205, 33, 21, 38, 112, 232, 242, 3, 141, 46–7, 258, 131, 190, 139, 134, 133, 176, 49, 43, 87, 44, 53, 105, 89, 34–5, 52, 76, 88, 51, 66, 238–41, 150, 228, 147, Pseudo-Augustine 'Ad Italicum', App, 1–15, 148, 262, 196, 80, 189, 18, 20, 19, 15, 5–7, 9, 10, 4). Additions: fol. 175, Augustine, *Epistolae*; fol. 178, Mico the Deacon, *Opus prosodiacum* (78 lines).	E	xii[1] Normandy or England; Exeter
657	Oxford, Bodleian Library, Bodley 289 (SC 2741)	Augustine, *Enarrationes in Psalmos* (I–L). Companion to Oxford, Bodleian Library, Bodley 272–3 (nos. 654–5).	E	xii[1] England or Normandy; Exeter
658 *	Oxford, Bodleian Library, Bodley 301 (SC 2739)	Augustine, *In Euangelium Iohannis*.	I(f)	xi/xii Normandy; Exeter
659	Oxford, Bodleian Library, Bodley 314 (SC 2129)	Gregory, *Homiliae xl in euangelia*. None of the spaces left for initials was filled.	P; U	xi/xii Exeter
660 ?*	Oxford, Bodleian Library, Bodley 317 (SC 2708)	Florus Lugdunensis (ex Augustine), *Expositio in epistolas beati Pauli ex operibus S. Augustini collecta* (II Cor., Gal., Eph., Phil., Col., I Thess., II Thess., I Tim., II Tim., Tit., Philem., Hebr.). Colophon. Companion to Cambridge, Trinity College, B. 4. 5 (no. 149).	I(f)	xii[in] ?Normandy; Canterbury, Christ Church
661	Oxford, Bodleian Library, Bodley 374 (SC 2484)	Augustine, *Retractatio; De ciuitate Dei*. Versus: '*Munere multiplici mirabilis enituisti / Augustine*' (mutiliated).	E/A	xii[1] Chichester
662	Oxford, Bodleian Library, Bodley 378 (SC 2748)	Augustine, *Retractatio; Epistola 174; De Trinitate*.	I	xii[1] Windsor
663	Oxford, Bodleian Library, Bodley 382, fols 1–53d (SC 2203)	Eusebius of Caesarea (trans. Jerome), *De situ et nominibus locorum hebraicorum*. Jerome, *De interpretatione Hebraicorum nominum*. Bede, *Nomina regionum atque locorum de Actibus Apostolorum*. This and the following two items comprise matching, contemporary but separable parts. These were evidently bound together at an early date: *teste* the *s.* xii contents list on fol. iv verso.	A	xii[1] Exeter

664	Oxford, Bodleian Library, Bodley 382, fols 54–68b (SC 2203)	Damasus, *Epistola ad Hieronymum.* Jerome, *Epistola ad Damasum de vii uindictis Cain; Epistola ad Euangelum de Melchisedech; Epistola ad Rufinum de iudicio Salomonis; Epistola ad Vitalem de Salomone et Achaz.* Eucherius, *Epistola de situ Iudeae.* Jerome, *Epistola ad Dardanum de Terra promissionis.* See note on previous item.	A	xii[1] Exeter
665	Oxford, Bodleian Library, Bodley 382, fols 69–91 (SC 2203)	Jerome, *Quaestiones hebraicae in Genesim.* See note on no. 663.	A	xii[1] Exeter
666	Oxford, Bodleian Library, Bodley 385 (SC 2210)	Jerome, *In Danielem.* Bede, *De tabernaculo.* Pseudo-Augustine, *Dialogus quaestionum lxv Orosii percontantis et Augustini respondentis.*	A	xi/xii Canterbury, Christ Church
667 †	Oxford, Bodleian Library, Bodley 387 (SC 2212)	Origen (trans. Rufinus), *Homiliae in Iosue.* Augustine, *De adulterinis coniugiis; De mendacio; Contra mendacium; De natura et origine animae.* *Sermo Arianorum.* Pseudo-Augustine (Syagrius), *Contra sermonem Arianorum.* Augustine, *Contra aduersarium legis et prophetarum.*	A	xii[in] (pre ?1124) Rochester; Windsor
668	Oxford, Bodleian Library, Bodley 391 (SC 2222)	Isidore, *De ortu et obitu patrum; Allegoriae sanctae scripturae.* Jerome, *De uiris illustribus.* Gelasius (attrib.), *Decretum de recipiendis et non recipiendis libris.* Gennadius, *Catalogus uirorum illustrium.* Isidore, *De uiris illustribus.* Augustine, *Retractationes.* Cassiodorus, *Institutiones* (Book I). Isidore, *De libris Noui Testamenti et Veteri prooemia.* Addition *s.* xii[2]: Antoninus Placentinus, *De situ ac mirabilibus terrae Hierosolymitanae.* The pastedown from the binding of the volume is now Lat. liturg. d. 16, fol. 9 (no. 735 below).	A	xi[ex]–xi/xii Canterbury, St Augustine's
669	Oxford, Bodleian Library, Bodley 392 (SC 2223)	Eusebius Gallicanus and Caesarius of Arles, *Homiliae.* Patrick of Dublin, *De tribus habitaculis animae.*	U/E	xi/xii Salisbury
670	Oxford, Bodleian Library, Bodley 444, fols 1–27 (SC 2385)	Isidore, *De nominibus legis et euangelii (Allegoriae sanctae scripturae); De libris Noui Testamenti et Veteri prooemia; De ortu et obitu patrum.*	U	xi/xii Salisbury
671	Oxford, Bodleian Library, Bodley 447 (SC 2680)	Bede, *De tabernaculo.*	I	xi/xii

672	Oxford, Bodleian Library, Bodley 451 (SC 2401)	Smaragdus of Saint-Mihiel, *Diadema monachorum*. Anon. treatise *De superbia et fornicatione* (Inc: '*Principaliter his duobus uitiis*'). Pseudo-Augustine, *Sermones* (12) mainly by Caesarius of Arles. Colophon (fol. 119v) signed by a *scriptrix*. Additions: fol. ii, *s.* xii^{med}, Note on Alfred, Neot and Edburga; fol. 120, *s.* xii$^{2/4}$, Account of miracle performed on blind woman.	A	xii^{in} Winchester, Nunna-minster
673	Oxford, Bodleian Library, Bodley 479 (SC 2013)	Bede, *De tabernaculo*.	U	xii^{1} Exeter ('Liber Clerobaldi')
674 ??*	Oxford, Bodleian Library, Bodley 517 (SC 2580)	William of Jumièges, *Gesta Normannorum Ducum* (incomplete: II,12–VII,42).	I	xi/xii Normandy; ?England
675	Oxford, Bodleian Library, Bodley 535, fols ii + 1–38 (SC 2254)	Hilduin of St Denis, *Passio S. Dionysii*. Flyleaf, fol. iir, contains a contemporary note, '*De preuaricatione regis Salomonis*'. Addition, *s.* xii$^{2/4}$, fol. 38: Godfrey of Winchester, *Poemata*.	U/E	xi/xii Winchester, Old Minster
676	Oxford, Bodleian Library, Bodley 535, fols 39–61	*Vita S. Neoti*. *Vita S. Mariae Magdalenae*.	E/A	xii^{in} Winchester, Old Minster
677	Oxford, Bodleian Library, Bodley 535, fols 62–94	*Vita S. Machutis*.	E	xii^{in} Winchester, Old Minster
678 ?*	Oxford, Bodleian Library, Bodley 569 (SC 2311)	Lanfranc, *De corpore et sanguine Domini aduersus Berengarium Turonensem*, embodying attributed quotations from Ambrose, Augustine, Cyprian, Gregory, Jerome, and Paul. Guitmund of Aversa, *De corpore et sanguine domini contra Berengarium*. Anselm, *De incarnatione Verbi*. Ernulf of Canterbury/Rochester, *De corpore et sanguine domini*. Addition, *s.* xii^{med}, fols 101v–2: Anselm, *Epistola de sacrificio Azimi et Fermentati*.	I(f)	xii^{1} England or Normandy; St Albans
679	Oxford, Bodleian Library, Bodley 582 (SC 2204)	Jerome, *In Ecclesiasten Salomonis*. Anon., *Expositiones in theologia* (Inc.: '*Sexto die formatur homo*'). Anon., *De nominibus Hebraicis interpretationes* (based on Eucherius, *Instructionum ad Salonium*, cc. 1–8).	I	xii^{1} Ely; Windsor
680 ?*	Oxford, Bodleian Library, Bodley 596, fols 175–214 (SC 2376)	Bede, *Vita S. Cuthberti; Vita S. Cuthberti* (verse extract). *Historia de S. Cuthberto* (incomplete). Lethaldus Miciacensis, *Vita S. Iuliani Cenomanensis antistitis* (of le Mans). Office of St Julian.	I	xi/xii ?France and Durham; Canterbury, St Augustine's (by *s.* xiv).
681 *	Oxford, Bodleian Library, Bodley 691 (SC 2740)	Augustine, *Retractatio; De ciuitate Dei*. Three original initials; others added *s.* xiv.	P; I	xi/xii Normandy; Exeter

682	Oxford, Bodleian Library, Bodley 698 (SC 2521)	Ambrose, *De Isaac et anima; De fuga saeculi; De Iacob et uita beata.* Anon., *De consecratione ecclesiarum liber.* Augustine, *De beata uita* (imperfect); *De duabus animabus.* Pseudo-Augustine (Quoduultdeus), *De quattuor uirtutibus caritatis; De tempore barbarico; De quarta feria tractatus; De tempore barbarico* (different readings).	A	xii[1] Salisbury
683 ?*	Oxford, Bodleian Library, Bodley 707 (SC 2608)	Gregory, *In Ezechielem.* Possibly the work of Normans in England.	I	xi[ex] ?Normandy; Exeter
684 *	Oxford, Bodleian Library, Bodley 717 (SC 2631)	Jerome, *In Isaiam.* Colophon-portrait of artist (Hugo Pictor).	D	xi/xii Normandy; Exeter
685	Oxford, Bodleian Library, Bodley 719 (SC 2633)	Gregory, *Homiliae xl in Euangelia.* Anselm, *Homilia super euangelium quod legitur in die assumptionis S. Mariae.* Tracts: *'Legitur in ecclesiastica historia Nabugodnosor rex Babylonie Ierusalem bellando destruxisse'; 'Noscat uestra caritas quod in diebus sollemnibus quantum possumus, altaria ornamus'.*	A	xii[1] Southwick
686 ?*	Oxford, Bodleian Library, Bodley 739 (SC 2736)	Ambrose, *De fide.* Gratianus Augustus, *Epistola ad Ambrosium.* Ambrose, *De Spiritu Sancto; De incarnationis dominicae sacramento.* Possibly the work of Normans in England.	I	xi/xii ?Normandy; Exeter
687	Oxford, Bodleian Library, Bodley 752 (SC 2522)	Ambrose, *De fide.* Gratianus Augustus, *Epistola ad Ambrosium.* Ambrose, *De Spiritu Sancto; De incarnationis dominicae sacramento.*	I	xii[1] St Albans; Oxford, Merton College
688	Oxford, Bodleian Library, Bodley 756 (SC 2526)	Ambrosiaster, *In Epistolas Pauli.*	U	xi[ex] Salisbury
689	Oxford, Bodleian Library, Bodley 762, fols 149–226 (SC 2536)	Gratianus Augustinus, *Epistola ad Ambrosium.* Ambrose, *De fide; De Spiritu Sancto.*	X; A	xi[ex] ?Ely
690	Oxford, Bodleian Library, Bodley 765, fols 1–9 (SC 2544)	Augustine, *Sermones* 351 and 393.	U	xi[ex] Salisbury
691	Oxford, Bodleian Library, Bodley 765, fols 10–77 (SC 2544)	Augustine, *De mendacio; Contra mendacium; De cura pro mortuis gerenda.* Cyprian, *De dominica oratione.* Ambrose, *Epistola* 63.	U/E	xi[ex] Salisbury
692	Oxford, Bodleian Library, Bodley 768 (SC 2550)	Ambrose, *De uirginibus; De uiduis; De uirginitate; Exhortatio uirginitatis.* Pseudo-Ambrose, *De lapsu uirginis consecratae.* Ambrose, *De mysteriis; De sacramentis.*	E	xi/xii Salisbury

693 *	Oxford, Bodleian Library, Bodley 783 (SC 2610)	Gregory, *Regula pastoralis*.	D	xi^{ex} Normandy; Exeter
694 ?*	Oxford, Bodleian Library, Bodley 792 (SC 2640)	Julian of Toledo, *Prognosticon futuri saeculi*. Ambrose, *De uirginitate; De uiduis; De uirginibus; Exhortatio ad uirgines*. Pseudo-Ambrose, *De lapsu uirginis consecratae*. Possibly the work of Normans in England.	I	xi/xii ?Normandy; Exeter
695	Oxford, Bodleian Library, Bodley 800 (SC 2658)	John Cassian, *Collationes*. Pseudo-Basil, *Monita ad monachos* (*Admonitio ad filium spiritualem*). Pseudo-Augustine, *De duodecim abusiuis saeculi*.	I	xii^{1}
696	Oxford, Bodleian Library, Bodley 804 (SC 2663)	Augustine, *Contra mendacium; De anima et eius origine* (Books I–III). Originally also contained Ambrose, *De sacramentis*; '*Ad Vercellenses*'. Plus added item: Eusebius Gallicanus, *Homiliae xii de pascha*. These seem to have been separated from the rest by *s.* xv.	E	xii^{in} Exeter
697 *	Oxford, Bodleian Library, Bodley 808 (SC 2667)	Jerome, *Quaestiones hebraicae in Genesim*. Pseudo-Jerome, *De decem temptationibus populi Israel in deserto; De quaestionibus hebraicis in libros Regum et Paralipomenon; Commentarium in Canticum Deborae; Commentarium in Lamentationes Ieremiae prophetae; Ad Dardanum de musicis instrumentis* (*De diuersis generibus musicorum*). Eusebius of Caesarea (trans. Jerome), *De situ et nominibus locorum hebraicorum*. Jerome, *De interpretatione Hebraicorum nominum*. Bede, *Nomina regionum atque locorum de Actibus Apostolorum*.	E	xi/xii Normandy; Exeter
698 ?*	Oxford, Bodleian Library, Bodley 810 (SC 2677)	*Canones apostolorum* (Lanfranc's collection). Probably the companion to Exeter Cathedral, 3512 (no. 295).	I	xii^{in} ?Normandy; Exeter
699 ?*	Oxford, Bodleian Library, Bodley 813 (SC 2681)	Augustine, *In epistolam Iohannis ad Parthos tractatus x*. Possibly the work of Normans in England.	I	xi^{ex} ?Normandy; Exeter
700	Oxford, Bodleian Library, Bodley 815 (SC 2759)	Augustine, *Retractatio; Confessiones* (NB: fols 13–20 are disordered). Includes small marginal sketch of Augustine's concubine, fol. 43v.	D; U	xi^{ex} Exeter
701 ?*	Oxford, Bodleian Library, Bodley 818 (SC 2697)	Origen, *In Matthaeum* (*uersio latina antiqua*): commentary on Matthew xvi, 13–xxvii, 64.	E/A	xii^{1} England or Normandy; Windsor
702	Oxford, Bodleian Library, Bodley 826, flyleaves (SC 2715)	Theodore of Mopsuestia, *Expositio in Psalmos* (frag.).	–	xii^{in} Canterbury, St Augustine's

703	Oxford, Bodleian Library, Bodley 826 (SC 2715)	Augustine, *Contra Faustum Manichaeum.*	I	xii^{1} Canterbury, St Augustine's
704 §	Oxford, Bodleian Library, Bodley 827 (SC 2718)	Gratianus Augustus, *Epistola ad Ambrosium.* Ambrose, *De fide; De Spiritu Sancto; De incarnationis dominicae sacramento.* See PLATE 14.	I	xi/xii–xii^{in} Canterbury, Christ Church
705	Oxford, Bodleian Library, Bodley 835 (SC 2545)	Ambrose, *De Ioseph patriarcha; De duodecim patriarchis; De paenitentia; De excessu fratris Satyri.*	U	xi/xii Salisbury
706 * ?	Oxford, Bodleian Library, Bodley 852 (SC 2611); + London, British Library, Cott. Vitellius D. xviii, fols 1–3	Fulbert of Chartres, *Vita S. Aichadri* (abbot of Jumièges). *Nomina abbatum Gemmeticensum* (from Philibert to Robert III with additions). *Vita S. Philiberti abbatis.* Pseudo-Ildefonsus (Pseudo-Jerome), *De natiuitate Dei genetricis semperque uirginis Mariae.* *Vita S. Vulganii.* At one time also included *Passiones SS. Paterni, Elphegi: teste s.* xv list. In Normandy in 1106; possibly at Malmesbury before 1125.	U	xi/xii Normandy (?Jumièges); Malmesbury
707	Oxford, Bodleian Library, Digby 20, fols 194–227	Bede, *Vita S. Cuthberti* (prose), plus chapters from *Historia ecclesiastica.* *Translatio S. Cuthberti* (extract).	I(f)	xii^{in} Durham
708	Oxford, Bodleian Library, Digby 39, fols 1–23	*Passio S. Theclae.* *Passio S. Blasii.*	U	xii^{in} Abingdon
709	Oxford, Bodleian Library, Digby 39, fols 24–39	'Hermann the Archdeacon' (attrib.), *Miracula S. Edmundi.*	U	xii^{in} Abingdon
710	Oxford, Bodleian Library, Digby 39, fols 40–9	Fulbert of Chartres, *Sermo de natiuitate BVM.* *Translatio Iacobi apostoli.*	U	xii^{in} Abingdon
711	Oxford, Bodleian Library, Digby 39, fols 50–89	Lections on Birinus from Bede, *Historia ecclesiastica* III, 7. Masses for the translation and deposition of Birinus. [Hymn to Birinus (now lacking).] *Vita S. Birini.* Osbern, *Vita S. Ælphegi.*	U	xii^{in} Abingdon
712 ?	Oxford, Bodleian Library, Digby 53, fol. 69	Antiphoner (frag.: part of one leaf, plus small strip of the conjoint leaf).	–	xi/xii England or France

713	Oxford, Bodleian Library, Digby 112, part I, fols 1–103	*Vita S. Swithuni.* *Vita S. Birini.* *Descriptio reliquiarum in magno palatio et in ecclesiis Constantinopolitanis conseruatarum cum uariis de eiusdem legendis.* *Loca sancta in ciuitate Ierusalem.* *Descriptio duodecim lapidum pro fundamentis muri coelestis ciuitatis positorum.* *Passio S. Marci Euangelistae.* *Vita Benedicti Biscop* (mainly from Bede, *Historia abbatum*). *Vita Ceolfridi* (mainly from the anonymous life, with interpolations from Bede, *Historia abbatum*). *Vita S. Egwini.* *Vita S. Maximi episcopi.* *Vita S. Eucharii episcopi.* John of Bobbio, *Vita S. Eustasii.* *Vita S. Burgundofare.* *Vita S. Saluii.* *Passio S. Indracti et sociorum eius.* Part II (fols 104–54) = Rhigyfarch, *Vita S. Davidis*; Godfrey of Winchester, *Poemata*, *s.* xii$^{2/4}$. The two parts were together by *s.* xii^{med}, *teste* contents list on the flyleaf ('i'v).	E	xii$^{1-2/4}$?Glastonbury or Winchester
714	Oxford, Bodleian Library, Digby 175	Bede, *Vitae S. Cuthberti* (prose, now begins imperfectly at the end of c. 8). *Narratio miraculosa de Ælfredo rege*, inc.: '*Deus omnipotens iuste misericors*'. Bede, *Vita Cuthberti* (verse). *Vitae SS. Oswaldi et Aidani* (ex Bede, *Historia ecclesiastica*, III: begins and ends imperfectly).	X; E	xii^{in} Durham
715	Oxford, Bodleian Library, Douce 330	Berengaudus, *In Apocalypsin.*	I	xii^{in} Lessness
716	Oxford, Bodleian Library, Douce 368	Bede, *Historia ecclesiastica.*	I(f)	xii$^{1-2/4}$ Winchcombe
717	Oxford, Bodleian Library, e Mus. 6 (SC 3567)	Augustine, *In Euangelium Iohannis.* Possidius, *Vita S. Augustini* (incomplete: stops in c. 30).	U	xii^{in} Bury St Edmunds
718	Oxford, Bodleian Library, e Mus. 7 (SC 3568)	Augustine, *Enarrationes in Psalmos* (CI–CL). Companion to Bodleian Library, e Mus. 8 (no. 719). Volume I is not known to survive.	U	xii^{in} Bury St Edmunds
719	Oxford, Bodleian Library, e Mus. 8 (SC 3569)	Augustine, *Enarrationes in Psalmos* (L–C). Companion to Bodleian Library, e Mus. 7 (no. 718). Volume I is not known to survive.	A	xii^{in} Bury St Edmunds
720	Oxford, Bodleian Library, e Mus. 26 (SC 3571)	Jerome, *In Prophetas minores* (Osee, Ioel, Amos, Abd., Ion., Mich.). Part one of a two-volume set; the second volume is not known to survive. Addition, p. 380: *Vita S. Macarii Romani.*	E	xi/xii Bury St Edmunds

721	Oxford, Bodleian Library, e Mus. 66 (SC 3655)	**A)** (fols 1–103) Bede, *In Cantica Canticorum allegorica expositio* including Gregory, *Excerpta in Cantica Canticorum.* **B)** (fols 104–54) Fulgentius of Afflighem, *Epistola* (to Franco). Franco of Afflighem, *De gratia Dei; Epistola, 'Quod monachus abiecto habitu non possit saluari'* (incomplete). Though produced to the same format and having the same style of decoration, the script of part B belongs to a later generation than that of part A.	A A	**A** xii^{1+} **B** xii$^{2/4}$ Canterbury, St Augustine's
—	Oxford, Bodleian Library, e Mus. 93	*See* Hereford Cathedral, P. V. 1, fols 29–152.		
722	Oxford, Bodleian Library, e Mus. 112 (SC 3578)	Jerome, *In Mattheum.* Anselm, *De libertate arbitrii; De concordia praescientiae et praedestinationis et gratiae Dei cum libero arbitrio; De conceptu uirginali et originali peccato.*	I	xii^{1} (1108–26) Bury St Edmunds
723	Oxford, Bodleian Library, Fairfax 12 (SC 3892)	Bede, *Historia ecclesiastica.* Cuthbert, *Epistola de obitu uenerabilis Bedae.* Abbo of Fleury, *Vita S. Edmundi.*	I(f)	xii^{1} Selby
—	Oxford, Bodleian Library, Fell 1	*See* Salisbury Cathedral, 222.		
724	Oxford, Bodleian Library, Fell 2, pp. 45–464 (SC 8690)	Passional, mainly for Nov. and Dec. (mutilated: leaves missing, initials excised). Part of 7 volume set; companion and successor to London, British Library, Arundel 91 (no. 357). Additions: Pp. 45–50, *s.* xii^{ex}, '*Relatio de ordinatione S. Augustini Cantuariensis*' (includes I(f) initial); *Libellus responsionum* (imperfect). Pp. 295–308, ?*s.* xii/xiii, Peter Manducator (Comestor), *Sermo in conceptione BVM.* Pp. 457(b)–9, *s.* xii^{med}, *Vita S. Pancratii.* Pp. 460–4, *s.* xii^{2}, Eadmer, *Vita S. Petri* (the first abbot of St Augustine's Abbey).	X; I I(f)	xii^{in-1} (?pre 1124×30) Canterbury, St Augustine's
—	Oxford, Bodleian Library, Fell 3	*See* Salisbury Cathedral, 223.		
—	Oxford, Bodleian Library, Fell 4	*See* Salisbury Cathedral, 221.		
725 §	Oxford, Bodleian Library, Hatton 23 (SC 4115)	John Cassian, *Collationes* (I–X). Bede, *In Tobiam.* Additions, fols 1 and 146v, *s.* xii^{1-ex}, Papal and episcopal letters. See PLATE 3.	I(f)	xi^{2+} Worcester; ?Great Malvern
—	Oxford, Bodleian Library, Hatton 48, fol. 77	*See* Bodleian Library, Lat. th. d. 33		
726	Oxford, Bodleian Library, Hatton 76, fols 131–9 (SC 4125)	Lapidary (Inc.: '*Hic continentur epistolae duae quas euax*').	U	xii^{in} Worcester

727	Oxford, Bodleian Library, Hatton 113 (SC 5210)	OE Homilies. Conceived as one volume with Bodleian Library, Hatton 114 (no. 728). Companion to Bodleian Library, Junius 121 (no. 732).	U	xi² (1064×83) Worcester
728	Oxford, Bodleian Library, Hatton 114 (SC 5134)	OE Homilies, including an ordered collection for Christmas to Pentecost (of which sixteen are from Ælfric, *Sermones catholici*), and for saints' days 1 May to 1 Nov. (also from the *Sermones catholici*). Conceived as one volume with Hatton 113 (no. 727). Companion to Bodleian Library, Junius 121 (no. 732).	U	xi² (1064×83) Worcester
729	Oxford, Bodleian Library, Hatton 115 (SC 5135), with Kansas, University of Kansas, Pryce MS C2:2	OE Homilies (many by Ælfric), including Ælfric, *Hexameron*. Additions, *s.* xi^ex, fol. 65, OE tract against idols ('*Ne dear ic for godes ege soðes suwian*); *s.* xii^2/4, fols 148–53, Significations.	U	xi^3/4 Worcester
730	Oxford, Bodleian Library, Hatton 116 (SC 5136)	OE Saints' lives and homilies (including many by Ælfric, and Ælfric's *Hexameron*).	U	xii¹ Worcester
731 ?	Oxford, Bodleian Library, Junius 85, front flyleaf (SC 5196)	Liturgica (frag: badly damaged).	–	xii^in England or Continent
732	Oxford, Bodleian Library, Junius 121 (SC 5232)	Wulfstan, '*Institutes of Polity*'; '*Canons of Edgar*'. OE Benedictine office. OE Penitentials. Ælfric, 2 OE Letters. OE Homilies (mainly by Ælfric). Additions, *s.* xi^2–ex, fols 1–4, Canons of councils including the Councils of Winchester 1070 and 1076; fols. 138–60, OE Homilies. Companion to Bodleian Library, Hatton 113 and 114 (nos. 727–8).	U	xi² (1064×83) Worcester
733	Oxford, Bodleian Library, Kennicott 13	Bible (Genesis-Judges)	X; I	xii¹
734 ★	Oxford, Bodleian Library Lat. bib. d. 10	Gospel book (frag.: Luke and John)	X	xi^ex Normandy; Exeter
735	Oxford, Bodleian Library Lat. liturg. d. 16, fol. 9	Sacramentary (frag.) Taken from the ?*s.* xvi binding of Oxford, Bodleian Library, Bodley 391 (no. 668), a manuscript of St Augustine's provenance and probable origin: this fragment presumptively has the same provenance.	–	xi² ?Canterbury, St Augustine's
736 ?★	Oxford, Bodleian Library, Lat. misc. b. 17, fols 1–2 and 3–4	Fols 1–2: *Vita S. Wandregesili* (Wandrille) (frag.). Fols 3–4: Paschasius Radbertus (Pseudo-Jerome), *De assumptione BVM* (Epistola, '*Cogitis me*') (frag.).	– U/E	xi/xii–xii^in France or England

737	Oxford, Bodleian Library, Lat. misc. b. 17, fol. 5	Isidore, *Etymologiae* (frag.: part of one leaf).	–	xii[1] ?Canterbury, Christ Church
738	Oxford, Bodleian Library, Lat. misc. b. 17, fol. 9	Ivo of Chartres, *Sermones* (frag.).	–	xii[1–2/4] England or France
739	Oxford, Bodleian Library, Lat. misc. b. 18, A. 7	Gradual (frag.: one damaged bifolium).	– A	xii[1] France or England
740	Oxford, Bodleian Library, Lat. misc. d. 13, fols 1–8, 11, 14, 17–24, 24a, 24b, 25, 27, 30, an 32 with Lat. misc. d. 30, fols 2–9, 12–13, 15, 17–18, and 20 (SC 30572)	Lat. misc. d. 13: Latin Chronicle of England (frag.). Lat. misc. d. 30: Latin Chronicle of Old Testament History (frag.). One further leaf is London, Private Collection CdH.	– E/A	xii[1] Canterbury, Christ Church
741	Oxford, Bodleian Library, Lat. th. b. 2, fol. 2 (SC 30588)	Augustine, *De Trinitate* (frag.).	–	xii[in] Canterbury, St Augustine's
742	Oxford, Bodleian Library Lat. th. c. 10. fols 100–101a	Augustine, *In euangelium Iohannis* (frag.: remains of one leaf (100) and one bifolium (101–1a)).	–	xi/xii
743 ?	Oxford, Bodleian Library, Lat. th. c. 10, fol. 103	Hrabanus Maurus, *Commentarium in libros IV Regum* (frag.).	–	xii[1] France or England
744 ?	Oxford, Bodleian Library Lat. th. d. 20	Augustine, *De ecclesiasticis dogmatibus*. Excerpta from Jerome, Ambrose, Gregory, and Augustine (including Augustine, *De ciuitate Dei; De uirtute Psalmorum*). *Decreta et epistolae paparum*. Germanus patriarch of Constantinople, *Ymnus in annunciatione et in omnibus festiuitatibus BVM cantandus*. Space left for a ?decorated initial on fol. 2r.	P U/E	xi[ex] (*c.* 1091) England or Normandy
745	Oxford, Bodleian Library, Lat. th. d. 33, with Hatton 48, fol. 77, and Oxford, St John's College, Ss. 7. 2, pastedown	Augustine, *Enchiridion* (frag.).	I	xi[ex] Worcester
746	Oxford, Bodleian Library, Lat. th. d. 34	Tertullian, *Apologeticum*. Pseudo-Ambrose, *Libellus de dignitate sacerdotali*. Ambrose, *Expositio de psalmo cxviii* (extracts).	U	xii[in]

747	Oxford, Bodleian Library, Lat. th. d. 46	Augustine, *Soliloquia; De immortalitate animae; De ordine rerum* (excerpts); *De diuersis quaestionibus lxxxiii.* Martin of Braga, *Formula honestae uitae.* Augustine, *De quantitate animae.* Addition, *s.* xii^{med}, fol. 103r: Martin of Braga, Preface to *Formula honestae uitae* = *Epistola Mironi Regi.*		xii$^{2/4}$ Winchcombe
748	Oxford, Bodleian Library, Laud Lat. 81	Psalter; Canticles; Litany; Prayers.	I	xi^{2}
749	Oxford, Bodleian Library, Laud Misc. 52	Ivo of Chartres, *De ecclesiasticis sacramentis* (1–5). Pseudo-Jerome, *Sententiae de essentia et inuisibilitate et immensitudine Dei.* Origen (trans. Jerome), *In Hieremiam* (8). Jerome, *Epistola* 8 (*De tribus uirtutibus*). Companion to Cambridge, Jesus College, Q. G. 4 (52) and Q. G. 5 (53) (nos. 101 and 104 above).		xii^{1} Durham
750	Oxford, Bodleian Library, Laud Misc. 140	Augustine, *Retractatio; Epistola 174; De Trinitate.*	I	xii^{in} York
751	Oxford, Bodleian Library, Laud Misc. 243	Bede, *Historia ecclesiastica.*	U	xii^{1}
752	Oxford, Bodleian Library, Laud Misc. 247	Victor of Vita, *Historia persecutionis Africanae prouinciae.* Paul the Deacon, *Historia Langobardorum.* Einhard, *Vita Caroli Magni.* Bestiary. ?Pseudo-Callisthenes (trans. Julius Valerius), *Historiae Alexandri Magni.* 'Alexander', *Epistola ad Aristotelem de mirabilibus Indiae.* *Epistolae Alexandri et Dindymi.* *Historia Apolloni regis Tyri.*	D	xii^{1}
753	Oxford, Bodleian Library, Laud Misc. 363	Ralph of Battle, *De peccatore qui desperat; Quod sint octo quae obseruant monachi; Fides exposita de ueritate corporis et sanguinis Domini; De perpetua uirginitate BVM; Meditatio de fide; De creatore et creatura; Preces; De nesciente et sciente; De inquirente et respondente.* Additions, *s.* xii^{2}, fols 163v–7v, Richard Pluto, *Aequiuoca*. Versus.	U	xii^{in} (??pre 1107) St Albans
754	Oxford, Bodleian Library Laud Misc. 364	Sulpicius Severus, *Vita S. Martini; Epistola de eodem; Dialogi.* Gregory of Tours, *De S. Bricii* (ex *Historia Francorum*). *Confessio de S. Trinitate.* Damasus, *Epistola de chorepiscopis.* *Acta et martyrium S. Vincentii.* Gregory of Tours, *De S. Vincentio* (ex *De gloria martyrum*). Augustine, *Sermones de S. Vincentio* (3). Jerome, *Vita S. Pauli.* *Lectiones in S. Martini festo.*	E	xii^{in} Thorney

755	Oxford, Bodleian Library, Laud Misc. 509, with London, British Library, Cott. Vesp. D. xxi, fols 18–40	OE Hexateuch. Ælfric, *Homilia de libro Judicum; Epistola ad Wulfgeatum; Libellus de Veteri Testamento et Nouo.* [Felix], OE *Vita S. Guthlaci.*	U	$xi^{3/4}$
756 ★	Oxford, Bodleian Library, Laud Misc. 546	Julian of Toledo, *Epistola praefatoria ad Idalium; Prognosticon futuri saeculi.*	E	xi^{ex} (pre 1096) Normandy; Durham; Finchale
757	Oxford, Bodleian Library, Laud. Misc. 636, fols 1–91	Anglo-Saxon Chronicle (E) ('The Peterborough Chronicle'). Fols 1–81 seemingly written in 1121. Additions, 1122–31, Annals written in six stages. Additions, *s.* xii^{med}, Annals for 1132–55.	A	xii^{1} (1121, 1122–31) Peterborough
758	Oxford, Bodleian Library, Rawl. C. 723	Jerome, *In Ezechielem.*	U	xi^{ex} Salisbury
759	Oxford, Bodleian Library, Rawl. G. 57 with G. 111	*Disticha Catonis* (incomplete) with glosses from Remigius of Auxerre's Commentary. Homer (Italicus), *Ilias Latina.* Verses. 'Martinus' (attrib.), *Cato nouus.* Avianus, *Epistola ad Theodosum imperatorem; Fabulae* with notes and glosses (some in OE). 'Aesopus', *Fabulae* (= '*Romulus metricus*').	U	xii^{in}
760	Oxford, Bodleian Library, Rawl. G. 139	Cicero, *Partitiones oratoriae; De officiis.* Pseudo-Quintilian, *Declamationes maiores xix.* Aulus Gellius, *Noctes atticae*, Bks 2–5 (excerpts).	U	xii^{1} Malmesbury
—	Oxford, Bodleian Library, Selden Supra 36★	*See* London, British Library, Royal 12 F. xiv.		
761	Oxford, Bodleian Library Wood Empt. 24 (SC 8612)	Augustine, *De quantitate animae.* Ambrose, *De bono mortis; De fuga saeculi; De uirginitate* (incomplete).	E	xii^{1} Durham
762	Oxford, Bodleian Library, Wood 106 (wrapper)	Virgil, *Aeneid* (frag.: one damaged folio, with part of Bk. IV). Used as a wrapper for Richard Stanyhurst, *The First Foure Bookes of Virgils Æneis* (London: Henrie Bynneman, 1583).	–	$xii^{1-2/4}$
—	Oxford, All Souls College, S. R. 58. f. 3	*See* Supplement.		
763	Oxford, All Souls College, S. R. 80. g. 8; with Eton College, 220,1; and Oxford, Merton College, 2. f. 10	Gaudentius of Brescia, *Tractatus* (frag.). Origen (trans. Rufinus), *Homiliae in Leuiticum* (frag.). Ten leaves in total.	–	xi^{ex}

764	Oxford, Balliol College, 173A, fols 74–119	Musical tracts including: Aurelianus Reomensis, *Musica disciplina* (extracts: cc. 8, 20). Pseudo-Jerome, *Ad Dardanum de musicis instrumentis.* Isidore, *Etymologiae* (extract). Guido of Arezzo, *Regulae rhythmicae.* Pseudo-Odo of Cluny, *Dialogus* (= *Explanatio artis musicae sub dialogo*).	I	xii^{1}
765	Oxford, Balliol College, 218, fols 2–70	Julian of Toledo, *Prognosticon futuri saeculi.* Addition, *s.* xii^{med}, fols 69v–70v, Decrees of the Council of Reims (1148).	I(f)	xii$^{2/4}$
766	Oxford, Balliol College, 272	Pseudo-Cicero, *Rhetorica ad Herennium.*	P	xii^{1}
767	Oxford, Balliol College, 273	Cicero, *De inuentione.*	I	xii^{1}
768	Oxford, Balliol College, 307	*Excerpta theologica* (from, *inter alia*, Augustine, *De Genesi ad litteram*; Origen, *Homiliae*; Basil, *Hexaemeron*; Anselm, *Monologion, Proslogion, De incarnatione Verbi*; Isidore, *Etymologiae*; Bernard of Clairvaux, *Homiliae.*)	I	xii$^{2/4}$ Northampton
769	Oxford, Christ Church, 95	*Epistolae Pauli*, with gloss.	I(f)	xii$^{1-2/4}$
770	Oxford, Christ Church, 115	Peter Damian, *Dominus uobiscum; Laus eremiticae uitae.* Augustine (attrib.), *Tractatus de libero arbitrio.* Bede, *De tabernaculo.*	I(f)	xii^{1} St Albans
771 ?	Oxford, Exeter College, 4	Priscian, *Institutiones grammaticae.*	I(f)	xi/xii England or Normandy
772	Oxford, Jesus College, 10, fols 1–6	Calendar. Numerous subsequent additions.		xii^{1} (1116–7×36) Gloucester
773	Oxford, Jesus College, 26	Ivo of Chartres, *Panormia.*		xii^{1} (1119×24)
774	Oxford, Jesus College, 37, fols 1–93, 95–155	John the Deacon, *Vita S. Gregorii.* Fol. 94 = inserted leaf of *s.* xii^{1}, with a sermon attibuted to Ambrose, '*Ergo a Christo non deficiunt ubera*' = parts of Ambrose, *De uirginibus* (PL 16, col. 197). Additions, *s.* xi$^{1-2/4}$, fols 156v–7, Anselm, *Epistolae* (to Odo, '*Dicitur quod tu quia sentis*' (ep. 436); and to Walther '*Litteras religiose dulcedinis tue*' (ep. 434)).	I	xii^{in} Hereford, St Guthlac
775	Oxford, Jesus College, 47, fols 5–16	Pseudo-Augustine, *Dialogus quaestionum lxv Orosii percontantis et Augustini respondentis.* Fols 1–4 are a self-contained quire which serves as flyleaves to the volume as a whole: 1v bears a note of lands pertaining to the Abbey of Pershore; and a Charter of Osbern de la Barbe; 2r has a Bull of Pope Alexander III. Though clearly bound together at an early date (*teste* contents list on fol. 2r), the quire signatures in part three and the differences in layout show that this and the following two items were originally separate.	U	xii$^{2/4}$ Pershore

776	Oxford, Jesus College, 47, fols 17–40	Leontius Neapolitanus (trans. Anastasius Bibliothecarius), *Vita S. Iohannis Eleemosynarii.* See note on previous item.	U/E	$xii^{2/4}$ Pershore
777	Oxford, Jesus College, 47 fols 41–96	Bede, *De tabernaculo.* Isidore, '*De ponderibus et mensuris*' (=*Etymologiae* xvi, 25–6). *Prophetia Sibyllae* ('*Decem sibillae fuerunt quae a doctis auctoribus celebrantur*'). Later addition: Versus: '*Res mundi uariabiles*' (Walther, 16633). See note on no. 775.	E	$xii^{1-2/4}$
778	Oxford, Jesus College 51, fol. 1	Antiphoner (frag.). Presumably had the same provenance as the main volume from *s.* xii, given that the binding is of that date.	–	xi^{2} ?Evesham
779	Oxford, Jesus College, 51, fols 2–105	Bede, *De Tabernaculo.* Isidore, '*De ponderibus et mensuris*' (*Etymologiae*, xvi, 25–6).	D	xii^{1} ?Evesham
780	Oxford, Jesus College, 54	Bede, *In Cantica Canticorum allegorica expositio*, including Gregory, *Excerpta in Cantica Canticorum.* Honorius Augustodunensis, *Sigillum Beatae Mariae.*	A	xii^{1} Evesham
781	Oxford, Jesus College, 69	Jerome, *Epistola* 83. *Quaestiones theologicae.* Bede, *In Epistolas Catholicas.* Fols. 110v–13r = near-contemporary additions.	I(f)	xii^{1}
782	Oxford, Jesus College, 102	Augustine, *Enarrationes in psalmos* (LI–C).	A	xii^{1} Winchcombe
783	Oxford, Keble College, 22	*Epistolae Pauli*, with prologues and gloss Additions, *s.* xi/xii, fols 1–3, Prologues to Romans. Fols 3–4v, Short extracts on the eucharist (from Paschasius Radbertus, *De corpore et sanguine Domini*; Hilary, *De Trinitate*; Ambrose, De sacramentis).	E	xi^{ex} Salisbury
784	Oxford, Lincoln College, lat. 27, fols 85–180	Macrobius, *Interpretatio in somnium Scipionis.*	D	xii^{in} Sempringham
785	Oxford, Lincoln College, lat. 100	Vegetius, *Epitome rei militaris.* Frontinus, *Stratagemata.* Eutropius, *Breuiarium historiae romanae ab urbe condita.* List of emperors in East and West up to Alexios Comnenos and Henry IV.		xii^{1} (?pre *c.* 1125) Malmesbury
786 ?	Oxford, Magdalen College, lat. 19	Boethius, *De musica.* '*De mensura fistularum*'.	D	xii^{1} England or Continent
787 ?	Oxford, Magdalen College, lat. 26	*Liber de ecclesiasticis sacramentis.*	I	xii^{1} England or Continent

788	Oxford, Magdalen College, lat. 172	William of Malmesbury, *Gesta pontificum Anglorum* (autograph copy).	U	xii^{1} (shortly after 1125) Malmesbury
789 ?	Oxford, Magdalen College, lat. 267, fols 60–1; with Oslo and London, Schøyen Collection, 79	Gregory, *Moralia in Iob* (frag.) The Schøyen fragment was Quaritch 1088, no. 17.	–	xii^{in} England or Continent
790	Oxford, Merton College, 181	Bede, *In Prouerbia Salomonis.* Jerome, *In Ecclesiasten Salomonis.* Alcuin, *In Ecclesiasten Salomonis.* Origen (trans. Jerome), *In Cantica Canticorum.* Honorius Augustodunensis, *In Cantica Canticorum.* Bede, *In Canctica Canticorum* allegorica expositio, including Gregory, *Excerpta in Cantica Canticorum.* John the Deacon, *Vita S. Gregorii.*	I	$xii^{1-2/4}$ Malmesbury
791	Oxford, Merton College, E. 3. 20	Priscian (frag.).	–	xii^{in}
—	Oxford, Merton College, 2. f. 10	*See* Oxford, All Souls College, SR 80. g. 8.		
—	Oxford, Merton College, Wrapper A. 35	*See* Oxford, Trinity College, C. 16. 11.		
792	Oxford, Oriel College, 42	*Collectio canonum paparum et decreta* ('*Collectio Quesnelliana*'). Leo, *Epistolae; Sermones.*	U	$xii^{1-2/4}$ Malmesbury
793	Oxford, Oriel College, 87, fols 3–10	Homiliarium (frag.; includes works by Caesarius of Arles).	–	$xii^{1-2/4}$
794	Oxford, St John's College, 17; with London, British Library, Cott. Nero C. vii, fols 80–4	Byrhtferth of Ramsey, *Epilogus.* Computistical Tables (many from the computus of Abbo of Fleury). Bede, *De temporibus; De natura rerum* (incomplete); *De temporum ratione.* Helperic, *De computo.* Dionysius Exiguus, *Epistolae duae de ratione festi paschae.* Paschal tables. *Computistica.* (See *Byrhtferth's Enchiridion*, ed. P. S. Baker and M. Lapidge (Oxford, 1995), pp. 373–427.)	D	xii^{in} (*c.* 1110) Thorney
795	Oxford, St John's College, 88	Hrabanus Maurus, *De universo* (*De rerum naturis*).	A	xii^{1} Chichester

796	Oxford, St John's College, 89	Bede, *In Apocalypsin*. Caesarius of Arles, *Expositio in Apocalypsin*.	U	xi/xii Canterbury, Christ Church
797	Oxford, St John's College, 128	Anastasius Bibliothecarius, *Epistola* ('*Inter caetera studia*'). Pseudo-Dionysius Areopagita, *De caelesti hierarchia* (Erigena's translation, 'T' version) with marginal glosses of Anastasius. John Scotus Erigena, *Epistola* ('*Valde quidem admiranda*'); *Epigrammata; Carmina*. Excerpts (from Policratus, Clement of Alexandria, and Philo). Methodius, *De principio saeculi*. Bede, *De locis sanctis*. Includes diagrams; initials unfinished.	D I(f)	xii^in
798 ?	Oxford, St John's College, 158	Anselm, *Cur Deus homo; Meditatio animae christianae; De conceptu uirginali et de originali peccato*. *Canones de poenitentia*. *Capitula de commemoratione defunctorum*. Ivo of Chartres, *Sermones* (*In dedicationem ecclesiae; De sacramentis neophytorum; De excellentia sacrorum ordinum et uita ordinandarum; De figuris et sacramentis ueteris legis; De figura crucis; De utroque Christi aduento*). Peter Damian, *Dominus uobiscum*.		xii^1 Southwick
—	Oxford, St John's College, Ss. 7. 2, pastedown	*See* Oxford, Bodleian Library, Lat. th. d. 33.		
799	Oxford, Trinity College, 28	Bede, *De tabernaculo*. '*Liber de Trinitate*' (Pseudo-Augustine, *De essentia diuinitatis*). Isidore, *De mensuris et ponderibus* (= *Etymologiae*, xvi, 25). Pseudo-Augustine (Caesarius of Arles), *Sermo de decem praeceptis legis et de decem plagis Aegyptii* (= sermo App. 21). Additions, *s*. xii, fol. 87v, margin: a neat foliage scroll drawn in lead.	U	xi^ex ??Durham; Winchester
800 §	Oxford, Trinity College, 39	Gregory, *Moralia in Iob* (I-X). Addition, *s*. xii, fol. iiv (first verso of a preliminary bifolium): Capitula for the *Moralia* as a whole. Part one of a three-volume set; volumes two and three are not known to have survived. See PLATE 20.	I	xii^in Lanthony
801	Oxford, Trinity College 60	Pseudo-Clement (Rufinus), *Recognitiones*.	E	xii^1
802 ?	Oxford, Trinity College, Old Library, C. 16. 11, rear pastedown; with Merton College, wrapper A. 35	Ivo of Chartres, *Decretum* (frag.). The Trinity portion comprises part of one bifolium. The volume (Antonius Chandeus, *Opera theologica* (Paris, 1593)) was formerly shelved at A* 8. 5.	–	xii^in England or France

803 §	Oxford, University College, 104	Julian of Toledo, *Prognosticon futuri saeculi.* See PLATE 4.	A	xi^{ex} Battle
804 ?	Oxford, University College, 114, fols 6–195	Priscian, *Institutiones grammaticae.* The additional fols 1–5 (which were clearly in place by *s.* xii^{med}) contain: Alphabet. Text on spelling, '*Rectae orthographiae ratio quae hic annotatur*' (similar to part of Lanfranc's Notes on Gregory's *Moralia*). '*Hii sunt omnes termini, Septuagesime, Quadragesime, Pasche, Rogationum, Pentecostes collecti simul*'. Versus, '*Qui petit a multis stipendia corrogat ille*'; '*Est barbarismus uerbi corruptio uilis*'. Greek alphabet.	A/E	xii^{1} Continent or England
805	Oxford, University College, 165	Bede, *Vita S. Cuthberti* (prose); plus two chs. from *Historia ecclesiastica*, and 7 miracles.	D	xii^{in} (*c.* 1100–4) Durham; Southwick
806	Oxford, Wadham College, 2 (A. 18. 3)	Gospels. Decoration remained unfinished.	D	xi^{ex}
807 †	Oxford, Worcester College, 273	*Vita S. Rumwoldi* (frag.: one leaf cut into three pieces). Probably part of a passional; and possibly part of the (otherwise lost) four-volume set recorded on the pre ?1124 booklist (EBL, 77, item 82).	–	xii^{1} (pre ?1124) Rochester
808	Paris, Bibliothèque de l'Arsenal, 236	Ambrose, *De uirginibus; De uiduis.* Pseudo-Ambrose, *De lapsu uirginis consecratae; Consolatio ad uirginem lapsam.* Ambrose, *De mysteriis; De sacramentis.* NB: the volume is foliated incorrectly: the numeration runs 'A, 1–27, then 23–151', '151' having been a pastedown at some point. The flyleaf, 'A' bears a fine but faint late medieval lead sketch of a seated male figure. There is also a crude ink drawing of the crucified Christ in the outer margin of the second fol. 25r. Though difficult to date with confidence, it is possibly *s.* xii^{1}, and conceivably the work of the hand which added corrections in the margin of 9r.	[D] U	?xii^{1}
809	Paris, Bibliothèque nationale, lat. 1751	Ambrose, *De uirginibus; De uiduis; De uirginitate; Exhortatio uirginitatis.* Pseudo-Ambrose, *De lapsu uirginis consecratae; Consolatio ad uirginem lapsam.* Ambrose, *De mysteriis; De sacramentis.* Pseudo-Jerome, *Epistola* 38 (*Homilia de corpore et sanguine Christi*).	E	xi^{ex} ?Canterbury, St Augustine's
810	Paris, Bibliothèque nationale, lat. 1906	Augustine, *Retractationes.* Cassiodorus, *Institutiones* (Book I). Isidore, *De libris Noui Testamenti et Veteri prooemia; De ortu et obitu patrum; Allegoriae sanctae scripturae.* Jerome, *De uiris illustribus.* Gelasius (attrib.), *Decretum de recipiendis et non recipiendis libris.* Gennadius, *De uiris illustribus* (abbreviated). Isidore, *De uiris illustribus.*	I(f)	xii^{1}

811	Paris, Bibliothèque nationale, lat. 2478	Anselm, *Epistolae.* Council of London (1102). *Versus in laudem S. Anselmi*, inc.: '*Haud habiture parem sumas pater alme*' (Walther, 7673). Contemporary addition, fols 136v–8v: List of Popes to Gelasius II (extended to Honorius II).	I(f)	xii$^{1-2/4}$
812	Paris, Bibliothèque nationale, lat. 12204	Augustine, *De Trinitate* (i). The script belongs to xii$^{1-2/4}$. The initials by contrast are retrospective both in style and design, mainly evoking work of xi/xii (two echo work of *c.* 1125): they would seem to be either the work of an old or conservative hand, or to have been largely copied from those in an exemplar produced a generation earlier.	I	xii$^{1-2/4}$ Saint-Germain-des-Prés
813	Paris, Bibliothèque nationale, lat. 14782	Gospels.	D	xi^{2} Exeter
814	Paris, Bibliothèque nationale, lat. 15170, fols 71–125	Macrobius, *Interpretatio in somnium Scipionis.*	I	xii^{in}
815 †	Rochester Cathedral, A. 3. 5, fols 1–118 (formerly deposited in Maidstone, Kent County Archives DRc/R1; now in Strood, Rochester-upon-Medway Studies Centre)	OE Laws; charm; *Institutiones Henrici I; Excommunicatio.* West Saxon genealogy; Anglo-Saxon royal genealogies; Lists of Popes, Emperors, Patriarchs, English Archbishops and Bishops. (The *Textus Roffensis*, part I.) A *s.* xiv note on fol. 1r associates the volume with Ernulf, bishop of Rochester 1114–24. NB: this and the following item, although originally separate were bound together by *s.* xiv.	U/E	xii^{1} (*post* 1122–3; ?pre 1124) Rochester
816	Rochester Cathedral, A. 3. 5, fols 119–229 (Strood, Rochester-upon-Medway Studies Centre, DRc/R1)	Cartulary of Rochester Cathedral priory in Latin and OE (including excerpt from Domesday Book). List of offices to be said for members of confraternity. Book list (incomplete). (The *Textus Roffensis*, part II.) Fols 164, 166, 181 = supply leaves. Additional leaves, *s.* xii^{2+}: fols 177–80, 193–4, 197, 203–8, 213, 217, 222, 230–5. See note on previous item.	I(f)	xii^{1} (*post* 1122–3) Rochester
817 †	Rochester Cathedral, A. 3. 16	Augustine, *De consensu euangelistarum; De sermone Domini in monte; De blasphemia in Spiritum Sanctum* (= sermo 71). Pseudo-Augustine (Caesarius of Arles), *Sermo de decem praeceptis legis et decem plagis Aegyptii* (= Pseudo-Augustine, Sermo App. 21).		xii^{1} (pre ?1124) Rochester
818	Rouen, Bibliothèque municipale, A. 21	Contemporary colophon explaining the commissioning of the book by Abbot Reginald of Abingdon for Jumièges. Gospel book.	D	xi^{ex} (1087×97) Abingdon; Jumièges
819	Rouen, Bibliothèque municipale, A. 44	Psalter (mutilated); Canticles; Litany; Prayers; Hymns; Monastic canticles.	X; I	xi/xii ?Canterbury, St Augustine's; Jumièges

820	Saint Lô, Archives de la Manche, 1	Gospel book (badly damaged).	D	xi$^{3/4}$ Saint Evroul de Mortain
—	St Petersburg, Public Library, O. v. I. 45	*See* Warsaw, Biblioteca Naradowa, I. 3311.		
821	Salisbury Cathedral, 4	Hilary, *De Trinitate; De synodis.*	U	xii^{1} Salisbury
822	Salisbury Cathedral, 5	Pelagius, *Commentarium in Epistolas Pauli.*	U	xii^{1} Salisbury
823 §	Salisbury Cathedral, 6	Augustine, *Retractatio; Confessiones.* See PLATE 10.	E(f)	xi^{ex} Salisbury
824	Salisbury Cathedral, 7	Isidore, *Liber sententiarum.*	U	xii^{1} Salisbury
825	Salisbury Cathedral, 9	Cyprian, *De dominica oratione; De bono patientiae; De opere et eleemosynis.* Gregory Nazianzenus (trans. Rufinus), *De Hieremia propheta* (= *Oratio* XVII). Cyprian, *De mortalitate; De catholicae ecclesiae unitate.* Caesarius of Arles, *Epistola 2.* Pseudo-Isidore (Sisbertus Toletanus), *Lamentum paenitentiae.* 'Versus beati Isidori' Texts in dialogue format. Questions and answers on biblical topics including Pelagius, *Libellus fidei ad Innocentium papam.* Additions, *s.* xii^{1}, fols 60v–81, monastic florilegium, including Pseudo-Jerome, Caesarius, Pseudo-Augustine (contents itemised in Webber, *Scribes and Scholars*, pp. 160–2).	U	xi/xii–xii^{in} Salisbury
826	Salisbury Cathedral, 10, fols 3–114	John Cassian, *Collationes* I–X, XIV, XV, XXIV, and XI.	I	xi^{ex} Salisbury
827	Salisbury Cathedral, 11	Pseudo-Clement (trans. Rufinus), *Recognitiones.*	U	xii^{1} Salisbury
828	Salisbury Cathedral, 12	Smaragdus, *Diadema monachorum.* Additions, *s.* xii^{1}, fols 56–60: Eutropius episcopus Valentinensis, *De districtione monachorum.* The *Rule of the Four Fathers* (imperfect). The manuscript originally also contained a '*Catalogus librorum Augustini*'.	U/E	xi/xii Salisbury
829	Salisbury Cathedral, 24	Jerome, *In Ieremiam.* The top of the first leaf is missing: it is possible an E initial has been lost.	X; U	xi/xii Salisbury
830	Salisbury Cathedral, 25	Jerome, *In Isaiam.*	U	xi/xii Salisbury
831	Salisbury Cathedral, 33	Gregory, *Moralia in Iob* (complete in one volume). NB: fols 1–66 (= Bks I–IV, plus part of V) were replaced, *s.* xii^{2}.	P I(f)	xi^{ex} Salisbury

832	Salisbury Cathedral, 35	Augustine, *Speculum quis ignorat.* Pseudo-Augustine, *Hypomnesticon contra Pelagianos et Caelestianos* (*Responsiones* i–iv). Pseudo-Augustine (Quoduultdeus), *De cataclysmo; De cantico nouo.* Pseudo-Augustine (Vigilius of Thapsus), *Contra Felicianum Arianum.* Augustine, *De symbolo ad catechumenos*, i–iv (ii–iv = Pseudo-Augustine [Quoduultdeus]); *Retractatio; De agone christiano; Sermones.* Pope Nicholas I, *Epistola.* *Concilium.*	U	xii^{1} Salisbury
833	Salisbury Cathedral, 37	Bede, *In euangelium Lucae expositio.*	U	xi/xii Salisbury
834	Salisbury Cathedral, 57	Augustine, *Enarrationes in Psalmos* (I–L). Companion to Salisbury Cathedral, 58 (no. 835).	E	xii^{1} Salisbury
835	Salisbury Cathedral, 58	Augustine, *Enarrationes in Psalmos* (L–C). Companion to Salisbury Cathedral, 57 (no. 834).	U	xii^{1} Salisbury
836	Salisbury Cathedral, 59	Cassiodorus, *Expositio psalmorum* (CI–CL).	E	xii^{1} Salisbury
837	Salisbury Cathedral, 61, fols 1–10	Augustine, *Sermones* (65, 53, 277, 330). Pseudo-Augustine, *Sermo de misericordia.*	U	xii^{1} Salisbury
838	Salisbury Cathedral, 61, fols 11–20	Augustine, *Epistola* 36. Pseudo-Augustine, (Ambrosius Autpertus), *De conflictu uitiorum et uirtutum.* Catena of extracts from Augustine and others.	U	xii^{1} Salisbury
839	Salisbury Cathedral, 61, fols 21–30	Augustine, *Retractatio; De natura boni.*	U	xii^{1} Salisbury
840	Salisbury Cathedral, 61, fols 31–52	Heriger of Lobbes, *De corpore et sanguine Domini* with enlarged Paschasian catena of eucharistic proof texts. Arnobius (Iunior), *Conflictus cum Serapione de Deo trino et uno.*	U	xii^{1} Salisbury
841	Salisbury Cathedral, 63	Augustine, *Retractatio; De agone christiano; De disciplina christiana; Sermo* (App. 252). Theodulf of Orléans, *De processione Spiritus Sancti.* Augustine, *De utilitate credendi; De gratia Noui Testamenti* (*epistola* 140); *Retractatio; De natura boni.* Pseudo-Augustine (Quoduultdeus), *Contra quinque haereses.*	U	xi^{ex} Salisbury
842	Salisbury Cathedral, 64	**A)** Augustine, *De pastoribus; De ouibus; De peccatorum meritis et remissione et de baptismo paruulorum; Epistola ad Marcellinum; De unico baptismo.* **B)** Augustine, *De baptismo contra Donatistas; De spiritu et littera.* One volume of two contemporary parts, which are currently bound in the wrong order. The above listing presents them in their original order.	E/I	xii^{1} Salisbury
843	Salisbury Cathedral, 65	Augustine, *Epistola* 200; *De nuptiis et concupiscentia; Epistola ad Claudium* (207); *Contra Iulianum.*	E/I	xii^{1} Salisbury

844	Salisbury Cathedral, 67	Augustine, *In euangelium Iohannis.* NB: fols 1–24 and 227–9 were replaced, *s.* xiii; the original beginning is lost.	X; E	xi^{ex} Salisbury
845	Salisbury Cathedral, 78	*Decreta pontificum et concilia* (Lanfranc's collection).	I	xi^{ex} Salisbury
846	Salisbury Cathedral, 88	Jerome, *De uiris illustribus.* Gelasius (attrib.), *Decretum de libris recipiendis et non recipiendis.* Gennadius, *De uiris illustribus.* Isidore, *De uiris illustribus.* Augustine, *Retractationes.* Cassiodorus, *Institutiones* (Book I). Isidore, *De libris Noui Testamenti et Veteri prooemia; De ecclesiasticis officiis* (I, 11–12); *De ortu et obitu patrum; Allegoriae sacrae scripturae.* Note on historical interpretation of Bible.	E	xi^{ex} Salisbury
847 ★	Salisbury Cathedral, 89	Gregory Nazianzenus (trans. Rufinus), *Orationes* (imperfect at the beginning). On the flyleaf (fol. 4r), Anglo-Norman *Laudes regiae.* On the endleaves (82v–3r), Tables.	I	xi^{2} Normandy (Fécamp); Salisbury
848	Salisbury Cathedral, 106	Augustine, *De doctrina christiana; De quantitate animae; Sermo 37;* part of an Easter sermon attrib. to Augustine; *De octo Dulcitii quaestionibus; De libero arbitrio; De natura boni; De uera religione; De disciplina christiana.*	U	xi^{ex} Salisbury
849	Salisbury Cathedral, 109, fols 1–8 with MS 114, fols 2–5, and MS 128, fols 1–4	Augustine, *De Genesi ad litteram* (frag.).	U	xi/xii Salisbury
850	Salisbury Cathedral, 109, fols 9–99	Prosper of Aquitaine, *De gratia Dei et libero arbitrio contra Collatrem; Pro Augustino responsiones ad capitula obiectionum Gallorum calumniantium; Pro Augustino responsiones ad capitula obiectionum Vincentianarum; Pro Augustino responsiones ad excerpta Genuensium.* Augustine, *De octo Dulcitii quaestionibus.* Pseudo-Augustine, *Hypomnesticon contra Pelagianos et Caelestianos.* Sermons for Christmas and Easter (by Augustine, Eusebius, Origen). Pseudo-Ambrose, *De Salomone (Sermo* 46). Ambrose, *De mysteriis; De Gedeone; De apologia prophetae David.*	E/I	xii^{1} Salisbury
851	Salisbury Cathedral, 110	Aethicus Ister (Virgil of Salzburg), *Cosmographia.*	U	xii^{1} Salisbury
852	Salisbury Cathedral, 110, flyleaf	Chalcidius, *Commentarium in Platonis Timaeum* (frag.).	–	xii^{1} Salisbury
853	Salisbury Cathedral, 112	?Correspondence between Isidore and Braulio, bishop of Saragossa. Isidore, *Etymologiae.*	U	xii^{1} Salisbury

—	Salisbury Cathedral, 114, fols 2–5	*See* Salisbury Cathedral, 109		
854	Salisbury Cathedral, 114, fols 6–122	Augustine, *De Genesi ad litteram.*	U	xi^{ex} Salisbury
855	Salisbury Cathedral, 115, with London, British Library, Royal 15 B. xix, fols 200–5	Gregory, *Moralia in Iob* (XVIII, extracts). Compendium in dialogue form (ex Pseudo-Augustine, *Dialogus quaestionum* lxv, and Eucherius, *Instructionum ad Salonium*). Gelasius (attrib.), *Decretum de libris recipiendis et non recipiendis.* Agnellus, *Epistola de ratione fidei ad Arminium.* Faustus of Reiez, *De ratione fidei.* Questions and answers on the Trinity; and on the Old and New Testaments. Symphosius, *Aenigmata.* Boniface, *Aenigmata de uirtutibus.*	U	xii^{1} Salisbury
856	Salisbury Cathedral, 116	Augustine, *Contra Faustum Manichaeum.*	E/I	xii^{1} Salisbury
857	Salisbury Cathedral, 118	Augustine, *De magistro; Confessiones* (extracts). Possidius, *Vita S. Augustini* (epitome). Augustine, *De decem chordis.*	U	xii^{1} Salisbury
858	Salisbury Cathedral, 119	Freculphus of Lisieux, *Chronicon*, Bk I.	U	xi/xii Salisbury
859	Salisbury Cathedral, 120	Freculphus of Lisieux, *Chronicon*, Bk I.	U	xi/xii Salisbury
860	Salisbury Cathedral, 124	Hilary, *In Mattheum.* Irish Pseudo-Hilary, *In septem epistolas catholicas.*	U	xii^{1} Salisbury
861	Salisbury Cathedral, 125	Isidore, *De differentiis.* Pseudo-Isidore, *Liber de uariis quaestionibus aduersos Iudaeos.*	U	xii^{1} Salisbury
—	Salisbury Cathedral, 128, fols 1–4	*See* Salisbury Cathedral, 109		
862	Salisbury Cathedral, 128, fols 5–116	Augustine, *De adulterinis coniugiis; De natura et origine animae.* *Sermo Arianorum.* Pseudo-Augustine (Syagrius), *Contra sermonem Arianorum.* Augustine, *Contra aduersarium legis et prophetarum.*	U	xi^{ex} Salisbury
863	Salisbury Cathedral, 129	Pseudo-Augustine (Ambrosiaster), *Quaestiones Veteris et Noui Testamenti CXXVII.*	U	xi/xii Salisbury
864	Salisbury Cathedral, 130	Paschasius Radbertus, *De corpore et sanguine Domini* (embodying Augustine, *Sermo* 52). Paulinus of Aquileia, *Liber exhortationis.*	U	xii^{1} Salisbury
865	Salisbury Cathedral, 131	Ephraim the Syrian, *Sermones* (*De compunctione cordis; De die Iudicii et de resurrectione et de regno caelorum; De beatitudine animae; De paenitentia; De luctaminibus; De die iudicii*).	I	xii^{1} Salisbury
866	Salisbury Cathedral, 132	Gregory, *Homiliae xl in Euangelia.*	U	xii^{in} Salisbury

867	Salisbury Cathedral, 135, fols 1–24	Treatise on church rites and observances: '*Signorum usus a Veteri Testamento sumptus est . . .*'.	U	xi/xii Salisbury
868	Salisbury Cathedral, 135, fols 25–59	Isidore, *Quaestiones in Vetus Testamentum* (unfinished).	U	xi^{ex} Salisbury
869	Salisbury Cathedral, 136	Bede, *In Samuelem prophetam allegorica expositio.*	U	xii^{1} Salisbury
870	Salisbury Cathedral, 137	Jerome, *In Mattheum.*	U	xii^{1} Salisbury
871	Salisbury Cathedral, 138	Augustine, *Epistolae 200; De nuptiis et concupiscentia; Epistola ad Claudium* (*Epistola* 207); *Contra Iulianum.*	U	xi^{ex} Salisbury
872	Salisbury Cathedral, 139	Eusebius of Caesarea (trans. Rufinus), *Historia ecclesiastica.*	I	xii^{1} Salisbury
873	Salisbury Cathedral, 140	Ambrose, *De fide; De Spiritu Sancto; De incarnationis dominicae sacramento.*	U	xi^{ex} Salisbury
874	Salisbury Cathedral, 140, flyleaves	Berengaudus, *In Apocalypsin* (frag. of unfinished copy).	U	xi/xii Salisbury
875	Salisbury Cathedral, 150 (gloss)	Continuous OE gloss added to psalter of s. x^{2}. The original book is decorated with I(f) initials.	–	xi/xii ?Wilton or Shaftesbury
876	Salisbury Cathedral, 154	Amalarius, *De ecclesiasticis officiis.*	U	xi^{ex} Salisbury
877 ??	Salisbury Cathedral, 157 (i)	Gregory, *Regula pastoralis.* Hymn to BVM. The early history of this and the following two, separable items is obscure. Certainly at Salisbury by *s.* xvii, it is unclear which side of the Channel they were written. A copy of a Norman charter of 1211 on the final leaf of part iii suggests it was in Normandy in *s.* xiii, but does not rule out an origin in England.		xi^{ex} Normandy or England
878 ??	Salisbury Cathedral, 157 (ii)	Augustine, *Enchiridion.* Pseudo-Augustine, *Dialogus quaestionum lxv Orosii percontantis et Augustini respondentis.* Augustine, *De orando Deo* (*Epistola* 130). [Gregory], *De iuramento episcoporum.* Service for the consecration of a church. See note on previous item.		xi^{ex} Normandy or England
879 ??	Salisbury Cathedral, 157 (iii)	Isidore, *Allegoriae sanctae scripturae; Quaestiones de Veteri et Nouo Testamento; De ortu et obitu patrum.* Fols 1–4, 171–4 = ?rejected leaves of Augustine, *Enchiridion.* See note on no. 877.		xi^{ex} Normandy or England
880	Salisbury Cathedral, 159	Origen (trans. Rufinus), *Homiliae in Exodum; Homiliae in Leuiticum.*	E	xi/xii Salisbury

881 ?*	Salisbury Cathedral, 160	Anon., *Commentarium in Psalmos et Cantica.*		xii¹ ?France; Salisbury (by *s.* xiii)
882	Salisbury Cathedral, 162, flyleaves	Berengaudus, *In Apocalypsin* (frag.).	–	xi/xii Salisbury
883	Salisbury Cathedral, 162, fols 3–18	Rufinus of Aquilea, *De Symbolo.*	U	xii¹ Salisbury
884	Salisbury Cathedral, 162, fols 19–27	*Scala uirtutum.*	U	xii¹ Salisbury
885	Salisbury Cathedral, 165, fols 1–10	Pseudo-Augustine (Vigilius of Thapsus), *Contra Felicianum Arianum.* This and the following two items were produced to the same format.	U	xi/xii Salisbury
886	Salisbury Cathedral, 165, fols 11–22	Pseudo-Methodius, *Reuelationes.* See note on previous item.	U	xi/xii Salisbury
887	Salisbury Cathedral, 165, fols 23–87	Bede, *De Tabernaculo.* See note on no. 885.	U	xi/xii–xii^in Salisbury
888	Salisbury Cathedral, 165, fols 88–107 (105–7 are blank)	Augustine, *De praesentia Dei.* Pseudo-Augustine (Pelagius), *De uita christiana ad sororem suam uiduam.* Pseudo-Augustine, *Ad inquisitiones Ianuarii* (I and II). Different format from nos. 885–7.	U	xii¹ Salisbury
889	Salisbury Cathedral, 165, fols 108–21	Augustine, *De diuersis haeresibus.*	E/U	xii^in Salisbury
890	Salisbury Cathedral, 165, fols 122–78	Alcuin, *De fide sanctae et indiuiduae Trinitatis; De Trinitate ad Fredegisum quaestiones xxviii; De animae ratione liber ad Eulalium.* Gennadius, *Liber siue diffinitio ecclesiasticorum dogmatum.* Gelasius (attrib.), *Decretum de libris recipiendis et non recipiendis.* Pseudo-Jerome, *De duodecim scriptoribus.* Two eucharistic miracle stories.	E	xi^ex Salisbury
891	Salisbury Cathedral, 168	Augustine, *De diuersis quaestionibus lxxxviii.* Pseudo-Augustine, *De duodecim abusiuis saeculi.* Bede, *De die iudicii.*	E	xi^ex Salisbury
892	Salisbury Cathedral 169	**A)** (fols 1–77r) Augustine, *De utilitate agendae paenitentiae.* Pseudo-Augustine, *Dialogus quaestionum lxv Orosii percontantis et Augustini respondentis.* Pseudo-Augustine (Vigilius of Thapsus), *Contra Felicianum Arianum.* Augustine, *De disciplina christiana; Sermo 37.* Part of Easter sermon attrib. to Augustine. Augustine, *De octo Dulcitii quaestionibus; De orando Deo* (*Epistola* 130). **B)** (fols 77v–91) Augustine, *Regula ad seruos Dei.* Bede, *In Tobiam.*	U U	xi/xii Salisbury xii¹

893	Salisbury Cathedral 179	Paul the Deacon, *Homiliarium* (*pars aestiualis* [imperfect]).	E	xi/xii Salisbury
894	Salisbury Cathedral, 197, with London, British Library, Royal App. 1	Augustine, *Epistola* 166; *De immortalitate animae.* Pseudo-Augustine, *Hypomnesticon contra Pelagianos et Caelestianos* (*Responsiones* i–iv). Jerome, *Altercatio Luciferiani et Orthodoxi.* Possidius, *Vita S. Augustini*, c. *xvii.* Augustine, *Epistolae 238–41; De Genesi ad litteram* (imperfect); *De opera monachorum; Epistola 259; De vita et moribus clericorum; Sermones.* Possidius, *Vita S. Augustini* (extract: c. 30). Augustine, *Epistola 228.*	U	xii[1] Salisbury
895	Salisbury Cathedral, 198 (*olim* Lancing College [Sotheby's, Dec. 1970, lot. 25])	Augustine, *Epistola 147* (= *De uidendo Deo*); *De fide et symbolo; Sermo 180; De agone christiano; De orando Deo* (= *Epistola 130*); *Sermo 291; De urbis excidio; Epistola 127.* Possidius, *Vita S. Augustini.* Augustine, *Sermones* (259, 350, 346–8). ?Anon., *Tractatus de fide*, inc.: '*Hoc dicimus et hoc docemus*'. Augustine, *Epistola 228; Sermo 82; De utilitate agendae paenitentiae.* Pseudo-Augustine, *Ad Inquisitiones Ianuarii* (I and II). Augustine, *De cura pro mortuis gerenda.*	E	xii[1] Salisbury
896	Salisbury Cathedral, 221 (*olim* Oxford, Bodleian Library, Fell 4)	Legendary (January–June; contents itemised in Webber, *Scribes and Scholars*, pp. 154–6; two lives missing). Additions, *s.* xii[in], fols 223–4, *Passio S. Blasii*; *s.* xii[1], fol. 278, Matthias.	E	xi[ex] Salisbury
897	Salisbury Cathedral, 222 (*olim* Oxford, Bodleian Library, Fell 1)	Legendary (July–December; contents itemised in Webber, *Scribes and Scholars*, pp. 156–7; begins imperfectly).	U/E	xi[ex] Salisbury
898	Salisbury Cathedral, 223, with MS 222, fol. 1 (*olim* Oxford, Bodleian Library, Fell 3)	*Vitae sanctorum* (mainly January–June; contents itemised in Webber, *Scribes and Scholars*, pp. 169–70). ?Companion to Dublin, Trinity College, 174 (no. 202 above).	U	xii[1] Salisbury
899 †	San Marino, Ca., Huntington Library, HM 62, vol. I	Bible (Genesis–Nehemiah, plus Matt.–John) (The 'Gundulf Bible'). Additions, *s.* xii[med], fols 240–1: Alcuin, Verses on the books of the Bible. Theodulf of Orléans, Verses on the books of the Bible. Six verses of an unidentified *Chanson de geste: 'Oor escutez seinurs que deus vus seit ami'.* *S.* xiii inscription on the flyleaf associates the volume with Bishop Gundulf. Companion to the next item.	E	xi[2] Rochester
900 †	San Marino, Ca., Huntington Library, HM 62, vol. II	Bible (Kings–Epistles, Baruch). *S.* xiii inscription on the flyleaf associates the volume with Bishop Gundulf. Companion to the previous item.	E	xi[2] Rochester

901 ★	Shrewsbury School, 21	Gregory, *Regula pastoralis.*	I	xi/xii Normandy; Durham
902	Shrewsbury School, 37	Juvenal, *Saturae cum scholiis.*	E	xii^{in}
903 ?	Stockholm, Kungliga Biblioteket, A. 128	Gradual (frag.) (six leaves, five of which are well preserved, apart from fold marks). Reused as wrappers.	– U/E	xi^{2-ex} Sweden
904	Stockholm, Riksarkivet, Fragm. 194 + 195	Augustine, *Sermones* (including *De baptismo paruulorum*) (frag.). Fragments from Östergötlands handlingar 1578:7:2 and 1578:7:3. Appearance is wholly Norman; however the Swedish provenance favours transmission via, or even origin in England.	– E	xi/xii Normandy or England; Sweden
–	Stockholm, Riksarkivet, Fragments	*See* supplement.		
905	Tokyo, Prof. T. Takamiya, 55 (*olim* Sotheby's 24 June, 1980)	Augustine, *Enarrationes in Psalmos* (frag.: portions from eight leaves). Part of volume II of a three-volume set: companion to Cambridge, Trinity College, B. 5. 26 and B. 5. 28 (nos. 158–9).	– A/E	xi/xii Canterbury, Christ Church
906 ??	Trier, Stadtbibliothek, 9	Psalter.	I	xii^{1} Ely
907 ?	Ushaw, St Cuthbert's College	Missal (frag.)	–	xii^{1} Ely
908 †	Vatican City, Biblioteca Apostolica Vaticana, Reg. lat. 458, fols 1–36; with 598, fol. 8; and 646, fols 1–49	Osbern, *Vita S. Ælphegi; Epistola de uita S. Dunstani; Vita S. Dunstani.* Mass for St Dunstan. Mass for St Ælphege. Originally also contained '*Sermones de dedicatione ecclesiae*', *teste* early library catalogue (EBL, 77, item 77).	E	xii^{1} (pre ?1124) Rochester
909 ★	Vatican City, Biblioteca Apostolica Vaticana, Reg. lat. 1351	Baudri of Bourgueil, *Poemata.* A seemingly composite manuscript, perhaps produced in Baudri's milieu, the principal separable sections being fols 5–108, 109–27+52, 128–47, and 148–51+1–4. Evidence for English provenance: *s.* xii^{1} English hand on fols 149 and 151v, the latter including, '*versus Baldrici archiepiscopi de organis Wigornensis ecclesiae*'. There is also a note in Middle English in the margin of fol. 3v.	U	xi/xii–xii^{1} France; England (by xii$^{2/4}$), ?Worcester
—	Vatican City, Biblioteca Apostolica Vaticana, Ross. 500	*See* Supplement.		
910 †	Vatican City, Biblioteca Apostolica Vaticana, Vat. lat. 4951	Homiliarium (temporale, sanctorale, commune sanctorum) (contents itemised in Richards, *Texts* and *Traditions*, pp. 112–17). Fol. 218^{v}: two faint but competent lead sketches of foliate scrolls, *s.* xii$^{2/4-med}$. The volume gives the impression of having been much used.	A D	xii^{1} Rochester

911	Verdun, Bibliothèque municipale, 70	Anselm, *Orationes et meditationes*. Some miniatures excised.	X; D	xii[1]
912 ??	Warsaw, Biblioteca Naradowa, I. 3311 (*olim* St Petersburg, Public Library, O. v. I. 45)	Psalter; Prayers Presently unlocatable: possibly destroyed.		?xi/xii
913	Winchester Cathedral, 2	Augustine, *In euangelium Iohannis*. Possidius, *Vita S. Augustini*. See note on no. 634.	I	xi/xii Winchester
914	Winchester College, 5	Paschasius Radbertus, *In Lamentationes*. Sketches of heads in the margins of fols 71v and 103v.	A; D	xii^{in} Winchester
915	Windsor, St George's Chapel, 5	Gregory, *In Ezechielem*. Bede, *In Prouerbia Salomonis*.	E	xii^{in} Canterbury, Christ Church
916	Wisbech and Fenland Museum, 1	Julianus Pomerius (Pseudo-Prosper), *De uita contemplatiua et actiua*.	A	xii^{in} ?Canterbury, Church; Bury St Edmunds
917	Wisbech and Fenland Museum, 9	Julianus Pomerius (Pseudo-Prosper), *De uita contemplatiua et actiua*. Bede, *In Tobiam*. Smaragdus, *Diadema monachorum*.	I	xii[1]
918	Woolhampton, Douai Abbey, 11	Service book (*Versarius*) (frag.: four leaves).		xii[1] ?Reading
919	Worcester Cathedral, F. 48, fols 1–48	Jerome, *Vita S. Pauli* (Paul of Thebes); *Vita S. Hilarionis*. Athanasius (trans. Evagrius of Antioch), *Vita S. Antonii*.	A	xi^{ex} Worcester
920	Worcester Cathedral, F. 81	Jerome, *In Psalmos* (begins imperfectly, but *not* as stated by Lambert, *Bibliotheca Hieronymiana Manuscripta* II, p. 207). Addition: Verses on final flyleaf: '*Cernens picturas homo rerum disce figuras*' = Walther, 2629 (where mistakenly labelled as 'Hereford').	X E/A	xii[1] Worcester
921	Worcester Cathedral, F. 92	Paul the Deacon, *Homiliarium* (Advent to Easter). Verses: '*Nobis uirgo pia miseris miserere Maria*' (Walther, 11880). Companion to Worcester Cathedral, F. 93–4 (nos. 922–3). Addition on flyleaf, s. xiii^{in}: Mauger, bishop of Worcester, *Epistola*.	E	xii^{in} Worcester
922	Worcester Cathedral, F. 93	Paul the Deacon, *Homiliarium* (Easter to Advent). Companion to Worcester Cathedral, F. 92, and F. 94 (nos. 921, 923).	E	xii^{in} Worcester

923	Worcester Cathedral, F. 94	Paul the Deacon, *Homiliarium* (Sanctorale: May to November; Commune sanctorum), beginning with Ralph d'Escures, *Homilia de assumptione Mariae.* Companion to Worcester Cathedral, F. 92–3 (nos. 921–2).	E	xii^{in} Worcester
924	Worcester Cathedral, Q. 1	Ivo of Chartres, *Epistolae.* Flyleaves bear papal bull, *s.* xiii^{in-1}.	I	xii^{1} Worcester
925 ?*	Worcester Cathedral, Q. 16 fols 112–99	Richard of Préaux, *Expositio in Cantica Canticorum* (ends imperfect). The initials to Books II–IV were not executed.	I(f) P	xii^{in} ?Normandy (??Préaux); Worcester (by xii^{1})
926	York Minster, xvi. Q. 1	Gregory, *Moralia in Iob* (I–X). Companion to York Minster, xvi. Q. 2 (no. 927). Volume three is not known to survive.	U	xi/xii ?York
927	York Minster xvi. Q.2	Gregory, *Moralia in Iob* (XI–XXII). Companion to York Minster, xvi. Q. 1 (no. 926). Volume three is not known to survive. Although vol. I (no. 926) is written in long lines while vol. II (no. 927) is in two columns, the shared provenance, the similarity of scribe iii of vol. I to scribe i of vol. II, and the comparable visual articulation of the two volumes suggests that they are indeed part of the same set.	U	xii^{in} ?York

SUPPLEMENT

928	Cambridge, University Library, Ii. 6. 5, fols 112–27	Hermannus Contractus, *De utilitatibus astrolabii* (extract). Near-contemporary additions: three short texts concerning the astrolabe, the second being, *Notae de mensurationibus astrolabio faciendis.*		xii^{1} Bury St Edmunds
929	Cambridge, Corpus Christi College, 184	Eusebius of Caesarea (trans. Rufinus), *Historia ecclesiastica* [omitting Book XI, cc. xxiii–xxix, suggesting it was copied from Cambridge, Corpus Christi College, 187 (no. 63)].	I(f)	xii^{1} Rochester
930	Cambridge, Corpus Christi College, 393	*Vita et miracula S. Ætheldredae.* Gregory of Ely, *Vita et miracula S. Ætheldredae metrice.* *Descriptio situs eliensis insulae et de quibusdam eiusdem insulae proprietatibus* (unfinished). *Virginis ut meritum testantia nobile factum.* *Vita S. Withburgae.* *In festiuitate S. Sexburgae.* *In natale S. Eormenildae.* Goscelin, *Vita S. Werburgae.* (The '*Historia Eliensis*'.)	I(f)	xii^{1} (1116x?35) Ely
931	Copenhagen, Kongelige Bibliotek, N. K. S. 1854 (2°)	Bede, *In Actus Apostolorum; Nomina regionum atque locorum de Actibus Apostolorum; Libellus retractationis in Actus Apostolorum.* Versus: '*Saepe sui quaedam praenuncia signa futura*'. NB: the volume is in a well-preserved, possibly original binding.	A	xii^{1}
932	London, British Library, Harley 488	Robert de Tumbalena, *Commentarium in Cantica Canticorum.* *Regula S. Benedicti.*	E	xii^{1}

933	London, British Library, Harley 988, fols 27–71	*Commentarium in Cantica Canticorum* (extracted from Jerome, *In Ecclesiasten Salomonis*), inc.: '*Tribus nominibus uocatum fuisse Salomonem scripturae manifestissime docent*'.	U/E	xii¹
934	Oxford, Bodleian Library, Auct. D. infra 2. 9, fols 111–142	*Apocalypsis* with scholia. The manuscript was ruled for all-round glossing.	U	xi²
935	Oxford, All Souls College, S. R. 58. f. 3 (*olim* S. R. 49. a. 11), pastedowns	Anselm, *De casu Diaboli* (frag. = two bifolia, one used as the front pastedown, the other as the back).	–	xii^in^ ? Kent
936	Stockholm, Riksarkivet, Fragm.?	Antiphoner (frag.) (one bifolium used as a wrapper). From Östergötlands handlingar 1597: 15	– A	xii¹ ?England; Sweden
937 ?*	Stockholm, Riksarkivet, Fragm. 2307	Office Lectionary (frag.) (two leaves used as a wrapper). Probably of French origin but certainly in England before xii^{ex}.	– U/E	xii¹ France or England; Sweden
938	Stockholm, Riksarkivet, Fragm. 2310	Office Lectionary (frag.) (two leaves used as a wrapper).	–	$xii^{2/4}$ Sweden
939	Vatican City, Biblioteca Apostolica Vaticana, Ross. 500	Priscian, *Institutiones grammaticae.* (Pseudo-)Priscian, *De accentibus*. In *s*. xv belonged to Poggio Bracciolini, then Domenico di Cristoforo da Brisighella – *teste* inscription on fol. 212^v.	I(f)	xii¹ ?Canterbury; Italy

INDEX OF AUTHORS AND TEXTS

Works and authors are listed in a continuous alphabetical sequence, excerpts and anonymous or unidentified tracts being included under their title or incipit. Pseudonymous works are presented after the main entries for the author in question. Each part of multi-volume works, such as bibles or lengthy texts like Gregory's *Moralia*, is recorded (the entries in the main inventory draw attention to companion volumes, as appropriate). Classes like 'Liturgica' and 'theologica' have been established for texts (often compilations or fragments) which cannot otherwise be classified briefly: they are not lists of all liturgical or theological books. Where a work was or is known under several titles, I have here supplied the major alternatives, although in the main inventory a 'standard' form has been preferred.

The siglum 'e' is used to indicate that the volume has only an extract from the text in question. Numbers in square brackets represent now lost items, for whose original existence, however, some evidence remains.

It should be stressed that this is an index to the Inventory of manuscripts: errors in attribution made there will be reflected here; correspondingly, texts that are not individually itemised in the main body of the work will not be separately listed here. Note that this index does not include references to the material documented on the booklists.

Anselm, ed. R. W. Southern and F. S. Schmitt (London, 1969), 352–4) 581
Cur Deus homo (*Sancti Anselmi Cantuariensis archiepiscopi Opera Omnia*, ed. F. S. Schmitt, II) 107, 128, 296, 592, 653, ?798
De casu Diaboli (*Opera Omnia*, ed. Schmitt, I) 106, 296, 592, 653, 935
(attrib.) *De cellarario domini* 505
De conceptu uirginali et originali peccato (*Opera Omnia*, ed. Schmitt, II) 107, 296, 363, 592, 653, 722, 798
De concordia praescientiae et praedestinationis et gratiae Dei cum libero arbitrio (*Opera Omnia*, ed. Schmitt, II) 592, 653, 722
De conuersatione monachorum 81
De grammatico (Bursill-Hall, 188.17; *Opera Omnia*, ed. Schmitt, I) 296, 592, 653
De humanis moribus per similitudines 505
De incarnatione Verbi / Liber de fide Trinitatis et de incarnatione Verbi (*Opera Omnia*, ed. Schmitt, I) 106, 296, 506, 592, 653, 678, 768e
De libertate arbitrii (*Opera Omnia*, ed. Schmitt, I) 106, 296, 506, 592, 653, 722
(attrib.) *De malo et nihil* 365
De processione Spiritus Sancti (*Opera Omnia*, ed. Schmitt, II) 5, 498, 506, 592, 653
(attrib.) *De similitudine temporalis et spiritualis militis* 505
De ueritate / Dialogus de ueritate (*Opera Omnia*, ed. Schmitt, I) 106, 296, 592, 653
Epistola de sacramentis ecclesiae 653
Epistola de sacrificio azimi et fermentati (= ep. 415) (*Opera Omnia*, ed. Schmitt, IV) 296, 498, 653
Epistolae (*Opera Omnia*, ed. Schmitt, III–V) 34 (two), 104 (one), 116 (one), 129 (two), 130, 269 (two), 312 (two), 365 (few), 376 (few), 391, 506, 581, 592, 774 (two), 811
Epitaphium Hugonis (*Memorials of St Anselm*, ed. Southern and Schmitt, 351–2) 581
(attrib.) *Hic ostendit archiepiscopus quid uere appetendum sit uel quid respuendum* 505
Homilia super euangelium quod legitur in die assumptionis BVM 685
Liber apologeticus contra Gaunilonem (*Responsio*) 106, 592
Meditatio animae christianae 296, 798
Meditatio de redemptione humana 592, 653
Meditationes, Orationes, Preces (*Opera Omnia*, ed. Schmitt, III) 296, 597, 601, 653, 911
Monologion (*Opera Omnia*, ed. Schmitt, I) 106, 131, 592, 611e, 653, 768e
Orationes → *Meditationes*
'Philosophical fragments' (*Memorials of St Anselm*, ed. Southern and Schmitt, 334–51) 581
Preces → *Meditationes*
Proslogion (*Opera Omnia*, ed. Schmitt, I) 106, 130, 592, 653, 768e
Quomodo grammaticus sit substantia et qualitas → *De grammatico*
Unde malum 592
(attrib.) *Utrum bono bonum siue malo malum possit esse contrarium* 505
Verses in praise of → *Haud habiture parem sumas pater alme*
See also Alexander of Canterbury, Eadmer
ANSELM OF LAON (Anselmus Laudunensis) (d. 1117),
In Apocalypsin (Stegmüller, 1361; PL, 162)) ?243
In Mattheum / Enarrationes in euangelium Matthei (Stegmüller, 1359; PL, 162)) 208
ANSO OF LOBBES (d. 800),
Vita Ermini (BHL, 2614) ?10
Anthologia Valerio-Gelliana 182
Antiphoner 205, 240, 323, 546, 614, ?615, 616, ?712, 778, 936
Apocalypsis Iohannis 189, 467, 478, 934
See also Bible
Apollonius of Tyre (*Historia Apolloni regis Tyri*) 752
Apothegms (OE) 178
Pseudo-APULEIUS,
Herbarium 622, 636
ARATOR (*s.* vi^in),
Historia apostolica (CPL, 1504) 557, 602
Arator, commentary on 558
Arator, note on the recitation of 557
ARATUS OF SOLI (d. before 240 B.C.),
(attrib.) *De signis caelestibus* 548
Phaenomena → Cicero
Archbishops → Bishops
Archbishops of Canterbury, short texts on the early ones → Goscelin
ARISTOTLE → 29
ARNOBIUS (Iunior) (fl. *c.* 450)
Conflictus cum Serapione de Deo trino et uno (CPL, 239) 840
Astronomica 404
See also Aratus, Cicero, Computistica, Dungalus, Hyginus
ATHANASIUS OF ALEXANDRIA (d. 373),
(attrib.) *De processione Spiritus Sancti* 366
Epistolae 641
(trans. Evagrius of Antioch) *Vita S. Antonii* (CPG, 2101b; BHL, 609; PL, 73) 919
See also Eusebius of Vercelli
Athanasius, account of libellus of 28

INDEX OF ADDITIONS
(*c.* $xii^{2/4}$–xiii^{in})

INDEX OF MEDIEVAL PROVENANCE

INDEX OF DATES

The first entry in each case comprises the manuscripts of English origin; manuscripts of certain or probable continental origin are listed separately thereafter. Where the date given to a manuscript in the inventory straddles two time bands, it is here indexed under the one which I regard as the more representative of the two.

$\mathrm{XI}^{3/4}$

XI^{2}

$\mathrm{XI}^{\mathrm{ex}}$

XI/XII

$\mathrm{XII}^{\mathrm{in}}$

XII^{1}

XII$^{2/4}$

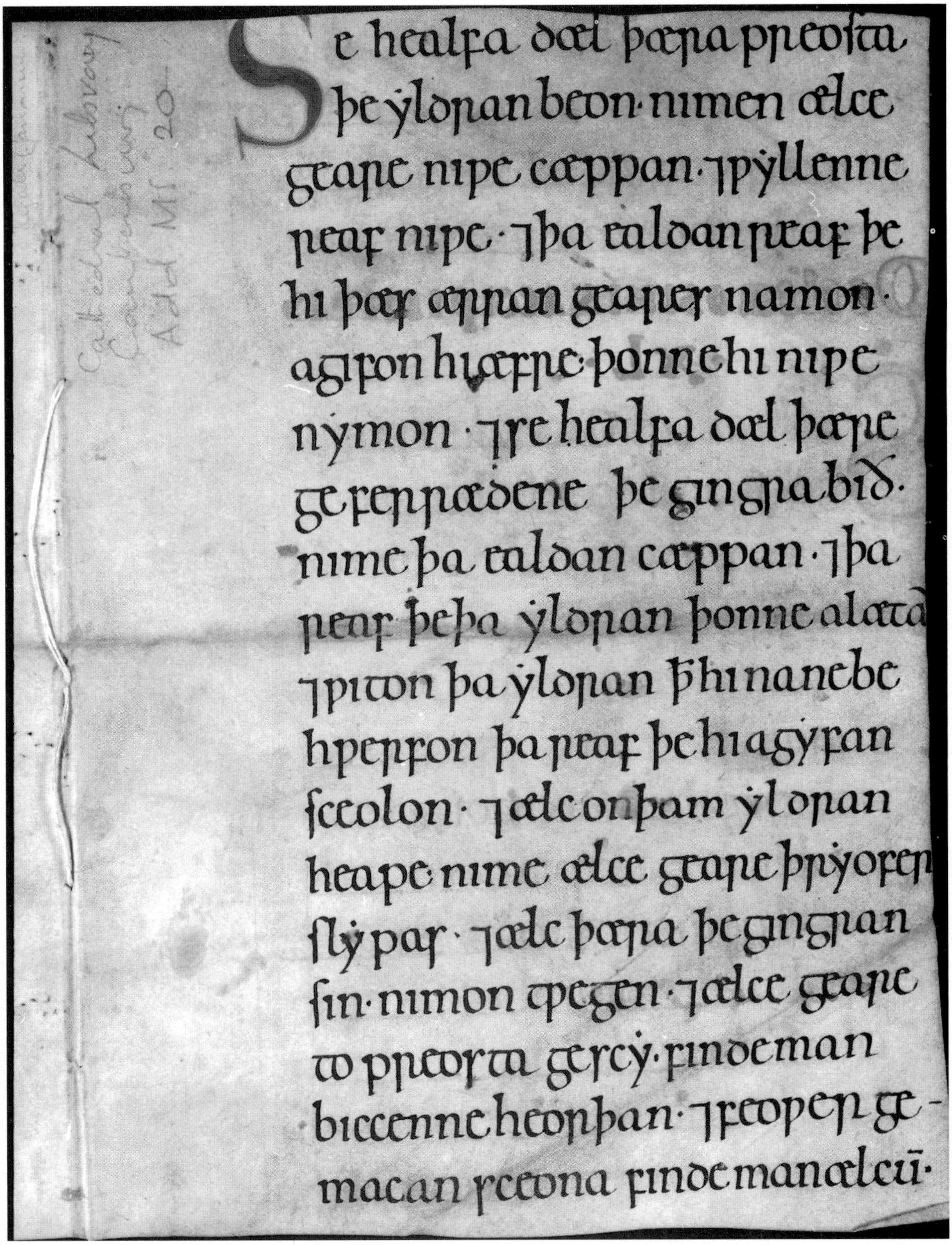

1 Canterbury Cathedral, Add. 20 (no. 187).
Chrodegang of Metz. *Saec.* xi[3/4]. Canterbury, Christ Church.
Written area: 224 × 115mm.

PLATE 2

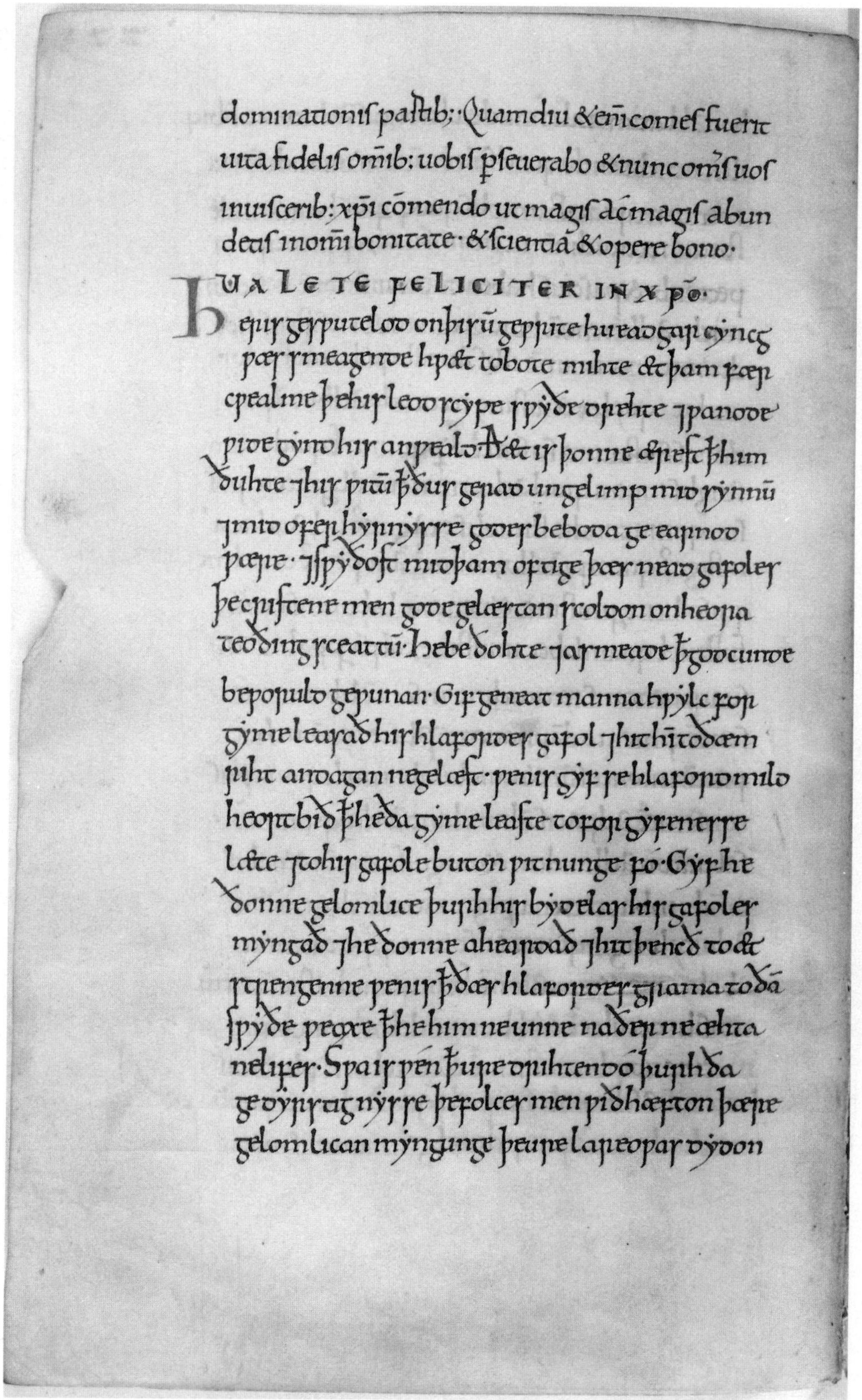
dominationis partib;· Quamdiu &enim comes fuerit
uita fidelis omnib: uobis perseuerabo &nunc omnis uos
in uisceribus xpi comendo ut magis acmagis abun
detis in omni bonitate· &scientia &opere bono·
Ualete feliciter in xpo·
Her is geswutelod on þisum gewrite hu eadgar cyng
wæs smeagende hwæt to bote mihte æt þam fær
cwealme þe his leodscipe swyðe drehte 7 panode
wide gynd his anweald. Þæt is þonne ærest þæt him
ðuhte 7 his witum þæt þus gerad ungelimp mid synnum
7 mid oferhyrnysse godes beboda geearnod
wære. 7 swyðost mid þam oftige þæs neadgafoles
þe cristene men gode gelæstan scoldon on heora
teoðingsceattum. He bebead ðohte 7 asmeade þæt godcunde
be woruldgewunan. Gif geneat manna hwylc for
gymeleasað his hlafordes gafol 7 hit him to ðæm
riht andagan ne gelæst. wenis gif se hlaford mild
heort bið þæt he ða gymeleaste to forgyfenesse
læte 7 to his gafole buton witnunge fo. Gif he
ðonne gelomlice þurh his bydelas his gafoles
myngað 7 he ðonne aheardað 7 hit þenceð to æt
standenne wenis þæt ðæs hlafordes grama to ðam
swyðe weaxe þæt he him ne unne naðer ne æhta
ne lifes. Swa is wen þæt ure drihten do þurh ða
gedyrstignysse þe folces men wiðhæfton þære
gelomlican myngunge þe ure lareowas dydon

2 Cambridge, Corpus Christi College, 265, p. 222 (no. 65).
Liturgica; Laws. *Saec.* xi[2]. Worcester.
Page size: 265 × 162mm. Written area: 198 × 102mm.

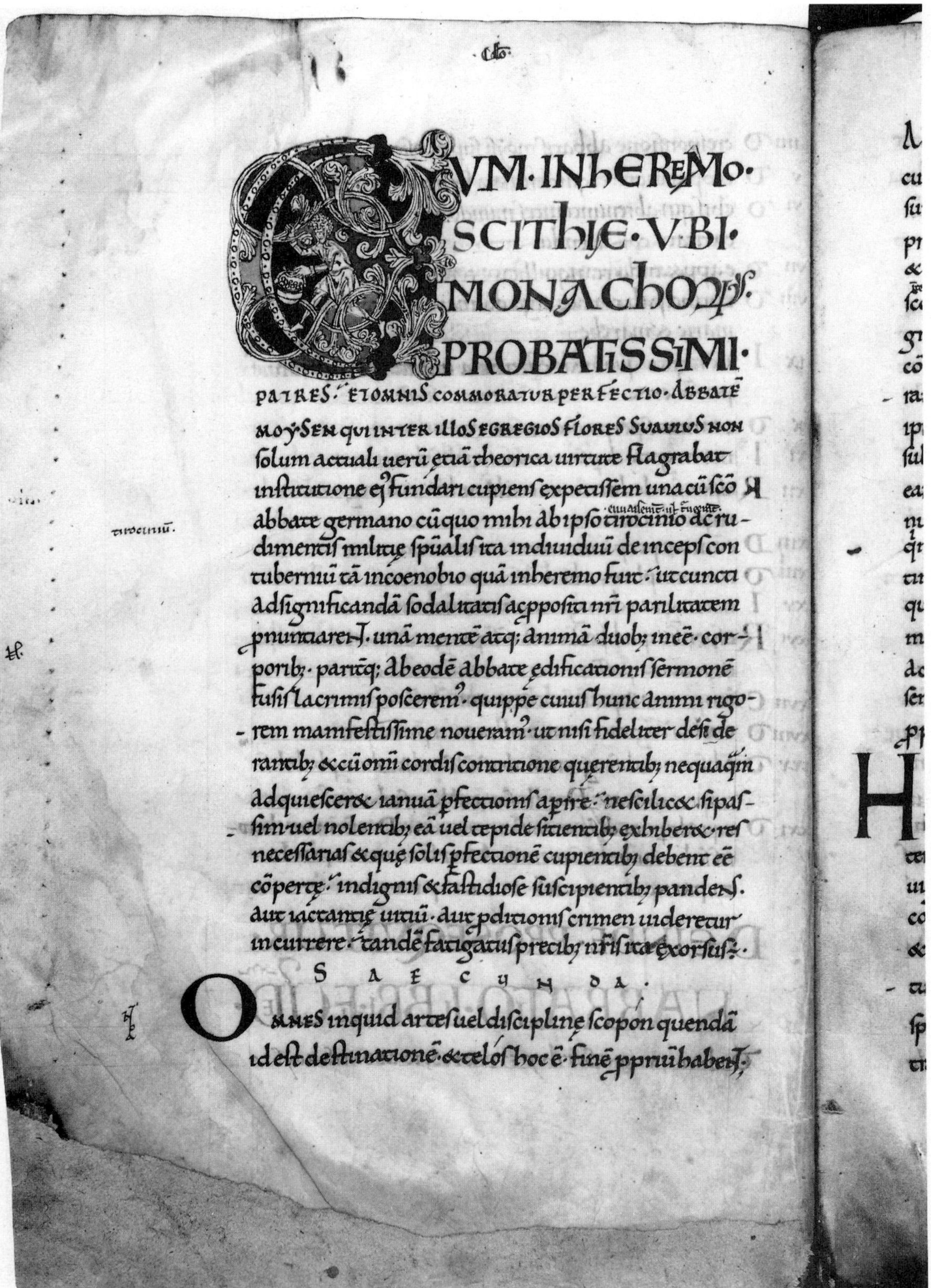
CUM IN HEREMO SCITHIE UBI MONACHORUM PROBATISSIMI PATRES ET OMNIS COMMORATUR PERFECTIO ABBATEM MOYSEN QUI INTER ILLOS EGREGIOS FLORES SUAUIUS NON solum actuali uerum etiam theorica uirtute flagrabat institutione eius fundari cupiens expetissem una cum sancto abbate germano cum quo mihi ab ipso tirocinio ac rudimentis militiae spiritualis ita indiuiduum deinceps contubernium tam in coenobio quam in heremo fuit ut cuncti ad significandam sodalitatis ac propositi nostri parilitatem pronuntiarent unam mentem atque animam duobus inesse corporibus pariterque ab eodem abbate edificationis sermonem fusis lacrimis posceremus quippe cuius hunc animi rigorem manifestissime noueramus ut nisi fideliter desiderantibus et cum omni cordis contritione querentibus nequaquam adquiesceret ianuam perfectionis aperire ne scilicet si passim uel nolentibus eam uel tepide sitientibus exhiberet res necessarias et quae solis perfectionem cupientibus debent esse compertae indignis et fastidiose suscipientibus pandens aut iactantiae uitium aut proditionis crimen uideretur incurrere tandem fatigatus precibus nostris ita exorsus est.

SAECUNDA.

OMNES inquid artes uel disciplinae scopon quendam id est destinationem et telos hoc est finem proprium habent

3 Oxford, Bodleian Library, Hatton 23, fol. 3v (no. 725).
John Cassian; Bede. *Saec.* xi². Worcester.
Page size: 300 × 190mm. Written area: 211 × 115mm.

PLATE 4

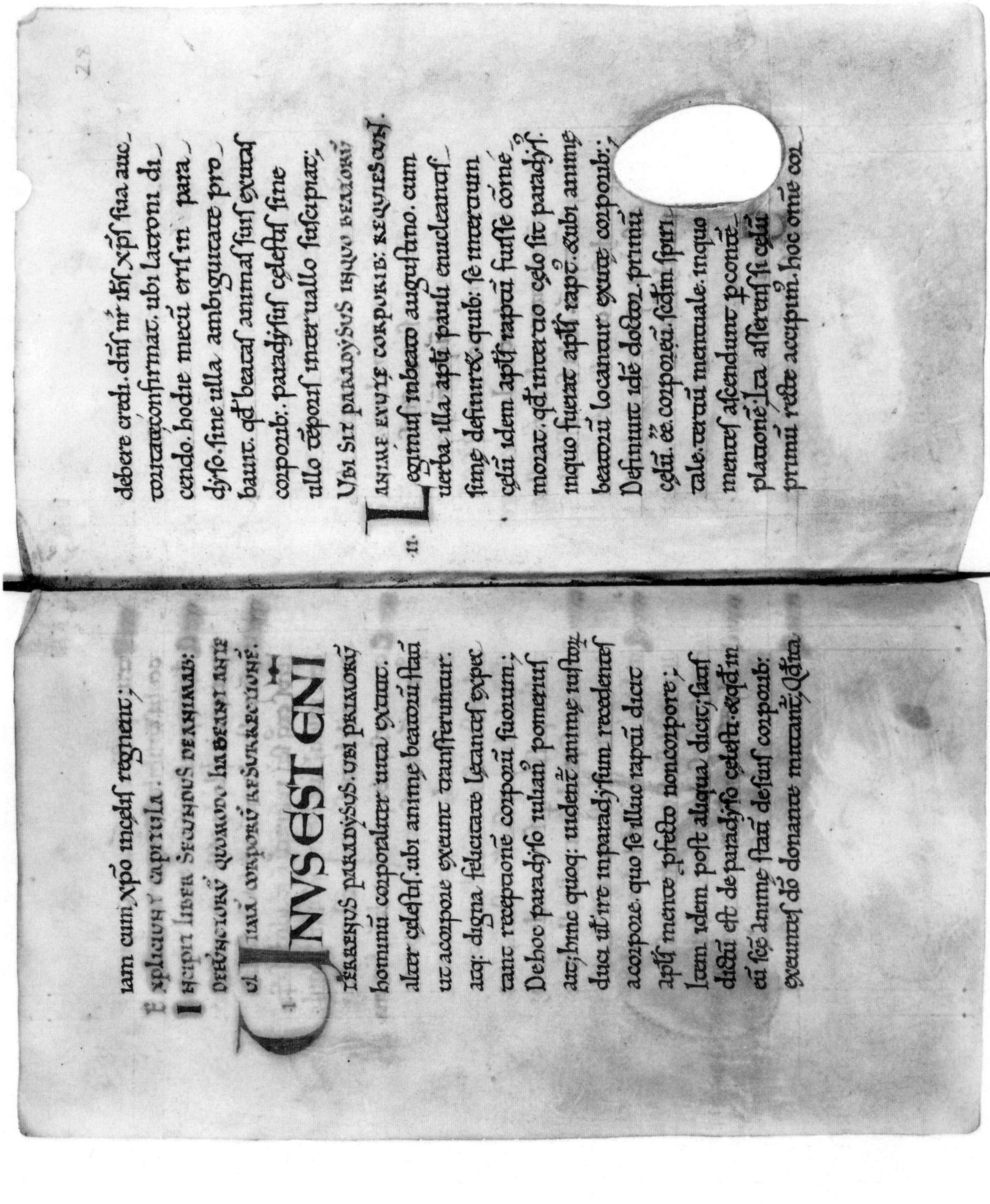

4 Oxford, University College, 104, fols. 27v+28r (no. 803). Julian of Toledo. *Saec.* xi^{ex}. Battle. Page size: 188 × 112mm. Written area: 131 × 66mm.

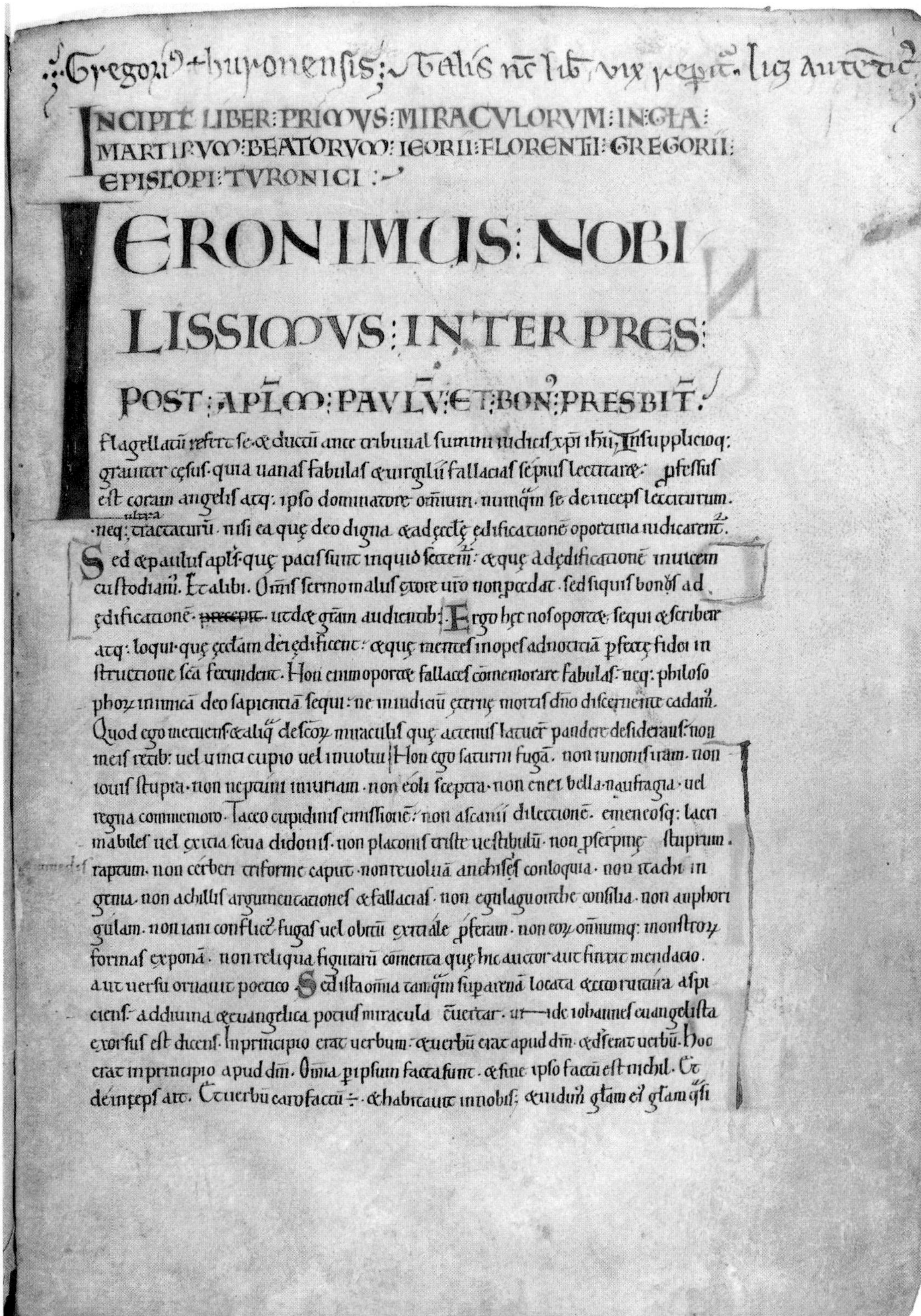

INCIPIT LIBER PRIMVS MIRACVLORVM IN GLA
MARTIRVM BEATORVM IEORII FLORENTII GREGORII
EPISCOPI TVRONICI
IERONIMUS NOBI
LISSIMVS INTERPRES
POST APLM PAVLV ET BON PRESBIT

5 Cambridge, Trinity College, O. 10. 23, fol. 1r (no. 171).
Gregory of Tours. *Saec.* xi[ex]. Exeter.
Page size: 292 × 210mm. Written area: 214 × 138mm.

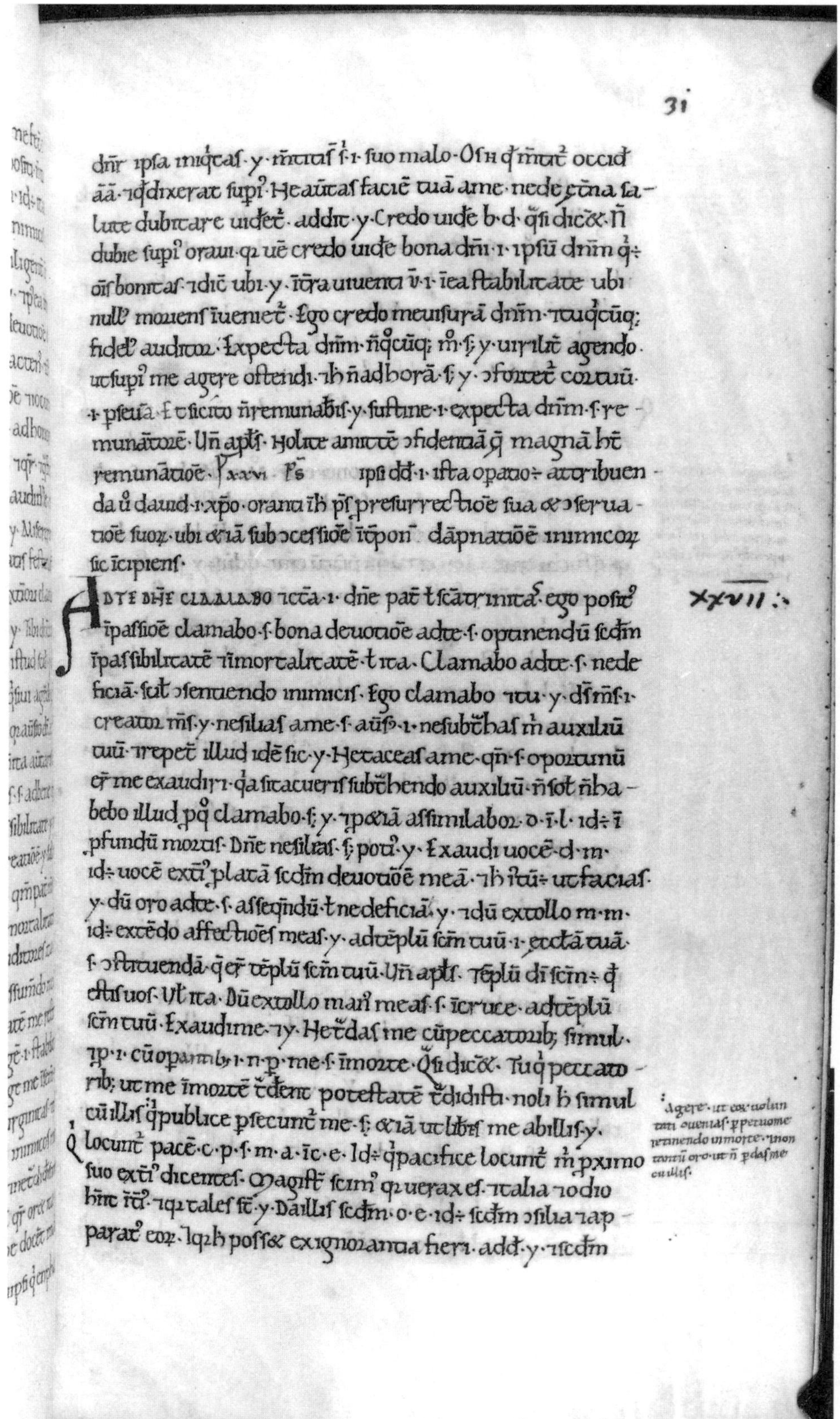

6 London, British Library, Arundel 235, fol. 31r (no. 361).
Hugh of Langres. *Saec.* xi[ex].
Page size: 233 × 144mm. Written area: 181 × 90mm.

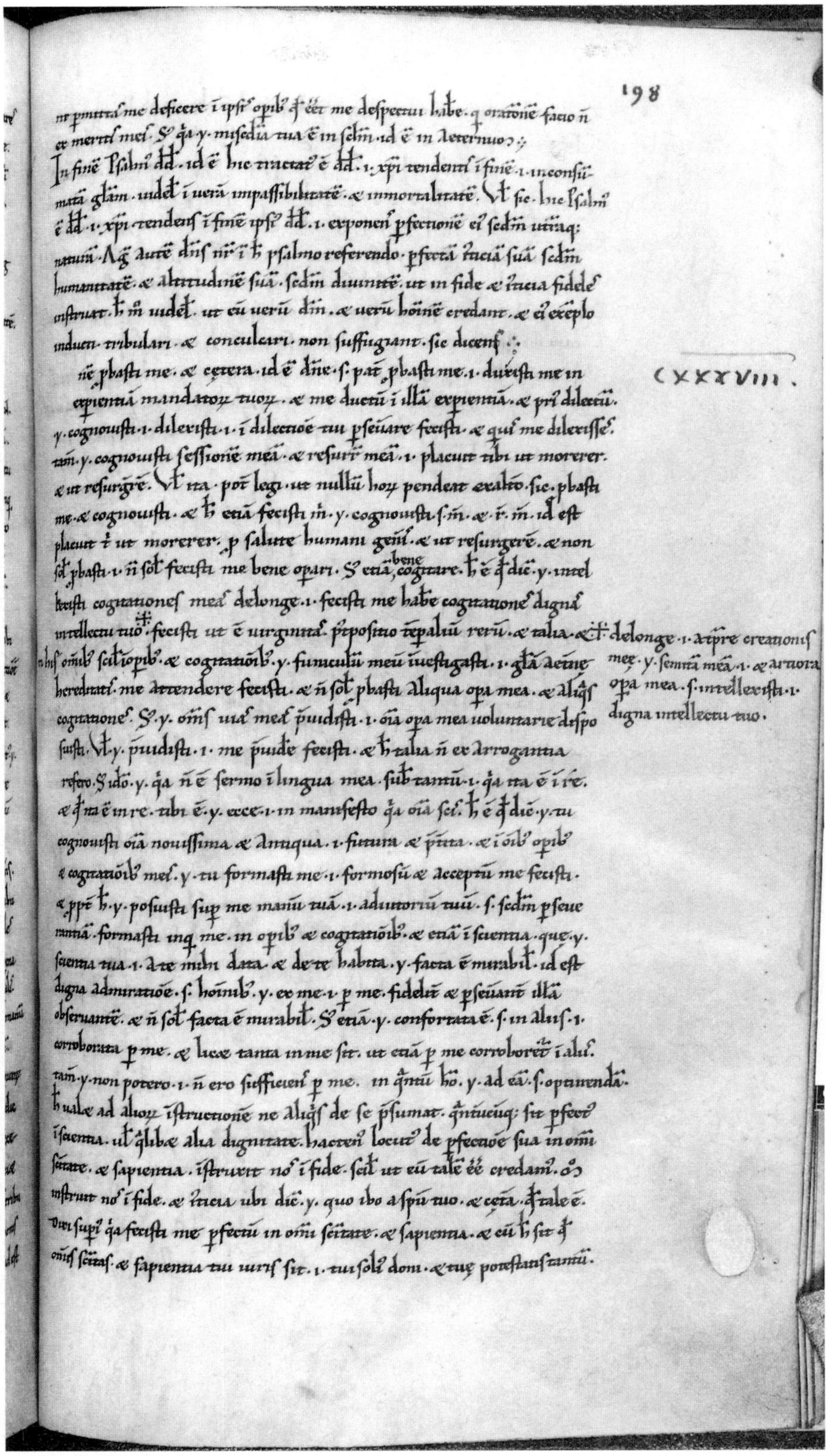

7 London, British Library, Arundel 235, fol. 198r

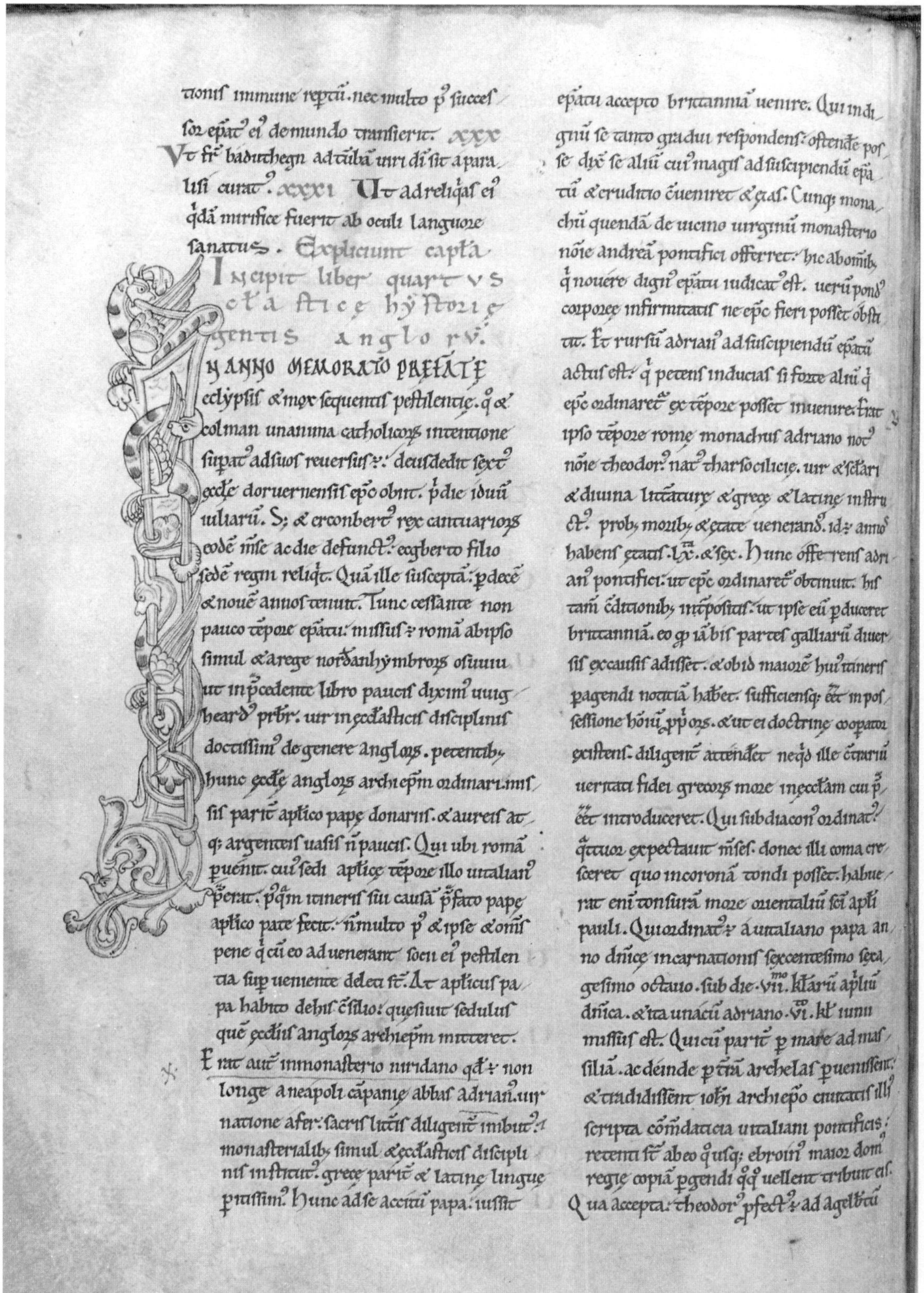

8 Durham Cathedral Library, B. II. 35, fol. 77v (no. 232).
Bede. *Saec.* xi[ex]. Durham.
Page size: 370 × 260mm. Written area: 285 × 175mm.

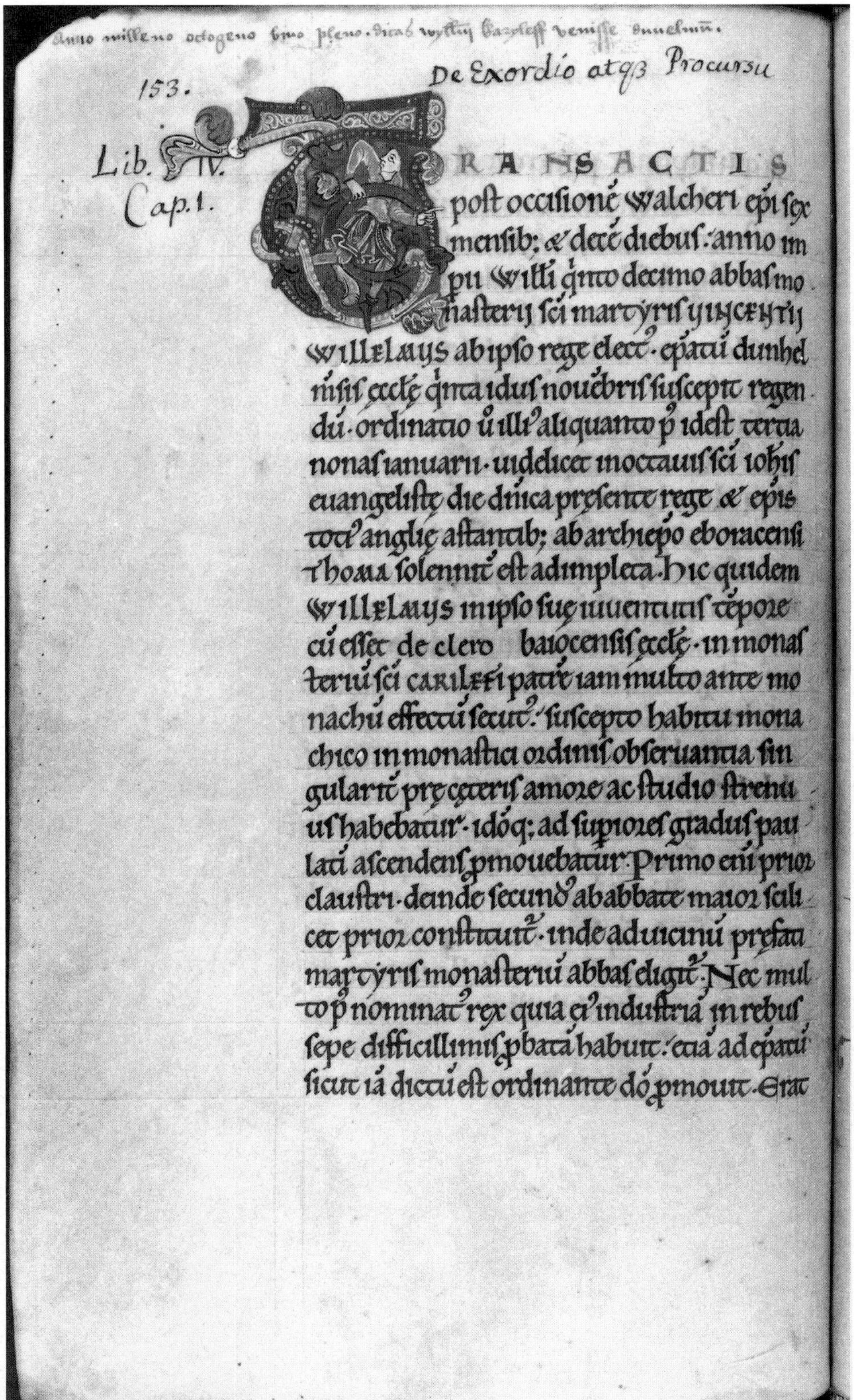
Anno milleno octogeno bino pleno. dicas wyllm karyleff venisse dunelmum.

153. De Exordio atque Procursu

Lib. IV. Cap. I.

TRANSACTIS
post occisionem walcheri episcopi sex
mensibus & decem diebus. anno im
perii Willelmi quinto decimo abbas mo
nasterii sancti martyris uincentii
willelmus ab ipso rege electus episcopatum dunhel
mensis ecclesie quinta idus nouembris suscepit regen
dum. ordinatio uero illius aliquanto post idest tertia
nonas ianuarii. uidelicet in octauis sancti iohannis
euangeliste die dominica presente rege & epis
copis totius anglie astantibus; ab archiepiscopo eboracensi
thoma solenniter est adimpleta. Hic quidem
Willelmus in ipso sue iuuentutis tempore
cum esset de clero baiocensis ecclesie. in monas
terium sancti carilefi patris iam multo ante mo
nachum effectum secutus. suscepto habitu mona
chico in monastica ordinis obseruantia sin
gulariter pre ceteris amore ac studio strenu
us habebatur. ideoque ad superiores gradus pau
latim ascendens promouebatur. Primo enim prior
claustri. deinde secundus ab abbate maior scili
cet prior constituitur. inde ad uicinum prefati
martyris monasterium abbas eligitur. Nec mul
to post nominatus rex quia eius industriam in rebus
sepe difficillimis probatam habuit. etiam ad episcopatum
sicut iam dictum est ordinante deo promouit. Erat

9 Durham University Library, Cosin V. ii. 6, fol. 77v (no. 283).
Symeon of Durham. *Saec.* xii[in]. Durham.
Page size: 295 × 175mm. Written area: 194 × 100mm.

PLATE 10

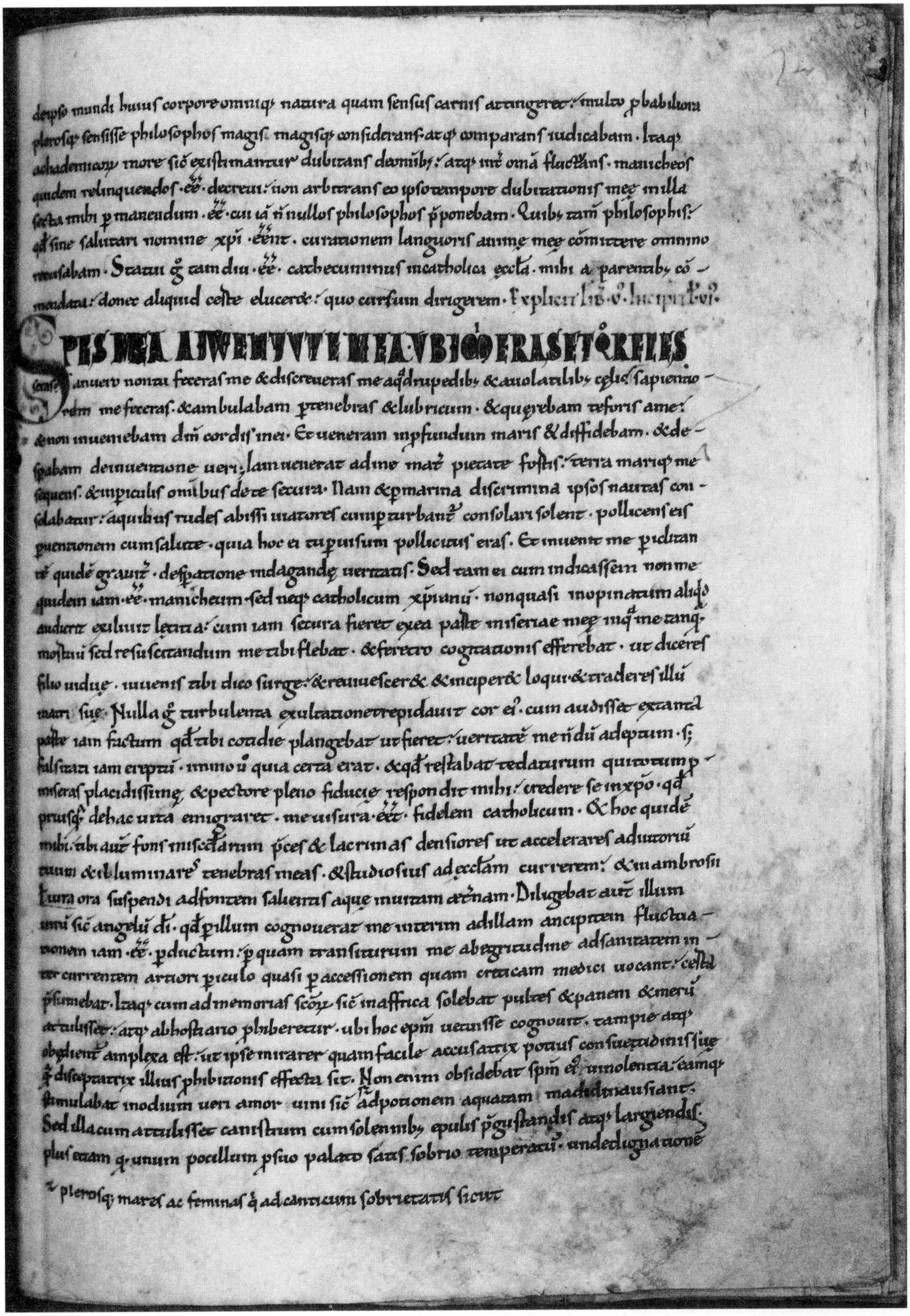

10 Salisbury Cathedral Library, 6, fol. 20r (no. 823).
Augustine. *Saec.* xi[ex]. Salisbury.
Page size: 290 × 212mm. Written area: 232 × 154mm.

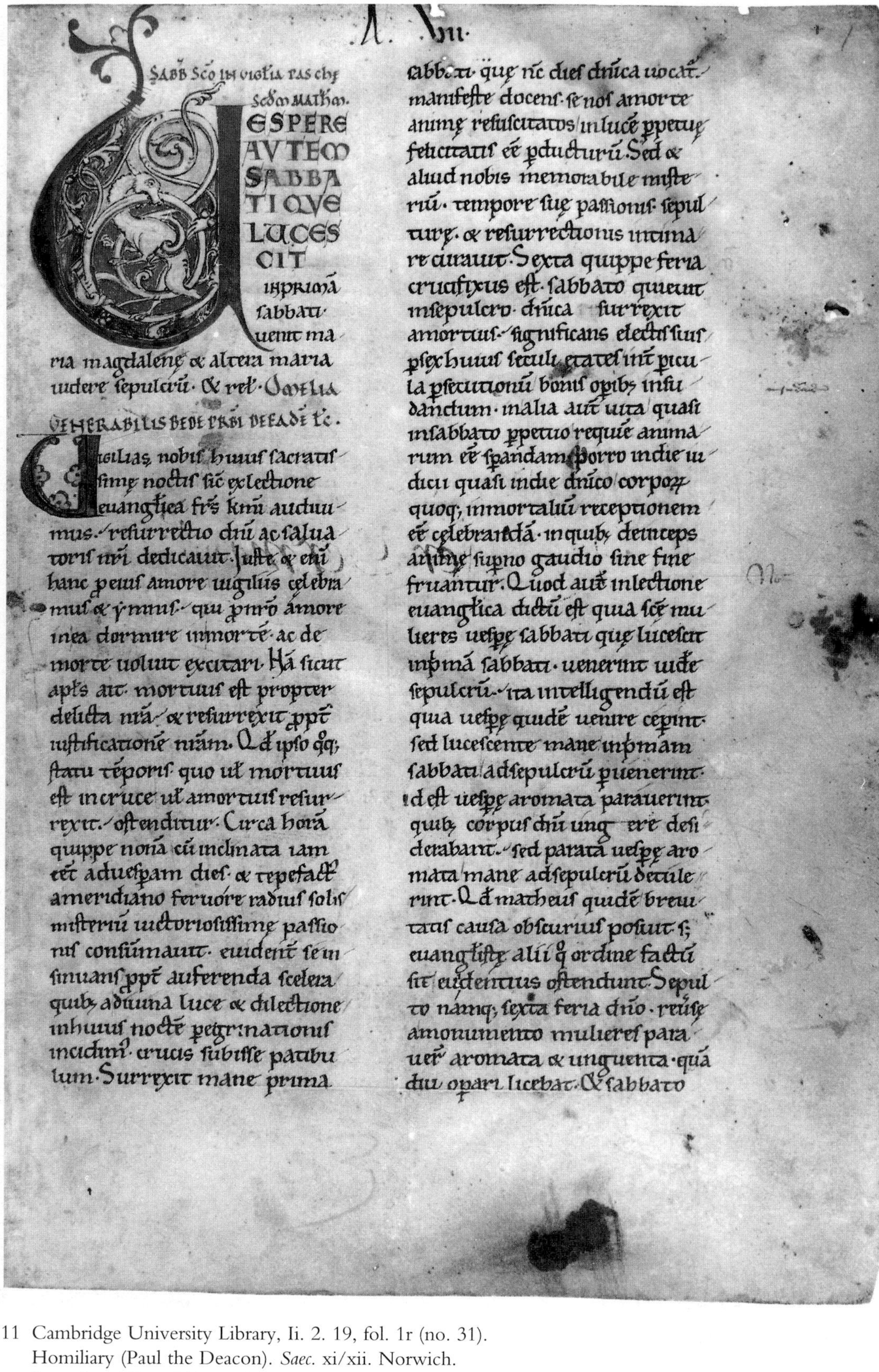

11 Cambridge University Library, Ii. 2. 19, fol. 1r (no. 31).
Homiliary (Paul the Deacon). *Saec.* xi/xii. Norwich.
Page size: 338 × 240mm. Written area: 266 × 168mm.

PLATE 12

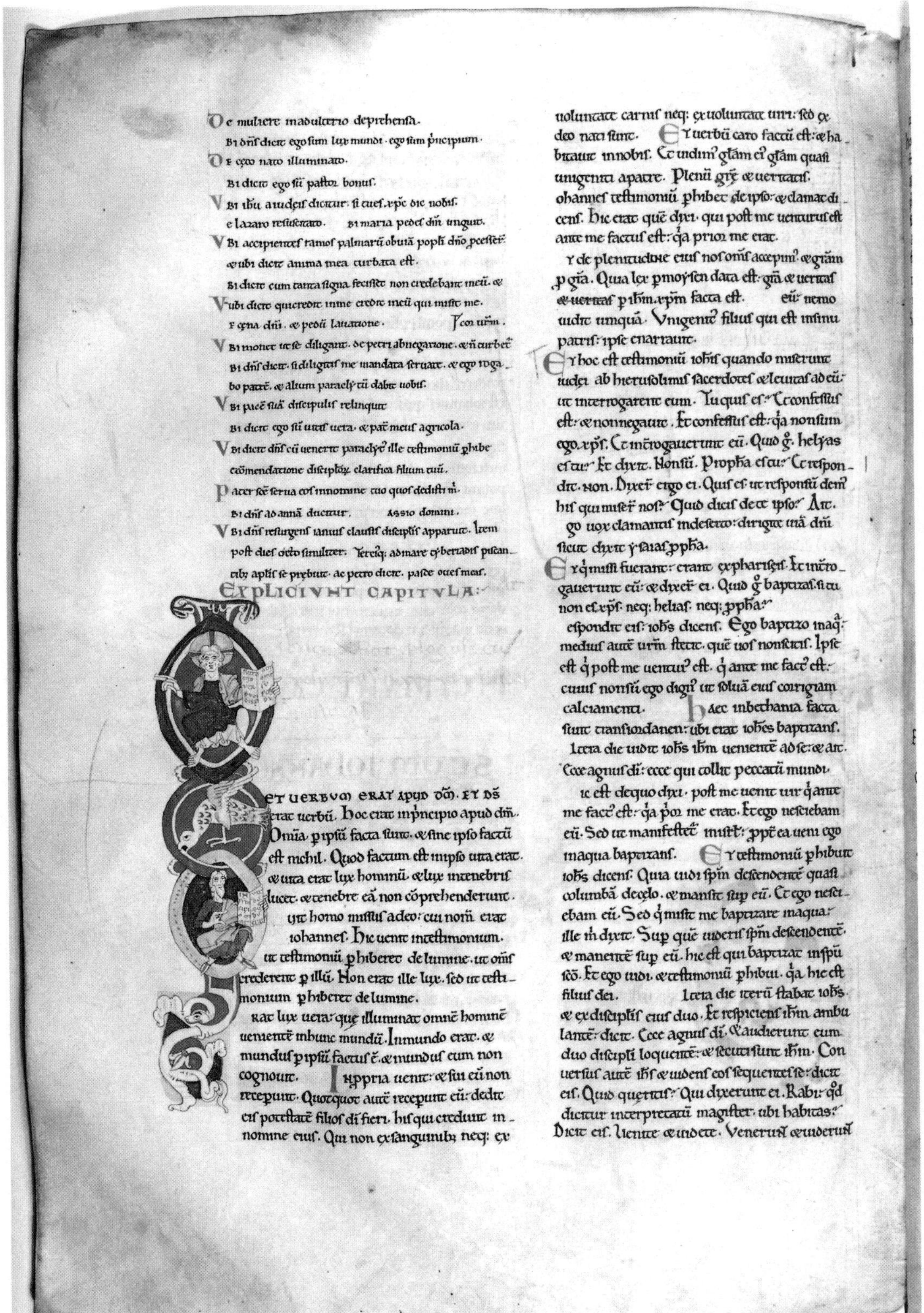

12 Cambridge, Trinity College, B. 5. 2, fol. 129v (no. 154).
Bible. *Saec.* xi/xii–xii[in]. Lincoln.
Page size: 480 × 330mm. Written area: 367 × 220mm.

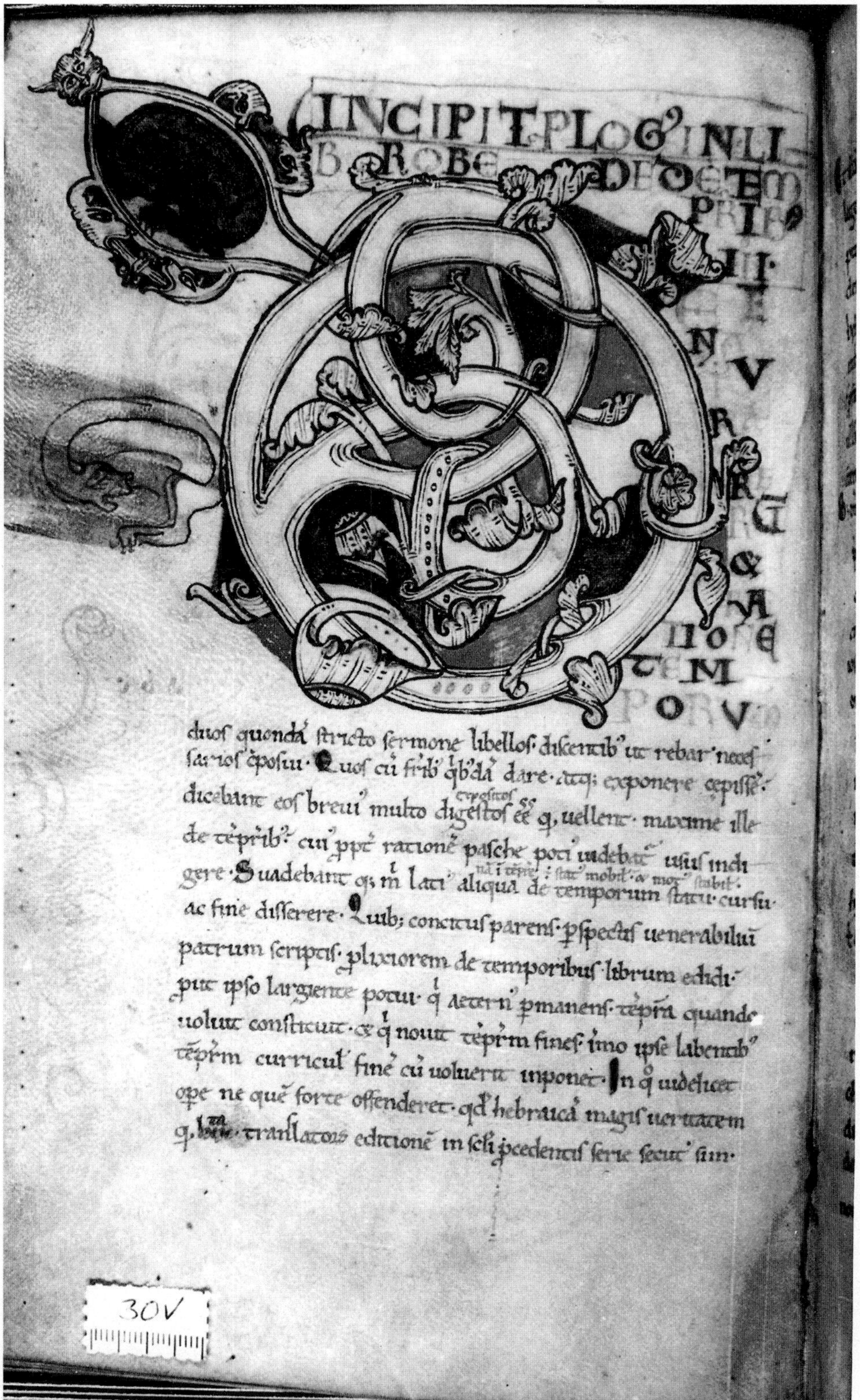

13 London, British Library, Royal 13 A. xi, fol. 30v (no. 548).
Computistica. *Saec.* xii[in]. England or France.
Page size: 236 × 150mm. Written area: 179 × 100mm.

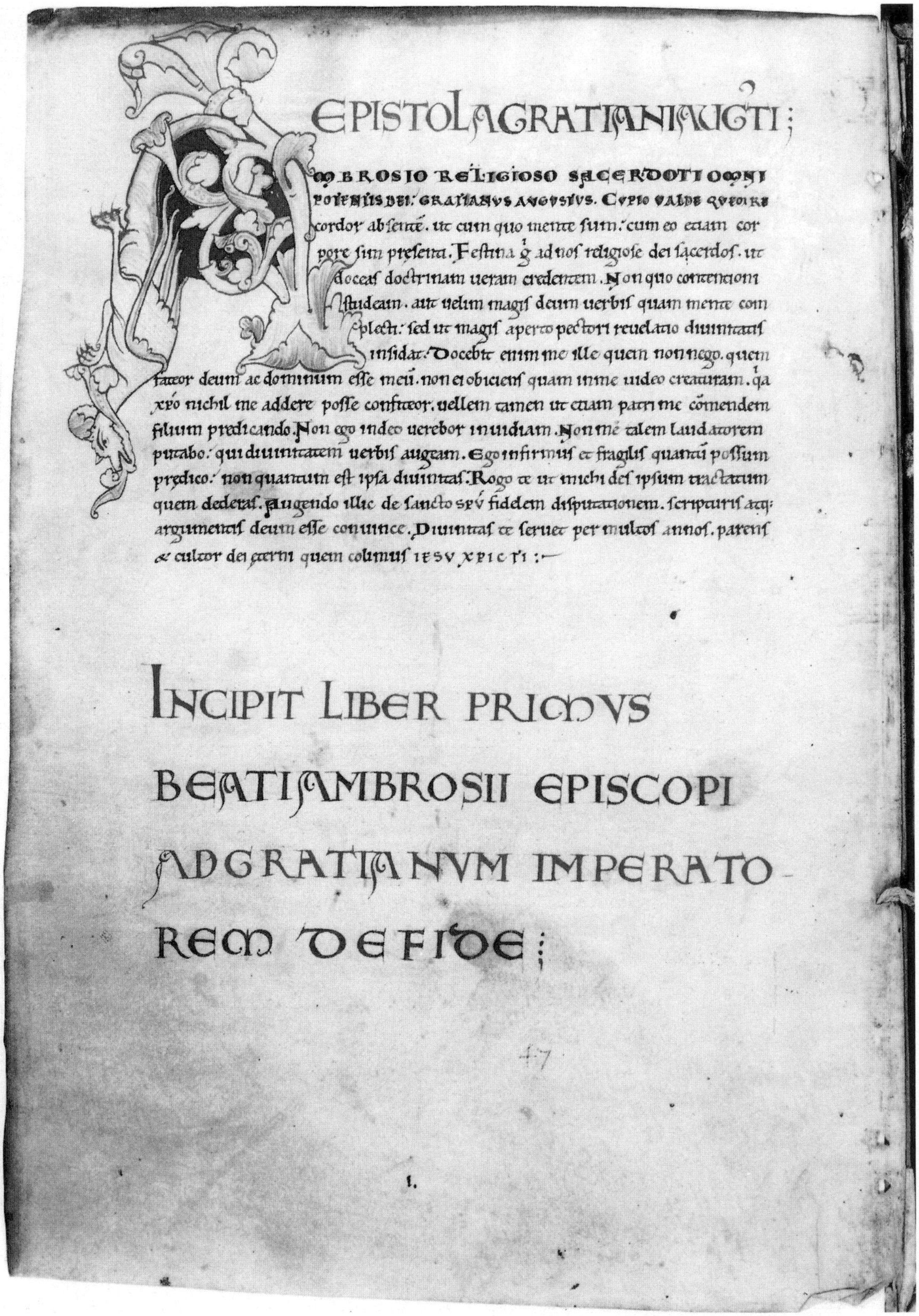

14 Oxford, Bodleian Library, Bodley 827, fol. 'i'v (no. 704).
Ambrose. *Saec.* xi/xii–xii[in]. Canterbury, Christ Church.
Page size: 283 × 202mm. Written area: 201 × 134mm.

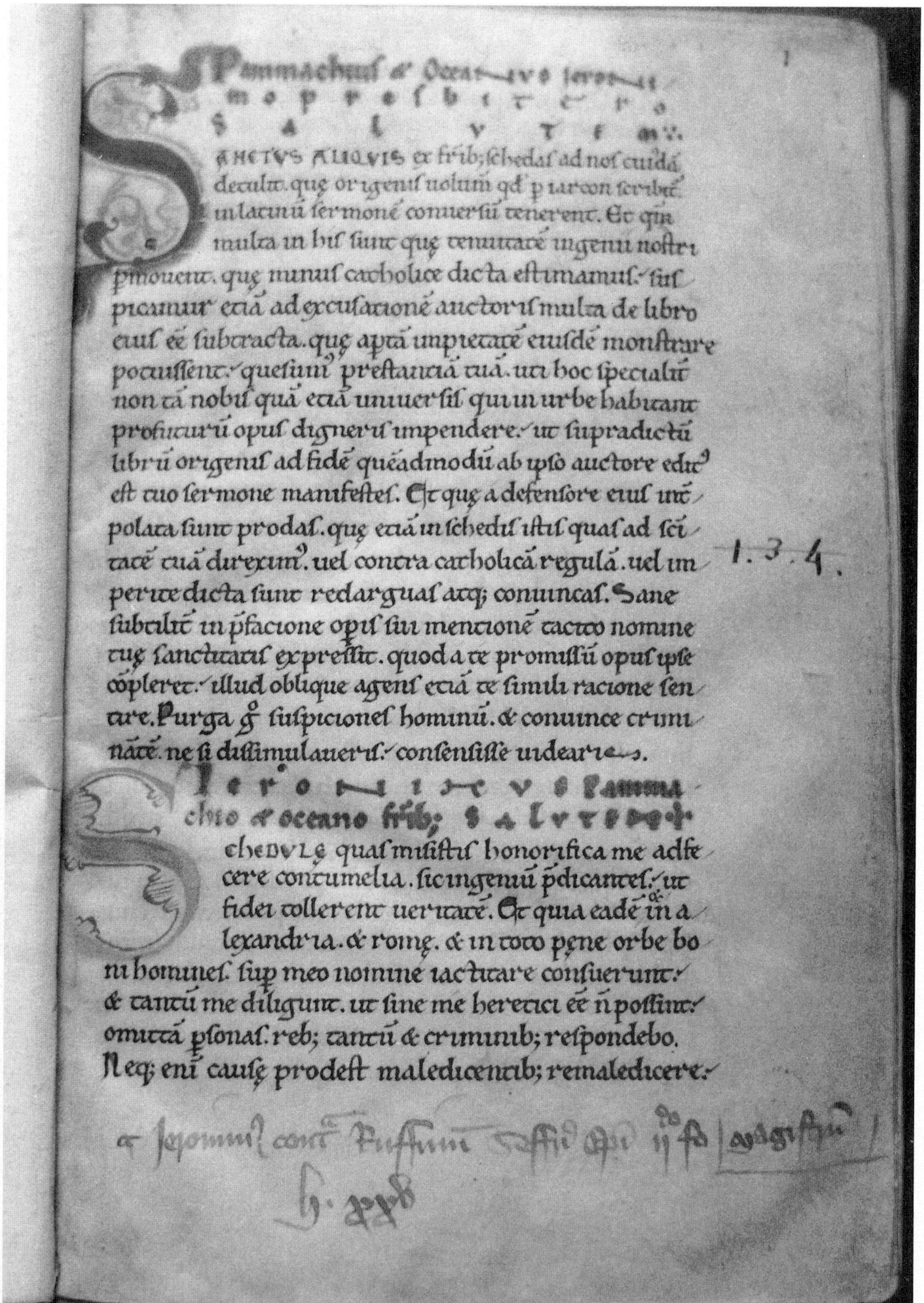

15 Cambridge, Emmanuel College, 25, fol. 1r (no. 93).
Jerome. *Saec.* xii[in]. ?Normandy; Chichester.
Page size: 240 × 155mm. Written area: 181 × 101mm.

PLATE 16

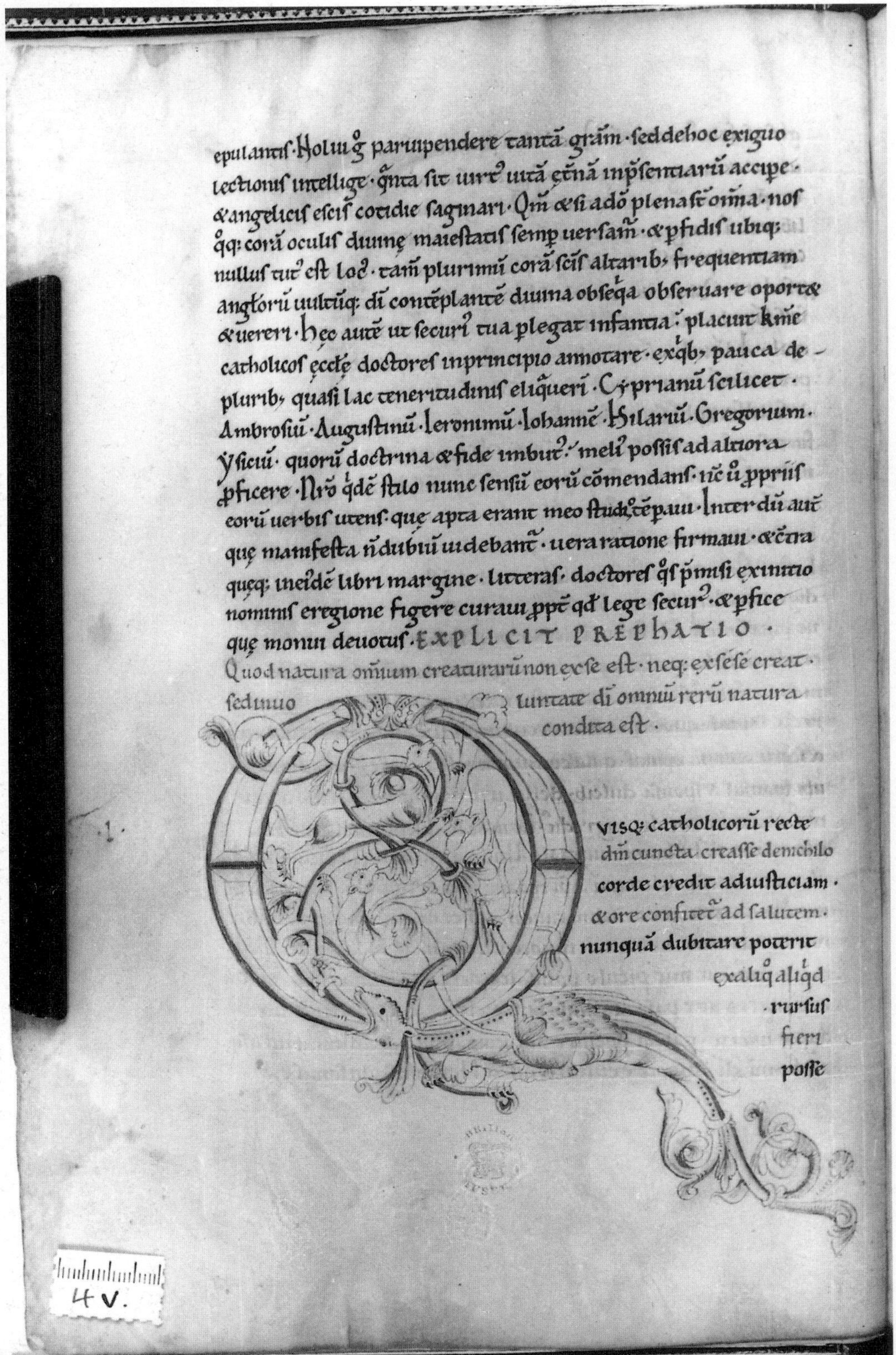

16 London, British Library, Harley 3061, fol. 4v (no. 445).
Paschasius; Lanfranc. *Saec.* xii[in]. ?Abingdon.
Page size: 265 × 180mm. Written area: 191 × 120mm.

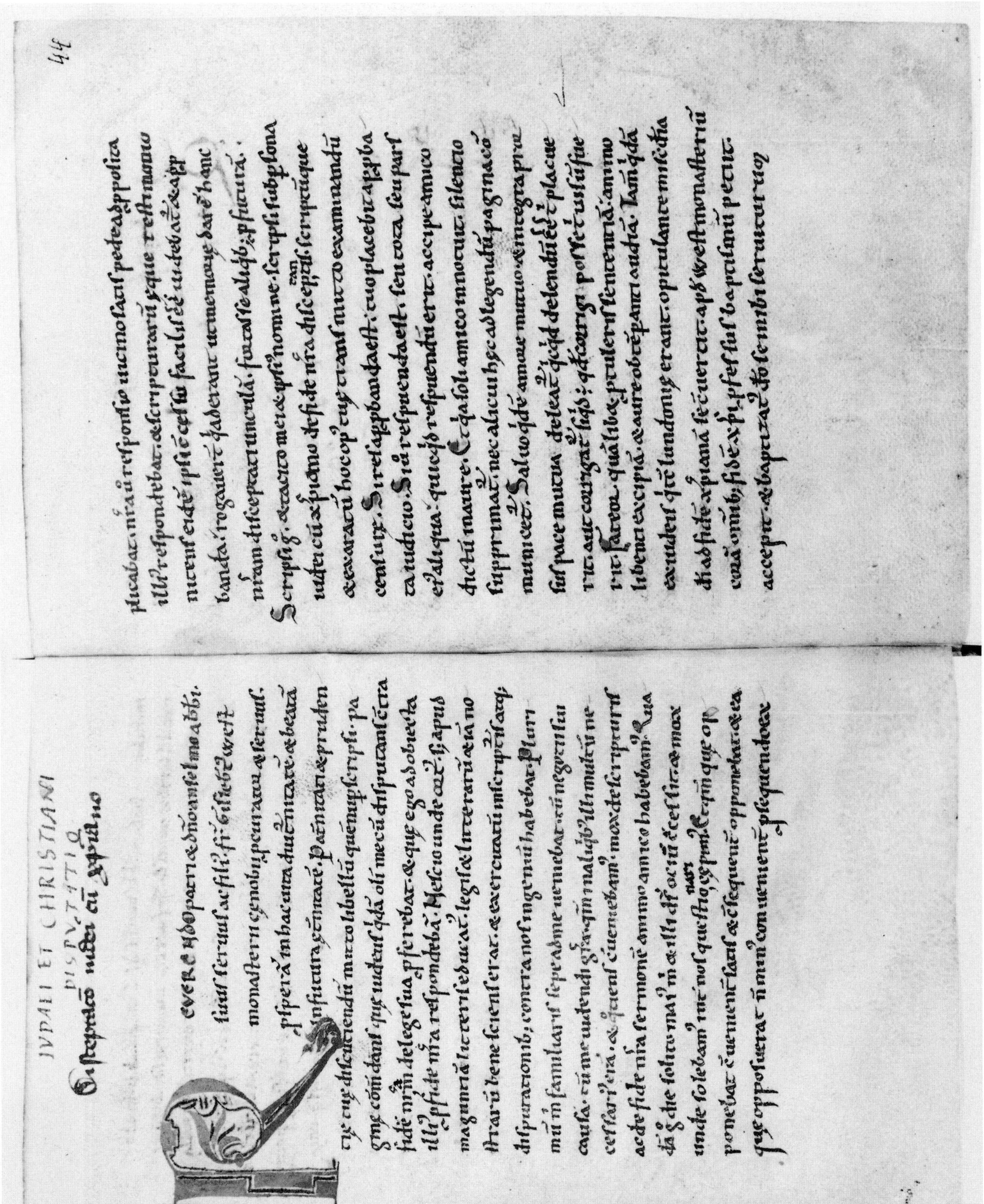

17 Brussels, Bibliothèque Royale, 8794–99 (1403), fols. 43v+44r (no. 13). Gilbert Crispin. *Saec.* xii^{in}. Rochester. Page size: 178 × 130mm. Written area: 118 × 84mm.

PLATE 18

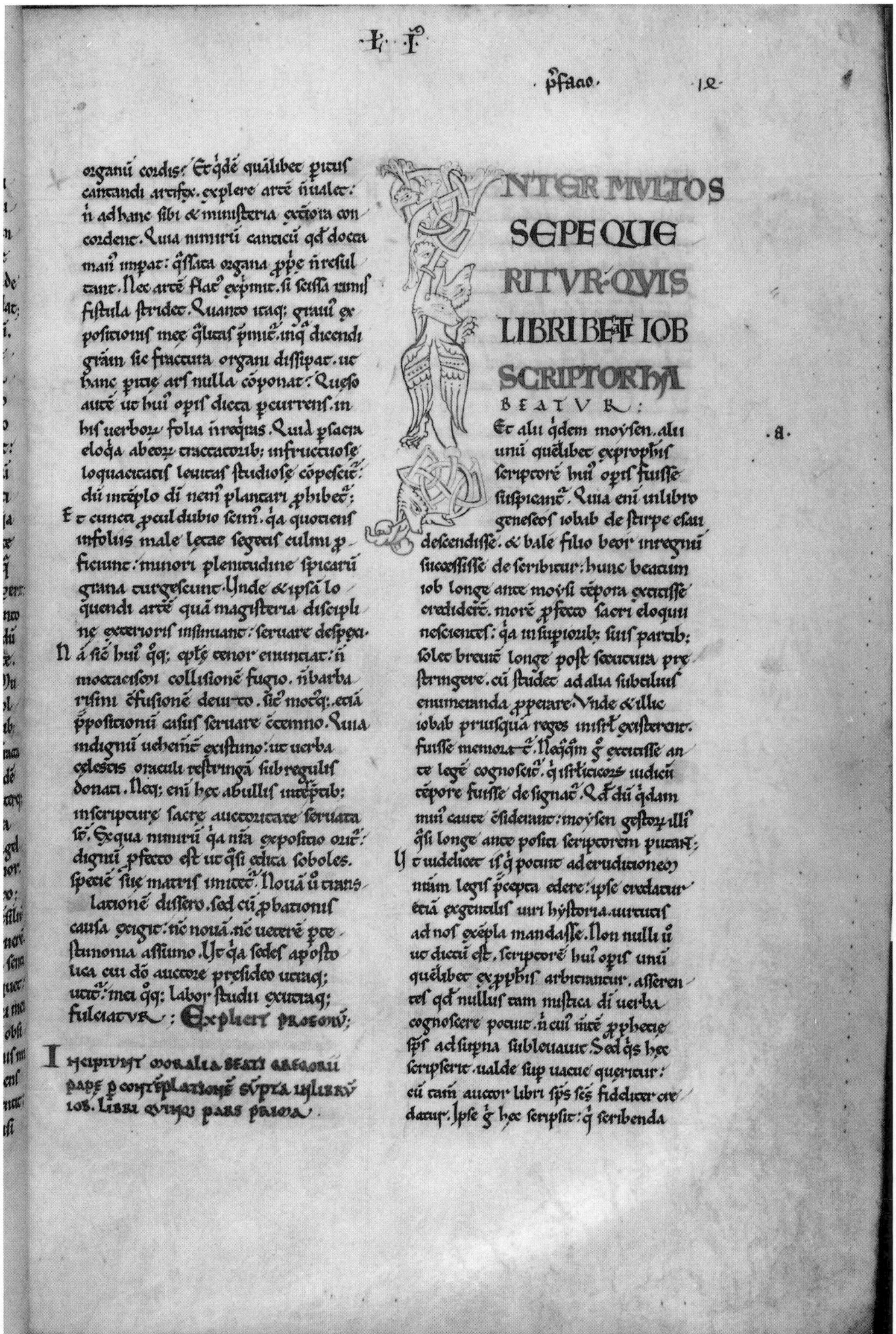

18 London, British Library, Royal, 3 C. iv, fol. 14r (no. 463).
Gregory the Great. *Saec.* xii[in]. Rochester.
Page size: 365 × 232mm. Written area: 260 × 164mm.

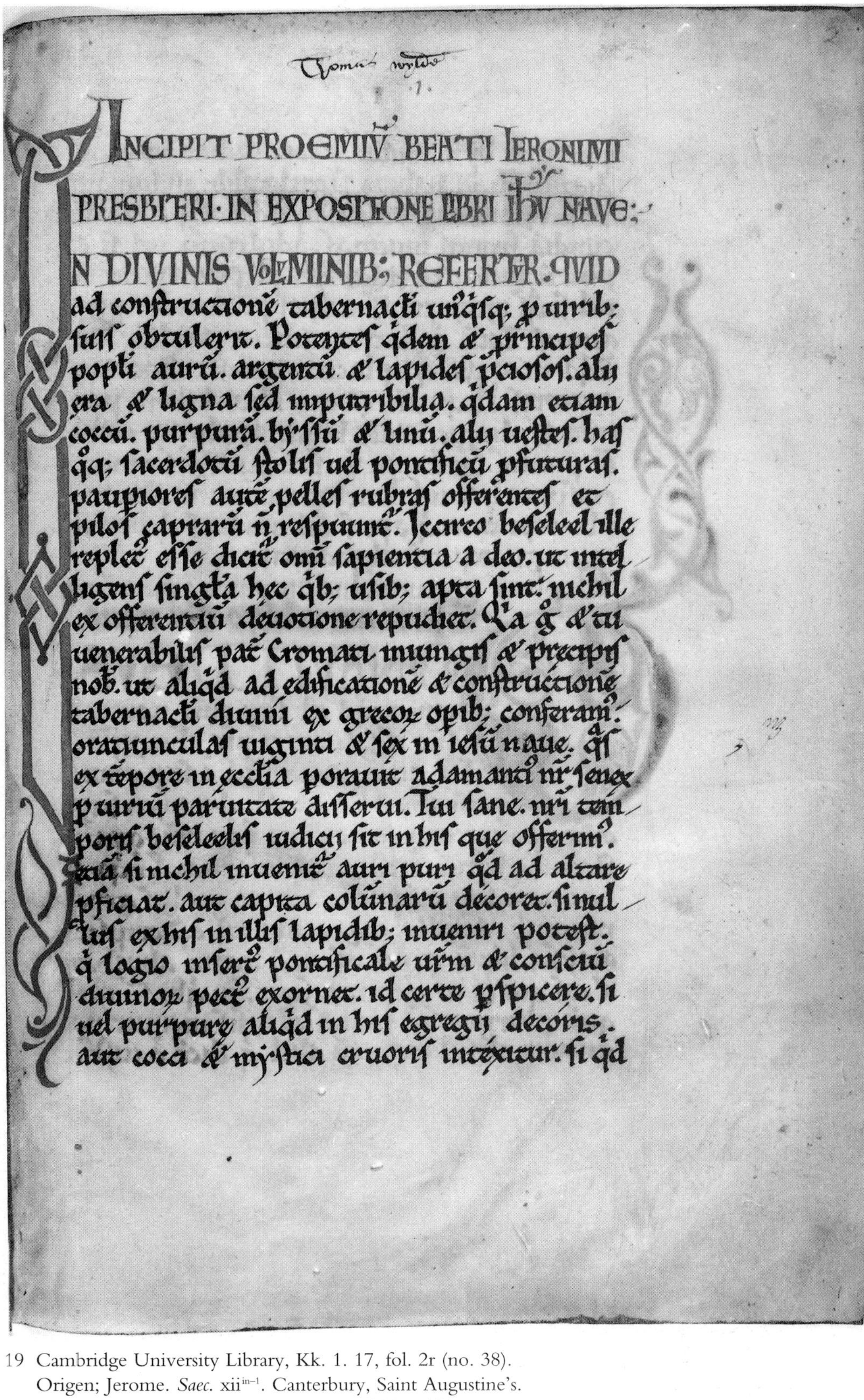

19 Cambridge University Library, Kk. 1. 17, fol. 2r (no. 38).
Origen; Jerome. *Saec.* xii^{in-1}. Canterbury, Saint Augustine's.
Page size: 295 × 205mm. Written area: 202 × 120mm.

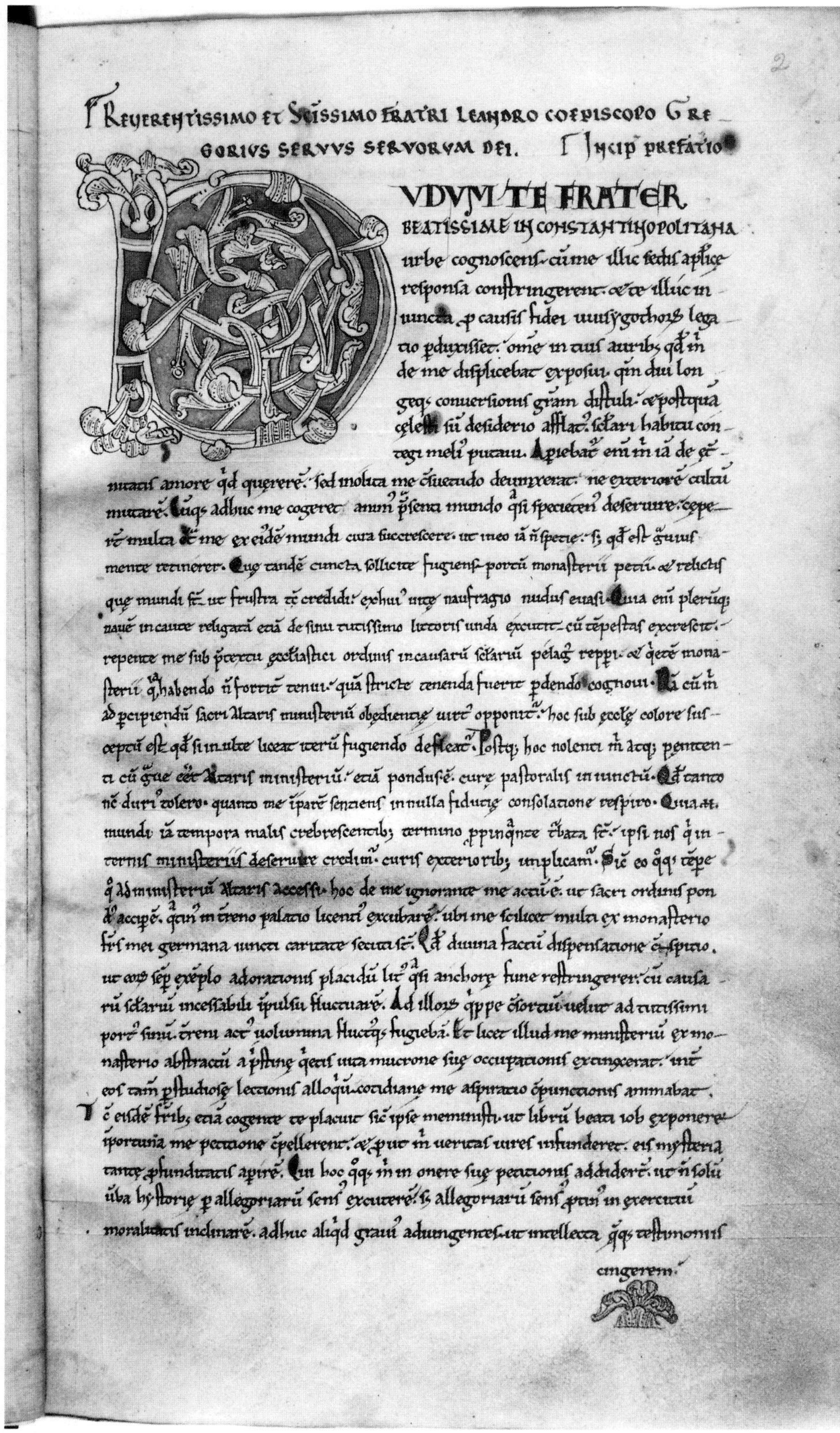

20 Oxford, Trinity College, 39, fol. 2r (no. 800).
Gregory the Great. *Saec.* xii^{in}. Lanthony.
Page size: 310 × 185mm. Written area: 239 × 130mm.

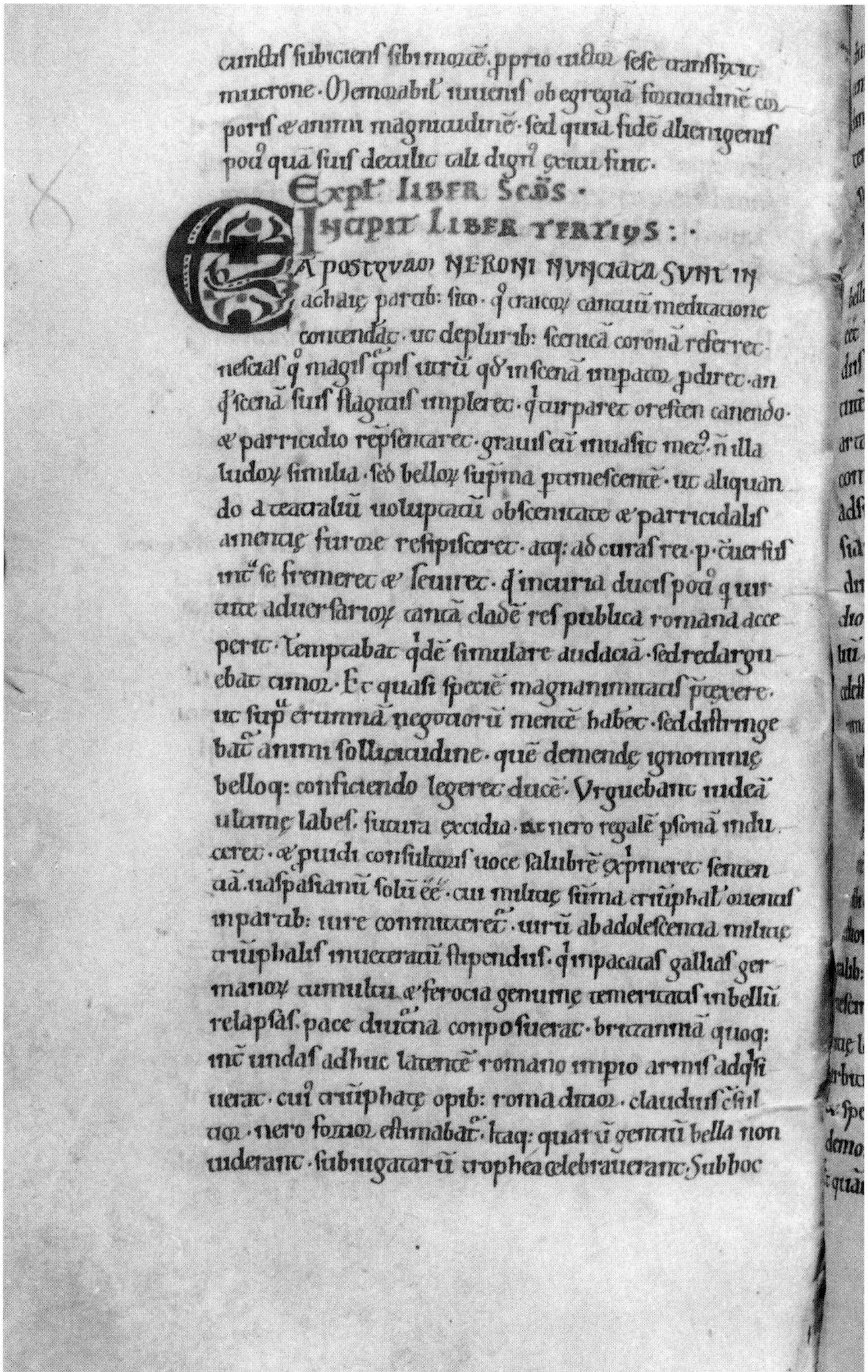

21 London, Lambeth Palace Library, 173, fol. 71v (no. 588).
Pseudo-Hegesippus. *Saec.* xii[in–1]. Lanthony.
Page size: 300 × 175mm. Written area: 218 × 115mm.

PLATE 22

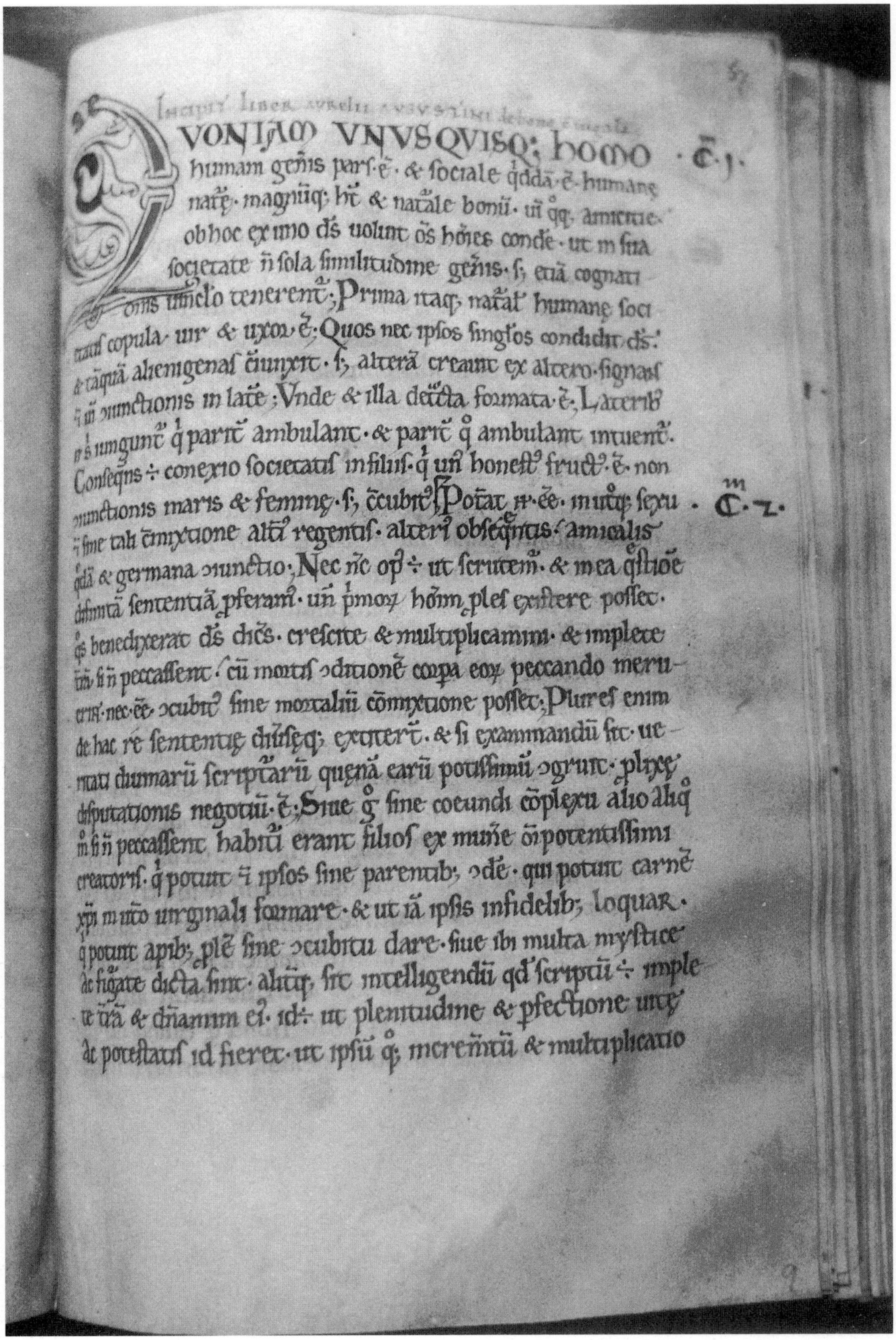

22 Cambridge, Emmanuel College, 26, fol. 67r (no. 94).
Jerome. *Saec.* xii[1]. Chichester.
Page size: 256 × 171mm. Written area: 185 × 118mm.

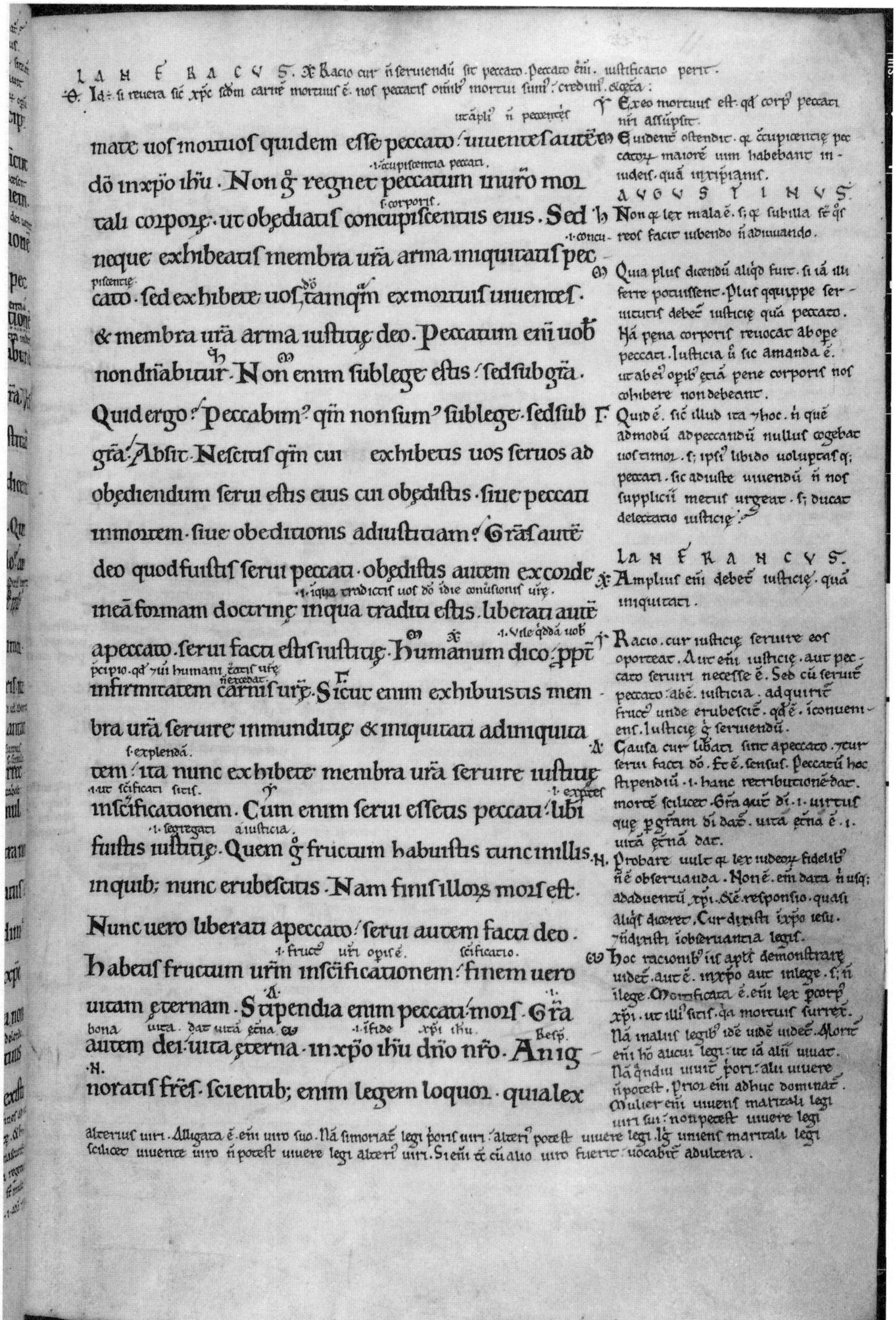

23 London, British Library, Royal, 4 B. iv, fol. 11r (no. 467).
Pauli Epistolae; Cantica Canticorum; etc. *Saec.* xii[1]. Worcester.
Page size: 280 × 193mm. Written area: 203 × 110mm.

PLATE 24

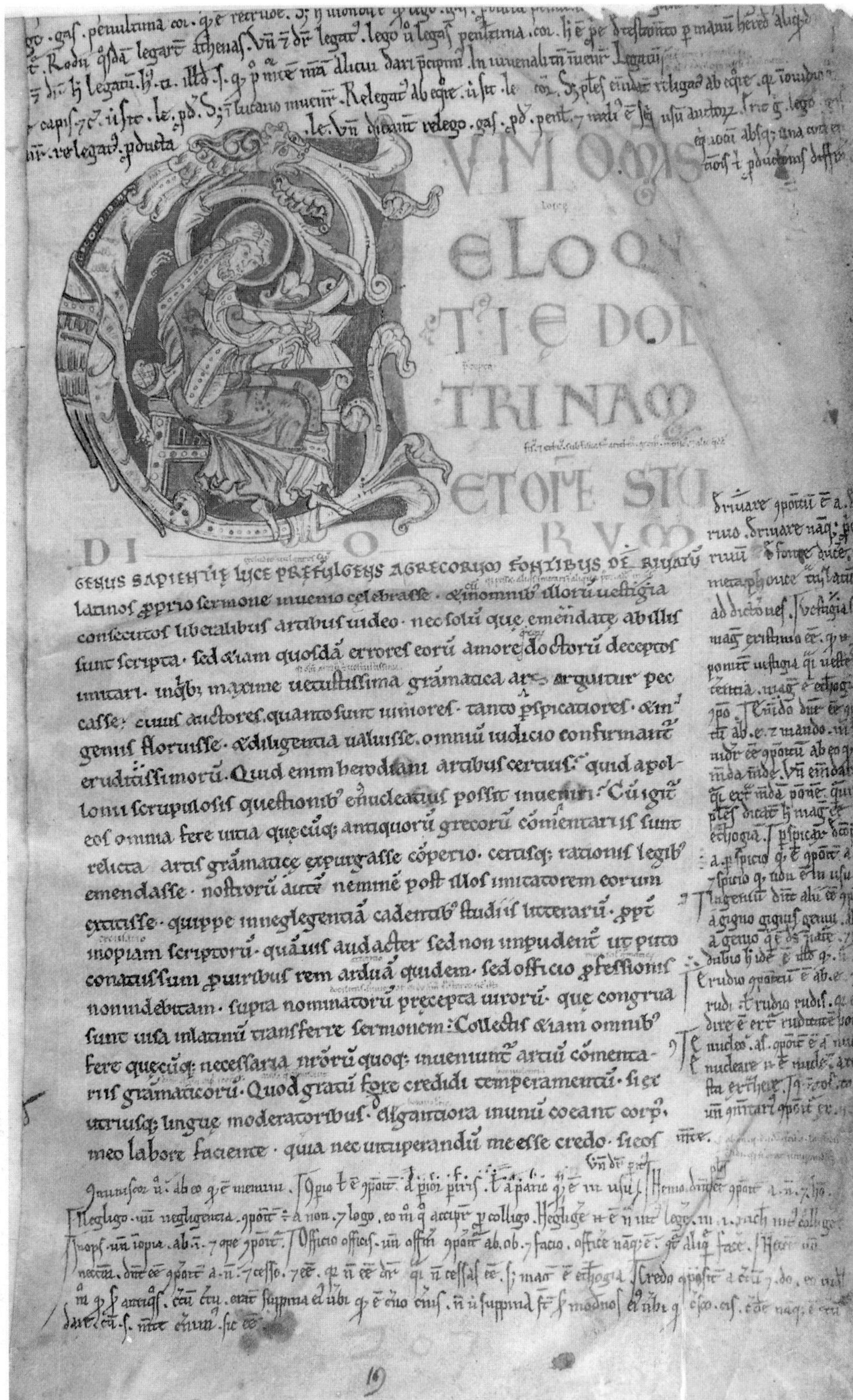

24 Cambridge University Library, Ii. 4. 34, fol. 1r (no. 35).
Priscian. *Saec.* xii[1]. Norwich.
Page size: 258 × 165mm. Written area: 200 × 108mm.